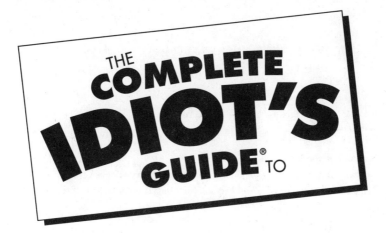

THE COMPLETE IDIOT'S GUIDE® TO

Learning German

Third Edition

Revisions by Lisa Graham

By Alicia Müller and Stephan Müller

ALPHA

A member of Penguin Group (USA) Inc.

This book is dedicated passionately to L. M. and Wendy.

ALPHA BOOKS

Published by the Penguin Group

Penguin Group (USA) Inc., 375 Hudson Street, New York, New York 10014, U.S.A.

Penguin Group (Canada), 10 Alcorn Avenue, Toronto, Ontario, Canada M4V 3B2 (a division of Pearson Penguin Canada Inc.)

Penguin Books Ltd, 80 Strand, London WC2R 0RL, England

Penguin Ireland, 25 St Stephen's Green, Dublin 2, Ireland (a division of Penguin Books Ltd)

Penguin Group (Australia), 250 Camberwell Road, Camberwell, Victoria 3124, Australia (a division of Pearson Australia Group Pty Ltd)

Penguin Books India Pvt Ltd, 11 Community Centre, Panchsheel Park, New Delhi—110 017, India

Penguin Group (NZ), cnr Airborne and Rosedale Roads, Albany, Auckland 1310, New Zealand (a division of Pearson New Zealand Ltd)

Penguin Books (South Africa) (Pty) Ltd, 24 Sturdee Avenue, Rosebank, Johannesburg 2196, South Africa

Penguin Books Ltd, Registered Offices: 80 Strand, London WC2R 0RL, England

International Standard Book Number: 1-59257-186-7
Library of Congress Catalog Card Number: 2003116931

08 07 06   8 7 6 5 4

Interpretation of the printing code: The rightmost number of the first series of numbers is the year of the book's printing; the rightmost number of the second series of numbers is the number of the book's printing. For example, a printing code of 04-1 shows that the first printing occurred in 2004.

Printed in the United States of America

Note: This publication contains the opinions and ideas of its authors. It is intended to provide helpful and informative material on the subject matter covered. It is sold with the understanding that the authors, book producer, and publisher are not engaged in rendering professional services in the book. If the reader requires personal assistance or advice, a competent professional should be consulted.

The authors, book producer, and publisher specifically disclaim any responsibility for any liability, loss, or risk, personal or otherwise, which is incurred as a consequence, directly or indirectly, of the use and application of any of the contents of this book.

Most Alpha books are available at special quantity discounts for bulk purchases for sales promotions, premiums, fundraising, or educational use. Special books, or book excerpts, can also be created to fit specific needs.

For details, write: Special Markets, Alpha Books, 375 Hudson Street, New York, NY 10014.

Publisher: *Marie Butler-Knight*
Product Manager: *Phil Kitchel*
Senior Managing Editor: *Jennifer Chisholm*
Senior Acquisitions Editor: *Mike Sanders*
Book Producer: *Lee Ann Chearney/Amaranth Illuminare*
Development Editor: *Ginny Bess Munroe*
Senior Production Editor: *Billy Fields*

Copy Editor: *Krista Hansing*
Illustrator: *Chris Eliopoulos*
Cover/Book Designer: *Trina Wurst*
Indexer: *Julie Bess*
Layout: *Angela Calvert, Rebecca Harmon*
Proofreading: *Donna Martin*

Contents at a Glance

Contents

Foreword

One of the most fascinating dictionaries published in recent years is the historical dictionary of *German Loanwords in English* (Pfeffer and Cannon: Cambridge University Press, 1994). It describes the more than 5,000 German loanwords that have entered English over the centuries that English speakers currently have at their disposal, enabling them to discuss topics ranging from angora to silicone, and apple strudel to Wagnerian opera. This linguistic exchange is, of course, a two-way street, with German speakers wearing Jeans (note that all German nouns are capitalized!) while logging on to their Computer and looking into RAM-chips and Userports.

In spite of Mark Twain's notorious reference to The Awful German Language, speakers of English and German are indeed linguistic relatives, with a long, common history of shared ideas and shared words. They are relatives who have been engaged in constant linguistic negotiation and exchange. Purists may lament linguistic contamination, but let us instead celebrate human ties. What better reason to learn German than to cement these ties and to become part of what has been and continues to be an extremely fruitful and exciting dialogue?

The Complete Idiot's Guide to Learning German, Third Edition, also points out that you know more than you think—the title of Chapter 4. This is not to claim that you already know all there is to know. Establishing any degree of intimacy always requires effort, commitment, and desire, and these are the three prerequisites you will have to bring to your attempt to "get to know" German. Knowledge of the already existing relationship should eliminate some of the fear of the unknown.

After many years of teaching German, not to mention my own attempts to learn some Russian and some French, I have come to believe that it is fear of the unknown, fear of failure, and fear of embarrassing oneself by being less than perfect that play the biggest roles in students' difficulties with learning a language. Language anxiety is as real as math anxiety. The charm of *The Complete Idiot's Guide to Learning German, Third Edition*, is that it does all it can to welcome you, introduce you, make you feel comfortable and at home, and encourage you to take risks. It could just as aptly be titled *German Without Fear.*

Americans have often heard that it's not necessary to learn another language because everyone speaks English anyway. This claim is, of course, patently false, especially if you plan to diverge from well-trodden tourist paths or if you confront recent immigrants to Germany who, while transporting you in their cab or taking your dinner order, are in the midst of their own efforts to learn German. The claim also ignores the access that knowing another language gives you to its culture, as well as the efforts made by non-native speakers of English to get closer to us. They, however, will not have forgotten and will truly appreciate your interest in them and your willingness to meet them at least halfway. And don't forget the tremendous sense of pride you will have in mastering a new skill and discovering a new talent.

—Dr. Evelyn M. Jacobson

Professor of German and Associate Vice Chancellor for Academic Affairs, University of Lincoln-Nebraska

Introduction

In the last hundred years, parts of the world that we would have had to travel months by boat to reach are now just a few hours away. There are, however, many other ways of traveling. We travel in books, in movies, and on the Internet, and we travel in our imaginations.

Some people believe that the soul of a culture resides in the grammatical patterns, in the linguistic intricacies, and in the phonetics of its language. The authors of this book share this view. If bank robberies aren't your thing, learning German may be the next most satisfying and effective way of enriching yourself fast.

The German language reveals German books, people, and customs in ways that are lost in translation. If you plan a trip to a German-speaking country, even before you get on a plane, you should have the basic tools with which to decipher the code of the culture you're about to enter. What are these tools? Traveler's checks, an elementary knowledge of the German language, and an open mind. You're going to have to get the traveler's checks and the open mind on your own; we'll help you with the German language.

Many chapters in this book are held together thematically as if you were off on an imaginary journey to a German-speaking land. In Chapter 11 you'll learn vocabulary related to air travel and airports. In Chapter 12 you'll learn how to tell your bus or taxi driver where you're going. By the end of Chapter 13 you'll be able to ask the desk clerk for the kind of room you want.

Each chapter builds on the one that preceded it, expanding on what you have learned. Learning a new language is, after all, a bit like evolving rapidly from infant to adult. First you learn to crawl through the new sounds of the language, and then you learn to walk proudly through basic grammar and vocabulary. When you can keep your balance with everything you've learned, you're well on your way to jogging through conversations with patient Berliners or the Viennese.

The Sum of Its Parts

Part 1, "Learning German Basics," starts by outlining why German is a tremendously important language and how it will be of use to you as a student, businessperson, or tourist. Not only will you learn all about the advantages of reading German texts in the original, but you'll also find out how much you already know (before you've even started learning anything). You'll also learn German consonant and vowel sounds.

Part 2, "Ready, Set, Go!" introduces you to a selection of common German idioms (expressions in which the meaning is not predictable from the usual meaning of the words that make it up) and slang. You'll get your first taste of German grammar, and you'll be able to use what you know of German through cognates. By the end of this section, you'll be engaging in and understanding simple conversations.

Part 3, "Up, Up, and Away," introduces you to the vocabulary and grammar you'll need to plan and take a trip to a German-speaking country. You'll use the real greetings Germans use with each other; you'll introduce yourself and give elementary descriptions. You'll ask basic questions. A chapter at a time, you'll arrive at an airport, catch a taxi or a bus, and make your way to the hotel of your choice. Most important, you'll be able to get the room you want furnished with all those indispensable things (cable television, extra blankets, hair dryers, and so on) that many of us cannot do without when we travel. Then you'll be able to go out and search for addresses, address a postcard, decipher a phone number, or exchange your dollars for Euros and Franks.

Part 4, "Out and About in Germany," furnishes you with the vocabulary you'll need to do practically anything fun, from playing tennis to going to the opera to nightclubbing. You'll also learn how to make sense out of the weather report, whether it's in the newspaper, on TV, or revealed to you via the aches and pains in the bones of the local baker. The chapter on food will help you understand where to buy all kinds of food in Germany and how to interpret a German menu. Finally, you'll be introduced to the phrases and vocabulary words you'll need to go on a shopping spree for chocolates, silk shirts, and Rolexes while the exchange rate is still high.

Part 5, "Angst: Solving Problems on the Go," prepares you for the inevitable difficulties that crop up when you travel. You'll learn how to make local and longdistance phone calls from a German phone and how to explain yourself to the operator if you have problems getting through. Is your watch broken? Do you need film for your camera? Did some food stain your new shirt? You'll be ready to take care of anything, to ask for help, and to explain what happened to your German friends or colleagues when your angst-ridden moments are (hopefully) distant memories.

Part 6, "When in Germany, Do As the Germans Do," instructs you in the terminology you'll need to spend, exchange, invest, borrow, and save money for an extended stay in Deutschland. By the end of this section, you should be able to buy or rent a house, an apartment, or even a castle (if extravagance appeals to you). You'll also be able to express your needs in the future tense.

In the appendixes, the **"Answer Key"** gives you the answers to the exercises you perform in this book. The **"Glossary"** summarizes the words defined throughout the book. The **"Lexicon: English to German, German to English"** translates essential vocabulary and lists the pronunciation of each.

By the time you finish this book, you will have the basic German language skills to embark on real journeys—in books, on planes, and in conversations. Be persistent, be patient, and be creative, and your rewards will speak (in German) for themselves.

Extras to Help You Along

Besides the idiomatic expressions, helpful phrases, lists of vocabulary words, and down-to-earth grammar, this book has useful information that is provided in sidebars throughout the text. These elements are distinguished by the following icons.

Many foreign words have been adopted by the German language and still retain their foreign pronunciation. These words do not follow the German pronunciation guide included in this book.

German Culture
These elements provide facts about interesting facets of life in Germany and other German-speaking cultures. They offer you quick glimpses into the German culture.

We Are Family
This box tells you all about the linguistic connections between German and our own language, English.

As a Rule

These sidebars highlight or expand on some aspect of German grammar that has been touched on in the text, usually summing it up in a rule so that it's easier to remember.

Achtung

Achtung boxes warn you of mistakes that are commonly made by those who are learning the German language and offer advice about how to avoid these mistakes yourself.

What's What

This box gives you definitions of grammatical terms.

Acknowledgments

The authors and reviser would like to acknowledge the support of the following people in the creation of this book: Angelika Müller, Francisca Muñoz, Margit Böckenkruger, Pat Muñoz, Manuel Muñoz, Maria Cabezas, Cristina Lopez, Jean Maurice Lacant, Elsie Jones, and Jennifer Charles. Also thanks to Lee Ann Chearney, creative director at Amaranth; and the team at Alpha: publisher Marie Butler-Knight, senior acquisitions editor Mike Sanders, development editor Ginny Bess, and senior production editor Billy Fields.

Special Thanks from the Publisher to the Reviser

The Complete Idiot's Guide to Learning German, Third Edition, has been thoroughly revised and updated by German language instructor and linguistics expert Lisa Graham. Lisa has held teaching positions at Washington College, the Boston Language Institute, and The Pennsylvania State University. She is a frequent presenter at foreign language and linguistic conferences, and has published several papers on the topic of German and English linguistics. Ms. Graham is a member of the Society for German Philology, the Modern Language Association, and the American Association of Teachers of German.

Special Thanks to the Technical Reviewer

The Complete Idiot's Guide to Learning German, Third Edition, was reviewed in page proofs by a reader with native proficiency in German. Our thanks to Dirk Lehmann for his careful eye. Dirk Lehmann has taught German at The Pennsylvania State University, the University of Missouri-Columbia, and is currently assistant professor of German at the New Mexico Military Institute.

Trademarks

All terms mentioned in this book that are known to be or are suspected of being trademarks or service marks have been appropriately capitalized. Alpha Books and Penguin Group (USA) Inc. cannot attest to the accuracy of this information. Use of a term in this book should not be regarded as affecting the validity of any trademark or service mark.

Part 1

Learning German Basics

Most people can think of a million reasons why they can't do something. In the first section of this book, you'll discover a great many reasons why you can learn the German language. Similarities abound! Whether you're a scholar interested in expanding your understanding of philosophy, art history, or literature, or simply someone who wants to have a working knowledge of Deutsch before embarking on their dream skiing holiday, this section will help you take the plunge and pronounce.

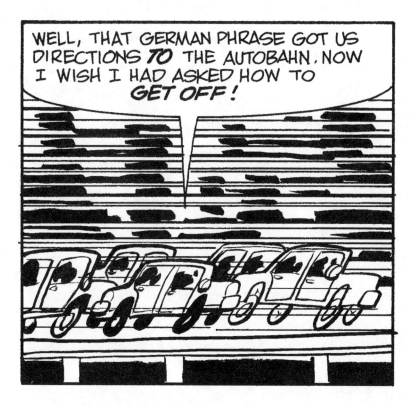

Learning German

In This Chapter

- ◆ German words in English

- ◆ Using a bilingual dictionary

- ◆ Why German and English are similar

It seems you can't pick up a textbook or even a courtroom thriller these days without bumping into German words and phrases. Say you're reading up on art history to dazzle your friends at the local brewpub, and you bump into *die Wanderlust*, *die Weltanschauung*, and *die Schadenfreude*. What's an inquisitive scholar to do? Learn the basic structural differences between German and English, that's what.

What Are All These German Words Doing Here?

German culture has shaped certain disciplines to such a degree that, in many schools and universities, you can't get away with not taking a basic German language course if you're studying art history, psychology, chemistry, or philosophy. About 1 in 10 books published throughout the world has been written in German. When you think about it, studying German makes sense. You'll have a much better understanding of these disciplines after you've studied the language and culture out of which many of the most important German, Austrian, and Swiss thinkers and creators came.

Business Benefits of German

In addition, many businesses, industries, and specialties such as medicine and science use German terms, particularly those with international markets or affiliations. The Federal Republic of Germany is one of the major industrial countries in the world. In terms of overall economic performance, it is the third largest, and with regard to world trade, it holds second place. Many German industrial enterprises are known throughout the world and have branches or research facilities overseas. The United States is one of Germany's most important trading partners and is the third largest market for German products. So get way ahead of your colleagues and learn German. Not only will you find it interesting and enriching, but it'll probably lead you to a greater appreciation of a foreign culture and enhance your global understanding.

> **German Culture**
>
> Many medical and scientific words are easy to understand in German and hard to understand in English. The word *der Blut-druckmesser* (*deyR blewt-dRook-me-suhR*) literally translated means "blood pressure monitor." The word for this same term in English is—ready?—*sphygmomanometer.* Try saying that three times fast!

Getting Serious About German

Having a clear sense of why you're learning German can help you maximize your efforts. Take a moment to consider your motives:

◆ If you're learning German to discuss the *Rheinheitsgebot* in your quest to discover the ultimate German beer, you may not need to spend a lot of time on cases and grammatical paradigms. Your knowledge of grammar will remain somewhat passive, outshined by your expansive knowledge of German vocabulary expressing finer aesthetic distinctions.

◆ If music is your thing, you'll have a head start with German musical terms such as *die Lieder* and *das Leitmotif* that pop up in music from Mozart to Madonna. And you'll be able to fine-tune your pronunciation so that even the last row will be able to understand your rendering of *die Walküren.*

◆ If your goal is to be able to read German, you may want to focus on the cognate section of this book—that is, the noun and verb sections. Additionally, figuring out how German structures its sentences will help you decipher who is doing what to whom and to develop the patience to wait for the verb. In German, the infinitive and past participle verb forms appear at the end of a sentence. Additionally, the finite (conjugated) form of a verb is sent to the end in a subordinate clause. Never fear! All this German grammar jargon will make perfect sense to you as you pursue your studies with this book as your guide.

If you determine what you want to achieve with your knowledge of the German language, you can easily tailor this book to your needs and use it to your advantage.

Look It Up

Whatever your particular needs are, a bilingual dictionary is essential to your learning. In addition to providing an accurate translation, a good German-English/English-German dictionary supplies grammatical information, field labels that differentiate various meanings of the word, and style labels that mark words and phrases that are not neutral in style level or that are no longer current in the language. What do you need to know to use a bilingual dictionary? Be forewarned: Using a bilingual dictionary is a little more involved than using an English dictionary. After finding the German translation for an English word in the English section, take a moment to look up the German word in the German section. It may not have the meaning you were intending—in English, we can "spend time and money," but German has two different words for "to spend": *verbringen (feR-bRin-guhn)*, with time, and *ausgeben (ous-gey-buhn)*, with money.

The next thing you should do is figure out what the grammatical abbreviations used in the definitions mean. Here are a few of them:

adj.   Adjective

adv.   Adverb

f.   Feminine noun

m.   Masculine noun

n.   Noun

nt.   Neuter noun

pl.   Plural noun

prep.   Preposition. Prepositions are words such as *above, along, beyond, before, through, in, to,* and *for* that are placed before nouns to indicate a relationship to other words in a sentence. Or, think of them in terms of "anywhere a cat can go." We discuss prepositions further in Chapter 11.

v.i.   Intransitive verb. An intransitive verb can stand alone, without a direct object, as *travel* does in the sentence "I travel."

v.r.   Reflexive verb. The object of a reflexive verb refers back to the subject itself, as in "I bought myself a car."

v.t.	Transitive verb. A transitive verb must be followed by a direct object, as in "I saw a cat." Unlike intransitive verbs, transitive verbs cannot stand on their own. Transitive verbs can be used passively, however, when the subject acts on itself, as in "I was interrupted."

In addition to labeling the parts of speech, dictionary entries often contain "field labels" which identify various subject areas that an entry may refer to and give the reader a better "sense" of the word. These include *comput. (computer), mech. (mechanical), sport, job, cook, hunt, chem. (chemistry), and zool (zoological)*. Words not used freely as part of the standard vocabulary are given "style labels" so that the reader can make useful judgments about the setting in which a term might be appropriate. Here are some possible style labels to guide actual language usage:

dated	This indicates that the word now sounds somewhat old-fashioned, although it is still occasionally used.
fig.	Figurative refers to non-literal, metaphorical uses of words, as in figures of speech.
form.	Formal. Formal language is used on official forms, for official communications, and in formal speeches.
inf./coll.	Informal or colloquial. Informal language is colloquial, typically used in an informal conversational context or in e-mail. It is inappropriate in more formal speech or writing.
old/obs	Old or obsolete refers to words that are no longer in current use and that the reader will normally only find in classical literature.
sl.	Slang. Slang words and phrases are highly informal and are appropriate only in very restricted contexts.
vulg.	Vulgar. Vulgar words are generally regarded as taboo and are likely to cause offense.

Identifying Parts of Speech

Learning how to use a bilingual dictionary takes a little grammatical know-how. For example, you should know how to use the basic parts of speech. Take the word *inside*. Look at how the meaning of the word changes in the following sentences when it is used as various parts of speech:

I'll meet you *inside* of an hour. (adverb)

They threw the marbles *inside* the circle. (preposition)

Do you like the *inside* of the building? (noun)

We have the *inside* story on the murder. (adjective)

Change *inside* to the plural, and its meaning changes:

He could feel it in his *insides*. (colloquial, noun)

If you look up the word in an English/German dictionary, you will see something like this:

inside [In'saId] 1. *adj.* inner, inwendig, Innen; (*coll.*) -*information*, direkte Informationen 2. *adv.* im Innern, drinnen, ins Innere; -*of*, innerhalb von, in weniger als. 3. *prep.* Innerhalb, im Innern (von or Gen.) 4. *n.* -s (*coll.*) der Magen.

Your Turn at Inside Information

Using the German definition of *inside* just given, figure out the part of speech for *inside* in each of the following sentences; then complete the translated sentences in German. Check your answers in Appendix A.

1. We will be home inside of two hours.

   Wir sind _____ zwei Stunden zu Hause.

2. He had inside information on the horse race.

   Er hatte _____ Informationen über das Pferderennen.

3. We go inside the cave.

   Wir gehen ins _____ der Höhle.

4. He hides the key inside the box.

   Er versteckt den Schlüssel im _____ der Schachtel.

5. The man's insides hurt.

   Der _____ des Mannes schmerzt.

Compounding Your German Vocabulary

You're likely to come across German compound words in everything you read from popular fiction to political essays, to letters to the editor in *Sports Illustrated*. Because the possible combinations of nouns are practically unlimited, you can actually create your own compound words pretty much as you please by linking nouns together. The ability to create words at will in German is one reason that this language has been so instrumental to many great thinkers. They have been able to express new concepts and ideas by *coining*, or making up, new words. The flip side to this flexibility is that these compound words are not easily translatable. To express the meaning of the single word *Zeitgeist* in English, for example, you have to use the cumbersome and rather spiritless phrase "spirit of the times." And this morphological process is not limited to combining two nouns to form a compound word. As in English, it's possible to combine adjectives such as *bittersweet* or verbs such as *sleepwalk* to form new words. There's even some mixing of the two languages, coupling the German preposition *über-* (*üb-buhR*), meaning "above," "beyond," and "super," with an English noun, as in *überbabe* or *überstar*.

As a Rule

Many German words in academic texts are compound words, and some of these compound words are not in the dictionary. A knowledge of basic German vocabulary will enable you to take apart those big, cumbersome compound words and look up their components one by one in a bilingual dictionary. The more you rely on and trust your powers of deduction, the easier learning a foreign language becomes!

The Genetic Relationship Between German and English

Even the casual student soon becomes aware of many similarities between German and English. Although vocabulary correspondences are perhaps the most obvious, the two languages also share structural secrets—consider the way they form the comparative and superlative (*blond, blonder, blondest*) or the striking parallels in the verbal systems (*sing, sang, gesungen*). Although these similarities seem fortuitous to the English-speaking learner of German (you!), English and German belong to the so-called Germanic family of languages, a relationship also shared by Danish, Icelandic, Norwegian, Swedish, and Dutch. Once upon a time, in fact, the Germanic languages were closely related to the following *linguistic* groups: Albanian, Armenian, Baltic, Celtic, Greek, Hittite, Indic, Iranian, Italian, Slavic, and Tocharian—all members of the Indo-European language family. Indo-European, spoken more than 6,000 years ago, was the predecessor language of English and most European languages, minus Finnish and Hungarian. But it took a German, Jacob Grimm, to figure out the sound correspondences between various branches of Indo-European and Germanic languages.

The Germanic languages can be subdivided according to geographical location: north, east, and west. North Germanic languages are Scandinavian, including Icelandic, Norwegian, Faroese, Swedish, and Danish; East Germanic is represented chiefly by Gothic, an extinct language preserved in a fourth-century Bible translation. The geographical grouping of West Germanic includes German, Dutch, Frisian, Yiddish, Afrikaans, and English. So what happened to cause the rift between English and German? An actual shift. No, not of earth, but of consonants, which occurred in the southernmost reaches of the German-speaking lands sometime around the fifth century. "Aha!" you exclaim triumphantly. That explains why it's *child* and *Kind*, *ship* and *Schiff*, *salt* and *Salz*.

> **What's What** _____
>
> **Linguistic**   Relates to language. Linguistics is the scientific study of human language.

> **What's What** _____
>
> **Grimm's law**   Named after the discoverer of the consonant shifts in Indo-European and Germanic, Jacob Grimm. The first shift (circa 500 B.C.E.) helped separate Germanic from its Indo-European siblings (Greek: *dêka*; Germanic: *zehan*, ten); the second shift around 500 C.E. differentiated German from English.

The Least You Need to Know

♦ Whether you're a student, a businessperson, or someone in the arts field, learning the German language will give you a head start in understanding and assimilating German terms and phrases.

♦ The particular meter of a piece of writing, the peculiarities of rhyme, and double meanings are all aspects of writing that can be partially, if not totally, lost in translation.

♦ A bilingual dictionary can help you tremendously in your study of German.

Pronounce It Properly: Vowels

In This Chapter

◆ Oh, the stress of it all

◆ Peculiarities of the German language

◆ Untie your tongue

You think you have it bad with German pronunciation? Consider the English *rain*, *reign*, and *rein*—three words with different spellings and meanings but with identical pronunciations. You're going to have a much easier time learning German pronunciation because what you see is what you hear. German is what is called a phonetic language; German words are pronounced exactly as they are spelled. You don't ever have to wonder whether the *e* at the end of a word is silent, which it sometimes is and sometimes isn't in English. In German, it is always pronounced. This rule makes it easy to spell as well. You need simply to learn what sounds are represented by the letters in German.

Before you can pronounce German words correctly, however, you'll have to learn how to say the vowels because the sounds of vowels in German are significantly different from the sounds of the same letters in English.

Also, you should get comfortable enunciating every letter in a word. This chapter helps you figure out how to pronounce German vowels.

Vowels That May Mutate

Three German *vowels*—*a*, *o*, and *u*—may be written as such and pronounced similar to these sounds in English, or they may be written with two dots above them. These two dots are called an *umlaut* and signal a change in the sound and meaning of a word. The sounds represented by ¨ and *o* are just as different as the English *a* versus *o*. *Schon* means "already"; *schön* means "beautiful" or "nice." This difference in sound is very significant. If you forget to pronounce the different vowel sound represented by the umlaut over *schwül*, the German word for "humid," and try to tell someone that you find a city humid, you could end up making a judgment about an entire city's sexual orientation (*schwul* means gay, or homosexual). When a vowel is represented orthographically (in spelling) with an umlaut, it becomes a *modified* or *mutated vowel*. These two dots over a vowel change the meaning of a German word as much as the variation of the English vowels *a* and *o* in *hat* versus *hot*. The vowel tables in this chapter provide hints, English examples, and the letters used as symbols to represent the sounds of vowels in German words.

What's What

Vowel   *a*, *e*, *i*, *o*, and *u* are vowels—sounds produced without significant constriction of air.

Umlaut   The term for the two dots (diacritics—additional markings on written symbols) that can be placed over the vowels *a*, *o*, and *u*.

Modified or mutated vowel   A vowel that takes an umlaut is referred to as a modified vowel, incurring a mutation of sound—the tongue moves forward in the oral cavity and the lips are rounded so that an *o* or a *u* (produced in the back of the mouth) moves up to the front, as if combined with an *ee* sound.

Linguistic Stress

No, linguistic stress isn't what happens to you when your Mercedes breaks down on the *Autobahn*. *Stress* is the emphasis placed on one or more syllables of a word when you pronounce it. If you say *ee*ther and I say *eye*ther, and you say tom*a*to and I say tom*ah*to, it doesn't necessarily mean we'll have to call the whole thing off. A general rule for determining the stressed syllable in German is that the emphasis is usually placed on the first syllable, as in the words *Bleistift* (pencil), *Schönheit* (beauty), and *Kaugummi* (chewing gum), thanks to the accenting established in early Germanic.

Foreign words such as *Hotel*, *Musik*, and *Philosophie* that have been assimilated into the German language, generally from Latin-based languages, do not follow German rules of stress, although they do acquire German pronunciation of vowels. Such words maintain the lender language's stress patterns. Hence, *Hotel* and *Musik* retain second syllable main stress, whereas *Philosophie*, also borrowed from English, stresses the final syllable.

What's What _____

Stress The emphasis placed on one or more syllables of a word when you pronounce it.

Assuming an Accent

Some people have no problem pronouncing new sounds in a foreign language. They were born rolling their R's, courtesy of genetics, and producing throaty gutturals. Not all of us have been so lucky.

To pronounce words correctly in a new language, you must retrain your tongue. After all, hasn't your tongue—the muscle that's been making the same sounds since you first opened your mouth as a baby to utter "mama"—been wrapping itself around the particular language known as English for as long as you can remember? Those intuitive skills you used to *acquire* your first language will enable you to *learn* a foreign language.

Don't worry if you can't make the exact German sound. As an adult language learner, you are able to monitor your utterances according to your conscious knowledge and correct yourself accordingly. This maturity and metalinguistic awareness enables you to strive for approximate perfection—chances are, what you're trying to communicate will be understood.

A Few Peculiarities of the German Language

The relationship between German pronunciation and spelling is much closer than the relationship between English pronunciation and spelling—no Great Vowel Shift or Norman Invasion to affect sound/symbol correspondences in German. After you learn how to pronounce German words correctly, reading them will be a breeze. You'll also be glad to hear that the German alphabet consists of the same 26 letters as the English alphabet, so you won't have to learn an entirely new alphabet as you would if you were studying Russian or Greek. Additionally, this same alphabet represents consistent sounds in German. There are, however, a few distinctly German language phenomena that you just can't do without.

The Umlaut

Remember those versatile two dots we spoke about earlier? In German, those two dots are known as an umlaut: literally, *um* ("around") + *Laut* ("sound"). The umlaut, really just a writing device to indicate another vowel sound, alters the sound of a vowel and results in a meaning change. Sometimes the change is grammatical, as in a plural form and in the comparison of an adjective, but most of the time the change is lexical—that is, it produces an entirely different word. Around the year 750, resulting from a change in word endings, the vowel *a*, formed in the back part of the oral cavity, slid forward, approximating the front vowel *i*. This phenomenon of partial assimilation is visible in the Germanization of *Attila* to *Etzel*. By the eleventh century, the umlaut had, in general, spread to include other back vowels, such as *o* and *u*, and to diphthongs. English has vestiges of the umlaut, observable in irregular forms such as *old/elder* and *foot/feet*. When you say *foot/feet*, you should be able to feel your tongue slide forward; that slide is vowel mutation!

> **CAUTION**
>
> **Achtung** _____
>
> An umlaut can be added only to *a*, *o*, or *u*. It can never be added to the front vowels, *e* or *i*.

Capitalizing on Nouns

When you see half a dozen capital letters in the middle of a German sentence, they're not typos. One of the differences between written English and written German is that German nouns are always capitalized. This convention goes back to the Reformation when Martin Luther opted to capitalize those nouns he deemed significant, such as *Glaube* (*glou-buh*), "faith" or "belief," and *Gott* (*got*), "God"—perhaps the e.e. cummings of his time!

Compare this English sentence with the translated German sentence. Don't be scared by the strange-looking *S* in the German text. It's known as an *es-tset* (you'll read all about it in the next chapter). Note the capital letters in the following sentences:

> Which famous German writer and philosopher said that pleasure is simply the absence of pain?

> Welcher berühmte deutsche Schriftsteller und Philosoph sagte, dass das Vergnügen schlicht die Abwesenheit von Kummer sei?

The answer is Arthur Schopenhauer.

Classification of Vowel Sounds

When it comes to the pronunciation of vowels, keep in mind that vowel sounds are organized into three principal types. These three types of vowel sounds are referred to throughout this book as vowels, modified vowels, and diphthongs. We've already discussed vowels and modified vowels. In German, both of these groups can have long vowel sounds, which, as their name suggests, have a drawn-out vowel sound (like the *o* sound in *snow*) or shorter vowel sounds, which have a shorter sound (like the *o* sound in *both*). *Diphthongs* are combinations of vowels that are treated as a single vowel. They begin with one vowel sound and end with a glide, a vowel-like *y* or *w* sound in the same syllable, as in the words *wine* and *bow*. Diphthongs represent a sliding together of two vowel sounds.

As a Rule _____

Generally, a vowel is long when it is followed by an *h*, as in *Mahl* (*mahl*), an orthographic device thought up by fifteenth-century spelling reformers. A vowel is also long when it is doubled, as in *Meer* (*meyR*) and *Aal* (*ahl*), or when it is followed by a single consonant, as in *Wagen* (*vah-guhn*). The vowel *i* is made into a long vowel when it is followed by an *e*—think *Bier* (*beeR*). In general, vowels are short when followed by two or more consonants, just as in English.

In the following pronunciation guide, each vowel appears in its own section. We try to give you an idea of how vowel sounds are pronounced by providing an English equivalent. Obviously, we cannot account for regional differences in either the German or English pronunciations of vowels and words. As you read this guide, remember that in English we have a tendency to glide, elongate, or "dipthongize" vowels, whereas in German vowels are "pure"—that is, they have a single sound. It may help to read the English pronunciation example first and then repeat each German word out loud for practice.

Say *a* as in *Modern*

For the short *a*, assume a British accent and make the sound of the vowel in the back of your throat. Say: *cast, fast.* Now read the following German words out loud:

Mann	Stadt	Rand	lachen	Matsch
mAn	*shtAt*	*rAnt*	*lA-CHuhn*	*mAtsh*
man, husband	city	frame	to laugh	mush

The long *a* is a prolongation of the short *a*. Pretend you're at the dentist's office and say: *ahhhhhhh*.

Wagen	haben	Staat	Mahl	lahm
vah-guhn	*hah-buhn*	*shtaht*	*mahl*	*lahm*
car	to have	state	meal	lame

German Letter	Symbol	Pronunciation Guide
a (short)	*A*	Close to *o* in *modern*
a, aa, ah (long)	*ah*	Say *a* as in *father*

Say *e* as in *Bed*

Smile while making the sound of the short stressed *e*, and your pronunciation will improve. This vowel is always flanked by double consonants in German.

Bett	Dreck	Fleck	nett
bet	*dRek*	*flek*	*net*
bed	dirt	spot	nice

When the *e* is unstressed, as it will be at the end of a word, it is pronounced like the *e* in *mother*, a phonetic representation lost in English.

Bitte	alle	bekommen	Dame	Hose
bi-tuh	*A-luh*	*buh-ko-muhn*	*dah-muh*	*hoh-zuh*
request	all	to receive	lady	trousers

There is no exact equivalent of the German long *e* sound in English, but you can approximate it by trying to make the sound of the stressed *e* and *ay* at the same time (be careful not to produce a diphthong—to add a *y* sound). Try saying these words:

Weg	Meer	Beet	Mehl	mehr
veyk	*meyR*	*beyt*	*meyl*	*meyR*
way	see	beet	flour	more

German Letter	Symbol	Pronunciation Guide
e (short, stressed)	*e*	Say *e* as in *bed*
e (short, unstressed)	*uh*	Say *uh* as in *ago*
e, ee, eh (long)	*ey*	Close to the *ey* in *hey*

Say *i* as in *Winter*

The short *i* is easy. It sounds like the *i* in the English words *wind* or *winter*. Try saying the following words:

Wind	Kind	schlimm	Himmel	hinter
vint	*kint*	*shlim*	*hi-muhl*	*hin-tuhR*
wind	child	bad	heaven	behind

For the long *i*, try saying *cheeeeeeeese* and widening your mouth!

Liter	Tiger	ihr	Fliege	schieben
lee-tuhR	*tee-guhR*	*eeR*	*flee-guh*	*shee-buhn*
liter	tiger	her; you	fly	to push

German Letter	Symbol	Pronunciation Guide
i (short)	*i*	Say *i* as in *winter*
i, ie, ih (long)	*ee*	Say *ee* as in *beet*

Say *o* as in *Lord*

In German, the sound of the short *o* should resonate slightly farther back in your mouth than the *o* sound in English.

Mord	Loch	kochen	Ort
moRt	*loCH*	*ko-CHuhn*	*oRt*
murder	hole	to cook	town

English does not have an exact equivalent of the German long *o*, but if you drop the *oow* sound at the end of *snow* and hold your jaw in place as the vibrations of the *o* sound come up your throat from your vocal chords, you'll be pretty darn close.

hoch	Boot	Ohr	loben
hohCH	*boht*	*ohR*	*loh-buhn*
high	boat	ear	to praise

German Letter	Symbol	Pronunciation Guide
o (short)	*o*	Say *o* as in *lord*
o, oo, oh (long)	*oh*	Close to *o* in *snow* (without the w glide)

Say *u* as in *Shook*

The sound of the short *u* has just a touch of the sound of the long *u* in it. If you can add a little *moon* to the sound of the short *o*, you'll be on the right track.

Mutter	Luft	Schuld	bunt	Geduld
moo-tuhR	*looft*	*shoolt*	*boont*	*guh-doolt*
mother	air	guild	bright	patience

Imitate your favorite cow (*Kuh*) for this long *u* sound: *mooo*.

zu	tun	Schuh	Uhr	Fuß
tsew	*tewn*	*shew*	*ewR*	*fews*
to	to do	shoe	clock	foot

German Letter	Symbol	Pronunciation Guide
u (short)	*oo*	Close to *oo* in *shook*
u, uh (long)	*ew*	Say *ew* as in *stew*

Achtung

Remember, the German *i* sounds like the English *e*. Usually the German *e* is soft, like the *e* in *effort* or the *a* in *ago*.

Be careful not to run the two *u*'s together when pronouncing *uu* in words like *Vakuum* (*va-koo-oom*) and *Individuum* (*in-dee-vee-doo-oom*). In most cases, the two letters are read as short *u*'s and are given equal stress. They should be treated as separate syllables, as they are in the English word *residuum*. Don't treat other vowels this way, however; this rule applies only to side-by-side *u*'s, not to the *a*, *e*, or *o*.

Modified Vowels

In German, an umlaut changes the way a vowel is pronounced. Many German words are consistently spelled with umlauts, but other words take an umlaut when they undergo some change in grammar—as with some nouns in the plural and monosyllabic adjectives in the comparative and superlative: *lang*, long; *länger*, longer; *(am) längsten*, longest. This guide treats each modified vowel separately, giving you hints to help you make the correct sounds. Focus on getting the sounds right one sound at a time.

Say ä as in *Fair*

The short *ä* is pronounced like the short *e* in German.

Stärke	Männer	hängen	ständig
shtäR-kuh	*mä-nuhR*	*hän-guhn*	*shtän-diH*
strength	men	to hang	constantly

The long *ä* is the same sound as the short *ä*, only with the sound prolonged—a quantitative rather than qualitative alteration.

ähnlich	Mähne	Bär	prägen
ähn-liH	*mäh-nuh*	*bähR*	*pRäh-guhn*
similar	mane	bear	to coin

German Letter	Symbol	Pronunciation Guide
ä (short)	*ä*	Say *ai* as in *fair*
ä, äh (long)	*äh*	Say *a* as in *fate*

Say ö as in *Fur*

This sound does not have an exact English equivalent. Round your lips and say an *ey* sound while tightening the muscles at the back of your throat.

Öffnung	möchten	Hölle	Löffel
öf-noong	*möH-tuhn*	*hö-luh*	*lö-fuhl*
opening	would like to	hell	spoon

Keep the long *ö* sound going for twice as long, just as you did the short *ö* sound.

hören	schön	fröhlich	Störung
höh-Ruhn	*shöhn*	*fRöh-liH*	*shtöh-Roong*
to hear	pretty	happy	disturbance

German Letter	Symbol	Pronunciation Guide
ö (short)	*ö*	Close to *u* in *fur*
ö, öh (long)	*öh*	Close to *u* in *hurt*

Say *ü* as in the French Word *Sûr*

This *ü* sound does not have an English equivalent. If you speak French, though, you're in luck: The *ü* is very close to the *u* sound in the French word *sûr*. Another way to accomplish this is to say *ee*, hold your jaw and tongue in this position, and then round your lips as if you were pronouncing *u*.

Glück	Mücke	Rücken	Rhythmus
glük	*mük-uh*	*Rü-kuhn*	*Rüt-moos*
luck	mosquito	back	rhythm

The long *ü* or *y* is the same sound, just held for a longer interval of time.

rühren	führen	Lüge	Pseudonym
Rüh-Ruhn	*füh-Ruhn*	*lüh-guh*	*psoy-doh-nühm*
to stir	to lead	lie	pseudonym

German Letter	Symbol	Pronunciation Guide
ü, y (short)	*ü*	Close to *oo* in *food*
ü, üh, y (long)	*üh*	Close to *oo* in *food*

As a Rule

If you've read through this pronunciation guide thoroughly, you may have already noticed a certain correlation between the spellings of words and their pronunciations. For example, a vowel is short when followed by two consonants. When a vowel is followed by an *h* and another consonant, or even by a single consonant, the vowel is long.

Diphthongs

Diphthongs are not a provocative new style of bikini. In English, we tend to dipthongize vowels in words like *sky*, where the *y* is pronounced *ah-ee*, and *go*, where the *o* is pronounced *oh-oo*. Following the pattern of German diphthong formation, the *o* and *u* in the English word *about* come together to create the diphthong *ah-oo*. You've seen diphthongs in vowels positioned back to back, as the *o* and the *e* are in the word *Noel*. Diphthongs are always made up of two different vowel sounds that glide in the same syllable. How do you recognize a diphthong? Listen. The first vowel

Achtung

Don't confuse *ie*, which is pronounced like *ee* in *feet*, with the diphthong *ei*, which is pronounced like the English word *eye*. Think *Bier* (*beeR*) versus *Wein* (*vayn*).

sound glides or "dips" into the next vowel sound. In German, they are vowels that travel in pairs.

Here are the diphthongs most frequently used in German. For other diphthongs, each vowel should be pronounced the same way it would be if pronounced separately: *Kollision (ko-lee-zeeohn), Familie (fah-mee-leeuh)*.

The Diphthongs *ei* and *ai*

To make the sound of these diphthongs, start with your mouth halfway open and end with your mouth almost—but not quite—closed. Practice with these words:

Bleistift	Mai	vielleicht	klein	fein
blay-shtift	*may*	*fee-layHt*	*klayn*	*fayn*
pencil	May	maybe	small	fine

German Letter(s)	Symbol	Pronunciation Guide
ei, ai	*ay*	Say *y* as in *cry*

The Diphthong *au*

Let's suppose that you've been trying so hard to pronounce these new sounds correctly that you bite your own tongue by mistake: Ow! That's precisely the sound of this next diphthong. Try making this *ow* sound as you say these words:

Haut	Braut	schauen	verdauen	Sauerkraut
hout	*bRout*	*shou-uhn*	*feR-dou-uhn*	*sou-eR-kRout*
skin	bride	to look	to digest	sauerkraut

German Letter(s)	Symbol	Pronunciation Guide
au	*ou*	Say *ou* as in *couch, mouse*

The Diphthongs *eu* and *äu*

Try saying this: "Boy oh boy oh boy oh boy oh boy." If you managed that without too much trouble, chances are, you have the sound of this diphthong down.

heute	Reue	neu	Schläuche	Häute
hoy-tuh	*Roy-uh*	*noy*	*shloy-Huh*	*hoy-tuh*
today	regret	new	hoses	skins

German Letter(s)	Symbol	Pronunciation Guide
eu, äu	*oy*	Say *oy* as in *toy*

We're finished with vowels. You might need a little time to get used to making sounds you've never made before. German friends (or, in the absence of live, German-speaking humans, German tapes or CDs from your local library) would come in handy now. You should try to listen to native German speakers, particularly because many of the modified vowel sounds do not have English equivalents. At this point, concentrate on getting the sounds right.

The Least You Need to Know

♦ Untie your tongue. Before you know it, you'll be pronouncing words like *Bratwurst* and *Fahrvergnügen* correctly.

♦ After you learn the basic pronunciation of German vowels, you will be able to read some German without too much difficulty.

♦ Umlauted vowels are only slightly different from pure vowels, but this difference significantly alters the meanings of words. Practice making the umlauted vowel sounds, just as you would any new sound.

Pronounce It Properly: Consonants

In This Chapter

- ◆ Consonants that sound the same
- ◆ Consonants to clear your throat
- ◆ Worthwhile combos
- ◆ Hissing and grrrring in German

By now you should be able to make the correct sounds of vowels in German. But what good are all the vowel sounds you learned in Chapter 2 without consonants? What good is Astaire without Rogers or hamburgers without catsup, lettuce, a tomato slice, and a pickle? The bottom line is, say *oo* or *ee* as often as you like: It won't get you a Big Mac at a Berlin McDonald's or a seat at the Vienna Opera without the help of a few consonants.

The good news is, the sounds of German consonants will not be as unfamiliar as many of the sounds you tried in the previous chapter. German consonants either are pronounced like their English counterparts or are pronounced like other consonants in English. The only German consonant sounds you won't encounter in English are the two sounds represented in this book by the symbol *H* (the *ch* in *ich*) and the symbol *CH* (the *ch* in *Loch* [*loCH*]).

In written German, you'll also come across a new letter: the consonant *ß*; this symbol is pronounced *es-tset*. It's a combination of the letters *s* and *z* and is considered a single consonant. When people can't find the es-tset key on their word processor, they often write the es-tset as a double *s* (*ss*). In either case, it should be pronounced like an *s*. And it gets simpler! In August 1998, German-speaking countries agreed to implement a spelling reform. Regarding when to spell with the es-tset and when to use a double *s*, the es-tset became less frequently used. It is used only after long vowels (a concept introduced in the last chapter). Until 2005, some latitude will exist with the acceptance of both spellings, after which the former *daß* ("that") must then appear written with two *s*'s—*dass*—because the *a* in this word (followed by a double consonant) is short.

Conquering Consonants

Before you start stuttering out *consonants*, we should probably tell you a little about how this section works. The consonants in the following tables are not given in alphabetical order. They are grouped according to pronunciation type. You should read the pronunciation guide carefully from beginning to end so that you'll know where to look later if you need to locate a specific consonant. For each letter, we provide English examples of how German consonants are pronounced, along with the symbols used throughout this book to represent the sounds. Keep in mind that the symbols (consonants or combinations of consonants, lowercase or uppercase) are not the standard ones used in the dictionary. We've tried to choose symbols that correspond closely to the sounds they represent and are easy for English speakers to recognize at a glance. Reading through these tables may seem like crossing a muddy field—progress is slow, each step requires effort, and at times it doesn't feel as if you're getting anywhere. But it's worth the effort: You want to speak German, don't you?

What's What

Consonants All the letters in the alphabet other than *a*, *e*, *i*, *o*, and *u*. Consonants are best described as involving some obstruction of the air stream, whereas vowels do not have any sort of obstruction.

Same Letters, Same Sounds

Many consonants are pronounced the same way in German and in English. When you see these letters, just go ahead and pronounce them the way you do in English words.

German Letter(s)	Symbol	Pronunciation Guide
f, h, k, l, m, n, p, t	The same as English letters	Pronounced the same as in English

Plosives: *b*, *d*, and *g*

Let's take a look at the letters *b*, *d*, and *g*. They are called *plosives* because of the way their sounds are articulated: with small explosions of air. At the beginning of a word (word initial) or when followed by a vowel, these sounds involving a stoppage of air utilize the vocal cords. Utter a *b* sound with a hand on your throat (where your vocal box is). You should feel vibrations because it is a voiced sound. Its countersound articulated at exactly the same place in the mouth, in exactly the same way but not involving the vocal cords, is a *p*, a voiceless sound.

Whisper, and you will not feel the vibrations in your vocal cords. This sound is heard in German at the end of a word yet is orthographically (spelling-wise) represented with a *b*. For example, at the beginning of a syllable, *b* is pronounced the same way as it is in English: *Bleistift* (*blay-shtift*), "pencil"; *braun* (*bRoun*), "brown"; and *aber* (*ah-buhR*), "but." When *b* occurs at the end of a syllable, however, it is pronounced like a *p* (without the use of the vocal cords): *Laub* (*loup*), "foliage"; or *Korb* (*koRp*), "basket."

> **CAUTION**
>
> **Achtung**
>
> The German *l* is not articulated in precisely the same place in the mouth as the English *l*. The English *l* is dark, formed with the tongue more relaxed. The German *l*—light, nearly as vibrant as the German *r*—is formed with the tip of the tongue just behind the upper front teeth.

German Letter	Symbol	Pronunciation Guide
b	*b*	Say *b* as in *big*
b at the end of a syllable	*p*	Say *p* as in *pipe*

At the beginning of a syllable, the *d* is *voiced* and pronounced like an English *d*: *Dach* (*dACH*), "stream"; *denken* (*den-kuhn*), "to think"; or like the first *d* in *Deutschland* (*doytch-lAnt*), "Germany." At the end of a syllable, the *d*, like its friend the *b*, loses its voicing and is pronounced like a *t*: *Leid* (*layt*), "sorrow," or like the last *d* in *Deutschland* (*doytch-lAnt*).

> **What's What**
>
> **Voicing**   The production of audible vibration—a buzzing sound—caused by air from the lungs passing through the vocal cords when they are partly closed.

German Letter	Symbol	Pronunciation Guide
d	*d*	Say *d* as in *dog*
d at the end of a syllable	*t*	Say *t* as in *tail*

At the beginning of a syllable, *g* is voiced and pronounced the same as it is in English: *Gott* (*got*), God. At the end of a syllable, *g* becomes voiceless and is pronounced like *k*: *Weg* (*veyk*), "way." But you already deduced that, didn't you? The consonant *g* has yet another pronunciation, thanks to foreign infiltration. In certain words, usually ones that have been assimilated into the German language from other languages—namely, French—pronounce the *g* as in *Massage* (*mA-sah-juh*).

German Letter	Symbol	Pronunciation Guide
g	g	Say *g* as in *God*
g at the end of a syllable	k	Say *k* as in *kitchen*
g in foreign language words	j	Say *j* as in *massage*

> ### As a Rule
>
> When the letters *-ig* occur at the end of a word, they are pronounced the way *ich* is pronounced in the German word *ich: traurig* (*tRou-RiH*). But check it out! We have the same word-building suffix in English, derived from Old English into Middle English, *-lic*, meaning "like," as in *childlike*. Eventually, this same suffix doubled its purpose and became the standard way to form an adverb, as in the present-day English *friendly* or *homely*.

Fricatives

Fricatives are consonants articulated when the air stream coming up the throat and out of the mouth meets an obstacle, causing—you guessed it—friction.

Got a Frog in Your Throat? *ch, chs, h, j*

There's no exact English equivalent to the *ch* sound in German, but when you say words like *hubris* and *human*, the sound you make when you pronounce the *h* at the very beginning of the word is very close to the correct pronunciation of the German *ch* in *ich* (this *ch* sound is one of the most difficult sounds, we might add, for English speakers learning to speak German). If you can draw out this *h* sound longer than you do in these two English words, you should have very little trouble pronouncing the following words accurately: *ich* (*iH*), "I"; *manchmal* (*mAnH-mahl*), "sometimes"; *vielleicht* (*fee-layHt*), "maybe."

The second *ch* sound is articulated at the same place in the back of the throat as *k*, but the tongue is lowered to allow air to come through. To approximate this sound (represented in this book by the symbol *CH*), make the altered *h* sound you just learned farther back in your throat—a little like gargling. Can you pronounce Johann Sebastian Bach's name correctly? Give this a shot: *Yoh-hAn zey-bAs-tee-ahn bahhhh* (gargle and hiss like a cat simultaneously at the end). Once you can do this, you have mastered this second *ch* sound. Practice by reading the following words aloud: *Buch* (*bewCH*), "book"; *hoch* (*hohCH*), "high"; *Rache* (*RA-CHuh*), "revenge." Take heart, however, because you don't have to be conscious of the variation between *H* and *CH*; you will automatically produce the one prompted by the preceding vowel. That is to say, if the vowel coming before the *ch* sound is produced in the front part of the oral cavity (linguistic term for "mouth") as in *ich*, the *ch* will come out less guttural than the *ch* after a back vowel, like the *a* in *Bach*.

In general, when *ch* occurs at the beginning of a word, it is pronounced like a *k*: *Chaos* (*kA-os*), *Charisma* (*kah-ris-mah*). Exceptions occur, however, as in *China*, where the *ch* may be pronounced like a *k* or the way it is in *ich*.

The *ch* has a fourth pronunciation: *sh*. This pronunciation is usually used only for foreign words that have been assimilated into the German language: *Chef* (*shef*), "boss"; *Chance* (*shahn-suh*).

German Letter(s)	Symbol	Pronunciation Guide
ch	*H*	Close to *h* in *human*
	CH	No English equivalent
	k	Say *k* as in *character*
	sh	Say *sh* as in *shape*

You won't have any trouble with the *chs* sound. Say *Fuchs* (*foox*), "fox"; *Büchse* (*büh-xuh*), "box."

German Letter(s)	Symbol	Pronunciation Guide
chs	*x*	Say *x* as in *fox*

The *h* is silent when it follows a vowel, to indicate that the vowel is long: *Stahl* (*shtahl*), "steel"—remember those spelling reformers of the fifteenth century? In some cases, *h* is silent when it follows a *t*, as in *Theater* (*tey-ah-tuhR*). Otherwise, the *h* is pronounced very much like the English *h*—just a little breathier, as in both the English "hello" and its German equivalent, *hallo* (*hA-loh*).

German Letter	Symbol	Pronunciation Guide
h	*h*	Say *h* as in *house*

As a Rule

The English *th* sound does not exist in German. Either the *h* is silent or both *t* and *h* are pronounced separately, as in the compound words *Stadthalle* (*shtAt-hA-luh*), "town hall"; and *Misthaufen* (*mist-hou-fuhn*), "dung heap," both of which are "divided" by a glottal stop between the syllables. You produce glottal stops all the time, believe it or not, whenever you disagree, shake your head, and utter *uh-uh*. That tiny pause between the syllables is referred to as a glottal stop!

Whenever you see a *j* in German, pronounce it like an English *y*: *Ja* (*yah*), "yes"; *Jaguar* (*yah-gwahR*).

German Letter	Symbol	Pronunciation Guide
j	*y*	Say *y* as in *yes*

Familiar Sound, Different Position: *z* and *c*

The *z* sound is made by combining the consonant sounds *t* and *s* into one sound: *zu* (*tsew*), "to"; *Zeug* (*tsoyk*), "thing"; *Kreuz* (*kRoyts*), "cross." Although this sound may *seem* new to you, English has the exact same sound—merely in a different position—word final, as in *cats*.

German Letter	Symbol	Pronunciation Guide
z	*ts*	Say *ts* as in *nuts*

In German, you will rarely run into a *c* that isn't followed by an *h*, but when you do, that *c* should be pronounced *ts* whenever it occurs before *ä*, *e*, *i*, or *ö*: *Cäsar* (*tsäh-zahR*), or like the first *c* in *circa* (*tseeR-kah*). Otherwise, it should be pronounced like a *k*: *Creme* (*kReym*), "cream"; *Computer* (*kom-pew-tuhR*); or the last *c* in *circa* (*tseeR-kah*).

German Letter	Symbol	Pronunciation Guide
c	*ts*	Say *ts* as in *nuts*
	k	Say *k* as in *killer*

Double or Nothing: *kn, ps, qu*

The combinations of consonants in this section are pronounced together—that is, one after another.

In English, the *k* is silent in words like *knight* and *knot*. In German, however, both *k* and *n* are pronounced: *Kneipe* (*knay-puh*), "pub"; *Knie* (*knee*), "knee."

German Letter(s)	Symbol	Pronunciation Guide
kn	*kn*	Say *k* as in *kitchen* and *n* as in *now*

As in English, the consonants *ph* are pronounced *f*: *Photograph* (*foh-toh-gRahf*), *Physik* (*füh-zik*).

In the other consonant combinations in this chart, both letters are pronounced: *Pfeife* (*pfay-fuh*), "whistle"; *Pferd* (*pfeRt*), "horse"; *Pseudonym* (*psoy-doh-nühm*); *Schlinge* (*shlin-guh*), "snare."

German Letter(s)	Symbol	Pronunciation Guide
pf	*pf*	No English equivalent
ph	*f*	Say *ph* as in *photo*
ps	*ps*	Say *ps* as in *psst*

The *qu* sound in German is a combination of the consonant sounds *k* and *v*: *Quantität* (*kvAn-tee-täht*); *Qual* (*kvahl*), "torment"; *Quatsch* (*kvAtsh*), "nonsense."

German Letter(s)	Symbol	Pronunciation Guide
qu	*kv*	No English equivalent

The German *r*

Mastering the German *r* will help you sound less American and more Germanlike. Whereas the American *r* is a hard *r*—that is to say, it is produced strongly near the front of the oral cavity—the German *r* is less strident and produced farther back.

To produce the German *r*, position your lips as if you are about to make the *r* sound, but then make the gargling sound you made for the German sound represented in this book by the symbol *CH*. The sound should come from somewhere in the back of your throat. The *r* sound can be soft, as in the words *Vater* (*fah-tuhR*), "father," and *Wasser* (*vA-suhR*), "water," or harder, as in the word *Reich* (*RayCH*), "kingdom." The distinction between these sounds is a subtle one. This book uses the same symbol (*R*) for both sounds.

German Letter	Symbol	Pronunciation Guide
r	*R*	No English equivalent

In southern Germany (München and Stuttgart), the *R* is rolled on the tip of the tongue, whereas in the north (Hamburg and Bremen), the *R* is pronounced deep at the back of the throat. This "uvular" pronunciation of the *R* is the most frequently used, but if you can't master it, try rolling your *R*'s (if someone asks about your accent, say you studied German in Stuttgart). Speaking of Hamburg, that accent is remarkably recognizable by its "sharp" *s*—instead of *Spitze* (*shpit-suh*), "point," you'll hear *spit-suh*.

s, ß, sch, st, tsch

The *s* is similar to the English *z* when followed by a vowel or surrounded by vowels: *Sohn* (*zohn*), "son"; *Seife* (*zay-fuh*), "soap"; *Rose* (*Roh-zuh*). At the end of a word, however, *s* is pronounced like the English *s*: *Maus* (*mous*), *Glas* (*glahs*)—note that there's no vowel following these *s*'s!

German Letter	Symbol	Pronunciation Guide
s	*z*	Say *z* as in *zero*
	s	Say *s* as in *house*

The letter *ß* (es-tset) and the letters *ss* are both pronounced like an unvoiced (no vocal cords in use) *s*: *nass* (*nAs*), "wet"; *dass* (*dAs*), "that"; *Masse* (*mah-suh*), "measure"; *Straße* (*shtRah-suh*), "street"; *Klasse* (*klA-suh*), "class"; *müssen* (*müs-uhn*), "to have to." According to the recently instated spelling reforms in German, the double *s* is used instead of *ß* after or between two short vowels.

German Letter	Symbol	Pronunciation Guide
ß, ss	*s*	Say *s* as in *salt*

The consonants *sch* are pronounced *sh: Scheibe* (*shay-buh*), "slice"; *Schatten* (*shA-tuhn*), "shadow"; *schießen* (*shee-suhn*), "to shoot."

German Letter(s)	Symbol	Pronunciation Guide
sch	*sh*	Say *sh* as in *shape*

In German, *sp* is a combination of the *sh* sound in *shake* and the *p* sound in *pat.* Try saying *ship* without the *i.* Now practice with these words: *Spiel* (*shpeel*), "game"; *Spanien* (*shpah-nee-uhn*), "Spain."

The word-initial *st* sound is a combination of the *sh* sound in *shake* and the *t* sound in *take.* Try saying *shot* without the *o* sound. Practice by saying the following words out loud: *steigen* (*shtay-guhn*), "to climb"; *stolz* (*shtolts*), "proud"; *Stuhl* (*shtewl*), "chair."

The *st* sound is pronounced the same way as it is in English when it occurs within a word or word-final in German: *Meister* (*may-stuhR*), "master"; *Nest* (*nest*), "nest."

German Letter(s)	Symbol	Pronunciation Guide
sp	*shp*	Say *ship* without the *i*
st	*sht*	Say *shot* without the *o*
	st	Say *st* as in *state*

Four consonants in a row! Don't panic. It's easier to read than it appears. *Tsch* is pronounced *tch,* as in the word *witch.* See? A breeze, right?: *Matsch* (*mAtch*), "sludge"; *lutschen* (*loo-tchuhn*), "to suckle"; *deutsch* (*doytch*), "German."

German Letter (s)	Symbol	Pronunciation Guide
tsch	*tch*	Say *tch* as in *switch*

Herbie the Love Bug: The Classic vw

In most cases, the *v* is pronounced like an *f: Vater* (*fah-tuhR*), "father"; *Verkehr* (*feR-keyR*), "traffic"; *viel* (*feel*), "many." In some cases, though, particularly with words that have been assimilated into the German language from Latin-based languages such as French, the *v* is pronounced *v: Vampir* (*vAm-peeR*), *Vase* (*vah-zuh*). You will readily recognize these because English has borrowed them from French as well!

German Letter	Symbol	Pronunciation Guide
v	*f*	Pronounced as the *f* in *father*
	v	Sometimes as the *v* in *voice*

The *w* is pronounced like a *v: wichtig* (*viH-tiH*), "important"; *Wasser* (*vA-suhR*), "water"; *Wurst* (*vuRst*) "sausage."

German Letter	Symbol	Pronunciation Guide
w	*v*	Say *v* as in *vast*

Pronunciation Guide

When you are further along in this book, you may not have time to flip through page after page looking for the letter or the symbol you want to pronounce. The following table is an abbreviated pronunciation guide of vowels, modified vowels, diphthongs, and consonants that differ in pronunciation from English consonants.

Abbreviated Pronunciation Guide

Letter(s)	Symbol	English Example	German Example
Vowels			
a (short)	*A*	Close to m*o*dern	M*a*nn
a (long)	*ah*	f*a*ther	L*a*ge
e (short, stressed)	*e*	b*e*d	B*e*tt
e (short, unstressed)	*uh*	*a*go	B*i*tte
e (long)	*ey*	Close to h*e*y	W*e*g
i (short)	*i*	w*i*nd	W*i*nd
i (long)	*ee*	s*ee*	w*i*r
o (short)	*o*	l*o*rd	*O*rt
o (long)	*oh*	Close to sn*o*w	Verb*o*t
u (short)	*oo*	sh*oo*k	M*u*tter
u (long)	*ew*	st*ew*	Vers*u*ch

Letter(s)	Symbol	English Example	German Example
Modified Vowels			
ä (short)	_ä_	f*ai*r	St*ä*rke
ä (long)	_äh_	Close to f*a*te	B*ä*r
ö (short)	_ö_	Close to f*u*r	L*ö*ffel
ö (long)	_öh_	Close to h*u*rt	sch*ö*n
ü (short)	_ü_	Close to f*oo*d	Gl*ü*ck
ü (long)	_üh_	Close to f*oo*d	l*ü*gen
Diphthongs			
ai, ei	_ay_	*I*	Bl*ei*stift
au	_ou_	c*ou*ch	Fr*au*
äu, eu	_oy_	t*oy*	h*eu*te
Consonants That Differ from English			
b	_b_	*b*ig	*B*leistift
	_p_	*p*ipe	o*b*wohl
c	_ts_	ba*ts*	*C*äsar
	_k_	*k*iller	*C*omputer
ch	_H_	Close to *h*uman	i*ch*
	_CH_	No equivalent	su*ch*en
	_k_	*ch*aracter	*Ch*aracter
	_sh_	*sh*ape	*Ch*ef
chs	_x_	fo*x*	Fu*chs*
d	_d_	*d*og	*D*ach
	_t_	*t*ime	Wan*d*
g	_g_	*g*ood	*g*roß
	_k_	*k*itten	We*g*
	_j_	Massa*g*e	Massa*g*e
h	_h_	*h*ouse	*H*eimat
j	_y_	*y*es	*j*a
kn	_kn_	No equivalent	*Kn*eipe
pf	_pf_	No equivalent	*Pf*eife
ph	_f_	*ph*oto	*Ph*oto
ps	_ps_	*ps*st!	*Ps*eudonym
ng	_ng_	sli*ng*	Schli*ng*e

continues

Abbreviated Pronunciation Guide   (continued)

Letter(s)	Symbol	English Example	German Example
qu	*kv*	No equivalent	*Quatsch*
r	*R*	No equivalent	*Reich*
s	*z*	*z*ero	*Suppe*
	s	mou*s*e	Gla*s*
ß, ss	*s*	*s*alt	Stra*ß*e, Ma*ss*e
sch	*sh*	*sh*ape	*Sch*atten
sp	*shp*	No equivalent	*sp*ielen
st	*sht*	No equivalent	*St*urm
	st	*st*ate	La*st*
tsch	*tch*	sni*tch*	deu*tsch*
v	*f*	*f*ather	*V*ater
	v	*v*oice	*V*ase
w	*v*	*v*ast	*w*ichtig
x	*x*	ta*x*i	ta*x*i
z	*ts*	ca*ts*	*Z*eug

Practicing Pronunciation

Have you practiced all these new sounds? If you have, we are willing to bet that you have succeeded in making most, if not all, of the sounds you will need to pronounce German words correctly. Now practice some more by reading the following sentences out loud.

German	English
Guten Tag, mein Name ist ….	Good day, my name is ….
Ich komme aus den Vereinigten Staaten.	I'm from the United States.
Ich spreche Englisch.	I speak English.
Ich habe gerade begonnen, Deutsch zu lernen.	I just started to learn German.
Die Aussprache ist nicht so schwer.	The pronunciation isn't so difficult.
Deutsch ist eine schöne Sprache.	German is a beautiful language.

The Least You Need to Know

◆ With some exceptions, German consonants are pronounced like their English equivalents.

◆ German is a phonetic language, in that every letter represented in orthography will be heard in its pronunciation. So, once you link a letter with a sound, you can pronounce a word 18 syllables long!

◆ Read whatever you can get your hands on that has been written in German; remember that the Internet is an invaluable resource for this! What seems peculiar in written German will quickly become familiar to you, and soon— particularly if you listen to the German being spoken on a tape or by a native speaker—you will begin to associate letters with their corresponding sounds.

◆ Speaking of the Internet, numerous websites offer pronunciation guides using breakthrough software. Just click on a sound or word and hear it produced.

Chapter 4

You Know More Than You Think

In This Chapter

- ◆ Cognates will help you understand German
- ◆ German words in the English language
- ◆ Beware of false friends

Chances are, you've been speaking German for years without even knowing it! *Kitsch, Wind, Mensch, Angst, Arm, blond, irrational*—the list of German words you already know is longer than you think. The reason you know so much German is that many words in German are similar to or exactly like their English counterparts. These words are called cognates. In addition, many German words have been used so much by English speakers that they have been swallowed whole, so to speak, into the English language to become a part of our vocabulary. Many other German words are so similar to English words that you can master their meanings and pronunciations with little effort. By the end of this chapter, you should be able to put together simple but meaningful sentences in German.

Cognates: What You Already Know Can Help You

Imagine that you've been invited to an art opening by an artist/friend you haven't seen in years. She has been living and teaching in Berlin for as long as you can remember, so you are surprised when you find the invitation in your mailbox. You have a thousand questions you want to ask her. What has it been like living in Berlin? Has she learned to speak German yet?

When the day of the show arrives, you go to the address on the invitation. Shortly after you push open the door and step into a noisy, crowded room, you conclude that something must be wrong. Everyone around you is speaking in tongues. Just as you are about to turn and leave, your friend pushes through the crowd and grabs you by the arm. You are in the right place. Almost all of her admirers are Berliners, she explains, and what you are hearing is German.

You stay close to your friend all night. You listen to the conversations she carries on with other people—*auf Deutsch* (*ouf doytch*). What surprises you most is not how well your friend speaks the language—it's how well you, having as little knowledge of it as you do, understand what is being said. You are able to pick up on certain words: *interessantes Object, gute Freundin, phantastische Party, modern, blau, braun.* Clearly, a new language—a hybrid, perhaps, of German and English—is being spoken, possibly even invented by this sophisticated crowd. How else would you be able to make sense of so many words?

The fact is, German and English are not just kissing cousins—they're sisters. Both languages like to borrow words from the same places—namely, Greek, Latin, and other Romance languages. Because both English and German are members of the Germanic family of languages, they share a lot of "genetic material"—*cognates*, for one thing. Another readily visible similarity is their word-building strategies—that is, add a little something to a noun or verb to make it an adjective: *child + ish = childish* in English; likewise, *Kind + isch = kindisch* auf Deutsch! But back to words that have the same meaning and similar form—the really great part about cognates is that they have the same meanings in German and in English. Pronunciation does vary, of course, but most of the time, these words are familiar to us. And don't forget the American influence on Germany. Since the late 1940s, thanks to postwar reconstruction and increasing globalization, the German language has taken many words from English without changing them at all, aside from capitalizing the nouns. Consider, for example, *team, fitness center, make-up, style, cool, e-mail, fair,* and *camping.*

What's What

Cognates Words that are historically derived from the same source. They may be similar to (near cognates) or exactly like (perfect cognates) counterparts in another language.

Perfect Cognates

The following table lists by article *perfect cognates*—words that are exactly the same in English and German. If you really want to get ahead of the game, use the pronunciation guide in Chapter 1 to pronounce these words the way a German would.

As a Rule

In English, we have only one definite article, *the*, which indicates specificity—a certain something is familiar and recognized in the referred-to situation. German has three definite articles:

- *der* (*deyR*), for masculine singular nouns
- *die* (*dee*), for feminine singular nouns
- *das* (*dAs*), for neuter singular nouns

We call this *grammatical gender*, as opposed to *biological gender*, because the noun following the article doesn't have to represent something male, female, or sexless. *Mädchen* (*mäht-Huhn*), for example, which means "girl," takes the neuter article *das*. Grammatical gender is arbitrary—unpredictable, in fact!

Remember, in German, all nouns are capitalized.

Nouns and their definite articles are explained in greater detail in Chapter 6.

Perfect Cognates

Adjectives		Nouns	
	der	*die*	*das*
ambulant *Am-bo-lAnt*	Alligator *A-li-gah-toR*	Adaptation *A-dAp-tA-tsion*	Auto *ou-to*
			Chaos *kah-os*
blond *blont*	Arm *ARm*	Bank *bAnk*	Element *eh-leh-ment*
elegant *e-le-gAnt*	Bandit *bAn-deet*	Basis *bAh-zis*	Folk *folk*
formal *foR-mahl*	Bus *boos*	Hand *hAnt*	Hotel *hoh-tel*
international *in-teR-nA-tsio-nahl*	Café *kah-fe*	Inspiration *in-spee-rA-tsion*	Museum *mew-zey-oom*
irrational *ee-RA-tsio-nahl*	Chef *shef*	Isolation *ee-zo-lA-tsion*	Nest *nest*

Perfect Cognates (continued)

Adjectives	Nouns		
	der	*die*	*das*
	Film		
	film		
irrelevant	Hamburger	Negation	Optimum
ee-Re-le-vAnt	*hAm-boor-guhR*	*ney-gA-tsion*	*op-tee-moom*
modern	Jaguar	Olive	Organ
moh-deRn	*yah-gwahR*	*oh-lee-vuh*	*oR-gahn*
nonstop	Moment	Pause	Panorama
non-shtop	*moh-ment*	*pou-suh*	*pA-no-Rah-mA*
parallel	Motor	Religion	Photo
pA-rA-lehl	*moh-tohr*	*rey-lee-geeohn*	*foh-to*
permanent	Name	Situation	Pseudonym
peR-mA-nent	*nah-muh*	*zee-too-A-tseeohn*	*psoy-doh-nähm*
	Tiger		Radio
	tee-guhR		*rA-dee-o*
total			System
toh-tahl			*süs-teym*
warm	Wind	Taxi	
vahRm	*vint*	*ta-xee*	
wild			Tennis
vilt			*te-nis*

How Much Do You Understand Already?

Now you could probably go back to your friend's art opening, or to some other gathering of Germans, and carry on a simple conversation in German. How do we recommend that you practice pronouncing these new words? If you haven't already developed the habit of talking to yourself, start talking now. Utilizing the following German noun and adjective cognates, build sentences by inserting the appropriate definite article before the noun (*der*, *die*, or *das*), the verb *ist* (expressing "is" in German), and the adjective. Check your sentences in Appendix A.

Example: You might say of a painting of a tiger in a jungle …

Tiger/wild: *Der Tiger ist wild.*

1. You might say of a painting of a cowboy in the Wild West …

   Bandit/blond:

2. You might say of a painting of a futuristic bank …

   Bank/modern:

3. You might say of an abstract painting of an olive …

   Olive/parallel:

4. You might say of the breeze coming in through the open window of the art gallery …

   Wind/warm:

5. You might say of an abstract-expressionistic piece of art hung upside down …

   Chaos/irrational:

*Did you remember to lead your noun with the grammatically correct form of "the" (der, die, das)?

Near Cognates

The following table lists *near cognates*, words that are spelled almost—but not quite—the same in English and German. Although their spellings differ, their meanings are the same. Now is a good time to recall the consonant shift that led to the separation and distinction of English from German. Consider, for example, the correspondence between the German *t* and English *d*. There's *taub* for "deaf," *tief* for "deep," *die Flut* for "flood," *das Bett* for "bed," and *hart* for "hard." If you vocalize both sounds, you will realize that both *t* and *d* are made in the same location in the mouth, in the same manner—the only difference is the utilization of the vocal cords. Practice pronouncing the German words correctly. Don't forget to gargle those *CH*'s and *R*'s!

Near Cognates

Adjectives		Nouns	
	der	*die*	*das*
akademisch	Aspekt	Adresse	Adjektiv
Ak-A-dey-mish	*As-pekt*	*A-dRe-suh*	*Ad-yek-teef*
akustisch	Autor	Realität	Ballett
A-koos-tish	*ou-tohR*	*Rey-ah-lee-tät*	*bA-let*

continues

Near Cognates   (continued)

Adjectives		Nouns	
	der	*die*	*das*
amerikanisch	Bruder	Bluse	Blut
A-mey-Ree-kah-nish	*bRew-duhR*	*blew-zuh*	*blewt*
äquivalent	Charakter	Energie	Buch
eh-kvi-vah-lent	*kA-Rak-tuhR*	*eh-neR-gee*	*bewH*
attraktiv	Detektiv	Existenz	Ding
A-tRAk-teef	*dey-tek-teef*	*egz-is-tents*	*ding*
blau	Disput	Familie	Ende
blou	*dis-pewt*	*fA-mee-lee-uh*	*en-duh*
direkt	Doktor	Gitarre	Glas
dee-Rekt	*dok-tohr*	*gee-tA-Ruh*	*glahs*
dumm	Elefant		Gras
doom	*ey-ley-fAnt*		*gRahs*
durstig	Fuß	Jacke	Haus
dooR-stiH	*fews*	*yA-kuh*	*hous*
frei	Kaffee	Kassette	Herz
fRay	*kA-fey*	*kA-se-tuh*	*heRts*
freundlich	Markt	Lampe	Licht
fRoynt-liH	*mARkt*	*lAm-puh*	*liHt*
gut	Muskel	Liste	Medikament
gewt	*moos-kuhl*	*lis-tuh*	*meh-dee-kah-ment*
		Nudel	
		new-dulh	
interessant	Onkel	Logik	
in-tuh-Re-sAnt	*on-kuhl*	*loh-gik*	
jung	Organismus	Medizin	Objekt
yoong	*oR-gah-nis-moos*	*meh-dee-tseen*	*ob-yekt*
kalt	Ozean	Methode	Papier
kAlt	*oh-tse-ahn*	*me-toh-duh*	*pah-peeR*
kompetent	Pfennig	Musik	Paradies
koom-pe-tent	*pfe-niH*	*mew-zeek*	*pA-RA-dees*
	Präsident		
	pRey-zee-dent		
lang	Preis	Nationalität	Parfüm
lAng	*pRays*	*nA-tseeo-nA-lee-tät*	*pAR-füm*

Adjectives	Nouns		
	der	*die*	*das*
mystisch *mühs-tish*	Salat *zA-laht*	Natur *nA-tooR*	Phänomen *fäh-noh-men*
		Nummer *Noo-muh*	
nervös *neR-vöhs*	Schock *shok*	Optik *op-tik*	Prinzip *pRin-tseep*
	Schuh *schew*	Oper *Ooh-puhR*	
passiv *pA-seef*	Skrupel *skRew-puhl*	Qualität *kvah-lee-tät*	Produkt *pRoh-dookt*
perfekt *peR-fekt*	Stamm *shtAm*	Rhetorik *Reh-toh-Rik*	Programm *pRo-gRAm*
platonisch *plah-toh-nish*	Strom *shtRom*	Skulptur *skoolp-tewR*	Resultat *Reh-zool-taht*
		Socke *so-kuh*	
populär *poh-pew-lähr*	Supermarkt *zew-peR-maRkt*	Theorie *te-oh-Ree*	Salz *zAlts*
primitiv *pRi-mee-teef*	Wein *vayn*	Tomate *toh-mah-tuh*	Schiff *shif*
sozial *zoh-tsee-ahl*	Wille *vi-luh*	Universität *Ew-nee-veR-zee-tät*	Skelett *skeh-let*
sportlich *shpoRt-liH*			
tropisch *tRo-pish*	Zickzack *tsik-tsAk*	Walnuß *wAl-noos*	Telefon *tey-ley-fohn*
typisch *tüh-pish*			
weis *vays*		Warnung *VaR-noong*	Zentrum *tsen-tRoom*

Cognate Conversation

Now imagine that you have just boarded a sleeper train from Köln to München. Only one other person is sharing your compartment. Use the adjective and noun cognates you have learned to engage your neighbor in conversation. Check your translations in Appendix A.

1. The weather is good.

2. Is the book interesting?

3. The author is popular.

4. The perfume is attractive.

5. The wind is warm.

6. The character is primitive.

7. The heart is wild.

8. *The salt is white.

You think to yourself, "Did I really mean to say that?"

Verb Cognates

It's time now to take a look at verb cognates in their infinitive forms. The *infinitive form* of a verb in German usually ends with an *-en*, as in the words *helfen* (*hel-fuhn*), "to help"; *lernen* (*leR-nuhn*), "to learn"; and *machen* (*mA-CHuhn*), "to do." However, sometimes an infinitive ends in a simple *-n*, as in *sammeln* (*zam-muhln*), "to collect." The following table is a list of verbs that are near cognates in their infinitive form.

What's What

Infinitive form   The unconjugated form of a verb. In German, the infinitive form of verbs end in *-en* or, in some cases, simply *-n*. Verbs are listed in the dictionary in the infinitive form. The English equivalent is *to + verb*. We utilize this infinitive form when using helping verbs such as *had*.

Verb Cognates

German	Pronunciation	English
backen	*bA-kuhn*	to bake
baden	*bah-duhn*	to bathe
beginnen	*buh-gi-nuhn*	to begin
binden	*bin-duhn*	to bind
brechen	*bRe-Huhn*	to break
bringen	*bRin-guhn*	to bring

German	Pronunciation	English
finden	*fin-duhn*	to find
fühlen	*füh-luhn*	to feel
haben	*hah-buhn*	to have
halten	*hAl-tuhn*	to hold
helfen	*hel-fuhn*	to help
kochen	*kO-CHuhn*	to cook
kommen	*ko-muhn*	to come
können	*kö-nuhn*	can
kosten	*kos-tuhn*	to cost
machen	*mA-Huhn*	to make
müssen	*mü-suhn*	must
öffnen	*öf-nuhn*	to open
packen	*pA-kuhn*	to pack
parken	*pAR-kuhn*	to park
planen	*plah-nuhn*	to plan
reservieren	*Rey-zeR-vee-Ruhn*	to reserve
rollen	*Ro-luhn*	to roll
sagen	*zah-guhn*	to say
schwimmen	*shvi-muhn*	to swim
senden	*zen-duhn*	to send
singen	*zin-guhn*	to sing
sinken	*zin-kuhn*	to sink
stinken	*shtin-kuhn*	to stink
sitzen	*zi-tsuhn*	to sit
spinnen	*shpi-nuhn*	to spin
telefonieren	*tey-ley-foh-nee-Ruhn*	to telephone
trinken	*tRin-kuhn*	to drink

Putting It All Together

This isn't so bad, is it? You can probably already read and understand the following fun and fanciful German sentences. Check your interpretations with the answers in Appendix A:

1. Der Präsident und der Bandit backen Tomaten.
   deyR pRä-zee-dent oont deyR bAn-deet bA-kuhn toh-mah-tuhn

2. Der Onkel trinkt Wein.
   deyR on-kuhl tRinkt vayn

3. Der Tiger und der Elefant schwimmen in dem Ozean.
   deyR tee-guhR oont deyR ey-ley-fahnt shvi-muhn in deym oh-tse-ahn

4. Der Film beginnt in einem Supermarkt.
   deyR film buh-gint in ay-nuhm zew-peR-mArkt

5. "Religion oder Chaos? Ein modernes Problem," sagt der junge, intelligente Autor.
   Rey-lee-geeohn oh-duhR kah-os? ayn moh-deR-nuhs pRo-bleym, zAkt deyR yoon-guh, in-te-lee-gen-tuh ou-tohR

6. Der Doktor und der Detektiv finden die Lampe interessant.
   deyR dok-tohr oont deyR dey-tek-teef fin-duhn dee lAm-puh in-tuh-Re-sAnt.

7. Mein Bruder hat eine Guitarre.
   mayn bRew-duhR hAt ay-nuh gee-tA-Ruh

8. Der Aligator kostet $10,000.
   deyR ah-lee-gah-toR kos-tet $10,000

> ⚠️ **Achtung**
>
> When you look up a verb in a dictionary, it's important that you look it up under its infinitive form—that is, under its unconjugated form—just as you would if you were looking up a verb in English. Otherwise, you'll have trouble finding the verb because many German verbs change significantly (as do many English verbs) after they are conjugated. They're changed to reflect logical (grammatical) agreement with the subject, as in *I am* and *she is*.

False Friends

No shortcut is without its pitfalls. Now that you've mastered the art of using words you already know to figure out words in German you didn't know you knew, we must warn you about false friends, or *falsche Freunde* (*fAl-shuh fRoyn-duh*). In language as in life, false friends are misleading. What are linguistic false friends? They are words spelled the same or almost the same in two languages that have different meanings. If you drink *Bier* (*beeR*) for two weeks straight at the Oktoberfest in München, for example, you may end up destroying your liver and lying on a *bier* shortly after your return to the United States. As you can see, these two words, which are spelled exactly the same, have totally different meanings. A word of caution: Cognates can be of help to you in learning German, but false friends can trip you up. Don't assume that you already know the meaning of *every* German word that looks like an English word. It's not always that simple. The following table lists some common false friends.

False Friends

English	Part of Speech	German	Part of Speech	Meaning
after	adverb	der After *Af-tuhR*	noun	anus
also	adverb	also *Al-zoh*	conjunction	so, therefore
bald	adjective	bald *bAlt*	adverb	soon
blaze, blase	noun	die Blase *blah-zuh*	noun	bladder, blister, or bubble
brief	adjective	der Brief *bReef*	noun	letter, official document
chef	noun	der Chef *shef*	noun	boss
closet	noun	das Klosett *kloh-zet*	noun	toilet bowl
fast	adjective	fast *fAst*	adverb	almost
gift	noun	das Gift *gift*	noun	poison
sympathetic	adjective	sympathisch *züm-pah-tish*	adjective	nice
kind	adjective	das Kind *kint*	noun	child
knack	noun	der Knacker *knA-kuhR*	noun	old fogy
lusty	adjective	lustig *loos-tiH*	adjective	funny
most	adjective	der Most *most*	noun	young wine
note	verb	die Note *noh-tuh*	noun	grade
rock	noun	der Rock *Rok*	noun	skirt
see	verb	der See *zey*	noun	lake
sin	noun	der Sinn *zin*	noun	sense

The Least You Need to Know

◆ By using cognates, you can express yourself in German with very little effort.

◆ Many German words and expressions are in use every day in English.

◆ Beware of false friends. Don't let them trick you into saying things you don't mean.

Chapter 5

Idioms: Say It the German Way

In This Chapter

◆ Idiomatic expressions

◆ Expressions of time, location, and direction

◆ Expressions you can use to get your opinion across

◆ German sayings

It's raining cats and dogs, and you're bored to tears, so you sit down to hit the books and study a little German. Today you're going to focus on common expressions in German, many of which are idioms. What are idioms? They are the peculiarities of a given language and must be entered into the mental lexicon as single items with their meanings specified.

Let's say you fall in love with a German politician and have a hasty wedding. He's anxious for you to meet his mother, and the two of you fly to Köln after your honeymoon. Unfortunately, he's called away suddenly on a top-secret mission. He arranges for you to have breakfast at the hotel with his mother the following morning. That night you're so worried about your *Mann* (*mAn*) that you are unable to sleep. You read a few children's stories to yourself, something that has always soothed and relaxed you, and soon you fall asleep. The following morning at breakfast your mother-in-law asks you how you managed to get through the night without her son. You have a working knowledge of German, and you know that *Bett* (*bet*) means "bed" and that *Geschichte* (*guh-shiH-tuh*) means "story," so you say, "*Mit einer Bettgeschichte.*" Your mother-in-law goes pale, rises from her chair, and stumbles from the room. Without realizing it, you have used the German idiom for having a one-night stand.

Idiomatic Expressions

The German expression for being lucky is *Schwein haben* (*shvayn hah-buhn*), which, literally translated, means "to have pig." Don't be too quick to take offense at something that

What's What

Idioms Fixed phrases whose meaning cannot be inferred from the meanings of the individual words. They tend to be frozen in form and thus do not readily enter into other combinations or allow the word order to change.

sounds like an insult; it may be an idiomatic expression. *Idiomatic expressions* are speech forms or expressions that cannot be understood by literal translation—they must be learned and memorized along with their meanings. Most differ greatly from their English counterparts in meaning as well as in construction, but perhaps an even greater number differ only slightly. In English you say, "I'm going home." In German you say, "*Ich gehe nach Hause*," or "I'm going *to* home." Because prepositions in general are idiomatic, it helps to learn them with certain expressions.

Idioms make a language colorful. Most idioms originate as metaphorical expressions that establish themselves in the language and become frozen in their form and meaning. Idiomatic expressions tend to be culturally specific because the lexical items that a certain language relies on to express nonliteral meanings generally have significance in that culture. For example, the German expression *seinen Senf dazugeben* (*zain-uhn zenft dA-tsew-gey-buhn*) literally means "to give his mustard to something." Huh? Well, mustard *does* play a rather prominent culinary role in German, so take a guess. Exactly—it means to give one's opinion—adding one's *two cents*. After all, would you rather have some mustard to go along with your *Wurst*, or two pennies?

To help you get a clearer idea of what idiomatic expressions are, here are a few in English:

sell down the river	haul over the coals
let one's hair down	put one's foot in one's mouth
snap out of it	bite your tongue
hit it off	eat your heart out

The following table lists some German idiomatic expressions that correspond, more or less, with their English equivalents.

Related German Idiomatic Expressions

Idiom	Pronunciation	Meaning
nicht in Frage kommen	*niHt in frah-guh ko-muhn*	to be out of the question
große Augen machen	*gRo-suh ou-guhn mA-CHuhn*	to be wide-eyed
vor die Hunde gehen	*foR dee hoon-duh gey-uhn*	to go to the dogs
Ende gut, alles gut.	*en-duh gewt A-luhs gewt*	All's well that ends well.
Es ist nur Theater.	*es ist noor tey-ah-tuhR*	It's just play-acting.
um ein Haar	*ewm ayn hahR*	by a whisker
ein wunder Punkt	*ayn voon-duhR poonkt*	a sore point
den Kopf voll haben	*deyn kopf fol hah-buhn*	to have a lot on one's mind
blinder Alarm	*blin-duhR A-lARm*	false alarm

More Idiomatic Expressions in German

You probably won't be using too much German slang at hotels and restaurants, but you will certainly find it useful to learn and memorize idiomatic expressions, which are expressions that cannot be literally translated without forfeiting some or all of their true meaning. They are worth committing to memory because knowing a language means knowing fixed phrases consisting of more than one word; you'll sound rather native and express yourself clearly by employing German idioms. The following table lists a few commonly used German idiomatic expressions, their corresponding English meanings, and their origins—the premise here being that knowing the sources of these idioms will help you remember them.

Common German Idiomatic Expressions

Idiom	Pronunciation	Meaning
reinen Tisch machen	*Ray-nuhn tish mA-CHuhn*	to clear the air (Origin: The picture is of a table having been cleared of dishes—a "fresh start.")

continues

Common German Idiomatic Expressions (continued)

Idiom	Pronunciation	Meaning
mit der Tür ins Haus fallen	*mit deyR tüR inz hous fA-luhn*	to come straight to the point (Origin: The picture is of someone in such a hurry to get into a house that he pushes the door off its hinges and then falls on top of it.)
jemandem auf den Zahn fühlen	*yey-mAnd-uhm ouf deyn tsahn füh-luhn*	to give someone a grilling (Origin: By feeling a horse's teeth, an expert can establish its age and value.)
nach Strich und Faden	*naCH striH oont fah-duhn*	good and proper (Origin: from weaving, referring to the two directions of the thread—warp and woof.)
in die Binsen gehen	*in dee bin-zuhn gey-uhn*	to go up in smoke (Origin: a hunting term—a wild duck took refuge from the hunter by hiding in the rushes (Binsen) of a pond or lake.)
wie am Schnürchen laufen	*vee Am schnüR-Hen lou-fuhn*	to go like clockwork (Origin: Die Schnur is the string from which a puppet is suspended and manipulated. Hence, this idiom implies "perfect control.")
den Bock zum Gärtner machen	*deyn bok tsewm gäRt-nuh mA-CHuhn*	to be asking for trouble (Origin: The picture is of a goat given freedom to roam in a well-tended garden. The goat's owner is obviously asking for trouble because goats eat garden plants and pee on flower beds.)
etwas auf die lange Bank schieben	*et-vAs ouf dee lAn-guh bAnk shee-buhn*	to put something off (Origin: In court, more important case files were placed next to the lawyer on his bench. Less urgent files were placed farther away.)

How?

Let's say you live in Wisconsin and you're going away for the weekend to your parents' farm in Vancouver, Canada. One of your new German friends (who doesn't speak any English) asks you how you're getting there. You are at a loss for words. The truth is that you'll be traveling by plane to Vancouver, then going by car from the airport to the lake on the other side of your parents' house, and then traveling by boat across the lake to the dock where a horse will be waiting for you, which you will then ride to the house—but how in the world are you going to start explaining this? What you need are some expressions for travel and transportation. Look at the following table for some suggestions.

German Culture
Literally translated, the German slang expression *Das ist mir Wurst* (*dAs ist meeR vooRst*) means "That's sausage to me." Although a great many Germans appear to love their sausage, this expression is used to show indifference. The idiomatic equivalent is *Das ist mir egal* (*das ist meeR ey-gahl*), which means "It's the same to me."

Expressions for Travel and Transportation

Expression	Pronunciation	Meaning
mit dem Bus	*mit deym boos*	by bus
mit dem Fahrrad	*mit deym fah-RAt*	by bicycle
mit dem Flugzeug	*mit deym flewk-tsoyk*	by plane
mit dem Motorrad	*mit deym moh-toh-RAt*	by motorcycle
mit dem Schiff	*mit deym shif*	by boat
mit der Straßenbahn	*mit deyR shtrah-suhn-bahn*	by streetcar
mit dem Zug	*mit deym tsewk*	by train
mit den Rollerblades	*mit deyn Rol-luhR-bleydz*	by rollerblades
mit der U-Bahn	*mit deyR ew-bahn*	by subway
mit einem Auto	*mit ay-nuhm ou-toh*	by car
mit einem Pferd/zu Pferd	*mit ay-nuhm pfeRt/tsew pfeRt*	on a horse
zu Fuß	*tsew fews*	by foot

Describing Travel

Now it's time to practice what you've learned. Use the preceding table to fill in the blanks of the following sentences with the correct German expressions. Check your answers in Appendix A.

1. Ich fahre _____ von Wisconsin nach Vancouver.
    (I travel _____ from Wisconsin to Vancouver.)

2. Ich fahre _____ vom Flughafen zum See.
    (I travel _____ from the airport to the lake.)

3. Ich fahre _____ über den See. (I go _____ over the lake.)

4. Ich fahre _____ in einer Großstadt. (I travel _____ in a big city.)

5. Ich gehe _____ an die Universität. (I walk to the university.)

When?

We've all benefited from—and suffered from—the vagaries of time expressions. What do people mean when they say "I'll see you soon," or "I'll see you later"? It's hard to say. Sometimes it means tomorrow—sometimes in 10 years. Many time expressions have a wide range of interpretations based on the perception of the speakers, whereas others are more grounded and specific. The following table has a few time expressions you will find useful.

Time Expressions

Expression	Pronunciation	Meaning
am Ende von	*Am en-duh fon*	at the end of
auf Wiedersehen	*ouf vee-deR-zey-uhn*	goodbye
bis bald	*bis bAlt*	see you soon
bis heute Abend	*bis hoy-tuh ah-buhnt*	see you this evening
bis Morgen	*bis moR-guhn*	see you tomorrow
bis später	*bis shpäh-tuhR*	see you later
(zu) früh	*(tsew) fRüh*	(too) early
früher	*fRüh-uhR*	earlier
(zu) spät	*(tsew) shpäht*	(too) late
später	*shpäh-tuhR*	later
gleichzeitig	*glayH-tsay-tiH*	simultaneously
guten Tag/Abend	*gew-tuhn tahk/ah-buhnt*	good day/evening
hallo	*hA-loh*	hello
heute	*hoy-tuh*	today
in einer Weile	*in ay-nuhR vay-luh*	in a while
jeden Tag	*yey-duhn tAk*	every day
jetzt	*yetst*	now
monatlich	*moh-nAt-liH*	monthly
plötzlich	*plöts-liH*	suddenly
pünktlich	*pünkt-liH*	punctually

Expression	Pronunciation	Meaning
regelmäßig	*rey-guhl-mäh-siH*	regularly
sofort	*zoh-foRt*	immediately
täglich	*tähk-liH*	daily
von morgens bis abends	*fon moR-guhnz bis ah-buhnts*	from morning till night
von Tag zu Tag	*fon tahk tsew tahk*	from day to day
von Zeit zu Zeit	*fon tsayt tsew tsayt*	from time to time
wöchentlich	*vö-Hent-liH*	weekly
zur gleichen Zeit	*tsewR glay-Huhn tsayt*	at the same time

Expressing Time

What German idioms of time would you use in the following situations? Check your mastery of time in Appendix A.

1. When your partner leaves on a business trip for the weekend, you say:

   _____

2. When you say goodbye to a friend you will be seeing later that evening, you say:

   _____

3. If the movie begins at 5 P.M. and you arrive at 5 P.M., you arrive: _____

4. If the movie begins at 5 P.M. and you arrive at 7 P.M., you arrive: _____

5. If the movie begins at 5 P.M. and you arrive at 4 P.M., you arrive: _____

6. If you watch TV every now and then, you watch it: _____

7. You should brush your teeth: _____

8. If you follow a ritual every Friday: _____

Where?

Some of the most useful vocabulary you can learn, particularly if you plan to travel in German-speaking countries, are the words for expressing location and direction. To use many of these expressions, you need to know about cases in German (see Chapter 7). The following table focuses on simple terms to help you get to wherever you're going.

Expressions Showing Location and Direction

Expression	Pronunciation	Meaning
draußen	*dRou-suhn*	outdoors
entlang	*ent-lAng*	along
gegenüber	*ge-gen-üh-buhR*	opposite, facing
geradeaus	*ge-Rah-duh-ous*	straight ahead
hinter	*hin-tuhR*	behind
(nach) links	*(nACH) links*	(to the) left
(nach) rechts	*(nACH) ReHts*	(to the) right
neben	*ney-buhn*	beside
seitlich	*zayt-liH*	at the side
über	*üh-buhR*	over, across
unter	*oon-tuhR*	beneath, below, under
vor	*fohr*	in front of

Stating Location

Now you can find anything, right? Here's a simplified map of a city street. Referring to the following map, see if you can fill in the blanks correctly by following the directions in German. Check your directional knowledge in Appendix A.

Getting around on a German street.

der Spielplatz

die Post

das Café

die Bäckerei

der Parkplatz

der Bahnhof

das Hotel

das Museum

Example: Rechts neben dem Café ist die Bäckerei.

1. Gegenüber der Post ist _____.

2. Vor dem Museum ist _____.

3. Links neben dem Hotel ist _____.

4. Hinter dem Café ist _____.

5. Gegenüber der Bäckerei ist _____.

So, What Do You Think?

Opinions—who doesn't have them? And who doesn't like to express them? People tell you how the food tastes, whether they liked the movie, and what they think of politics and religion. Now it's your turn: Express yourself in German—*auf Deutsch, bitte* (*ouf doytch, bi-tuh*). (See the following table.)

Expressing Your Opinions

Expression	Pronunciation	Meaning
Mir geht es ähnlich.	*meer geyt es ähn-liH*	I feel similarly.
bestimmt	*buh-shtimt*	certainly
Das ist mir egal.	*dAs ist meeR ey-gahl*	That's all the same to me.
Das macht nichts.	*dAs mACHt niHts*	It doesn't matter.
genau	*guh-nou*	exactly
Ich habe keine Ahnung.	*iH hA-buh kay-nuh ah-noong*	I have no idea.
Ich weiß nicht.	*iH vays niHt*	I don't know.
natürlich	*nah-tüR-liH*	of course
offensichtlich/klar/ einleuchtend	*o-fen-ziHt-liH/klAR/ ayn-loyH-tend*	obviously
ohne Zweifel/zweifellos	*oh-nuh tsvay-fuhl/ tsvay-fuhl-lohs*	without a doubt; doubtless
Du hast Recht.	*dew hAst Reht*	You are right. (inf.)
Sie haben Recht.	*zee hah-buhn ReHt*	You are right. (form.)
selbstverständlich	*zelpst-feR-shtänt-liH*	self-evident
Das ist falsch.	*dAs ist fAlsh*	That is wrong.
Das ist viel besser.	*dAs ist feel be-suhR*	That's much better.
Das ist völlig richtig.	*dAs ist fö-liH riH-tiH*	That's entirely correct.

continues

Expressing Your Opinions (continued)

Expression	Pronunciation	Meaning
Das finde ich gut/schlecht.	*dAs fin-duh iH gewt/shleHt*	That's good/bad.
Das ist eine tolle/ schlechte Idee.	*dAs ist ay-nuh to-luh/ shleH-tuh ee-dey*	That's a good/bad idea.
danke	*dAn-kuh*	thanks
keine Ursache	*kay-nuh ooR-zah-CHuh*	no need (no problem)

What's Your Opinion?

Imagine this: You're spending the weekend with a friend. She (or he) suggests ways for the two of you to spend the afternoon. Fill in the blanks with the appropriate German suggestions and the English meanings. Check your responses in Appendix A.

Your friend: Heute scheint ein schöner Tag zu sein. Denkst du, dass es regnen wird? (Today looks like a beautiful day. Do you think it will rain?)

You: _____. Ich habe den Wetterbericht nicht gelesen. (_____. I haven't read the weather report today.)

Your friend: Hast du Lust, heute Nachmittag schwimmen zu gehen? (Do you feel like going swimming this afternoon?)

You: _____. Ich schwimme sehr gern! (_____. I love swimming!)

Your friend: Vielleicht sollten wir zunächst den Wetterbericht lesen. Das Wetter könnte sich ändern. (Maybe we should read the weather forecast first. The weather may change.)

You: _____. Das ist mir schon oft passiert. (_____. It's happened to me before.)

Your friend: Welche Zeitung sollen wir kaufen? (Which newspaper should we buy?)

You: _____. Ich glaube in jeder Zeitung finden wir einen Wetterbericht. (_____. I think that we can find a weather report in any newspaper.)

Your friend: Gehen wir ins Kino? (Should we go to a movie?)

You: _____. Ich will den neusten Arnold Schwarzenegger Film sehen!

How Do You Feel?

Many physical and emotional conditions in German can be expressed with the verb *sein* (*zayn*), which means "to be," just as they would be in English: "I am sad," "I am happy," and so on. To express many other conditions, however, you must use the verb *haben* (*hA-buhn*), "to have." For example, in German you would say *Ich habe Angst* (*iH hah-buh Ankst*), literally, "I have fear." To express certain physical conditions, you can use both *sein* and *haben*. It's important to memorize the German expressions that clearly deviate from the English ones because you might create an embarrassing misunderstanding otherwise. Feelings that are expressed with the verb *haben* are followed by a noun. Feelings that are expressed with the verb *sein* are followed by an adjective. Chapters 9 and 10 discuss these verbs and how their form changes to *agree* with the subject. For now, concentrate on expressing how *you* feel: *ich bin* (*iH bin*) for expressions with *sein*, and *ich habe* (*iH hah-buh*) for expressions with *haben*. (See the following table.)

Physical Conditions

Expression	Pronunciation	Meaning
… Jahre alt sein	… yah-Ruh Alt zayn	to be … years old
Angst haben (vor)	Ankst hah-buhn (foR)	to be afraid (of)
beleidigt sein	buh-lay-diHt zayn	to be offended
beschämt sein	buh-shämt zayn	to be ashamed (of)
besorgt sein/Sorgen haben	buh-zoRkt zayn/zoR-guhn hah-buhn	to be worried/to have worries
durstig sein/Durst haben	dooR-stiH zayn/dooRst hah-buhn	to be thirsty
fertig sein	feR-tiH zayn	to be finished
fit sein	fit zayn	to be in shape
glücklich sein	glük-liH zayn	to be happy
gut/schlecht gelaunt sein	gewt/shleHt guh-lount zayn	to be in a good/foul mood
häßlich sein	häs-liH zayn	to be ugly
hungrig sein/Hunger haben	hun-gRiH zayn/ hun-guhRh A-buhn	to be hungry
Mir ist kalt.	meeR ist kAlt	I am cold.
Mir ist heiß.	meeR ist hays	I am hot.
müde sein	müh-duh zayn	to be tired
schlapp sein	schlAp zayn	to be worn out

continues

Physical Conditions (continued)

Expression	Pronunciation	Meaning
Schmerzen haben	*shmeR-tsuhn hah-buhn*	to have an ache, to be in pain
schön sein	*shöhn zayn*	to be beautiful
traurig sein	*tRou-RiH zayn*	to be sad
verliebt sein	*feR-leept zayn*	to be in love

How Are You?

Express how you feel using the expressions in the preceding table. Check your accuracy in Appendix A.

1. Ich bin _____. (I am tired.)

2. Mir ist _____. (I am cold.)

3. Sie weint. Sie ist _____. (She cries. She is sad.)

4. Ich bin _____, dass das Wetter gut ist. (I'm happy that the weather is good.)

5. Mein Magen knurrt. Ich bin _____. (My stomach is growling. I'm hungry.)

6. Ich bin _____. (I'm in love.)

7. Ich kann nicht mehr! Ich bin_____. (I just can't do anymore! I'm finished.)

8. Ich trainiere jeden Tag und mache Bodybuilding. Ich bin _____. (I train every day and do bodybuilding. I am in shape.)

9. Ich esse jetzt mein Lieblingseis. Ich bin _____. (I'm eating my favorite ice cream. I'm in a good mood.)

Achtung

If you say, "I am hot" in German, you are certain to be misunderstood. *Ich bin heiß* (*iH bin hays*) expresses the speaker's level of sexual arousal. To express that you are hot physically, you would say, "*Mir ist heiß*" (*meeR ist hays*)—literally, "It's hot to me."

You know the saying "The early bird gets the worm?" Sayings are everywhere in language, embodying familiar truths and generally accepted beliefs in colorful, expressive language. Here are a few German sayings and their English counterparts.

Sayings

German Saying	Pronunciation	English Equivalent
Wer zuerst kommt, mahlt zuerst.	*veyR tsew-eRst komt, mahlt tsew-eRst*	The early bird gets the worm.
Was ich nicht weis, macht mich nicht heiß.	*vas iH niHt vays, mACHt miH niHt hays*	What I don't know can't hurt me.
Wer zuletzt lacht, lacht am Besten.	*veyR tsew-letst lACHt, lACHt Am bes-tuhn*	He who laughs last, laughs best.
Wer lügt, der stiehlt.	*veyR lühkt, deyR shteelt*	He who lies, steals.
Iss, was gar ist, trink, was klar ist, sprich, was wahr ist.	*is, vAs gahR ist, tRink, vAs klahR ist, shpriH, vAs vahR ist*	Eat what is cooked, drink what is clear, speak what is true.
Ein Unglück kommt selten allein.	*ain oon-glük kOmt zel-tuhn uh-layn*	It never rains, but it pours.
Wer wagt, gewinnt.	*veR vAkt, guh-vint*	Nothing ventured, nothing gained.
Kommt Zeit, kommt Rat.	*komt tsayt, komt Rat*	Time will tell.
Andere Länder, andere Sitten.	*An-duh-ruh län-duhR, An-duh-ruh zi-tuhn*	When in Rome, do as the Romans do.

The Least You Need to Know

◆ Every language has idiomatic expressions that are specific to it. Such colorful expressions help personalize and individualize a language—rendering it culture-specific.

◆ Certain terms, phrases, and expressions in German will be useful when you want to express location or direction.

◆ The verbs with the highest frequency in both English and German are "to have" and "to be." Start learning them and express your opinions and feelings.

◆ When you use popular sayings, don't translate from English to German. Although the sense may be the same in both languages, they use different words. Your best bet is to learn these sayings by rote and sound multicultural.

Part 2

Ready, Set, Go!

Now that you can pronounce German, it's time for some more vocabulary and a little structure. Even if you're not a glutton for grammar, a little reintroduction to some grammatical principles will take you a long way in sounding like a German. In this section of the book, you'll acquire not only the basics—nouns, verbs, sentence structure—but you'll also learn how to express yourself more colorfully.

Chapter 6

The Joy of Gender

In This Chapter

- ◆ How to determine the sex of words
- ◆ Sex changes
- ◆ Pluralities

Think a girl is female (*das Mädchen*)? Think your female baby-sitter is female (*der Babysitter*)? Think your infant girl is female (*der Säugling*)? Not to a German. In this chapter, you'll learn everything you need to know about the gender of German nouns.

Determining Gender

If you have taken any French or Spanish, you have already dealt with nouns that have two genders. In German, it's more complex: German nouns have *three* distinct genders. Believe it or not, the English language used to share this fixation on gender with its German sister. But very early on, even before Chaucer was writing his bawdy *Canterbury Tales*, English speakers were quite politically correct. We began referring to everything as a genderless *the*. If you've been reading this book carefully, you've probably already noticed that German nouns are preceded by three distinct *definite articles:* the masculine article *der* (*deyR*), the feminine article *die* (*dee*), or the neuter article *das* (*dAs*). All plural nouns are preceded by the plural article *die* (*dee*).

Although the natural, or biological, gender of the noun and the grammatical gender of the definite article may work the way you'd expect them to—*Herr* (*heR*), for example, the noun for "man," takes the masculine article *der* (*deyR*)—determining linguistic gender can be tricky. Gender is divided into three linguistic classes that don't correspond to the real world. The fact of the matter is that grammatical gender is arbitrary and unpredictable—basically, a matter of rote memorization.

Don't expect to get the article for a noun just by looking at it. Without committing a noun's gender to memory, you'll need to constantly rely on looking up the noun in a dictionary; masculine nouns are followed by *m.*, feminine nouns by *f.*, and neuter nouns by *n.* Thousands of years ago, gender was based on word classes generally stemming from vowels in the Indo-European culture. Unfortunately for the modern-day German learner, these distinctions have become lost in the sea of language change. In modern German, there are no longer obvious rules or explanations for determining gender. Consider this: Why is the meat you eat at dinner neuter (*das Fleisch*), the potato feminine (*die Kartoffel*), and the cauliflower masculine (*der Rosenkohl*)?

The only fail-safe way of ensuring that you are about to use the correct gender of a German noun is to learn the gender and plural of a noun along with the noun itself.

> **What's What**
>
> **Definite article** The masculine (*der*), feminine (*die*), or neuter (*das*) article that precedes German nouns corresponds to *the* in English. Unlike the English *the*, these articles show the gender and number of a noun, but both English and German definite articles indicate specificity.

Visualize nouns as triangles: One angle is the spelling, one is the gender, and the other is its plural. Inside the triangle is the meaning you attach to the noun. Bear in mind that the gender of a noun affects its relationship to other words in a sentence, and if you learn the definite articles along with the nouns, it will be easier for you to form sentences correctly later. Nevertheless, a few tricks can help you determine the gender of certain nouns as well as alter the gender of certain other nouns, as in English when you change the word *waiter* to *waitress*. We'll share them with you later in this chapter. Keep reading!

Definite Articles

Before you get into German nouns, you must take into account one little diversion: the noun marker that precedes most singular nouns. We use the term *noun marker* to refer to an article or adjective—something that indicates the gender of the noun— whether it is masculine (m.), feminine (f.), neuter (n.), singular (s.), or plural (p.) The most common noun markers, shown in the following table, are definite articles expressing "the" and indefinite articles expressing "a," "an," or "one."

Singular Noun Markers

Noun Marker	Masculine	Feminine	Neuter
the	der	die	das
one, a, an	ein	eine	ein

As a Rule

The noun marker for plural nouns (*die*) should not be confused with the feminine singular definite article (*die*). Although on the surface they share the same form (as you'll find with several grammatical forms in German), their function is different. Because of this homophony in form, only the singular noun markers (*der, die, das*) clearly indicate the grammatical gender of a noun.

Singular Nouns

The nouns in the following table are easy to remember. An obvious correspondence exists between the grammatical gender of the noun marker and the natural, biological gender of the noun. Even the different types of mothers remain predictably feminine, while the different types of fathers are masculine in gender. Later in this chapter, you'll learn how to predict the gender of compound nouns. But for now, become acquainted with family terms.

Gender-Obvious Nouns

Masculine Noun	Pronunciation	English	Feminine Noun	Pronunciation	English
der Bruder	*deyR bRew-duhR*	the brother	die Schwester	*dee shves-tuhR*	the sister
der Kousin	*deyR koo-zin*	the cousin	die Kousine	*dee koo-zee-nuh*	the cousin
der Freund	*deyR fRoynt*	the friend	die Freundin	*dee froyn-din*	the friend
der Onkel	*deyR on-kuhl*	the uncle	die Tante	*dee tAn-tuh*	the aunt
der Opa	*deyR oh-pah*	the grand-father	die Oma	*dee oh-mah*	the grand-mother
der Vater	*deyR fah-tuhR*	the father	die Mutter	*dee moo-tuhR*	the mother
der Stiefvater	*deyR steef-fah-tuhR*	the step-father	die Stiefmutter	*dee shteef-moo-tuhR*	the step-mother
der Schwieger-vater	*deyR shvee-guhR-fah-tuhR*	the father-in-law	die Schwieger-mutter	*dee shvee-guhR-moo-tuhR*	the mother-in-law
ein Mann	*ayn mAn*	the man	eine Frau	*ay-nuh fRou*	the woman
ein Sohn	*ayn zohn*	the son	eine Tochter	*ay-nuh toCH-tuhR*	the daughter

Even in a world where hardly anything is what it seems, you can still determine the gender of certain kinds of nouns even if you haven't memorized their definite articles. For example, nouns referring to male persons (*der Mann, der Sohn*); nouns of professions ending in *-er, -or, -ler,* or *-ner* (*der Pastor, der Bäcker*); and most nouns referring to male animals of a species (*der Tiger, der Elefant*) take the article *der*. But don't worry about gender equality, because you'll soon learn a sure-fire way to effeminate masculine persons and animals! The following tables group endings that will help you to identify the gender of nouns.

Masculine Nouns

Masculine Endings	Example	Pronunciation	English Meaning
-ich	der Strich	*deyR shtRiH*	the line
-ig	der Honig	*deyR hoh-niH*	the honey
-ing	der Ring	*deyR Ring*	the ring
-ling	der Sträfling	*deyR shtRähf-ling*	the prisoner

Exception: das Ding (dAs ding), "the thing"

Even if you aren't a botanist, it may be helpful to keep in mind that most trees and flowers take the feminine article: *die Tulpe* (*dee tool-puh*), *die Rose* (*dee Roh-zuh*), *die Eiche* (*dee ay-Huh*). Generally, two-syllable nouns ending in *-e*, such as *Sonne* (*zo-nuh*) and *Blume* (*blew-muh*), take the feminine article *die*.

Feminine Nouns

Feminine Endings	Example	Pronunciation	English Meaning
-ei	die Malerei	*dee mah-luh-Ray*	the painting
-heit	die Gesundheit	*dee guh-zoont-hayt*	the health
-keit	die Leichtigkeit	*dee layH-tiH-kayt*	the lightness

Feminine Endings	Example	Pronunciation	English Meaning
-schaft	die Gesellschaft	*dee guh-zel-shAft*	the company
-ung	die Wanderung	*dee vAn-duh-Rung*	the walking tour

Das Berlin, das Deutschland, das Paris—most countries, towns, and cities all take the neuter article *das*, as do the letters of the alphabet: *das A, das B, das C, das D,* and so on. So will *most* words borrowed directly into German from other languages: *das Hotel, das Poster,* and so on.

Neuter Nouns

Neuter Endings	Example	Pronunciation	English Meaning
-lein	das Büchlein	*dAs büH-layn*	the little book
-chen	das Kätzchen	*dAs käts-Huhn*	the kitty
-nis	das Ergebnis	*dAs eR-gep-nis*	the result
-tel	das Drittel	*dAs dRi-tuhl*	the third
-tum	das Eigentum	*dAs ay-guhn-tewm*	the property

Exceptions: *der Irrtum (deyR iR-tewm),* "the error"; *der Reichtum (deyR RayH-tewm),* "the wealth"; *die Erlaubnis (dee eR-loup-nis),* "the permission"; and *die Erkenntnis (dee eR-kent-nis),* "the knowledge."

As a Rule _____

When added to a noun, the suffix *–lein* (layn) or *–chen* (Huhn) alters the meaning of the noun, changing it to a diminutive. These nouns are always neuter: *die Stadt* (dee shtAt), "the city," becomes *das Städtchen* (dAs shtät-Huhn), "the little city." Mono-syllabic nouns with *o, u,* or *a* incur an umlaut in this linguistic process of making a noun refer to something smaller.

Certain German nouns never change gender, regardless of whether they refer to a male or a female person or animal. Here are a few of them.

German	Pronunciation	English
das Kind	*dAs kint*	the child
das Model	*dAs moh-del*	the model

continues

continued

German	Pronunciation	English
das Individuum	*dAs in-dee-vee-doo-oom*	the individual
der Flüchtling	*deyR flüHt-ling*	the refugee
das Opfer	*dAs op-feR*	the victim
das Genie	*dAs jey-nee*	the genius
die Person	*dee peR-zohn*	the person

In most cases, making nouns feminine is as easy as changing the definite article from *der* to *die*, dropping the vowel (if the noun ends in a vowel), adding *-in* to the masculine noun, and, if the noun contains an *a*, an *o*, or a *u*, modifying this vowel: *der Koch* (*deyR koCH*), for example, becomes *die Köchin* (*dee kö-Hin*). This convention makes sense if you just think back to what an *umlaut* is all about: When the *–in* suffix is added to the noun, the *i* sound, produced in the front of the mouth, coaxes the back vowels of *a*, *o*, or *u* to slide a little forward as well—hence, sound change! The following table lists some common nouns that can undergo sex changes.

Sex Changes

Masculine Ending	Pronunciation	Feminine Ending	Pronunciation	Meaning
der Lehrer	*deyR ley-Ruhr*	die Lehrerin	*dee ley-Ruh-Rin*	the teacher
der Schüler	*dey R shüh-luhR*	die Schülerin	*dee shüh-luh-Rin*	the school boy/girl
der Arzt	*deyR ARtst*	die ärztin	*dee äRts-tin*	the doctor
der Bauer	*deyR bou-uhr*	die Bäuerin	*dee boy-uhR-in*	the farmer
der Löwe	*deyR löh-wuh*	die Löwin	*dee löh-vin*	the lion
der Anwalt	*deyR An-vAlt*	die Anwältin	*dee An-väl-tin*	the attorney

Compound Nouns (gz)

Meeresgrundforschungslaborauswertungsbericht—pronounced *mey-Ruhs-gRoont-foR-shoongz-lah-bohR-ous-veR-toongz-buh-RiHt*—what in the world, you may ask, is that? Believe it or not, *that* is a word—a compound noun, to be exact. It means "sea-floor research lab evaluation report." While English joins words together to form new, compound words such as *bittersweet*, *homework*, or *spoonfeed*, compound nouns of the cargo-train variety are a German phenomenon. Don't let these words frighten you. If you can recognize the individual nouns, adjectives, or verbs within the longer word, you should have no trouble figuring out the meaning. In the first table of this section, you learned that *die Mutter* means "the mother" and *der Vater* means "the father." It didn't take you long to figure out that the particle *Stief* adds a layer of meaning—"step"—and that *Schwieger* adds "in-law." You also noticed that *all* forms of mothers were feminine—that is to say, they took the feminine marker, *die*. Hmmm …. Is a pattern emerging here? Why, yes! German looks to the right end of a noun to determine its gender. Another way to think of it is that the (directional) right end governs the entire noun. And, after all, government likes to tell us how to do things, and nouns must abide by these very same rules!

As a Rule

Compound nouns combine two or more nouns into one. They are written as one word in German and take the gender of the last noun in the compound. Likewise, compound nouns, being governed by the right end of things, take the plural form of the last noun. *Der Zahnarzt (deyR tsahn-ARtst)*, for example, is made up of the two words *der Zahn* and *der Arzt (deyR ARtst)*. Because *Arzt* comes last, it is the only part of the compound noun that can become plural.

See whether you can put the following words together to form compound nouns and consult Appendix A to verify your new nouns:

Example:

 die Zeit ("time") + der Geist ("spirit") = *der Zeitgeist*

1. das Hotel ("hotel") + die Kette ("chain") = _____

2. die Musik ("music") + das Geschäft ("store") = _____

3. das Geschenk ("gift") + das Papier ("paper") = _____

4. das Telefon ("telephone") + die Nummer ("number") = _____

5. der Brief ("letter") + der Kasten ("box") = _____

6. schwer ("heavy") + die Kraft ("power") = *_____

7. treff (from "to meet") + der Punkt ("point") = *_____

 * Don't forget to capitalize the newly formed compound noun!

An *n* or an *s* is sometimes used between nouns to connect them:

die Tomate ("tomato") + der Saft ("juice") = der Tomatensaft

die Liebe ("love") + die Erklärung ("declarations") = die Liebeserklärung

More Than One

In English, talking about more than one thing is relatively easy—usually, you just add an -*s* to a word. But there are plurals that stump learners of our language. How many *childs* do you have—or, rather, *children?* Are they silly little *gooses*, uh, *geese?* German plurals seem to be confusing, too, but there is a method to the madness. The German language has rules about forming plurals, stemming from that time in German language history when every German noun fit into a "class" of nouns and took many different endings (back when gender was categorical). As this system of *inflecting* nouns declined in the eleventh and twelfth centuries, some of the features of these classes were retained as plural endings. This historical curiosity is what makes forming plurals in German such a challenging experience. Nonetheless, when a noun becomes plural in German, the *noun marker* becomes plural with it, and the articles *der, die*, and *das* all become *die* in their plural forms.

> **What's What**
>
> **Noun marker** Any of a variety of articles, such as *der, die, das*, or *die* (the equivalent of *the* for plural nouns); *ein* (the equivalent of *a* for masculine or neuter nouns); or *eine* (the equivalent of *a* for feminine nouns).

Pluralities

Every English speaker knows that if you have more than one cat, you have cats. In German, however, it's a little trickier. When nouns become plural in German, the noun may remain unchanged (*Mädchen*, for example, remains *Mädchen* in the plural); may take an ending such as -*e*, -*er*, -*n*, -*en*, or -*s*; and/or may undergo a vowel modification. Altering the vowel this way reflects such a noun's history; we can deduce that many hundreds of years ago, an -*i* or -*ja* ending coerced the vowel to shift to the front. Rest assured, there are rules for forming plurals in German, and with enough attention and devotion, you will develop a linguistic feel for them, a type of *Sprachgefühl*. For now, the best way to be sure that you are forming the plural of a noun correctly is to memorize it along with the noun and the article according to the triangle scheme. The following tables give you some basic rules on how to form plurals.

When the nouns in the following two tables become plural, they take either *-n* or *-en*. A majority of German nouns fall into this group, including most feminine nouns. The nouns in this group never take an umlaut in the plural, but if they already have one in the singular, it is retained.

When the nouns ending in *-e*, *-el*, and *-er* in the following table become plural, they take *-n*.

Plural Nouns: Group I

German Noun Singular	Pronunciation	German Noun Plural	Pronunciation	English Meaning
das Auge	*dAs ou-guh*	die Augen	*dee ou-guhn*	eye(s)
der Bauer	*deyR bou-uhR*	die Bauern	*dee bou-uhRn*	farmer(s)
der Junge	*deyR yoon-guh*	die Jungen	*dee yoon-guhn*	boy(s)
der Name	*deyR nah-muh*	die Namen	*dee nah-muhn*	name(s)
die Gruppe	*dee gRoo-puh*	die Gruppen	*dee gRoo-puhn*	group(s)
die Kartoffel	*dee kAR-to-fuhl*	die Kartoffeln	*dee kAR-to-fuhln*	potato(es)
die Schüssel	*dee shü-suhl*	die Schüsseln	*dee shü-suhln*	bowl(s)
die Steuer	*dee shtoy-uhR*	die Steuern	*dee shtoy-uhRn*	tax(es)

Most of the nouns in the following table that take the ending *-en* in the plural are feminine nouns ending in *-ung*, *-ion*, *-keit*, *-heit*, *-schaft*, and *-tät*. All nouns referring to female persons or animals ending in *-in* double the *n* in the plural form before adding the plural *-en*. This convention keeps the *i* sound short—no mutation here, my friend!

Plural Nouns: Group II

German Noun Singular	Pronunciation	German Noun Plural	Pronunciation	English Meaning
das Herz	*dAs heRts*	die Herzen	*dee heR-tsuhn*	heart(s)
das Ohr	*dAs ohR*	die Ohren	*dee oh-Ruhn*	ear(s)
der Mensch	*deyR mensh*	die Menschen	*dee men-shuhn*	human being(s)
die Freiheit	*dee fRay-hayt*	die Freiheiten	*dee fRay-hay-tuhn*	liberty(ies)
die Königin	*dee köh-ni-gin*	die Königinnen	*dee köh-ni-gi-nuhn*	the queens(s)
die Löwin	*dee löh-vin*	die Löwinnen	*dee löh-vi-nuhn*	the lioness(es)
die Mannschaft	*dee mAn-shAft*	die Mannschaften	*dee mAn-shAf- tuhn*	crew(s), team(s)

continues

Plural Nouns: Group II   (continued)

German Noun Singular	Pronunciation	German Noun Plural	Pronunciation	English Meaning
die Möglich-keit	*dee mö-kliH-kayt*	die Möglich-keiten	*dee mö-kliH-kay-tuhn*	possibilities
die Qualität	*dee kvah-lee-täht*	die Qualitäten	*dee kvah-lee-täh-tuhn*	quality(ies)
die Religion	*dee Rey-lee-gee-ohn*	die Religionen	*dee Rey-lee-gee-oh-nuhn*	religion(s)
die Zeit	*dee tsayt*	die Zeiten	*dee tsay-tuhn*	time(s)
die Zeitung	*dee tsay-toong*	die Zeitungen	*dee tsay-toon-guhn*	newspaper(s)

The nouns in the following table take no ending in their plural form. Some of the masculine nouns in the group undergo a vowel modification (because they have since lost their ending), as do the only two feminine nouns in this group. The neuter nouns don't change.

Plural Nouns: Group III

German Noun Singular	Pronunciation	German Noun Plural	Pronunciation	English Meaning
das Mittel	*dAs mi-tuhl*	die Mittel	*dee mi-tuhl*	the mean(s)
das Zimmer	*dAs tsi-muhR*	die Zimmer	*dee tsi-muhR*	the room(s)
das Fenster	*dAs fen-stuhR*	die Fenster	*dee fen-stuhR*	the window(s)
der Garten	*deyR gAR-tuhn*	die Gärten	*dee gäR-tuhn*	the garden(s)
der Lehrer	*deyR ley-RuhR*	die Lehrer	*dee ley-RuhR*	the teacher(s)
der Vater	*deyR fah-tuhR*	die Väter	*dee fäh-tuhR*	the father(s)
die Mutter	*dee moo-tuhR*	die Mütter	*dee mü-tuhR*	the mother(s)
die Tochter	*dee toCH-tuhR*	die Töchter	*dee töH-tuhR*	the daughter(s)

When the nouns in the following table become plural, they take the ending *-e*. All neuter and feminine nouns that end in *-nis* double the *s* in the plural form before adding *-e*, again ensuring that the *i* sound remains short. Take note that some mono-syllabic nouns incur a vowel modification along with assuming the *-e* plural ending.

Plural Nouns: Group IV

German Noun Singular	Pronunciation	German Noun Plural	Pronunciation	English Meaning
das Ereignis	*dAs eR-ayk-nis*	die Ereignisse	*dee eR-ayk-ni-suh*	the event(s)
das Gedicht	*dAs guh-diHt*	die Gedichte	*dee guh-diH-tuh*	the poem(s)
das Jahr	*dAs yahR*	die Jahre	*dee yah-Ruh*	the year(s)
das Pferd	*dAs pfeRt*	die Pferde	*dee pfeR-duh*	the horse(s)
der Baum	*deyR boum*	die Bäume	*dee boy-muh*	the tree(s)
der Brief	*deyR bReef*	die Briefe	*dee bRee-fuh*	the letter(s)
die Kenntnis	*dee kent-nis*	die Kenntnisse	*dee kent-ni-suh*	the knowledge
die Kunst	*dee koonst*	die Künste	*dee küns-tuh*	the art(s)
die Wand	*dee vAnt*	die Wände	*dee vän-duh*	the wall(s)

The plurals of the nouns in the following table end in *-er*. Wherever possible, vowels are modified. When they cannot be modified, as in the noun *das Bild* (the vowels *e* and *i* never take an umlaut in German—they're already "front" vowels), the word takes the *-er* ending. Note that all the words that follow have only one syllable.

Plural Nouns: Group V

German Noun Singular	Pronunciation	German Noun Plural	Pronunciation	English Meaning
das Bild	*dAs bilt*	die Bilder	*dee bil-duhR*	the painting(s)
das Buch	*dAs bewCH*	die Bücher	*dee bü-HuhR*	the book(s)
das Land	*dAs lAnt*	die Länder	*dee län-duhR*	the country(ies)
der Geist	*deyR gayst*	die Geister	*dee gay-stuhr*	the ghost(s)
der Mann	*deyR mAn*	die Männer	*dee mä-nuhR*	the man (men)

Practice Those Plurals

Here is a list of singular items found around the house. Rewrite the list, changing the nouns into their appropriate plural form (all preceded by *die*!). Check Appendix A to verify your plural forms:

Ex. das Haus   **die Häuser**

1. das Zimmer

2. der Garten

3. die Wand

4. das Bild

5. das Buch

6. die Schüssel

7. der Brief

8. die Zeitung

Noteworthy Plurals

As in English, some nouns in German are used only in their plural forms. These are worth noting, particularly because you don't have to worry about whether the articles preceding them are masculine, feminine, or neuter. They always take the plural article *die*. One exception worth mentioning is the English plural noun for spectacles, "glasses," which is singular in German: *die Brille* (*dee bri-luh*).

German	Pronunciation	English
die Ferien	*dee fey-Ree-uhn*	vacation
die Geschwister	*dee guh-shvis-tuhr*	brothers and sisters
die Leute	*dee loy-tuh*	people
die Eltern	*dee el-tuhrn*	parents

A few nouns in German (usually words ending in *a*, *i*, or *o*) take an *-s* to form the plural, as in *das Lotto* (*die Lottos*). In addition, add *-s* in the plural for nouns of foreign origin, such as *die Kamera* (*die Kameras*), *das Café* (*die Cafés*), and *das Büro* (*die Büros*). German abbreviated nouns also add an *-s* in the plural: *der/die Azubi* (*die Azubis*), being an abbreviation for *der/die Auszubildende*, a type of student undertaking further education.

The Least You Need to Know

♦ The only sure-fire way to know a noun's gender is to memorize the definite article with the noun.

♦ Most nouns referring to male persons and animals become feminine nouns when -*in* is added.

♦ Compound nouns in German are easy to formulate and instantly increase your vocabulary power. Figuring out their gender or their plural form won't be a problem because gender and plural forms of even the longest compound words are always determined by the rightmost constituents.

♦ There are many exceptions to rules about forming plurals. Plural forms of nouns should be learned along with the noun and the definite article. If you think of nouns in terms of a triangle—one point being the noun; the second, its gender; and the third, its plural form—you'll be learning three parcels of information for the price of one!

Chapter 7

Fitting Form with Function

In This Chapter

◆ Cases in German

◆ Definite articles

◆ An introduction to subject pronouns

◆ Formality issues

Before we start, we should probably warn you that this chapter introduces some new grammatical concepts and that it just might take some time before you fully understand them. More understanding will come with time and exposure to the language. We all know that learning grammar can be about as exciting as watching grass grow, but lots of people have done it and are now happy, German-speaking individuals.

Now that you have familiarized yourself with nouns, it's time to start forming sentences. In English, once you have the subject, the verb, and the direct object, forming a sentence is easy enough; you put the words in the right order and start talking. It doesn't work this way in German, however. Word order—the position of words in a sentence—isn't as crucial in German as it is in English because German has retained many of the inflections that English dropped along the way. German nouns, pronouns, articles, adjectives, and pronouns are inflected—that is to say, they have overt markings showing their grammatical relations and functions in sentences.

The Four Cases in German

You don't have to be Sherlock Holmes to figure out cases in German. Cases are the forms that articles, adjectives, pronouns, and a few nouns take in a sentence, depending on their function. When we speak of cases and nouns, we are speaking of their articles because the article that precedes a noun is the primary indicator of its gender, number, and—you guessed it—*case*. German uses four cases to express grammatical relations between sentence parts: nominative, accusative, dative, and genitive. By altering the form of *the, a,* or an adjective, you can figure out what's happening to whom, no matter where the nouns are in the sentence. So don't be put off. Although at first you might scowl at such grammatical-sounding terms, you figured all this out intuitively when you *acquired* English as a native language—you just didn't have to consciously label grammatical relations as you do when you *learn* a foreign language. In a nutshell, the nominative case indicates the subject of a sentence, the accusative case indicates the direct object of a sentence, and the dative case indicates the indirect object of a sentence. The genitive case shows possession.

> **What's What**
>
> **Case**   The form that articles, adjectives, pronouns, and a few nouns in German take, depending on their grammatical function in a sentence. Cases make it clear whether a noun phrase is functioning as a subject of a verb or an object of a verb or preposition.

Subject	Verb	Indirect Object	Direct Object
The girl	buys	the cat	a fish
Das Mädchen	*kauft*	*der Katze*	*einen Fisch*

In German, cases enable you to vary the order of nouns and pronouns without changing the overall meaning of the sentence, allowing you to place focus on whatever element of the sentence you like!

> Das Mädchen kauft den Fisch.
>
> Den Fisch kauft das Mädchen.

Although the second sentence might make you think that the fish is buying the girl, it isn't, thanks to the cases taken by the nouns *das Mädchen* (nom.) and *den Fisch* (acc.). Despite the position of the nouns, the noun markers remain the same in both sentences, clearly indicating that the fish is being bought by the girl, not that the girl is being bought by the fish.

Naming the Nominative Case

Nominative is the case of the *subject* of a sentence—that is, of the noun or pronoun performing the action (or undergoing the state of being) of the verb. Think of the nominative case as "naming" who or what is performing the action in the sentence.

Nominative (Subject)	Verb
Ich (I)	denke (think)

What Gets the Action: The Accusative Case

The accusative case is used with the direct object. The *direct object* tells you to whom or what the action of the verb is being directed. You also use the accusative case with time and in measuring data that specifies how short, how soon, how often, how much, and how old, and after certain prepositions. Some varieties in English still express the accusative case (in English it's called the *objective* case) by using the alternative form of who: *whom*. Think of the accusative case as expressing whom or what is being "accused" by the verb.

Nominative (Subject)	Verb	Accusative (Direct Object)
Ich (I)	schicke (send)	ein Paket (a package)

Indirectly: The Dative Case

The dative case can be used instead of a possessive adjective with parts of the body and after certain verbs, prepositions, and adjectives. It is used primarily to indicate the indirect object, however. The *indirect object* is the object for whose benefit or in whose interest the action of the verb is being performed. Think of giving, helping, pleasing, and such—an animate object is receiving the action and usually something else (the direct object), to boot! English has lost most of its inflectional endings reflecting this case, so it relies on *word order* and prepositions, such as *to* and *for*, to express the dative function.

What's What

Word order   The order of the basic sentence elements—subject, object, and verb—that contributes to the meaning or *sense* of a sentence.

Nominative (Subject)	Verb	Dative (Indirect Object)	Accusative (Direct Object)
Er (he)	schickt (sends)	seinem Bruder (his brother)	ein Paket (a package)

Possessing the Genitive Case

The genitive case indicates possession. Whereas English uses an -s, as in "the neighbor's yard" or the preposition *of* in "the yard *of* the neighbor" to express possession, German can use either an -s (without an apostrophe) after a person's name or the German prepositional equivalent—in this case, *von*. Most of the time, however, German marks possession on both the noun marker (the article or adjective preceding the noun) and, with neuter and masculine nouns, after the noun with -(e)s. Although this construction might seem confusing at first, think of it in terms of the word *possessive*; look at all of those -s additions. Why not latch on to that idea in German?

Nominative Object)	Verb	Dative (Indirect Object)	Genitive (Possessive)	Accusative (Direct Object)
Er (he)	schickt (sends)	der Frau (the wife)	seines Bruders (of his brother)	ein Paket (a package)

Marking Who's Doing What to Whom

If you've been exposed to Latin or a Slavic language such as Polish or Russian, you might have heard about *declension*, the term used to talk about the changes occurring in a word to indicate different cases.

Declension refers to the patterns of change followed by different groups of words in each case. Declension in German is pretty much limited to articles, adjectives, and a few instances of nouns. In addition, pronouns change form according to their function, but this change is very similar to English: *he* versus *him* and such. Be sure that when you are looking up a noun, you look for it under its base form, not its plural or possessive form. The nominative singular is the form under which nouns appear in the dictionary, just as the infinitive is the form under which verbs appear.

What's What

Declension The pattern of inflectional markings that occurs in articles, adjectives, pronouns, and a few nouns in each of the four cases in German.

The Case of the Definite Article

German has four possible declensions for each definite article (remember, definite articles are used when you are speaking about a particular person or thing). In addition, the plurals of *der*, *die*, and *das* have separate declensions. Commit this chart to memory, rewrite it on a card, use a different color for each case—do anything and everything to help yourself conceptualize the case system. This system is your springboard, and you won't be able to dive in if you don't learn this *paradigm*. In addition, you will be able to plug in new information as you go along.

What's What

Paradigm A grammatical chart, organized in a regular way so that new information may be plugged in and easily assimilated.

Case	Masculine	Feminine	Neuter	Plural
Nom.	der	die	das	die
	deyR	*dee*	*dAs*	*dee*
Acc.	den	die	das	die
	deyn	*dee*	*dAs*	*dee*
Dat.	dem	der	dem	den
	deym	*deyR*	*deym*	*deyn*
Gen.	des	der	des	der
	des	*deyR*	*des*	*deyR*

As a Rule

An easy way to remember the definite article, or *der*-word, paradigm is with the pneumonic device reflecting the last sound of each of the genders, numbers, and cases represented left to right, top to bottom: RESE (*Ree-see*), NESE (*nee-see*), MRMN (*muhR-muhN*), SRSR (*suhR-suhR*).

Masculine Nouns

Using the same paradigm—the same setup of cases in descending order of nominative, accusative, dative, genitive—we can plug in actual masculine nouns. Notice the noun endings in the genitive case. You'll observe that a monosyllabic noun gets an *-e* before its genitive *-s*. A masculine noun of more than one syllable in the genitive case requires a mere *-s*.

Case	Noun	Pronunciation	Noun	Pronunciation
Nom.	der Fall	*deyR fAl*	der Vater	*deyR fah-tuhR*
Acc.	den Fall	*deyn fAl*	den Vater	*deyn fah-tuhR*
Dat.	dem Falle	*deym fA-luh*	dem Vater	*deym fah-tuhR*
Gen.	des Falles	*des fA-luhs*	des Vaters	*des fah-tuhRs*

Remember those Indo-European noun classes that once ruled supreme? Well, trace vestiges occur with a few masculine nouns that take an *-(e)n* ending in all cases except the nominative. These are usually referred to as *weak nouns* because they're too weak to stand on their own in any sentence function except as the subject. Because they get an *-(e)n* in the genitive, you don't need to add that usual *-(e)s*. This group includes many nouns of foreign origin that are accented on the last syllable, such as *der Assistent, der Demokrat, der Polizist, der Präsident, der Tourist*; Germanic masculine nouns that end in an unstressed *-e*, such as *der Löwe* ("lion"), *der Kunde* ("customer"), and *der Junge* ("boy"); and in a few monosyllabic nouns, such as *der Mensch* ("human being"), *der Held* ("hero"), and *der Herr* ("man").

Case	Noun	Pronunciation	Noun	Pronunciation
Nom.	der Student	*deyR shtew-dent*	der Junge	*deyR yoon-guh*
Acc.	den Studenten	*deyn shtew-den-tuhn*	den Jungen	*deyn yoon-guhn*
Dat.	dem Studenten	*deym shtew-den-tuhn*	dem Jungen	*deym yoon-guhn*
Gen.	des Studenten	*des shtew-den-tuhn*	des Jungen	*des yoon-guhn*

Feminine Nouns

Fair's fair, so here are a few feminine nouns plugged into our paradigm. Notice that, unlike the masculine nouns, feminine nouns do not need endings. They remain unchanged.

Case	Noun	Pronunciation	Noun	Pronunciation
Nom.	die Lust	*dee loost*	die Blume	*dee blew-muh*
Acc.	die Lust	*dee loost*	die Blume	*dee blew-muh*
Dat.	der Lust	*deyR loost*	der Blume	*deyR blew-muh*
Gen.	der Lust	*deyR loost*	der Blume	*deyR blew-muh*

Neuter Nouns

And now for the neuter nouns. Just like the masculine ones, the monosyllabic neuter noun takes that vestigal -*e* ending in the dative and -(*e*)*s* in the genitive case.

Case	Noun	Pronunciation	Noun	Pronunciation
Nom.	das Jahr	*dAs yahR*	das Licht	*dAs liHt*
Acc.	das Jahr	*dAs yahR*	das Licht	*dAs liHt*
Dat.	dem Jahre	*deym yah-Ruh*	dem Lichte	*deym liHt*
Gen.	des Jahres	*des yah-Ruhs*	des Lichtes	*des liHts*

Plurals

Coming now to the right side of the original paradigm, we can plug in the plural nouns for *father* and *child*, only augmenting them with an -*n* in the dative case. If the plural form already ends in an -*n*, as in *Katzen* ("cats"), you have nothing to worry about. All plurals in the dative case take an additional -*n*, if possible.

Case	Plural	Pronunciation	Plural	Pronunciation
Nom.	die Väter	*dee fäh-tuhR*	die Kinder	*dee kin-duhR*
Acc.	die Väter	*dee fäh-tuhR*	die Kinder	*dee kin-duhR*
Dat.	den Vätern	*deyn fäh-tuhRn*	den Kindern	*deyn kin-duhRn*
Gen.	der Väter	*deyR fäh-tuhR*	der Kinder	*deyR kin-duhR*

Identifying Function

Now it's time to apply form to function. Underline the subject (in the nominative case), put parentheses around the direct object (accusative case), and brackets around the indirect object (dative case) in the following sentences. Not all sentences have both an indirect and a direct object! Check your analyses in Appendix A.

1. Den Studenten findet der Detektiv intelligent.

2. Dem Vater schicken die Kinder den Kaffee.

3. Die Menschen helfen den Kindern.

4. Das Paket packt der Lehrer.

5. Die Mütter bringen den Vätern die Blumen.

Indefinite Articles

The English equivalent of the indefinite article is *a* or *an*. *Indefinite articles* are used when you are speaking about a noun in general, not about a specific noun. Only three declensions are possible for the indefinite article because indefinite articles do not occur in the plural. Just as in English, it's not possible or logical to talk about *a books*. Again, we're using that original paradigm and plugging in this *new* information that really isn't all that *new*. If you compare this chart of indefinite articles (the *ein*-word paradigm) with the definite article chart (the *der*-word paradigm), you'll see that all the feminine endings exactly resemble the ends of the feminine definite articles: *die, eine; die, eine; der, einer; der, einer.* Now look for correspondences in the masculine and neuter. Sure enough, only three new bits of information are actually on this chart, provided that you've done your homework and learned the other paradigm: Masculine and neuter nominative and neuter accusative indefinite articles (*ein*) don't take an ending. See? German *is* simple, after all!

What's What

Indefinite article

Article used when you are speaking about a noun in general, not about a specific noun. The indefinite article is used to introduce a topic into discourse.

Case	Masculine	Feminine	Neuter	Plural
Nom.	ein	eine	ein	none
	ayn	*ay-nuh*	*ayn*	
Acc.	einen	eine	ein	none
	ay-nuhn	*ay-nuh*	*ayn*	
Dat.	einem	einer	einem	none
	ay-nuhm	*ay-nuhR*	*ay-nuhm*	
Gen.	eines	einer	eines	none
	ay-nuhs	*ay-nuhR*	*ay-nuhs*	

Subject Pronouns

Before you can form sentences with verbs in German, you have to know something about subject pronouns. A subject pronoun is, as its name suggests, the subject of a sentence—the who or what that performs the action. The verb must agree with the subject pronoun (grammatically speaking, that is, in person and number—we all know verbs don't have opinions of their own). You can link this bit of information to what you already know about cases. The case of the subject is nominative, so you can also think about these pronouns as nominative personal pronouns. The German subject pronouns in the following table have a person (first person is *I*, second person is *you*, and third person is *he*, *she*, or *it*) just as subject pronouns do in English, and a number (singular or plural). If you've ever studied literature, you may recall discussing narrators' perspectives: First person omniscient or limited was told by the narrator using *I*; third person objective had the narrators talking about the story and characters using *he* and *she*. So what is second person all about? It involves directly addressing someone—talking to someone.

As a Rule

It used to be considered polite in German society to use the third person plural to refer to someone you were talking to. One speaker would look directly at another and use "they" when referring to that person! Hence, the German formal pronouns are *exactly* the same as the third person plural pronouns. Less to learn!

Subject Pronouns

Person	Singular	English	Plural	English
First	ich *iH*	I	wir *veer*	we
Second	du *dew*	you	ihr *eer*	you
Third	er, sie, es *eR, zee, es*	he, she, it	sie *zee*	they
Formal Second	Sie *zee*	you	Sie *zee*	you

Du and *Ihr* Versus *Sie:* Informal Versus Formal

When was the last time you got up from your seat on a crowded bus, turned to someone, and said, "Would thee like to sit down?" Today the only place you're going to come across *thee* is in Shakespeare ("Shall I compare thee to a summer's day?") In German, however, *Sie* (the polite form for "you") is still very much a part of German discourse. Generally, *Sie* is used with a single person or persons you don't know, or to indicate respect. *Du*, the informal "you," is used more casually—with a single peer, a family member, a close friend, a pet, or God—whereas *ihr* is the informal plural used with more than one of your peers or with those you know well. See whether you can figure out which of the following questions you would address to your teacher and which you would use to initiate a conversation with a fellow student.

Wie heißt du?
vee hayst dew   What's your name?

Wie heißen Sie?
vee hay-suhn zee   What's your name?

We Are Family

Stepping back into the not-so-mythical linguistic past, both English and German used to decline nouns. Our English possessive -s is a remnant. All nouns in German and English used to take an ending. You may thank your lucky stars that in present day German, only trace vestiges of this complex system remain. In the fifth century, neuter and masculine monosyllabic nouns were members of the same *class* of nouns; reflective of this history, an -e ending remains with neuter and masculine monosyllabic nouns in the dative case. This practice of declension is gradually falling by the wayside, yet is *fossilized* in such fixed expressions as *im Jahre and zu Hause*.

Du, Ihr, or Sie?

How would you address the following people? Formally or informally? If informally, in the singular (*du*) or in the plural (*ihr*)? Check your pronoun mastery in Appendix A.

1. Ein Tourist aus Amerika:

   Wie ("how") finden _____ Amerika?

2. Frau und Herr Wootten:

   Was ("what") machen _____ ?

3. 4 Kinder:

   Was bringt _____ zum Park?

4. Ein Student:

   Was trinkst _____ ?

5. Eine Katze:

   Warum ("why") stinkst _____ ?

6. Der Präsident:

   Was planen _____ ?

Pronouns, items that can substitute for a noun (Christoph) or a noun phrase (the very handsome man), streamline your speech. You'll note from the following examples that the gender of the pronoun must correspond to the gender of the noun. As in English, the same "they" (*sie*) is used to refer to more than one person, be they of mixed company, all feminine, or all masculine.

Noun(s)	Pronouns
Christoph	er
Bettina	sie
Kerstin und Frank	sie
Tania und Anne	sie
Julia und Klaus	sie

You can also use pronouns to replace the name of a common noun referring to a place, thing, or idea. Whereas in English we use the blanket pronoun *it* to refer to anything inanimate, the gender of the pronoun in German must correspond to the gender of the noun that you have so diligently memorized.

Noun	Pronunciation	Pronoun	Meaning
das Café und das Kino	*dAs kah-fey oont dAs kee-noh*	sie	the café and the movie theater
der Hafen und das Schiff	*deyR hah-fuhn oont dAs shif*	sie	the harbor and the ship
die Straße und die Kirche	*dee ShtRah-suh oont dee KeeR-Huh*	sie	the street and the church
das Geschäft und die Schuhe	*dAs guh-shäft oont dee shew-uh*	sie	the store and the shoes

Er, Sie, Es?

Imagine that your boss marries a woman young enough to be his granddaughter. You attend the wedding reception with your best friend. Toward the end of the *Feier (fay-uhR)*, his ex-wife barges in and takes a hatchet to the wedding cake. Eventually, she is subdued and escorted to the door. The guests recover their poise, and the festivities continue. You and your friend don't get a chance to talk about this scandalous turn of events until you are in the elevator on your way to the parking lot. You don't know exactly who is in the elevator with you, so you try to keep your use of

Achtung

Don't confuse the singular *sie* ("she") with the plural *sie* ("they"). The verb form that you will encounter in the next chapter indicates whether the pronoun *sie* is being used as third person singular or third person plural. The formal *Sie* (pronoun) is always capitalized and further designated by its verb form.

people's names to a minimum. Which pronouns would you use to talk about the in-laws? the bride? the groom? Which pronoun would you use to talk about the hatchet? the party? the hotel? the other people in the elevator? Check your choices with those in Appendix A.

Example: Der Ehemann küsste seine Frau.

Answer: Er küsste seine Frau.

1. Die Schwiegereltern tanzten.

2. Die Musik war heiter.

3. Die Mutter des Ehemanns weinte.

4. Der Onkel der Ehefrau war betrunken.

5. Das Kind der neuen Frau ist groß.

The Least You Need to Know

◆ The function of German nouns and pronouns in a sentence is indicated by their case, which can be nominative, accusative, dative, or genitive.

◆ The declension of articles and some nouns is the pattern of changes a word undergoes to express various grammatical functions, as represented by the four cases.

◆ Subject (nominative) pronouns streamline your speech. The gender of the pronoun must correspond to the gender of the noun.

◆ Because you're probably accustomed to the largely uninflected English language, these concepts might take a little getting used to. Refer to this chapter—or to the cards reflecting paradigms you've artistically created—as you work through this book, and try to assimilate the basic concepts of cases and declensions gradually.

There's No Place Like Deutschland

In This Chapter

◆ Understanding subject pronouns

◆ Conjugating weak and strong verbs

◆ Using common weak and strong verbs

◆ Learning how to ask questions

In the preceding chapter, you learned about determining the gender, number, and case of nouns, and you were introduced to German pronouns. Now it's time to move on to verbs. Verbs, the building blocks in language, convey action in a sentence. To communicate, you must have a basic understanding of verbs. In this chapter, you're introduced to weak and strong verbs, thereby acquiring the tools to set the world in motion!

What's the Subject?

Imagine that you sign up for a special travel package to Germany that includes hotel accommodations and airfare. What this package also includes—and this becomes clear to you as you are on the airplane

What's What

Imperative form The form a verb takes to express a command, request, or directive. This form is easily deduced from the conjugated second person verb. In the imperative form, the expressed or understood subject is always *you*.

listening to others who have signed up for this deal—is spending your week of vacation with 10 other people, each with his or her own agenda. *You* want to take quiet, relaxing strolls through churches and parks. The woman to your left wants the group to spend three days shopping in Zürich. The mother-and-daughter team sitting in the row ahead tell you that *they* intend to hang out at nightclubs to experience what they refer to as "the real Germany." The tour guide is standing in the aisle looking at all of you and rolling his eyes.

To express what people want to do, you need verbs—and verbs, of course, require a subject to set the course in action:

> *You* want to take quiet, relaxing strolls through churches and parks. *The woman* wants to spend three days shopping in Zürich.

When a sentence takes the *imperative form*, the form of a command, the subject (*you*) is understood: Go shopping!

Subjects can be either nouns or pronouns that replace nouns:

> *The man* ate the entire pizza. *He* ate the entire pizza.

As a Rule

Unlike German nouns, which are capitalized no matter where they appear in a sentence, most pronouns take a capital letter only when they begin a sentence. This makes a lot of sense if you think of personal pronouns as representing nouns—not quite achieving noun status, and thus not attaining upper-case orthographic status. The only exception to this rule is the pronoun *Sie* (the polite form for *du* and *ihr*), which is capitalized no matter where it appears in a sentence. The uppercase spelling of the formal *Sie* helps distinguish it from its lowercase twins, *sie* and *sie*. Furthermore, don't let yourself be influenced by the capitalization of the English *I*, whose German equivalent is the lowercase *ich*.

Verb Basics

It's easier to understand how a plane takes off if you know something about its parts. The same is true of verbs. Here are some basic things you should know about verbs before you start using them.

The *stem* of a verb refers to what you get when you remove the ending *-en* from the German infinitive. The *stem vowel* refers to the vowel within this stem. In English, for example, when you conjugate the verb *run* (I run, you run, she runs), it retains the same stem vowel throughout the conjugation, marking the third person singular (he/she/it runs) with the addition of the inflectional suffix *-s. Conjugation* refers to the changes the verb undergoes, internally and externally (by the addition of inflectional endings), that keep the verb in agreement with the subject.

What's What

Conjugation The changes of the verb, the inflection attached to a verb, that occur to indicate who or what is performing the action (or undergoing the state of being) of the verb and when the action (or state of being) of the verb is occurring: in the present, the past, or the future.

Verbs in Motion

We need verbs to express action, motion, or states of being. When you acquired English, you very readily discerned the difference between being able to add a little something to a verb to express yesterday, as in *pushed* and *pulled,* and changing the verb internally: *sing, sang, sung.* Little did you know it then, but you were differentiating between two classes of verbs: *weak* and *strong.* Perhaps you learned to refer to them in school as *regular* and *irregular.* In German, as well, the most common way of grouping verbs is weak (*schwach*), strong (*stark*), or mixed (*schwark*). When verbs are conjugated to indicate that an action has already occurred, a relatively predictable pattern of endings is attached to the stem of weak verbs, as occurs in English (*-ed* in the past tense). Strong verbs have a relatively predictable pattern of endings when they are conjugated in the *present tense* (the form a verb takes to indicate that action is occurring in the present), but the stem undergoes a sound change in the past tense. Mixed verbs have features of both weak and strong verbs, hence the innovative term *schwark*—a blend of *schw*ach and st*ark.* The rest of this chapter examines *schwach* and *stark* verbs in the present tense. Mixed (*schwark*) verbs are discussed in Chapter 22.

Weak Verbs

In Chapter 4 you learned about the infinitive, or unconjugated, form of verbs. Weak verbs are verbs that, when conjugated, follow a set pattern of rules and retain the same stem vowel throughout. Think of them as being too weak to alter the sound patterns they've already established. Let's follow the weak English verb *kiss* through its full conjugation.

Person	Singular	Plural
First	I kiss	we kiss
Second	you kiss	you kiss
Third	he/she/it kisses	they kiss

A large majority of German verbs and all newly coined verbs fall into the category of *schwach* verbs (see the following table). But with either *schwach* or *stark*, the present tense inflectional endings remain the same. Only one paradigm to learn, lucky you!

Your first step is to determine the stem of the verb. That's right, lop off the *-en* of the infinitive. Second, add a little something to this stem, just as you add an *-s* in the English third person singular. Looking at the *schwach* verb "to live," you can observe just how the verb endings differ with each subject pronoun.

Weak Verb Conjugation: *leben*

Person	Singular	English	Plural	English
First	ich leb**e** *iH ley-buh*	I live	wir leb**en** *veeR ley-buhn*	we live
Second	du leb**st** *dew leypst*	you live	ihr leb**t** *eeR leypt*	you live
Third	er, sie, es leb**t** *eR, zee, es leypt*	he, she, it lives	sie leb**en** *zee ley-buhn*	they live
Formal	Sie leb**en** *zee ley-buhn*	you live	Sie leb**en** *zee ley-buhn*	you live

Verbs with stems ending in *-d or -t*, such as *finden* or *kosten*, add an *-e* before the *-st* (*du*) or *-t* (*er/sie/es* and *ihr*) endings. Why add the *-e*? A simple matter of lingual practicality—without it, your tongue would get tangled and you'd end up tripping. The verb endings are exactly the same as for those verbs that don't end in a *d* or *t*, with the tiny addition of that *-e* to facilitate pronunciation. The following table spells out the conjugation of *finden*, a verb stem that ends in *d*. But this time, just one third person singular pronoun, *er*, is used.

Weak Verb Conjugation: *finden*

Person	Singular	English	Plural	English
First	ich find**e** *iH fin-duh*	I find	wir find**en** *veeR fin-duhn*	we find
Second	du find**est** *dew fin-duhst*	you find	ihr find**et** *eeR fin-duht*	you find
Third	er ... find**et** *eR fin-duht*	he ... finds	sie find**en** *zee fin-duhn*	they find
Formal	Sie find**en** *zee fin-duhn*	you find	Sie find**en** *zee fin-duhn*	you find

CAUTION

Achtung

Now that you are becoming attuned to the ease of articulation when it comes to verb endings, it should make perfect sense that when a verb stem ends in ß, s, or z, the du form is identical with the er/sie/es form. Hence, the verb for "to dance," tanzen, is conjugated as du tanzt and er/sie/es tanzt.

Verb Endings

Think of *weak verbs* as timid, law-abiding creatures that would never cross the street when the light is red. The easy thing about weak verbs (*schwach* means both "weak" as well as "easy") is that they obey grammar laws and follow a predictable pattern of conjugation, even in the past tense. Once you've learned this pattern (and the few exceptions to stems ending in *d, t, ß, s,* and *z*), you can conjugate present tense verbs in German without too much difficulty: Drop the *-en* from the infinitive and then add the endings shown in the following table. Here's your verb paradigm to be *memorized* and written out on a card!

What's What

Weak verbs Verbs (*schwach*) that follow a set pattern of rules and retain the same stem vowel throughout their conjugation. Compare this pattern with the English verbs that form their past tense with the addition of *-ed.*

Person	Singular	Ending	Plural	Ending
First	ich	**-e**	wir	**-en**
Second	du	**-(e)st**	ihr	**-(e)t**
Third	er, sie, es	**-(e)t**	sie	**-en**
Formal	Sie	**-en**	Sie	**-en**

Painless Conjugation

Now it's time to practice a little of what you've learned. See whether you can apply an ending to creat the correct form of the verbs in the following sentences. Remember, the verb must agree with the subject and you can check your verbs in Appendix A.

1. (suchen) Ich _____ das Museum.

2. (reservieren) Klaus _____ ein Hotelzimmer.

3. (warten) Sie (Anne und Otto) _____ auf den Bus.

4. (mieten) Ihr _____ ein Auto.

5. (fragen) Wir _____ nach der Adresse.

6. (lernen) Ich _____ Deutsch.

7. (reisen) Ich _____ nach Hamburg.

8. (brauchen) Er _____ ein Taxi.

9. (besuchen) Du _____ deine Mutter.

10. (bestellen) Tina _____ ein Glas Wein.

11. (tanzen) Christoph, du _____ gut!

12. (arbeiten) Der Professor _____ jeden Tag.

13. (öffnen) Die Professorin _____ das Fenster.

14. (kosten) Die Pizza _____ nur 7 Euro.

In the following table, you will find some of the most commonly used weak verbs in German. Read the list a few times and try to commit these verbs to memory.

Common Weak Verbs

Verb	Pronunciation	Meaning
antworten	*Ant-voR-tuhn*	to answer
arbeiten	*AR-bay-tuhn*	to work
bestellen	*buh-shte-luhn*	to order
blicken	*bli-kuhn*	to look, glance
brauchen	*bRou-CHuhn*	to need
danken	*dAn-kuhn*	to thank
fragen	*fRah-guhn*	to ask
glauben	*glou-buhn*	to believe
kochen	*ko-CHuhn*	to cook
kosten	*ko-stuhn*	to cost, to taste, to try
heiraten	*hay-rA-tuhn*	to marry
lernen	*leR-nuhn*	to learn, to study
lieben	*lee-buhn*	to love
machen	*mA-CHuhn*	to make, to do
mieten	*mee-tuhn*	to rent
öffnen	*öf-nuhn*	to open

Verb	Pronunciation	Meaning
rauchen	*Rou-CHuhn*	to smoke
regnen	*reyk-nuhn*	to rain
reisen	*ray-zuhn*	to travel
reservieren	*ruh-zeR-vee-Ruhn*	to reserve
sagen	*zah-guhn*	to say, to tell
schicken	*shi-kuhn*	to send
sehen	*zey-uhn*	to see
spielen	*shpee-luhn*	to play
studieren	*shtew-dee-Ruhn*	to look over, to be enrolled
suchen	*zew-CHuhn*	to look for
schwänzen	*shvän-tsuhn*	to skip class
tanzen	*tAn-tsuhn*	to dance
telefonieren	*tey-ley-foh-nee-Ruhn*	to telephone
weinen	*vay-nuhn*	to cry
warten	*vAR-tuhn*	to wait
wohnen	*voh-nuhn*	to reside
zeichnen	*tsayCH-nuhn*	to draw
zeigen	*tsay-guhn*	to show, to indicate

As a Rule _____

Studieren refers to enrollment at a college or university: *Bernadette studiert an der Universität Mainz.* It also indicates a student's major: *Gretchen studiert Germanistik. Ich studiere die Liste* means "look over carefully." *Lernen* means "to study," in the sense of studying for a test or learning specific skills: *Sie lernen Deutsch!*

Strong Verbs

Of course, verbs don't lift weights or have muscles. You can't tell the difference between *strong verbs* and weak verbs just by looking at them. The only way you can distinguish between them is to memorize them as such. Of course, as an English speaker, you will have the advantage of already being familiar with strong verbs, and those strong verbs in English are just as *stark* in German.

Strong Verbs Exhibit Their Strength

Strong verbs can be deemed "strong" because they are strong enough to sustain a stem vowel change in the past tense, unlike weak verbs. This pattern becomes readily evident in the past tense (recall *pushed* versus *drank*). Some strong verbs change their stem vowel in the present tense—they are "very strong," *sehr stark*. Present tense endings, however, are the same for both weak and strong verbs. With the *sehr stark* verbs, vowel alterations occur only in the second and third persons (*du* and *er/sie/es*) in the stem vowel. Although *everything* in German might seem to be an exception, all German verbs actually stem from seven older (800 C.E.) verb classes to which no new verbs may be added! So take heart; vowel changes follow a limited number of patterns. As far as present tense stem changes, the only permutations are these:

> *a(u)*, *o*, *u* may become *ä(u)*, *ö*, or *ü*.
> *e* may become *i* or *ie*.

> **We Are Family**
>
> English and German share many features when it comes to strong verbs. The irregular forms—such as *take*, *took*, *taken*, or *drink*, *drank*, *drunk*—date back more than 6,000 years! They are examples of original Indo-European verbs and haven't changed too much since.

The following tables illustrate the stem changing of some *sehr stark* verbs. Note that the stem *-e* changes to *-ie* only in the second and third person singular! Other verbs that incur this stem change (because their stem vowel is the long *ey*) include *lesen*, *befehlen*, *empfehlen*, and *geschehen*. Very strong verbs that modify their stem vowel from *e* to *i* (without the subsequent *e*) include *essen*, *nehmen*, *geben*, and *sprechen* (again, an *ey* sound in the stem).

Very Strong Verb Conjugation: *sehen (e→ie)*

Person	Singular	English	Plural	English
First	ich sehe *iH zey-uh*	I see	wir sehen *veeR zey-uhn*	we see
Second	du siehst *dew zeest*	you see	ihr seht *eeR zeyt*	you see
Third	er ... sieht *eR zeet*	he ... sees	sie sehen *zee zey-uhn*	they see
Formal	Sie sehen *zee zey-uhn*	you see	Sie sehen *zee zay-uhn*	you see

Again, note that in the following table, *a* changes to *ä* only in the second and third person singular! Other verbs that incur this stem change include *fahren, fangen, halten, laden, lassen, laufen, schlafen, tragen, wachsen,* and *waschen*.

The Other Very Strong Verb Conjugation: *fallen (a→ä)*

Person	Singular	English	Plural	English
First	ich falle *iH fA-luh*	I fall	wir fallen *veeR fA-luhn*	we fall
Second	du fällst *dew fälst*	you fall	ihr fallt *eeR fAlt*	you fall
Third	er ... fällt *eR fält*	he ... falls	sie fallen *zee fA-luhn*	they fall
Formal	Sie fallen *zee fA-luhn*	you fall	Sie fallen *zee fA-luhn*	you fall

Bear the Sound Change and Conjugate

Although most *stark* verbs do not incur a sound change in the present tense, you might as well become well versed in the handful that do. See whether you can conjugate these *very* strong verbs in the following sentences and check your answers in Appendix A.

Note that the verbs followed by an asterisk do not incur a stem change in the present tense.

1. (essen) Hans _____ gern Bratwurst.

2. (geben) Er _____ mir einen guten Tip.

3. (sehen) Christoph _____ einen Biergarten.

4. (treffen) Petra _____ ihre deutsche Brieffreundin.

5. (sprechen) Du _____ sehr gut Englisch.

6. (lesen) Karl _____ die Süddeutsche Zeitung.

7. (fahren) Almut _____ nach Köln.

8. (halten) Der Bus _____ vor der Kirche.

9. (blasen) Der Bayer _____ das Horn.

10. (empfehlen) Meine Freundin _____ das Restaurant.

11. (scheinen) Die Sonne _____ sehr hell.*

12. (waschen) Du _____ die Wäsche jede Woche.

13. (laufen) Paul _____ sehr schnell und oft.

CAUTION **Achtung**

The infinitives of a few verbs take *-n*, not *-en*. The conjugated form of these verbs in the first and third person plural is the same as the infinitive form. *Handeln (hAn-duhln)*, which means "to act," becomes *wir/sie handeln* or "we/they act" in the first and third person plural.

Strong verb   A verb whose stem vowel undergoes a change or a modification when conjugated in the past tense. Only some strong (*stark*) verbs undergo a vowel modification in the present tense (*sehr stark*).

14. (genießen) Er _____ sein Bier.*

15. (tragen) Die Professorin _____ einen Mikro-rock.

The following table lists some commonly used strong verbs. Read through them a few times, as you did with the weak verbs. The very strong-verb vowel changes are indicated in parentheses after the infinitive. You shouldn't have too much trouble memorizing them—many are near cognates. Don't forget to learn the present tense stem change, if there is one!

Common Strong Verbs

Verb	Pronunciation	Meaning
befehlen (ie)	*buh-fey-luhn*	to command
beginnen	*buh-gi-nuhn*	to begin
besitzen	*buh-zi-tsuhn*	to possess
beweisen	*buh-vay-zuhn*	to prove
bieten	*bee-tuhn*	to offer
blasen (ä)	*blah-zuhn*	to blow
bleiben	*blay-buhn*	to remain
empfangen (ä)	*em-pfAn-guhn*	to receive
empfehlen (ie)	*em-pfey-luhn*	to recommend
essen (i)	*es-uhn*	to eat
fahren (ä)	*fah-Ruhn*	to drive
fallen (ä)	*fA-luhn*	to fall
fangen (ä)	*fAn-guhn*	to catch
finden	*fin-duhn*	to find
fliegen	*flee-guhn*	to fly
geben (i)	*gey-buhn*	to give
gehen	*gey-uhn*	to go
genießen	*guh-nee-suhn*	to enjoy
geschehen (ie)	*guh-shey-uhn*	to happen
halten (ä)*	*hAl-tuhn*	to hold, to stop
hängen	*hän-guhn*	to hang
helfen (i)	*hel-fuhn*	to help
laden (ä)	*lah-duhn*	to load

Verb	Pronunciation	Meaning
lassen (ä)	*lA-suhn*	to leave, to let
laufen (ä)	*lou-fuhn*	to run
leiden	*lay-duhn*	to suffer
leihen	*lay-uhn*	to lend, to borrow
lesen (ie)	*ley-zuhn*	to read
liegen	*lee-guhn*	to lie, to be situated
nehmen (i)*	*ney-muhn*	to take
raten (ä)	*Rah-tuhn*	to advise
reißen	*Ray-suhn*	to tear
reiten	*Ray-tuhn*	to ride
rufen	*ewR-fuhn*	to call
scheinen	*shay-nuhn*	to shine, to seem
schießen	*shee-suhn*	to shoot
schlafen (ä)	*shlah-fuhn*	to sleep
schlagen (ä)	*schlah-guhn*	to hit
schreiben	*shray-buhn*	to write
schweigen	*shvay-guhn*	to be silent
schwimmen	*shvi-muhn*	to swim
sehen	*zey-uhn*	to see
singen	*zin-guhn*	to sing
sitzen	*zi-tsuhn*	to sit
sprechen (i)	*shpRe-Huhn*	to speak
stehen	*shtey-uhn*	to stand
stinken	*shtin-kuhn*	to stink
tragen (ä)	*trah-guhn*	to wear, to carry
treffen (i)	*tRe-fuhn*	to meet
trinken	*tRin-kuhn*	to drink
tun	*tewn*	to do
vergessen	*feR-ge-suhn*	to forget
versprechen (i)	*feR-shpRe-Huhn*	to promise
wachsen (ä)	*vACH-suhn*	to grow
waschen (ä)	*va-shuhn*	to wash
ziehen	*tsee-uhn*	to pull

halten → er/sie/es hält (no additional -(e)t); nehmen → du nimmst and er/sie/es nimmt. (doubling of "m")

As a Rule _____

While German has a considerable number of verbs with a stem vowel change in the *du* and *er/sie/es* forms, it really is simpler than it appears. There are only three types of stem vowel changes: *e* changes to *ie*, *e* to *i*, and *a(u)* to *ä(u)*. You have to learn the stem changes associated with such strong verbs only once. Adding a prefix to a stem does *not* alter the conjugation. The verb *sprechen* (stem change from *e* to *i*) "to speak" becomes *du sprichst* "you speak," and *er spricht* "he speaks." Likewise, *versprechen* "to promise" contains the stem, *sprechen,* and thus incurs the same stem vowel change: *du versprichst* "you promise" and *er verspricht* "he promises."

Ask Me Anything

Okay, now go back to where you were at the beginning of this chapter: planning a trip. Suppose that you're planning another trip—alone this time. You'll probably want to ask a lot of questions when you get to your destination. Stick to the easy questions, the ones that can be answered with a simple yes or no. You'll deal with more complicated questions in Chapter 9.

There are other ways, besides the confused look on your face, to show that you're asking a yes/no question: through intonation, the addition of the tag *nicht wahr,* and inversion.

Intonation

One of the easiest ways to indicate that you're asking a question is by simply raising your voice slightly at the end of the sentence. To do so, speak with a rising *inflection.*

Du denkst an die Reise?
Dew denkst An dee Ray-zuh
Are you thinking about the trip?

Nicht Wahr?

Another easy way of forming questions in German is by adding the tag *nicht wahr* (*niHt vahR*) to your statements. *Nicht wahr* means "Right?" or "Isn't this true?"

Du denkst an die Reise, nicht wahr?
Dew denkst An dee Ray-zuh, niHt vahR
You think about the trip, don't you?

Inversion

The final way of forming a yes/no question is by *inversion*. Inversion is what you do when you reverse the word order of the subject and the conjugated verb. We use inversion all the time in English with the addition of *do* as a helper to the verb. Statement: He eats pie. Question: Does he eat pie? If you're up to the challenge of inversion, follow these rules:

What's What _____

Inversion   Reversing the word order of the subject noun or pronoun and the conjugated form of the verb to make a statement a question.

◆ Avoid inverting with *ich*. It's awkward and rarely done.

◆ Invert subject nouns or pronouns only with conjugated verbs. The following examples will give you a feel for how inversion works:

Du gehst nach Hause.	Gehst du nach Hause?
Er spricht Deutsch.	Spricht er Deutsch?
Wir reisen nach Cottbus.	Reisen wir nach Cottbus?
Ihr esst Sauerkraut.	Esst ihr Sauerkraut?
Sie trinken Bier.	Trinken sie Bier?
Du fährst mit dem Zug.	Fährst du mit dem Zug?

Remember that whether you are using intonation, *nicht wahr*, or inversion, you are asking for exactly the same information: a yes or no (*ja oder nein*) answer.

Ask Me If You Can

Now it's time to put what you've learned about inversion to use. You're in an airport, and you need information. After waiting in line at the information counter, it's finally your turn. See whether you can use inversion (flipping around the subject and the verb) to provide the questions for the following statements. Check your word order in Appendix A.

Example: Das Flugzeug fliegt um 10 Uhr. (The plane leaves at 10.)

Answer: Fliegt das Flugzeug um 10 Uhr?

1. Das Ticket kostet 200 Euro. (The ticket costs 200 Euros.)

2. Das ist das Terminal für internationale Flüge. (This is the terminal for international flights.)

3. Die Flugnummer steht auf dem Ticket. (The flight number is indicated on the ticket.)

4. Es gibt Toiletten auf dieser Etage. (There are bathrooms on this floor.)

5. Der Flug dauert zwei Stunden. (The flight is two hours long.)

6. Das Abendessen ist inklusiv. (The evening meal is included.)

And the Answer Is ...

If you generally look on the bright side of things, you'll probably want to know how to say "yes." To answer in the affirmative, use *ja* (*yah*) and then give your statement.

Sprichst du Deutsch?   Ja, ich spreche Deutsch.
shpRiHst dew doytch   *yah, iH shpRe-Huh doytch*

Or, if your time is valuable and you are constantly being harangued to do things you have no interest in doing, you should probably learn to say "no." To answer negatively, use *nein* (*nayn*) at the beginning of the statement and then add *nicht* (*niHt*) at the end of the statement.

Rauchen Sie?   Nein, ich rauche nicht.
Rou-CHuhn zee   *nayn, iH Rou-CHuh niHt*

You can vary the forms of your negative answers by putting the following negative phrases after the conjugated verb.

… nie(mals) *nee(mahlz)*	never
Ich rauche nie(mals). *iH Rou-CHuh nee(mahlz)*	I never smoke.
… nicht mehr *niHt meyR*	no longer
Ich rauche nicht mehr. *iH Rou-CHuh niHt meyR*	I no longer smoke.
… (gar)nichts (*gAR*)*niHts*	(absolutely) nothing
Ich rauche nichts. *iH Rou-CHuh niHts*	I'm not smoking anything.

If you want to form simple sentences in the present tense, you'll need to have as many verbs as possible at the tip of your tongue. Refer to the lists of verbs earlier in the chapter for help.

The Least You Need to Know

♦ Weak verbs never incur a sound mutation and follow a set pattern of rules.

♦ Strong verbs always undergo a stem-vowel change in the past tense, and some also undergo a vowel change in the present tense.

♦ To formulate a yes/no question to elicit information, invert the subject and the verb so that the verb begins the question.

♦ You can ask questions by using intonation, inversion, or the tag *nicht wahr.*

Part 3

Up, Up, and Away!

After you learn the basics, the next step is to start to converse (don't worry about being left behind—we'll be taking baby steps throughout this section). One of the first things you'll acquire is a working knowledge of common introductory phrases that German speakers use in various situations. You can use these phrases to start conversations and to expand your vocabulary.

WHY DO I NEED TO LEARN TO ORDER IN GERMAN? I ALREADY KNOW ALL I NEED TO ASK FOR — BEER AND BRATWURST.

Chapter 9

Haven't We Met Before? Making Friends

In This Chapter

- ◆ Common greetings
- ◆ The verb *sein*
- ◆ Professions
- ◆ Getting the information you need

In the previous chapter, you learned how to create simple German sentences (using subject nouns, pronouns, and verbs) and how to ask basic yes or no questions. Now you're going to put some of what you learned to work. It's time to start engaging in conversation.

You are sitting alone on an airplane, admiring the view of clouds and sky through the window. The person in the seat next to you is German; you want to use this opportunity to test some of your newly acquired language skills.

Conversation Openers

Let's face it: You can listen to a thousand tapes or CDs at the library, and you can read every language book in the bookstore—the moment of truth arrives only when you are face to face with someone who is speaking to you in German. If this person is sitting next to you on the airplane, all the better because he or she can't get away. Each and every German speaker you meet before arriving at your destination will give you the chance to practice what you've learned so far. You may find the following conversation openers useful.

German Culture

One of the subtle differences between German and American cultures is the use of the phrase "How are you?" In America, it's almost an extension of a greeting, and usually the response an American expects is the simple answer "I'm fine." If you ask a German, "How are you?" be prepared for a lengthy dissertation. Your question will probably be taken seriously rather than rhetorically.

Formal Greetings and Salutations

Using the *du* form of address with someone who isn't a friend or relative is considered rude. Because you don't know the person you're speaking to, you'll probably want to take the formal approach. It is worth noting, however, that younger generations are tending to use the informal *du* form more extensively.

German	Pronunciation	Meaning
Guten Tag.	*gew-tuhn tahk*	Hello.
Guten Abend.	*gew-tuhn ah-bent*	Good evening.
mein Herr	*mayn heR*	Sir
meine Dame	*may-nuh dah-muh*	Miss, Mrs.
Ich heiße …	*iH hay-suh*	My name is …
Wie heißen Sie?	*vee hay-suhn zee*	What is your name?
Wie geht es Ihnen?	*vee geyt es ee-nuhn*	How are you?
Danke, sehr gut.	*dAn-kuh, zeyR gewt*	Thank you, very well.
Danke, nicht schlecht.	*dAn-kuh, niHt shleHt*	Thank you, not bad.
Danke, es geht so.	*DAn-kuh, es geyt zo*	Thank you, so so.

Informal Greetings and Salutations

You hit it off with your plane buddy right away, and he says, "*Dutzen Sie mich, bitte* (*dew-tsuhn zee miH, bi-tuh*)," which means, "Please, use *du* with me." His request means that you've earned the right to a certain degree of linguistic intimacy with this person. You can now use the following phrases:

German	Pronunciation	Meaning
Hallo!	*hA-lo*	Hi!
Ich heiße …	*iH hay-suh*	My name is …
Wie heißt du?	*vee hayst dew*	What is your name?
Wie geht's?	*vee geyts*	How are you?
Wie geht es dir?	*vee geyt es deeR*	How's it going with you?
Was machst du so?	*vAs mACHst dew zo*	What's up?
Ganz gut.	*gAns gewt*	Okay.
Ich kann nicht klagen.	*iH kAn niHt klah-guhn*	I can't complain.
Mal so, mal so.	*mahl zo, mahl zo*	So so.
Na ja.	*nA-yah*	All right.

Where Are You From?

After you have made your initial introductions, if you decide to continue the conversation with your seatmate, you will probably wonder about his idiosyncrasies—the peculiar lilt in his voice when he speaks, certain gestures you have never seen anyone make, and his use of idioms. Eventually, you are going to want to know where this person is from. You'll also want to be able to respond correctly when he asks where you are from. To continue this conversation, you will need to familiarize yourself with the strong verb *kommen* (*ko-muhn*). Take out your verb-ending chart, lop the *-en* off the infinitive to produce the stem (*komm-*), and try to come up with a match to the following table.

> **What's What**
>
> **Saying hello** *Hallo* is informal for "hello" practically everywhere, but in southern Germany and Austria, the term *Grüß Gott* (*gRüs got*), literally, "God greets you," is used formally instead of *Guten Tag* (*gew-tuhn tAhk*).

The Verb: *kommen*

Person	Singular	English	Plural	English
First	ich komm**e** *iH ko-muh*	I come	wir komm**en** *veeR ko-muhn*	we come
Second	du komm**st** *dew komst*	you come	ihr komm**t** *eeR komt*	you come
Third	er, sie, es komm**t** *eR, zee, es komt*	he, she, it comes	sie komm**en** *zee ko-muhn*	they come
(Formal)	Sie komm**en** *zee ko-muhn*	you come	Sie komm**en** *zee ko-muhn*	you come

---

German Culture

You should address a man as Herr (*heR*) So-and-So and a woman as Frau (*fRou*) So-and-So. Although Fräulein (*fRoy-layn*) does mean "Miss," most young women in Germany prefer to be addressed as Frau. Unlike Mister, Madam, and Miss in English, *Herr*, *Frau*, and *Fräulein* cannot be used on their own.

To question someone about his or her origins, try the following:

Formal:

> Woher kommen Sie?
> *voh-heR ko-muhn zee*
> Where are you from?

Informal:

> Woher kommst du?
> *voh-heR komst dew*
> Where are you from?

Response:

> Ich komme aus …
> *iH ko-muh ous …*
> I come from …

You might recall from Chapter 6 that most countries, towns, and cities are neuter nouns and take the article *das*. *Die USA* (*dee ew-es-ah*) and *die Vereinigten Staaten* (*dee feR-ay-nik-tuhn shtah-tuhn*), "The United States," are exceptions; because they are plural, they take the plural article *die*. Some other countries that don't take *das* are *die Schweiz* (*dee shvayts*), "Switzerland"; *die Türkei* (*dee tüR-kay*), "Turkey"; *der Irak* (*deyR ee-Rahk*), "Iraq"; *der Iran* (*deyR ee-Rahn*), "Iran"; *der Libanon* (*deyR lee-bah-non*), "Lebanon," and *der Kongo* (*deyR kon-go*), "The Congo."

When you use countries, cities, or towns with the neuter article, drop the article *das*:

> Ich komme aus New York.
> *iH ko-muh ous new yoRk*

> Ich komme aus Amerika.
> *iH ko-muh ous ah-mey-Ree-kah*

CAUTION

Achtung _____

Using informal language to address someone with whom you have not established a friendship or bond is generally considered quite rude. To *dutzen* (*dew-tsuhn*) someone—in other words, to use the informal *du* form of address with a person—may alienate the stranger, neighbor, distant relative, or business acquaintance you are addressing. Generally, you have to earn the privilege to use the informal *du* with people you don't know.

Be careful with countries that take *der* and *die* articles. These articles are not dropped, and they must be declined correctly (that is, they must take the appropriate case).

Die USA, which is plural, takes the dative plural article *den* because it follows *aus*, which is a dative preposition:

> Ich komme aus den USA.
> *iH ko-muh ous deyn ew-es-ah*

Die Schweiz, which is feminine, takes the feminine dative article *der*, following the dative preposition *aus*:

> Ich komme aus der Schweiz.
> *iH ko-muh ous deyR shvayts*

Der Libanon, which is masculine, takes the masculine dative article *dem*:

> Ich komme aus dem Libanon.
> *iH ko-muh ous deym lee-bah-non*

To Be or Not to Be?

After you've established where someone is from, you will probably want to find out more about what that person does. But what if, instead of answering you directly, he smiles whimsically and say, "*Raten Sie mal (Rah-tuhn zee mahl)*," which means, "Guess." What can you do? You'll probably have to recite a list of professions in the hopes that sooner or later you'll happen on the right one. To do so, you should learn the conjugation of the irregular verb *sein (zayn)*, or "to be," and learn some professions. The following table illustrates the conjugation of *sein*, "to be."

The Verb: *sein*

Person	Singular	English	Plural	English
First	ich bin *iH bin*	I am	wir sind *veeR zint*	we are
Second	du bist *dew bist*	you are	ihr seid *eeR zayt*	you are
Third	er, sie, es ist *eR, zee, es ist*	he, she, it is	sie sind *zee zint*	they are
(Formal)	Sie sind *zee zint*	you are		

The following phrase may help you illicit information about someone and tell about yourself. Note the forms of *sein* that agree with the subject pronoun.

Formal:

> Was sind Sie von Beruf?
> *VAs sint zee fon buh-Rewf*
> What is your profession?

What's What

Sein One of the four irregular verbs in German. These verbs vary from strong verbs, which follow a regular sound-shift pattern in stem vowels, because consonants as well as vowels change in the truly unpredictable irregular verbs.

Informal:

> Was bist du von Beruf?   Was machst du?
> *VAs bist dew fon buh-Rewf* *vAs maCHst dew*
> What is your profession? What do you do?

Response:

> Ich bin …
> *iH bin …*
> I am …

The following table lists a few professions with the feminine form in parenthesis.

Professions

Profession	Pronunciation	English
der Architekt (die Architektin)	*deyR AR-Hi-tekt* *(dee Ar-Hi-tek-tin)*	architect
der Arzt (die Ärztin)	*deyR ARtst* *(dee äRts-tin)*	doctor

Profession	Pronunciation	English
der Bäcker (die Bäckerin)	*deyR bäh-kuhR* (*dee bäh-kuh-Rin*)	baker
der Beamte (die Beamtin)	*deyR buh-Am-tuh* (*dee buh-Am-tin*)	government employee
der Bibliothekar (die Bibliothekarin)	*deyR bib-lee-oh-tay-kAhR* (*dee bib-lee-oh-tay-kA-Rin*)	librarian
der Chemiker (die Chemikerin)	*deyR He-mee-kuhR* (*dee He-mee-kuh-Rin*)	chemist
der Elektriker (die Elektrikerin)	*deyR ey-lek-tRi-kuhR* (*dee ey-lek-tRi-kuh-Rin*)	electrician
der Flugbegleiter (die Flugbegleiterin)	*deyR flook-buh-glay-tuhR* (*dee flook-buh-glay-tuh-Rin*)	flight attendant
der Friseur (die Frieseuse)	*deyR fRee-zühR* (*dee fRee-züh-zuh*)	hairdresser
der Geschäftsführer (die Geschäftsführerin)	*deyR guh-shäfts-füh-RuhR* (*dee guh-shäfts-füh-Ruh-Rin*)	business manager
der Informatiker (die Informatikerin)	*deyR in-foR-mah-tee-kuhR* (*dee in-foR-mah-tee-kuh-Rin*)	computer scientist
der Kaufmann (die Kauffrau)	*deyR kouf-mAn* (*dee kou-frou*)	merchant, shopkeeper
der Kellner (dieKellnerin)	*deyR kel-nuhR* (*dee kel-nuh-Rin*)	waiter, waitress
der Krankenpfleger (die Krankenschwester)	*deyR kRAn-kuhn-pfley-guhR* (*dee kRAn-kuhn-shves-tuhR*)	nurse
der Künstler (die Künstlerin)	*deyR kün-stluhR* (*dee kün-stluh-Rin*)	artist
der Mechaniker (die Mechanikerin)	*deyR mey-Hah-ni-kuhR* (*dee mey-Hah-ni-kuh-Rin*)	mechanic
der Musiker (die Musikerin)	*deyR mew-zee-kuhR* (*dee mew-zee-kuh-Rin*)	musician
der Politiker (die Politikerin)	*deyR poh-lee-tee-kuhR* (*dee poh-lee-tee-kuh-Rin*)	politician
der Polizist (die Polizistin)	*deyR poh-lee-tsist* (*dee poh-lee-tsis-tin*)	police officer
der Professor (die Professorin)	*deyR proh-fe-soR* (*dee proh-fe-soh-Rin*)	professor
der Rechtsanwalt (die Rechtsanwältin)	*deyR ReHts-An-vAlt* (*dee ReHts-An-väl-tin*)	lawyer
der Schauspieler (die Schauspielerin)	*deyR shou-shpee-luhR* (*dee shou-shpee-luh-Rin*)	actor, actress

continues

Professions   (continued)

Profession	Pronunciation	English
der Schriftsteller (die Schriftstellerin)	*deyR shrift-shte-luhR* (*dee shrift-shte-luh-Rin*)	writer
der Sekretär (die Sekretärin)	*deyR sek-Re-tähR* (*dee sek-Re-täRin*)	secretary
der Student (die Studentin)	*deyR shtew-dent* (*dee shtew-den-tin*)	student

As a Rule

In German, the indefinite article *ein*(e) is generally not used when a person states his profession, unless the profession is qualified by an adjective. To say, "I'm a policeman," you would say, "*Ich bin Polizist* (*ich bin poh-lee-tsist*)." To say "I'm a good policeman," however, you would say, "*Ich bin ein guter Polizist* (*iH bin ayn gew-tuhR poh-lee-tsist*)."

You've been introduced to the verb *sein* and to some of the most common professions. But what's the use of all this newly acquired information if you can't use it? Put what you've learned to use by translating the following sentences into German. Pay attention to the gender of the pronoun and check your translations in Appendix A.

1. I am a waiter.

2. He is a nurse.

3. She is a doctor.

4. I am a lawyer.

5. You are a student.

6. He is a police officer.

7. She is a business manager.

8. You are a writer.

Finding Things Out

When you learn a new language, you often revert to what feels like a somewhat infantile state of existence. You have a limited vocabulary and, at best, a somewhat sketchy understanding of grammar. You point to things a lot and ask, "What is that?", "*Was ist das? (vAs ist dAs)*"; or "What does that mean?", "*Was bedeutet das? (vAs buh-doy-tuht dAs)*." Yet even someone with a limited knowledge of a language can convey a broad range of meaning.

We Are Family

Have you noticed how the endings for professions in both English and German are often *-er*? This goes back to way back when because both languages share the same lexical morphology for forming agentive suffixes. That is to say, an additional *-er* suffix turns the verb into a doer of the verb: One who sings is a sing*er*, or a *Sänger*. Note that there is no plural suffix added to the German masculine form: one or a room full of *Sänger*.

One advantage of learning a new language is that you can get away with sounding a little childlike. So start learning by asking about everything. Here are some interrogative helpers:

Information Question Expressions

German	Pronunciation	English
mit wem	*mit veym*	with whom
um wie viel Uhr	*ewm vee-feel ooR*	at what time
von wem	*fon veym*	of, about, from whom
wann	*vAn*	when
warum/wieso/weshalb	*va-Rum/vee-zoh/ves-hAlp*	why
was	*vAs*	what
wer	*veR*	who
wie	*vee*	how
wie lange	*vee lAn-guh*	how long
wie viel/viele	*veefeel*	how much, many
wo	*voh*	where
woher	*voh-heR*	from where
wohin	*voh-hin*	where (to)
womit/mit was	*voh-mit/mit vAs*	with what

continues

Information Question Expressions (continued)

German	Pronunciation	English
worüber	*voh-Rüh-buhR*	what about
wovon/von was	*voh-fon/fon vAs*	of, about, from what
zu wem	*tsew veym*	to whom

As a Rule

The interrogative pronouns *wen* and *wem* are used with a preposition to refer only to persons. The interrogative pronoun *was* refers to things and ideas. As an object of a preposition, *was* may be replaced by a *wo*-compound: *wo-* is added as a prefix to prepositions, as in *womit?*, "with what?"; or *wofür?*, "for what?" In colloquial German, the preposition may be followed by *was: Vor was hast du Angst?* which means "What are you afraid of?" *Wo-* expands to *wor-* when the preposition begins with a vowel: *Worüber sprechen wir?*

Gleaning Information

An interesting-looking person is sitting across from you on a train. You have a long journey in front of you and have finally mustered up the courage to say something. What's your opening line? You put aside "You look like a movie star" as too trite. How about "Hi, where are you from?" If you're charming and sincere enough, you might get away with it. Here are some other ways to break the ice.

Formal	Informal	English
Mit wem reisen Sie? *mit veym Ray-zuhn zee*	Mit wem reist du? *mit veym Rayst dew*	With whom are you traveling?
Warum reisen Sie? *vah-Room Ray-zuhn zee*	Warum reist du? *vah-Room Rayst dew*	Why are you traveling?
Wie lange reisen Sie? *vee lAn-guh Ray-zuhn zee*	Wie lange reist du? *vee lAn-guh Rayst dew*	How long are you traveling for?
Wohin reisen Sie? *voh-hin Ray-zuhn zee*	Wohin reist du? *voh-hin Rayst dew*	Where are you traveling?
Wie finden Sie das Land? *vee fin-duhn zee dAs lAnt*	Wie findest du das Land? *vee fin-duhst dew dAs lAnt*	How do you like the country?
Wo wohnen Sie? *voh voh-nuhn zee*	Wo wohnst du? *voh vohnst dew*	Where do you live?

Formal	Informal	English
Woher kommen Sie? *vo-heR ko-muhn zee*	Woher kommst du? *vo-her komst dew*	Where are you (coming) from?
Wovon sprechen Sie? *voh-fon shpRe-chuhn zee*	Wovon sprichst du? *voh-fon shpriHst dew*	What are you speaking about?
Wie viele Kinder haben Sie? *vee-fee-luh kin-duhR hah-buhn zee*	*Wie viele Kinder hast du?* *vee-fee-luh kin-duhR hAst dew*	How many children do you have?
Wann reisen Sie zurück? *vAn Ray-zuhn zee tsu-Rük?*	Wann reist du zurück? *vAn Rayst dew tsü-Rük*	When are you traveling home?

As a Rule

To express directions of motion, the adverb particles *her-* and *hin-* may be used with the interrogative *wo* to suggest motion toward the speaker (*woher*, "where from") or motion away from the speaker (*wohin*, "where to"). In spoken German, the question words *wohin* and *woher* are often separated: *wo* is placed at the start of the question; *hin* and *her* appear at the end: *Wohin geht Christine?* or *Wo geht Christine hin?* In a statement, *hin* and *her* occupy the last position in the sentence.

Ask Away

Each of the following statements is an answer to a question. Try to ask the questions that elicit these statements. In the first example, use the informal *du* to pose questions to Klaus. In the second example, use the third person singular *sie* to pose questions about Frau Sahlmann. Don't forget what you learned about inversion in Chapter 8. Your questions may be simple or conjoined by "and"—*und*. Verify your questions in Appendix A.

Example: Ich heiße Klaus. **Question:** Wie heißt du?

A. Ich heiße Klaus und ich komme aus Köln. Ich reise mit meiner Schwester nach München. Ich trinke Bier auf der Wiesú (at Oktoberfest) für zwei Wochen (for two weeks) in München.

B. Ich bin Frau Sahlmann und komme aus Kiel. Ich reise einen Monat lang (for a month) in der Schweiz. Ich finde die Schweiz sehr schön. Ich reise nie zurück.

The Least You Need to Know

- Don't use *du* with strangers or with your superiors! The greetings you use depend on your familiarity with a person.

- The verb *kommen* with the question word *woher* is used to ask people where they're from.

- For most professions, simply add an *-in* to speak about a female.

- You can get information by learning and asking a few key questions.

Chapter 10

I'd Like to Get to Know You

In This Chapter

- Introducing your relatives
- Expressing possession two ways
- Introducing and talking about yourself
- The irregular verb *haben* and adjectives

By now you should be well on your way to introducing yourself and your friends to other people. But what if your mother, father, uncle, and in-laws are all traveling with you, peering over your shoulder every time you strike up a conversation? Perhaps the best thing to do is to find people to introduce them to. Introducing your relatives is the first thing you'll learn to do in this chapter.

The next thing you'll learn is how to find out about other people. One approach is to ask the objects of your curiosity what they think about themselves: Do they consider themselves to be creative, intelligent, sensitive, or adventurous? To ask these kinds of questions, you're going to need adjectives. And to use adjectives correctly, you must attach the appropriate ending to them so that they agree in gender and case with the noun they are modifying. This process is similar to changing the definite (*der*) and indefinite (*ein*) articles according to their gender and grammatical function, as you did in Chapter 7.

Family Matters

Have you ever been introduced to a group of people sitting around a table and said, "Oh, and this must be your lovely daughter," only to find yourself the object of puzzled, nervous glances? Was the silence broken when the gentleman you were addressing said, "Actually, no. This is my wife."? Of course, if you find yourself putting your foot in your mouth in German, you can always claim that you are still learning your vocabulary. Start practicing now with the words for family members in the following table, some of which you were exposed to in Chapter 6.

Family Members

Male	Pronunciation	English	Female	Pronunciation	English
das Kind	*dAs kint*	child	das Kind	*dAs kint*	child
der (Ehe) Mann	*deyR (ey-yuh) mAn*	husband	die (Ehe) Frau	*dee (ey-yuh) fRou*	wife
der Bruder	*deyR brew-duhR*	brother	die Schwester	*dee shves-tuhR*	sister
der Cousin	*deyR kew-zahN*	cousin	die Cousine	*dee kew-see-nuh*	cousin
der Enkel	*deyR en-kuhl*	grandson	die Enkelin	*dee en-kuh-lin*	grand-daughter
der Freund	*deyR fRoynt*	boyfriend	die Freundin	*dee fRoyn-din*	girl-friend
der Neffe	*deyR ne-fuh*	nephew	die Nichte	*dee niH-tuh*	niece
der Onkel	*deyR on-kuhl*	uncle	die Tante	*dee tAn-tuh*	aunt
der Opa/ Großvater	*deyR oh-pah/ gRohs-fah-tuhR*	grand-father	die Oma/ Großmutter	*dee oh-mah/ gRohs-moo-tuhR*	grand-mother
der Schwie-gersohn	*deyR shvee-guhR-zohn*	son-in-law	die Schwie-gertochter	*dee shvee-guhR-toCH-tuhR*	daughter-in-law
der Schwie-gervater	*deyR shvee-guhR-fah-tuhR*	father-in-law	die Schwie-germutter	*dee shvee-guhR-moo-tuhR*	mother-in-law
der Sohn	*deyR zohn*	son	die Tochter	*dee toCH-tuhR*	daughter
der Stiefbruder	*deyR shteef-bRew-duhR*	step-brother	die Stief-schwester	*dee shteef-shves-tuhR*	step-sister
der Stiefsohn	*deyR shteef-zohn*	stepson	die Stief-tochter	*die shteef-toCH-tuhR*	step-daughter
der Vater	*deyR fah-tuhR*	father	die Mutter	*dee moo-tuhR*	mother

Here are some useful plurals and their spellings:

Plural	Pronunciation	English
die Kinder	*dee kin-duhR*	the children
die Eltern	*dee el-tuhRn*	the parents

Plural	Pronunciation	English
die Großeltern	*dee gRohs-el-tuhRn*	the grandparents
die Schwiegereltern	*dee shvee-guhR-el-tuhRn*	the in-laws

Marking Relations?

We're all connected somehow. You're your mother's daughter or son, your uncle's nephew or niece, your wife's husband, or your husband's wife. There are two principal ways of showing possession in German: by using the genitive case and by using possessive adjectives.

The Genitive Case: Showing Possession

The genitive case shows possession or dependence. However, to show possession, you must also decline the noun and the noun marker correctly. Have you forgotten what a noun marker is? Noun markers refer to the definite article *the*, including the nominative *der, die, das,* or *die*; the indefinite article *ein,* the equivalent of *a* for nominative masculine or neuter nouns; or *eine,* the equivalent of *a* for nominative feminine nouns. Remember from Chapter 7 that masculine and neuter nouns take an ending, -(e)s, in the genitive case. Here is an abbreviated version of the genitive declension of the definite articles. When you use proper names or are speaking of family members expressing ownership or possession, you can use the *genitive -s* (add the -s without an apostrophe to the end of the word).

What's What

Genitive -s This method of showing possession can be used with family members and proper names. For example, *Stephanies Vater* (ste-fah-nees fah-tuhR) means "Stephanie's father," and *Vaters Tochter* (fah-tuhRs toH-tuhR) means "father's daughter."

Masculine	Feminine	Neuter	Plural (All Genders)
des	der	des	der

English frequently relies on the preposition *of* to express ownership, especially with inanimate objects. Note that the order of objects in German closely corresponds to the English possessive construction: *the X of the Y,* as in *die Farbe des Hauses,* or "the color of the house." In German, you identify the object first and then specify its owner, since logically, the most relevant item is that which is being modified—owned, possessed, had.

German	Pronunciation	Meaning
Das ist der Sohn des Mannes.	*dAs ist deyR zohn des mA-nuhs*	That is the man's son. (That is the son of the man.)
Das ist der Ehemann der Frau.	*dAs ist deyR ey-yuh-mAn deyR fRou*	That is the woman's husband. (That is the husband of the woman.)
Die Mutter des Kindes ist schön.	*dee moo-tuhR des kin-duhs ist shöhn*	The child's mother is beautiful. (The mother of the child is beautiful.)

Mine, All Mine

The *possessive adjectives my, your, his, her,* and so on show that something belongs to some-body. In German, possessive adjectives agree in number and gender with the noun they are describing (that is, with the thing being possessed rather than with the possessor, since the *his* or *her* part of the adjective already refers to the possessor). Singular possessive adjectives use the same endings as the declension of the indefinite article *ein* (declined in Chapter 7 and written out on a card by *you!*). You can think of this chart as the "*ein Wort*" chart—all of its members take the same endings and sort of rhyme: *ein, mein, dein, sein,* ... well, you get my drift. The following examples show someone loving someone. The *someone* is the direct object and, therefore, takes the accusative case.

What's What

Possessive adjectives
The adjectives *mein, dein, sein, ihr, unser, euer,* and *ihr* show that something belongs to someone, indicating possession or a special relationship. These are almost always followed by a noun and, therefore, like the *ein* words, need an ending.

English	German +	Pronunciation
He loves his father.	Er liebt **seinen** Vater.	*eyR leept zay-nuhn fah-tuhR*
He loves his mother.	Er liebt **seine** Mutter.	*eyR leept zay-nuh moo-tuhR*
She loves her father.	Sie liebt **ihren** Vater.	*zee leept ee-Ruhn fah-tuhR*
She loves her mother.	Sie liebt **ihre** Mutter.	*zee leept ee-Ruh moo-tuhR*

The following table lists the possessive adjectives.

Possessive Adjectives

Person	Singular	Meaning	Plural	Meaning
First	mein *mayn*	my	unser *oon-zuhR*	our
Second	dein *dayn*	your	euer *oy-uhR*	your
Third	sein, ihr, sein *zayn, eeR, zayn*	his, her, its	ihr *eeR*	their
(Formal)	Ihr *eer*	your	Ihr *eer*	your

The following two tables review the declension of possessive adjectives that exactly mirror the declension of the indefinite article, *ein*. Do recall that the only way the following paradigm deviates from the definite article (*der Wort*) paradigm is that the masculine nominative, neuter nominative, and neuter accusative take no endings. Otherwise, it resembles your *der Wort* paradigm.

The Declension of Singular Possessive Adjectives

Nom.	dein Mann *dayn mAn*	deine Frau *day-nuh fRou*	dein Kind *dayn kint*
Acc.	deinen Mann *day-nuhn mAn*	deine Frau *day-nuh fRou*	dein Kind *dayn kint*
Dat.	deinem Mann *day-nuhm mAn*	deiner Frau *day-nuhR fRou*	deinem Kind *day-nuhm kint*
Gen.	deines Mann(e)s *day-nuhs mAn(uh)s*	deiner Frau *day-nuhR fRou*	deines Kind(e)s *day-nuhs kind(uh)s*

The Declension of Plural Possessive Adjectives

Case	Plural ("your children")
Nom.	deine Kinder *day-nuh kin-duhR*
Acc.	deine Kinder *day-nuh kin-duhR*
Dat.	deinen Kindern *day-nuhn kin-duhRn*
Gen.	deiner Kinder *day-nuhR kin-duhR*

Now that you know how to express possession with the genitive case and with possessive adjectives, see whether you can express these relationships in German. Check your answers in Appendix A.

Example: her father

Answer: ihr Vater

1. his sister

2. my uncle

3. our family

4. your (informal, pl.) children

5. the girl's brother

6. the man's mother

7. the child's parents

8. the husband of my sister

9. the parents of his wife

10. the aunt of your (informal, sg.) cousin (m.)

Using Possessive Adjectives to Show Your Preference

Everyone has favorites. What's your favorite color, song, or city? German uses the adjective *lieblings-* (*leep-links*) to express "favorite" after the appropriate possessive adjective: *mein* for a masculine (*der*) noun, *meine* for a feminine (*die*) noun, and *mein* for a neuter (*das*) noun in the nominative case. The word *lieblings-* is linked to the noun to form a compound noun: *die Lieblingsfarbe* (*leep-links-fAR-buh*) for "favorite color," *das Lieblingslied* (*leep-links-leet*) for "favorite song," and *die Lieblingsstadt* (*leep-links-shtAt*) for "favorite city." Recall that the gender of this new word will be determined by the gender of its component on the right.

Here's an example:

Mein Lieblingsschauspieler ist Robert de Niro.
mayn leep-links-shou-shpee-luhR ist Roh-beRt de nee-Roh
My favorite actor is Robert de Niro.

Catharines Lieblingsfilm ist *Der Englische Patient.*
Kah-tuh-Ree-nuhs leep-links-film ist deyR en-gli-shuh pah-tsi-uhnt
Catharine's favorite movie is *The English Patient.*

Try forming five sentences to express your favorite things! Sentence beginnings are in Appendix A.

Example: das Gemüse (*guh-mü-zuh*), vegetable

Answer: Mein Lieblingsgemüse ist Spinat.

1. der Film (movie)

2. die Schriftstellerin (woman writer)

3. das Buch (book)

4. die Stadt (city)

5. der Sänger (singer)

 **Achtung**

The German word *ihr* (*eeR*) has many meanings. As a possessive adjective, it can mean "her," "their," or "your." One way of avoiding confusion in written German is by remembering to capitalize *Ihr* when it means "your."

Introductions

Introductions keep people from standing on opposite sides of the room staring at their feet all evening. Introductions break more ice than the *Titanic*, and whether you like them or not, it's pretty tough to get by without them. Practice a few of the following phrases to get the hang of introducing yourself.

German	Pronunciation	English
Darf ich mich vorstellen? Mein Name ist ….	*dARf iH miH foR-shte-luhn? Mayn nah-muh ist*	May I introduce myself? My name is ….
Kennen Sie (kennst du) meine Schwester Kathrin?	*ke-nuhn zee (kenst dew) may-nuh shves-tuhR kah-tReen*	Do you know my sister Katrin?
Kommen Sie (komm), ich stelle Ihnen (dir) meine Schwester Kathrin vor.	*ko-muhn zee (kom), iH shte-luh ee-nuhn (deeR) may-nuh shves-tuhR kah-tReen foR*	Come on, let me introduce my sister Katrin.
Das ist meine Schwester Kathrin.	*dAs ist may-nuh shves-tuhR kah-treen*	This is my sister Katrin.

You wouldn't greet the prime minister of England with a quick, "Hey, man, what's happenin'?" German has similar rules about the proper and improper way to deal with formal introductions. If you are being introduced to the head of a company at a business meeting, you will be given a formal introduction. Your response, in turn, should be expressed formally. Here are some formal ways of responding to an introduction:

Es freut mich, Sie kennenzulernen.
es froyt miH, zee ke-nuhn-tsew-leR-nuhn
It is a pleasure to meet you.

You're at a party and a friend wants to introduce you to someone; you'll probably find yourself caught up in an informal introduction. Here are some informal ways of responding to an introduction:

Es freut mich, dich kennenzulernen.
es froyt miH, diH ke-nuhn-tsew-leR-nuhn
Great meeting you.

To reply to an informal introduction, say:

Freut mich.
froyt miH
What a pleasure.

Schön, dich kennenzulernen.
shön, diH ke-nuhn-tswe-leR-nuhn
Nice to meet you.

Angenehm.
An-guh-neym
Pleasant.

> **German Culture**
>
> You don't have to go to Germany to find somebody who will help you practice your German. Go to Canada or to Latin America, or travel across the United States in a convertible shouting *Guten Tag!* at stoplights; sooner or later, someone will shout back *Guten Tag!* Millions of native German speakers live in the United States, Canada, and Latin America.

Breaking the Ice

Okay, you've learned all about family names, possession, and introductions. Now you're ready to get out there and converse! Imagine that you and a few members of your family are taking a bus to a local museum. Soon after you board, an individual whom you seem to remember having seen somewhere before sits next to you and begins flipping through a magazine. See whether you can do the following. Check your accuracy in Appendix A.

1. Introduce yourself.

2. Tell where you are from.

3. Say what you do.

4. Ask your new acquaintance where she comes from.

5. Ask her whether she knows a member of your family.

6. Introduce a member of your family to her.

7. Imagine that she introduces herself to you, and express pleasure at having met her.

Getting Involved in Conversation

One very useful verb is *haben* (*hah-buhn*), "to have." You can use this verb to express many things concerning yourself. Like the verb *sein*, *haben* is irregular (the second of the four irregular verbs in German). You'll have to memorize its conjugation, which shouldn't be too difficult—the irregularities of losing the *b* occur in the second and third person singular forms, exactly where the vowel changes occur in very strong verbs.

The Verb: *haben*

Person	Singular	Meaning	Plural	Meaning
First	ich habe *iH hah-buh*	I have	wir haben *veeR hah-buhn*	we have
Second	du hast *dew hAst*	you have	ihr habt *eeR hAbt*	you have
Third	er, sie, es, hat *eR, zee, es, hAt*	he, she, it, has	sie haben *zee hah-buhn*	they have
Formal	Sie haben *zee hah-buhn*	you have	Sie haben *zee hah-buhn*	you have

Express Yourself with *haben*

You can take a look at Chapter 5 to review the idioms with *haben* that express physical conditions. Here you'll pick up some new expressions with *haben*. Maybe you want to express how happy you are to have the opportunity (*die Gelegenheit haben*) to engage in conversation with someone, or how lucky you are (*wie viel Glück du hast*) to be able to visit Germany. The following table lists some idiomatic phrases that use *haben* to express luck, intention, and opportunity. You need merely combine these with the rest of your thoughts, involving another verb and possibly an idea housed in an infinitive phrase, to complete these expressions.

Expressions with *haben*

Idiom	Pronunciation	Meaning
die Gelegenheit haben	*dee guh-ley-guhn-hayt hah-buhn*	to have the opportunity
es hat keinen Zweck	*es hat kay-nuhn tsvek*	There's no point.
keine Lust haben	*kay-nuh loost hah-buhn*	to have no desire
die Zeit haben	*dee tsayt hah-buhn*	to have time
die (An)Gewohnheit haben	*dee (An)guh-vohn-hayt hah-buhn*	to have the habit to

continues

Expressions with *haben*   (continued)

Idiom	Pronunciation	Meaning
die Absicht haben	*dee Ap-siHt hah-buhn*	to have the intention
das Recht haben	*dAs ReHt hah-buhn*	to have the right
den Mut haben	*deyn moot hah-buhn*	to have the courage

Be sure to conjugate the verb *haben* correctly when you use it in a sentence.

German	English
Du hast die Gelegenheit, reich zu werden.	You have the opportunity to become rich.
Ich habe keine Zeit (zu arbeiten).	I have no time (to work).
Sie haben das Recht zu schweigen.	You have the right to be silent.
Ihr habt den Mut, laut zu singen.	You all have the courage to sing loudly.
Er hat die Absicht, sie zu heiraten.	He has the intention to marry her.
Es hat keinen Zweck, die Möbel auf der Titanic zu arrangieren.	There's no point to arranging the furniture on the Titanic.

As a Rule

In English, dependent infinitives used with most verbs are preceded by *to*. In German, dependent infinitives used with most verbs are preceded by *zu*. The German infinitive phrase is normally at the end of a sentence, is composed of *zu* and an infinitive, and is separated with a comma when the clause includes more than just the infinitive and *zu*. Although in English other parts of the phrase (modifiers and objects) follow the infinitive phrase, in German these elements precede it. Some verbs that can be followed by *zu* + an infinitive include: *beginnen, brachen, lernen, scheinen,* and *vergessen,* as in *Vergiss nicht zu essen!,* "Don't forget to eat!"; or *Wir beginnen, Deutsch zu lernen!,* "We are beginning to learn German!"

Using Idioms with *Haben*

These idiomatic expressions are of little use to you in their base infinitive forms. See how successfully you've memorized them by completing the following sentences with the correctly conjugated form of the verb *haben*. Check your idioms in Appendix A.

das Glück haben	die Gewohnheit haben
die Absicht haben	die Zeit haben
keine Lust haben	den Mut haben

1. Dirk ist nicht fröhlich. Er _____ mitzukommen.

2. Eva ist sehr abenteuerlich (adventurous). Sie _____ , Bungy-Jumping zu machen.

3. Hans ist verliebt. Er _____ zu heiraten.

4. Es sind Ferien. Anne und Mark _____ , eine Reise nach Deutschland zu machen.

5. Ihr habt in der Lotterie gewonnen. Ihr _____ im Spiel.

What's It Like?

What good is an artist if she's not creative and ground-breaking? Or a Marine if he's not courageous and strong? Without adjectives—words that describe nouns—describing someone is about as easy as brain surgery. With them, you can paint pictures with words. If you want to describe someone or something, you will need to use descriptive adjectives. German adjectives take an ending when they come immediately before a noun so that noun and adjective agree in gender (masculine, feminine, or neuter), number (singular or plural), and case (nominative, accusative, dative, or genitive)—seems to be a recurring theme, eh? If an adjective doesn't precede a noun, but rather comes after the verb, the adjective doesn't need an ending.

An attributive adjective—one taking an ending expressing agreement:

> Die freundliche Katze schnurrt viel.
> *dee froint-li-Huh kah-tsuh shnoort feel*
> The friendly cat purrs a lot.

A predicate (nonattributive) adjective—no noun follows it:

> Die Katze ist freundlich.
> *dee kah-tsuh ist froint-liH*
> The cat is friendly.

As a Rule _____

Adjectives that follow verbs, as in *Der Wein ist gut*, do not take endings. Because such adjectives are in the verb half of the sentence, they are referred to as predicate adjectives. However, if an adjective precedes the noun it modifies, its role becomes attributive and it takes an ending. All consecutive adjectives, no matter how many, that precede a noun have the same ending: *das schöne, lustige, kleine, intelligente Kind* (the pretty, funny, small, intelligent child).

Figuring Out Adjective Endings

Adjectives can take different endings depending on the type of word that precedes them; these words are commonly referred to as "limiting" words. When a *der Wort* (definite article) precedes an adjective, it performs the arduous task of expressing gender and grammatical function (case). Hence, the following adjective ending doesn't need to reflect this information and takes a so-called weak (*schwach*) ending (*-e/-en*): *der gute Film; Die nette Schwester besucht den faulen Bruder.* If no limiting word comes before the adjective (which would mark gender and case), the adjective has to take on this responsibility and needs to be "strong" (*stark*) enough to indicate gender and case: *deusbches Bier; französischer Wein.* In the middle of this spectrum are adjectives that come after certain "*ein*" words. *Ein* words share characteristics of both weak and strong declensions. The grammatically ambiguous masculine nominative, neuter nominative, and neuter accusative *ein* words (*ein/ein/ein*) depend on the adjective for grammatical expression: *ein rotes Auto, mein neuer Ball.* The good news is that these declensions are all quite regular, and once you learn the corresponding paradigms, you won't have any trouble.

Some words, referred to as *der* words, are inflected just like the definite article *der*. These words behave just like definite articles, expressing all of the grammar in front of a noun, so the adjective that follows takes a weak ending. *Der* words include *der* ("the"), *dies-* ("this"), *jed-* ("each"), *jen-* ("that"), *manch-* ("many a"), *solch-* ("such"), and *welch-* ("which, what"). The following table gives *der* word declension with the corresponding adjective ending. You can make a useful chart to illustrate the adjective endings for adjectives preceded by a *der* word by setting up your paradigm with cases and genders and then filling in the bold-faced endings shown here.

The Weak (-e/-en) Declension of an Adjective Preceded by a *der Wort*

Case	Masculine "the little boy"	Feminine "the little cat"	Neuter "the little pig"	Plural "the little pigs"
Nom.	der klein**e** Junge	die klein**e** Katze	das klein**e** Schwein	die klein**en** Schweine
	deyR klay-nuh yoon-guh	*dee klay-nuh kA-tsuh*	*dAs klay-nuh shvayn*	*dee klay-nuhn shvay-nuh*
Acc.	den klein**en** Jungen	die klein**e** Katze	das klein**e** Schwein	die klein**en** Schweine
	deyn klay-nuhn yoon-guhn	*dee klay-nuh kA-tsuh*	*dAs klay-nuh shvayn*	*dee klay-nuh shvay-nuh*
Dat.	dem klein**en** Jungen	der klein**en** Katze	dem klein**en** Schwein	den klein**en** Schweinen
	deym klay-nuhn yoon-guhn	*deyR klay-nuhn kA-tsuh*	*deym klay-nuhn shvayn*	*dehn klay-nuhn shvay-nuh*

Case	Masculine "the little boy"	Feminine "the little cat"	Neuter "the little pig"	Plural "the little pigs"
Gen.	des klein**en** Jungen	der klein**en** Katze	des kleinen Schweins	der kleinen Schweine
	des klay-nuhn yoon-guhn	*deyR klay-nuhn kA-tsuh*	*des klay-nuhn shvayns*	*deyR klay-nuhn shvay-nuh*

As you can see in the preceding table, all adjectives following a *der* word in the dative and genitive cases or in the plural take the ending *-en*.

Adjectives not preceded by a definite article, a *der* word, an indefinite article, or an *ein* word must indicate the gender and case of the noun they modify. Thus, when no article precedes a noun, adjectives take the strong declension and resemble a *der* word in their endings: *Schönes Wetter, was? (shö-nuhs ve-tuhR, vAs)*, "Nice weather, isn't it?" The following table illustrates this similarity between unpreceded adjective endings and the *der* words, with the only exception found in the masculine and neuter genitive adjective endings.

The strong declension also is used in the salutation of a letter because no limiting word precedes the adjective:

> Lieber Vater
> *lee-buhR fah-tuhR*
> Dear father

The Strong Declension of an Adjective Not Preceded by a Limiting Word (Unpreceded Adjective Endings)

Case	Masculine "green salad"	Feminine "cold milk"	Neuter "warm bread"	Plural "fresh fish"
Nom.	grün**er** Salat	kalt**e** Milch	warm**es** Brot	frisch**e** Fische
	grü-nuhR zah-lAt	*kAl-tuh milH*	*vAR-muhs bRot*	*fri-shuh fi-shuh*
Acc.	grün**en** Salat	kalt**e** Milch	warm**es** Brot	frisch**e** Fische
	grü-nuhn zah-lAt	*kAl-tuh milH*	*vAr-muhs bRot*	*fri-shuh fi-shuh*

continues

The Strong Declension of an Adjective Not Preceded by a Limiting Word (Unpreceded Adjective Endings) (continued)

Case	Masculine "green salad"	Feminine "cold milk"	Neuter "warm bread"	Plural "fresh fish"
Dat.	grün**em** Salat	kalt**er** Milch	warm**em** Brot	frisch**en** Fischen
	grü-nuhm zah-lAt	*kAl-tuhR milH*	*vAr-muhm bRot*	*fri-shuhn fi-shuhn*
Gen.	grün**en*** Salats	kalt**er** Milch	warm**en*** Brotes	frisch**er** Fische
	grü-nuhn zah-lAts	*kAl-tuhR milH*	*vAr-muhn bRo-tuhs*	*fri-shuhR fi-shuh*

*Note that the only adjective endings that do not resemble the der Wort paradigm are the genitive masculine and neuter, which take an -en rather than the predicted -es ending. But you still get to inflect the genitive masculine and neuter noun with an -(e)s, so take heart!

When adjectives come after an *ein Wort*, they have the responsibility to indicate the grammar *only* if the preceding limiting word doesn't—this is indicated by an asterisk in the following table. For the most part, the adjectives become wishy-washy and weak. Remember, *ein* words include *ein, mein, dein, sein* (m.), *ihr* (f.), *sein* (n.), *unser, euer, ihr* (pl.), and *Ihr* (formal).

Adjective Endings Following an *ein Wort*

Case	Masculine "green salad"	Feminine "cold milk"	Neuter "warm bread"	Plural "fresh fish"
Nom.	mein groß**er*** Bruder *mayn gRoh-suhR bRew-duhR*	meine große Schwester *may-nuh gRoh-suh shve-stuhR*	mein groß**es*** Haus *mayn gRoh-suhs hous*	meine groß**en** Häuser *may-nuh gRoh-suhn hoy-zuhR*
Acc.	meinen groß**en** Bruder *may-nuhn gRoh-suhn bRew-duhR*	meine große Schwester *may-nuh gRoh-suh shve-stuhR*	mein groß**es*** Haus *mayn gRoh-suhs hous*	meine groß**en** Häuser *may-nuh gRoh-suhn hoy-zuhRn*
Dat.	meinem groß**en** Bruder *mayn-uhm gRoh-suhn bRew-duhR*	meiner groß**en** Schwester *may-nuhR gRoh-suhn shve-stuhR*	meinem groß**en** Haus *may-nuhm gRoh-suhn hous*	meinen groß**en** Häusern *may-nuhn gRoh-suhn hoy-zuhRn*

Case	Masculine "my big brother"	Feminine "my big sister"	Neuter "my big house"	Plural "my big houses"
Gen.	meines groß**en** Bruders *may-nuhs gRoh-suhn bRew-duhRs*	meiner groß**en** Schwester *may-nuhR gRoh-suhn shve-stuhR*	meines groß**en** Hauses *may-nuhs gRoh suhn hou-zuhs*	meiner groß**en** Häuser *may-nuhR gRoh-suhn hoy-zuhR*

Denotes instances in which the ein *word itself has no ending; thus, it becomes the responsibility of the adjective to reflect case and gender.*

Note that, just like adjectives following a *der Wort*, all adjectives following an *ein Wort* in the dative and genitive cases, as well as all plurals, get the easy *-en*.

Adjectives and Their Antonyms

Are you fickle? Knowing adjectives and their opposites comes in handy if you're constantly changing your mind. If you find something interesting one moment and boring the next, you may want to memorize the adjectives in the following table along with their opposites. Besides, if you learn adjectives with their opposites, you are economically acquiring two words for the memory price of one!

A List of Useful Adjectives

German	Pronunciation	Meaning	German	Pronunciation	Meaning
alt	*Alt*	old, aged	jung	*yoong*	young
dick	*dik*	fat or thick	dünn	*dün*	thin
blöd	*blöd*	stupid	intelligent	*in-te-li-gent*	intelligent
fleißig	*flay-siH*	industrious	faul	*foul*	lazy
gesund	*guh-zoont*	healthy	krank	*kRAnk*	sick
groß	*gRohs*	big	klein	*klayn*	small
hart	*hArt*	hard	weich	*vayH*	soft
hell	*hel*	bright	dunkel	*doon-kuhl*	dark
hoch	*hoCH*	high	tief	*teef*	low
interessant	*in-tey-re-sAnt*	interesting	langweilig	*lAng-vay-liH*	boring
kalt	*kAlt*	cold	warm	*vahRm*	warm
klug	*klewk*	smart	dumm	*doom*	dumb
lang	*lAng*	long	kurz	*kooRts*	short
lustig	*loos-tiH*	funny	ernst	*eRnst*	serious

continues

A List of Useful Adjectives   (continued)

German	Pronunciation	Meaning	German	Pronunciation	Meaning
müde	*müh-duh*	tired	munter	*moon-tuhR*	awake
mutig	*mew-tiH*	brave	feige	*fay-guh*	cowardly
naß	*nAs*	wet	trocken	*tRo-kuhn*	dry
reich	*RayH*	rich	arm	*Arm*	poor
scharf	*shArf*	sharp	stumpf	*shtoompf*	blunt
schön	*shöhn*	beautiful	häßlich	*häs-liH*	ugly
schwer	*shveR*	hard or heavy	leicht	*layHt*	easy or light
stark	*shtARk*	strong	schwach	*shvACH*	weak
süß	*zühs*	sweet	sauer	*zou-uhR*	sour
tolerant	*to-luh-Rant*	tolerant	intolerant	*in-to-luh-Rant*	intolerant
teuer	*toy-uhR*	expensive	billig	*bi-liH*	cheap
traurig	*tRou-RiH*	sad	glücklich	*glük-liH*	happy
weiß	*vays*	white	schwarz	*shvARts*	black
dreckig	*dRe-kiH*	dirty	sauber	*zou-buhR*	clean
leer	*leyR*	empty	voll	*fol*	full
falsch	*fAlsh*	wrong	richtig	*RiH-tiH*	right
wahr	*vahR*	true	falsch	*fAlsh*	untrue
stolz	*shtolts*	proud	bescheiden	*buh-shay-duhn*	humble

Applying Adjectives

You're deep in conversation with a new friend and are excited about sharing your views. Use the rules you've learned in this chapter to complete the following descriptions with German adjectives. Remember to first determine which type (if any) of limiting word precedes the adjective, and the case and the gender of the noun to be modified. To help you start, we've divided the following exercise into three parts. We'll let you figure out which limiting word is involved in each grouping! Check your accuracy in Appendix A.

A. 1. Wo spielt dieser interessant _____ Film?

2. Ich nehme das kalt _____ Bier.

3. Jedes rot _____ T-Shirt ist billig.

4. Wir besuchen die klein _____ Stadt.

5. Sie lesen den best _____ Autor!

B. 1. Das ist warm _____ Brot.

2. Sie hat kluge _____ Ideen. (pl.)

3. Frisch _____ Salat ist gesund.

4. Haben Sie schön _____ Blumen?

5. Lieb _____ Kerstin, ….

C. 1. Mainz ist eine schön _____, alt _____ Stadt.

2. Er ist mein best _____ Freund.

3. Ich sehe seine jung _____ Schwester.

4. Wo ist ein gut _____ Restaurant?

5. Wir kaufen ein neu _____ Auto.

The Least You Need to Know

♦ To show possession in German, use the genitive case or possessive adjectives.

♦ *Haben* isn't just an important irregular verb that expresses physical conditions; it also can be used in certain idiomatic expressions of luck, intention, and opportunity.

♦ German adjectives agree with the noun they modify in gender, number, and case, and take endings according to which kind of limiting word precedes them.

Chapter 11

At the Airport

In This Chapter

- Plane travel
- The verbs *gehen* and *fahren*
- Giving and receiving directions
- Prepositions that are useful for getting around

You've done it. You've planned a trip, you've driven to the airport, you have your passport, and you have run your shoes through security. You've finally boarded the plane. You've even managed to have a somewhat stilted but successful chat with a German who has given you the names of a few good hotels in the city where you plan to spend a few relaxing, fun-filled days and nights.

A voice on the overhead speaker tells you that your plane will be landing soon. You take a deep breath, close your eyes, and begin to make a mental list of all the things you have to do before you find a hotel. You have to pick up your bags, pass customs, and figure out whether you're going to take a taxi or locate a bus or commuter train that goes to the city. What if no one at the airport speaks English? Don't worry: By the end of this chapter, you'll be able to accomplish all of these things in German.

Inside the Plane

Even if you're not afraid of heights, claustrophobic, or allergic to perfume, you may find it tough sitting sardinelike in the window seat. If this should happen to you, you might want to get the flight attendant's attention to find out whether you can move to a different seat. This section gives you the vocabulary you need to solve plane problems.

Mainly on the Plane

Soon after the plane takes off, a voice on the overhead speaker begins referring to items on the plane that are above and around you. This familiarizes the passengers with safety features and with the actions taken in the event of an emergency. The vocabulary in the following table will help you understand this information as well as solve various flight-related problems.

Inside the Plane

German	Pronunciation	English
(nicht) Raucher	*(niHt) Rou-CHubR*	(no) smoking
die Fluggesellschaft or die Fluglinie	*dee flook-guh-zel-shAft* *dee flook-li-nyah*	airline
das Flugzeug	*dAs flook-tsoyk*	airplane
die Maschine	*dee mA-shee-nuh*	
der Flughafen	*deyR flook-hah-fuhn*	airport
am Fenster	*Am fen-stuhR*	by the window
der Notausgang	*deyR noht-ous-gAng*	emergency exit
im Notfall	*im noht-fAl*	in an emergency
notwendig	*noht-ven-diH*	necessary
der Flugsteig	*deyR flook-shtayk*	gate
das Handgepäck	*dAs hAnt-guh-päk*	hand luggage
die Landung	*dee lAn-dung*	landing
die Rettungsweste or Schwimmweste	*dee Re-toongz-ves-tuh* *shvim-ves-tuh*	life vest
am Gang	*im gAng*	on the aisle
der Passagier or der Fluggast	*deyR pA-sA-jeeR* *deyR flook-gAst*	passenger
die Sicherheitsvorkehrungen	*dee zi-HuhR-hayts-for-key-Run-guhn*	safety precautions
der Sitz	*deyR zits*	seat

German	Pronunciation	English
der Abflug	*deyR ap-flook*	takeoff
das Terminal	*dAs teR-mee-nahl*	terminal
aus dem Flugzeug aussteigen	*ous deym flook-tsoyk ous-shtay-guhn*	to get off of or exit the plane
rauchen	*Rou-CHuhn*	to smoke

On the Inside

Overall, you've had a pleasant flight. Finally, the plane lands. There is a mad scramble for the aisle, and passengers begin opening the overhead compartments. As you leave the plane, there are signs everywhere, all of them pointing in different directions. You make it through customs without any difficulties and drag your bags off the luggage belt. Where should you go now?

Negotiating the Airport

You may want to ask someone where the baggage carts are. After that, you'll probably want to hit an ATM or change some money the old-fashioned way at an exchange booth. Perhaps you need to freshen up a little. You can wander around looking for those signs with the generic men and women on them, or you can ask someone where the nearest *Toilette* (*toy-le-tuh*) is. The following table gives you much of the vocabulary you'll need to get around the airport.

Inside the Airport

German	Pronunciation	English
die Ankunft	*dee An-koonft*	arrival
die Ankunftszeit	*dee An-koonf-tsayt*	arrival time
die Gepäckausgabe	*dee guh-pak-ous-gah-buh*	baggage claim
der Gepäckwagen	*deyR guh-pak-vah-guhn*	luggage cart
die Toilette	*dee toy-le-tuh*	bathroom
die Bushaltestelle	*dee boos-hAl-tuh-shte-luh*	bus stop
der Autoverleih	*deyR ou-toh-feR-lay*	car rental
der Abflug	*deyR Ap-flook*	departure
die Abflugszeit	*dee Ap-flook-tsayt*	departure time
das Flugziel	*dAs flook-tseel*	destination
der Aufzug	*deyR ouf-tsook*	elevator

continues

Inside the Airport   (continued)

German	Pronunciation	English
der Ausgang	*deyR ous-gAng*	exit
der Flug	*deyR flook*	flight
die Flugnummer	*dee flook-noo-muhR*	flight number
die Information	*dee in-foR-mah-tseeohn*	information
die Geldwechselstube	*dee gelt-vek-suhl-shtew-buh*	money exchange office
die Passkontrolle	*dee pAs-kon-tRo-luh*	passport control
kontrollieren	*kon-tRo-lee-Ruhn*	to inspect
die Sicherheitskontrolle	*dee zi-HuhR-hayts-kon-tRo-luh*	security check
der Grund	*deyR gRoont*	the reason
der Zwischenstop	*deyR tsvi-shuhn-shtop*	stopover
das Gepäckstück	*dAs guh-päk-shtük*	piece of luggage
der Koffer	*deyR ko-fuhR*	suitcase
das Taxi	*dAs tah-xee*	taxi
das Ticket	*dAs ti-ket*	ticket
einen Flug verpassen	*ay-nuhn flook veR-pA-suhn*	to miss a flight

Signage

Airline security has always been pretty tight on international flights. But if you've traveled within the United States after 9/11, you've already encountered this type of heightened security. Just in case, it would be comforting to be able to decipher signs giving travelers tips and warnings and indicating rules and regulations in German. The following signs provide examples of information you might see in an airport that serves German-speaking populations. Read the signs carefully and then try to match the sign with its corresponding bulleted question from the list that follows. Check your answers in Appendix A.

A. ACHTUNG:

Gefährden Sie nicht Ihre eigene Sicherheit: Nehmen Sie keine Gepäckstücke von anderen Personen an.

B. Ihr gesammtes Gepäck, einschließlich Ihres Handgepäcks, wird kontrolliert.

C. Das Benutzen von Gepäckwagen ist außschließlich im Flughafen gestattet.

D. ACHTUNG:

Aus Sicherheitsgründen werden alle zurückgelassenen Gepäckstücke von der Sicherheitspolizei zerstört.

Es ist dehalb notwendig, dass Sie Ihr GepÄck ständig mit sich führen.

E. AN DIE FLUGÄSTE

Das Mitführen von versteckten Waffen an Bord eines Flugzeuges ist gesetzlich verboten.

Es ist gesetzlich vorgeschrieben, dass alle Gepäckstücke, einschließlich des Handgepäcks, von der Sicherheitskontrolle überprüft werden.

Diese Durchsuchung kann verweigert werden. Passagiere, welche die Durchsuchung verweigern, sind nicht befugt, die Sicherheitskontrolle zu passieren.

Identify the sign that tells you:

1. _____ If you leave something behind, it might be destroyed.

2. _____ All of your luggage will be checked, even carry-on.

3. _____ Carrying a concealed weapon onboard is forbidden.

4. _____ You can use the baggage carts only within the airport.

5. _____ You shouldn't accept packages from strangers or from anyone you know if you don't know what's in the package.

Getting Around

You will undoubtedly find the strong verb *gehen* ("to go") handy as you make your way out of the airport to the taxi stand. As you learned in Chapter 8, you must conjugate present tense verbs so that they agree with the subject. Now you need to apply these inflections (sg. *-e, -st, -t* and pl. *-en, -t, -en*) to the stem *geh-*. The verb for "to travel" is *fahren*. *Fahren*, being a very strong verb, incurs a sound change (*a→ä*) in the present tense, like *fallen* does. The following table reviews this type of change, which occurs only in the second and third person singular forms.

The Very Strong Verb: *fahren*

Person	Singular	English	Plural	English
First	ich fahre *iH fah-Ruh*	I travel	wir fahren *veeR fah-Ruhn*	we travel
Second	du fährst *dew fähRst*	you travel	ihr fahrt *eeR fahrt*	you travel
Third	er, sie, es fährt *eR, zee, es fähRt*	he, she, it travels	sie fahren *zee fah-Ruhn*	they travel
Formal	Sie fahren *zee fah-Ruhn*	you travel	Sie fahren *zee fah-Ruhn*	you travel

Contractions with *Gehen*

The verb *gehen* is often followed by the preposition *zu* (to). *Zu* is a preposition that always takes the dative case; therefore, when this preposition is used to indicate location, the entire prepositional phrase is in the dative. Recall the declination of the dative *der* words—*dem* (m.), *die* (f.), *dem* (n.). If the noun after the preposition is masculine or neuter (*dem*), *zu* can contract with the article *dem* to become *zum* ("to the"). A *contraction* is a single word made out of two words, as in the word *it's*. In German, contractions don't take an apostrophe. Some prepositions in German may take the accusative or dative. *Auf* and *in* are two prepositions that can be used to indicate motion, and when *gehen* is followed by one of these prepositions, the prepositional phrase is in the accusative (*den, die, das*). Because contractions make it faster and easier to express things, we can again combine the prepositions *in* and *auf* with the accusative neuter *das* to come up with *ins* and *aufs*. Here are some examples of these contractions, with the illustration of gender and case in parentheses—case is determined by the preceding preposition.

> **What's What**
>
> **Contraction**   A shortened linguistic form attached to an adjacent form. In German, it's (a contraction in English!) a fusion of forms. Unlike their English counterparts, German contractions do not use apostrophes.

Ich gehe zum Bahnhof. (*der* Bahnhof + dative → dem)
iH gey-uh tsewm bahn-hohf
I'm going to the train station.

Ich gehe zum Geschäft. (*das* Geschäft + dative → dem)
iH gey-uh tsewm guh-shäft
I'm going to the store.

If the location toward which the subject is heading is feminine, *zu* ("to") can contract with the feminine dative article *der* ("the") to become *zur* ("to the").

Ich gehe *zur* Kirche. (*die* Kirche + dative → der)
iH gey-uh tsewR keeR-Huh
I'm going to the church.

Ich gehe *ins* Kino. (*das* Kino + accusative → das)
ich gey-uh inz kee-noh
I go to the movies.

Er geht *aufs* Polizeirevier. (*das* Polizeirevier + accusative → das)
eR geyt oufs po-lee-zay-Ruh-veeR
He goes to the police station.

How Do You Get To ...?

You may get disoriented in a new place; the best thing to do is to ask someone how to get to wherever you want to go. Here are some ways of asking questions:

Wo ist der Ausgang?
voh ist deyR ous-gAng
Where is the exit?

Der Ausgang, bitte.
deyR ous-gAng, bi-tuh
The exit, please.

Wo sind die Taxis?
voh zint dee tah-xees
Where are the taxis?

Die Taxis, bitte.
dee tah-ksees, bi-tuh
The taxis, please.

If you're not sure whether what you're looking for is nearby, or if you just want to know whether whatever you're looking for is in the vicinity, use the phrase *gibt es* ("is there," "are there") and the prepositional phrase *in der Nähe* ("nearby"). It's a useful way of finding things out. To answer a question affirmatively, reverse the word order, beginning with the subject, *es*.

Gibt es Toiletten in der Nähe?
gipt es toy-le-tuhn in deyR näh-uh
Are there toilets nearby?

Ja, es gibt Toiletten in der Nähe.
yah, es gipt toy-le-tuhn in deyR näh-uh
Yes, there are toilets nearby.

In certain situations, you use the preposition *nach* to indicate where you are going.

With continents, countries, and towns:

Ich fahre nach Berlin.
iH fah-Ruh nACH beR-lin
I'm going to Berlin.

With prepositions that show direction:

Er geht nach rechts.
eR geyt nACH reHts
He's going to the right.

On the other hand, the preposition *zu* (along with the dative case) is used to indicate motion if the object is a person:

Ich gehe zum Arzt.
iH ge-uh tsewm ARtst
I'm going to the doctor.

And for going to places other than cities, regions, and countries—think of closer locations:

Wir fahren zum Flughafen.
veer fah-Ruhn tsewm flook-hah-fuhn
We're going/traveling to the airport.

You Can't Get There from Here ...

What if the place you're looking for isn't within pointing distance? In this case, you'd better know the verbs people use when they give directions.

Verbs Used When Giving Directions

German	Pronunciation	English
abbiegen*	*Ap-bee-guhn*	to turn
gehen	*gey-uhn*	to go
laufen[s]	*lou-fuhn*	to walk

German	Pronunciation	English
mitfahren*[S]	*mit-fah-Ruhn*	to ride with/along
nehmen[S]	*ney-muhn*	to take
weitergehen*	*vay-tuhR-gey-uhn*	to go on, to continue

indicates a separable prefix verb.

[S] *indicates a very strong verb, incurring a sound change in the second and third person singular.*

Verbs with Separable Prefixes

Some verbs in the preceding table (the ones with asterisks next to them) have *separable prefixes*, verbal complements that are placed at the end of the sentence when the verb is conjugated (separable prefixes are addressed at greater length in Chapter 13). Some of the most common separable prefixes include *auf, hinüber, aus, an, hinunter, hinauf, weiter, bei, mit, nach,* and *zu.* Although many of these indicate direction, all of them add a little layer of meaning to the stem verb. When you use a verb with separable prefixes, the verb comes near the beginning of the sentence next to the subject, and the prefix comes at the end. Incidentally, the verbs marked with a superscript *S* are the *very strong,* or *sehr stark* verbs—those that incur a vowel change in the second and third person singular.

Du biegst rechts ab.
dew beekst reHts Ap
You turn right.

Er geht zum Terminal weiter.
eR geyt tsewm teR-mee-nahl vay-tuhR
He continues to the terminal.

Sie fährt mit?
zee fähRt mit?
Is she riding along/with?

> **What's What**
>
> **Separable prefix**
> Verbal complements comprised of prepositions, adverbs, or particles that are placed at the end of the sentence when the verb is conjugated. This produces a two-part verb that alters or in some way affects the meaning of the main verb. These prefixes are always stressed.

Giving Commands

When someone tells you how to get somewhere, generally you are receiving a command, an imperative. Imperatives express commands, requests, or directives. The subject of the imperative is *you.* Because you can address someone formally or informally in German, and speak to one or more than one person, German has several easily deducible imperative forms corresponding to the three grammatical forms expressing the second person pronoun "you": *Sie, du,* and *ihr.* Try to figure out which of the following *imperative* forms correspond to *du, ihr,* and *Sie.* The answers are in Appendix A.

A. Gehen Sie nach rechts.
gey-uhn zee nACH reHts
Go right.

B. Geht nach rechts.
geyt nACH ReHts
Go right.

C. Geh(e) nach rechts.
Gey(-uh) nACH reHts
Go right.

We Are Family

English has numerous verbs that extend their meanings by adding certain prepositions, called *complements:* to go out, to come along/with, to drive back. German very neatly attaches this *complement* to the infinitive—hence, you get very similar constructions of *ausgehen, mitkommen, zurückfahren.* These separable prefixes occur sentence-final in statements and in questions. Some varieties of American English retain German word order, as in "Are you coming with?"

If you deduced that answer A was the formal (*Sie*-address) imperative form, identical to the present-tense form, give yourself a point. Because it is a command, it begins with the verb because action is tantamount in getting one's way. And answer B? You guessed it—the familiar plural (*ihr*-address) imperative is identical to the *ihr* form in the present tense, except that the pronoun, *ihr*, is omitted. This pattern is easy enough to account for: Commands in the familiar realm do not need to be formal, so we can omit the pronoun. Likewise, we can account for answer C being the familiar singular (*du*-address) imperative, omitting the pronoun and even the ending (-*st*) on the verb! To pronounce that type of sliced-off stem more easily, often an -*e* is added, as in *Warte!* ("Wait!") or *Finde den Flugsteig!* ("Find the gate!")

As a Rule

In an imperative, the prefix from a separable prefix verb still goes to the end of the command, as illustrated with the verb *aufstehen*, "to get up": *Stehen Sie auf! Steht auf!* or *Steh auf!* ("Get up!") Also noteworthy is the fact that the umlaut stem change from a(u)→ becomes ä(u) in a *sehr stark* verb is not retained in the *du* form of the imperative (whereas the e changing into ie or i stem change persists). Consider: *Gib her!* ("Hand over!") and *Fall nicht hin!* ("Don't fall down!"). See how easy it was to form the imperative with very strong separable prefix verbs?

Giving Orders

You need to practice giving and receiving commands before you can effectively do either. Complete the following exercise by filling in the appropriate command forms and their meanings. The entire chart appears in Appendix A.

Verb	du	ihr	Sie	English
abbiegen*	_____	_____	_____	Turn!
gehen	Geh(e)!	Geht!	Gehen Sie!	Go!
weitergehen*	_____	_____	_____	Continue!
laufen[s]	_____	_____	_____	Walk!
mitfahren*[s]	_____	_____	_____	Ride along!

*indicates a separable prefix verb.

[s] indicates a very strong verb, incurring a sound change in the second and third person singular.

Prepositions: Little Words Can Make a Big Difference

Prepositions are useful for giving and receiving directions. They show the relationship of a noun to another word, adding supplemental information to a basic subject/verb sentence. Prepositions locate something— an entity, event, or situation—in relation to another referent in terms of space or time, or to designate the source and/or direction of motion. The following table contains some useful prepositions for getting where you want to go.

What's What

Preposition   A word or phrase that shows the relation of a noun to another word in a sentence.

Prepositions

German	Pronunciation	English
an	*an*	to go to, on (vertical)
auf	*ouf*	to, in, at, on (horizontal)
aus	*ous*	out of
bei	*bay*	at, near
bis	*bis*	until, as far as
durch	*dooRCH*	through
gegen	*gey-guhn*	against
hinter	*hin-tuhR*	behind

continues

Prepositions (continued)

German	Pronunciation	English
in	*in*	in
nach	*nACH*	after
neben	*ney-buhn*	next to
ohne	*oh-nuh*	without
um	*ewm*	around
unter	*oon-tuhR*	under
von	*fon*	from
vor	*foR*	in front of
zu, nach	*tsew, nACH*	to, at
zwischen	*tsvi-shuhn*	between

Prepositions Are Particular!

Although the preceding table lists German prepositions, not all prepositions are created equal. Sure, you had it made in English, knowing that it's *for him* rather than *for he*. You intuitively and automatically change the case from nominative to objective after a preposition in English. German changes the form of the noun phrase (which might be a pronoun or a noun) after the preposition as well, relying on its various cases after specific prepositions. The following table contains the prepositions from the preceding table that are always dative. Although a few other prepositions also take the dative case—that is, what comes after the preposition will appear in the dative case—for now, let's limit this exercise to prepositions that are helpful for getting around and indicating time. Note how some dative prepositions contract with the following definite article, as in *beim* and *zur*.

Dative Prepositions

German	Example	English
aus	aus dem Haus	out of the house
bei	beim Postamt	at the post office
	beim Artz	at the doctor's
nach	nach einer Stunde	after an hour
	nach Wien	to Vienna
von	von Hamburg	from Hamburg
	von meinen Eltern	from my parents
zu	zur Bushaltestelle	to the bus stop

See whether you can fill in the correct form of the dative in the following dative prepositional phrases. Check your responses in Appendix A.

1. aus _____ Flugzeug (n.) (out of the airplane)

2. bei _____ Flughafen (m.) (near the airport)

3. von sein _____ Arbeit (f.) (from his workplace)

4. zu _____ Hotel (h.) (to the hotel)

Likewise, some prepositions always take the accusative case. Those relating to direction and duration are listed in the following table.

Accusative Prepositions

German	Example	English
bis	bis nächste Woche bis Mainz	by/until next week as far as Mainz
durch	durch die Stadt	through the city
ohne	ohne den Bus	without the bus
um	um die Ecke	around the corner

Use the accusative case to finish these prepositional phrases. Check your responses in Appendix A.

1. durch _____ Land (n.) (through the country)

2. ohne _____ Ticket (n.) (without the ticket)

3. um _____ Sitz (m.) (around the seat)

4. bis _____ Sicherheitskontrolle (f.) (until the security check)

The prepositions *in* and *auf* belong to a nifty group of prepositions that can govern either the dative or the accusative, depending on the context. With verbs like *gehen* and *fahren* (introduced earlier in this chapter) that indicate motion *toward* a place, the preposition governs the accusative. To indicate moving around *within* a place, the preposition governs the dative. The following table provides examples of both instances for the two-way prepositions listed earlier in the table titled "Prepositions":

Two-Way Prepositions

German	Example	English
an	Ich gehe ans Fenster. Ich bin am Fenster.	I'm going to the window. I'm at the window.
auf	Geh auf den Marktplatz! Parke auf dem Marktplatz!	Go to the town square! Park on the town square!
hinter	Fahr hinter die Garage! Das Auto ist hinter der Garage.	Drive behind the garage! The car is behind the garage.
in	Ich gehe in das Terminal. Ich bin im Terminal.	I'm going (in)to the terminal. I'm in the terminal.
neben	Mein Koffer liegt neben dem Gepäckablage.	My suitcase is lying next to the luggage rack.
unter	Die Rettungsweste ist unter dem Sitz.	The life vest is under the seat.
vor	Die Taxis warten vor dem Flughafen.	The taxis are waiting in front of the airport.
zwischen	Die Paßkontrolle liegt zwischen der Sicherheitskontrolle und dem Flugsteig.	The passport control is between the security check and the gate.

Care to finish off your prepositional preoccupation with a few more exercises, this time concerning the two-way prepositions? Check your answers in Appendix A.

1. Ich werfe deinen Koffer auf dein _____ Sitz. (I'm throwing your suitcase onto your seat.)

2. Es gibt eine Paßkontrolle an _____ Grenze. (There is passport control on/at the border.)

3. Klaus ist in _____ Toilette. (Klaus is in the bathroom.)

4. Stell dein Handgepäck neben _____ Bett (neut.). (Put your hand luggage next to the bed.)

5. Mein Ticket ist unter dein _____ Handgepäck! (My ticket is under your carry-on luggage!)

Pardon Me?

We've all asked for directions and then immediately regretted it. Such remorse generally happens when the direction-giver enumerates more rights and lefts than we can handle. Thus, knowing how to show lack of understanding in a foreign country is extremely useful. In addition to scratching your head and cocking it to one side, use some of the phrases in the following table to let people know that you just don't understand.

Expressing Incomprehension and Confusion

German	Pronunciation	English
Entschuldigen Sie!	*ent-shool-dee-guhn zee*	Excuse me! (formal)
Entschuldigung, ich habe Sie nicht verstanden.	*ent-shool-dee-goong, iH hah-buh zee niHt feR-shtAn-duhn*	Excuse me, I didn't understand you.
Ich verstehe nicht.	*iH feR-shtey-uh niHt*	I don't understand.
Sprechen Sie langsamer, bitte.	*shpRe-Hun zee lAng-zah-muhR, bi-tuh.*	Please speak more slowly.
Was haben Sie gesagt?	*vAs hah-buhn zee guh-zAkt*	What did you say?
Wiederholen Sie, bitte.	*vee-deR-hoh-luhn zee, bi-tuh*	Please repeat (what you just said).

The Least You Need to Know

 ♦ Learning a few useful vocabulary words will help you figure out airport traveling in German.

 ♦ The strong verb *gehen* is used to give directions. Useful also is the very strong verb *fahren*.

 ♦ German has three ways of forming commands, depending on the degree of formality and the number of addressees.

 ♦ Prepositions are useful tools in expressing direction. Some of them govern the dative case, others govern the accusative, and still others can't quite make up their minds.

 ♦ If you don't understand the directions being given to you, don't be afraid to say, "Ich verstehe nicht. Wiederholen Sie, bitte (*iH feR-shtey-uh niHt, vee-deR-hoh-luhn zee, bi-tuh*)."

Chapter 12

Heading for the Hotel

In This Chapter

- ◆ Getting around
- ◆ Renting a car
- ◆ Determining *which*, *this*, *every*, or *such*
- ◆ Counting with cardinal numbers
- ◆ Telling time

We're going to take it for granted that, when you step outside the international departures terminal, there are no taxis in sight, so you find a bus and take it into the center of the city. Now you have to find a reasonably priced but comfortable hotel where you can settle down and begin to figure out how to get a number of things done, including renting a car (that rather adventurous bus ride to the hotel has made you eager to arrange for a car as soon as possible). This chapter examines ways to get things done effectively and efficiently.

Ticket to Ride

The only way to get to know a city is to travel around in it. You have a number of options, of course. Walking is fun and cheap; taking a bus affords an overhead view of the shops, sidewalks, and people along the streets; and taking a taxi is convenient and comfortable. The mode of travel you choose will depend on many factors, including how near or distant your destination is. Whichever mode of travel is right for you, you should familiarize yourself with some terms.

Modes of Transportation

Whether you see yourself zipping along on the Autobahn or hobnobbing with the locals on a bus, knowing the words listed here will help you get around. You've already seen this vocabulary used with the dative preposition *mit* to indicate "by means of" in Chapter 5.

German	Pronunciation	English
das Auto	*dAs ou-toh*	car
der Wagen	*deyR vah-guhn*	car
der Sportwagen	*deyR shpoRt-vah-guhn*	sportscar
das Taxi	*dAs tah-xee*	taxi
der Bus	*deyR boos*	bus
der Zug	*deyR tsewk*	train
die S-Bahn	*dee es-bahn*	commuter train
die U-Bahn	*dee ew-bahn*	subway
die Straßenbahn	*dee shtRah-suhn-bahn*	streetcar

A Means to an End

You'll use the verb *nehmen* (*ney-muhn*), "to take," to express how you are going to get from where you are to where you are going. *Nehmen* is a very strong verb whose stem vowel changes from *e* to *i* in the second and third person singular. Because we're not only changing the quality of the *e* sound but also shortening it quantitatively, we'll reflect that in the spelling by dropping that "lengthening *h*" and adding a second *m* so that the *i* comes out short. Of course, you need only remember that *e→i*. (See the following table.)

The Verb *nehmen*

Person	Singular	English	Plural	English
First	ich nehme *iH ney-muh*	I take	wir nehmen *veeR ney-muhn*	we take

Person	Singular	English	Plural	English
Second	du nimmst *dew nimst*	you take	ihr nehmt *eeR neymt*	you take
Third	er, sie, es nimmt *eR, zee, es nimt*	he, she, it takes	sie nehmen *zee ney-muhn*	they take
Formal	Sie nehmen *zee ney-muhn*	you take	Sie nehmen *zee ney-muhn*	you take

This stem-vowel change from *e →i* might summon images of the very strong verb *sehen*, which also involves the addition of an *i*, as in *sehen → er, sie, es sieht*. Other verbs that incur the change from *e → i*, and thus very much resemble *nehmen*, include *geben*, "to give"; *essen*, "to eat"; *sprechen*, "to talk"; *werfen*, "to throw"; and *sterben*, "to die."

See whether you can fill in the blanks in these sentences with the correct form of the verb *nehmen*. Check your answers in Appendix A.

1. Ich _____ ein Taxi, um zum Geschäft zu kommen.

   I take the bus to get to the store.

2. Wir _____ die Straßenbahn, um in die Innenstadt zu kommen.

   We take the streetcar to get downtown.

3. Er _____ das Auto, um zur Kirche zu fahren.

   He takes the car to get to the church.

4. Du _____ das Fahrrad, um aufs Land zu fahren.

   You take the bicycle to ride to the country.

Which One?

Someone tells you that to get to the local museum, you must go straight past a building and then take a left on a street. *Which* building is the person talking about? *Which* street does he or she mean? When you're traveling—and particularly when you're asking directions—one word in German will be indispensable to you: *welcher* (*vel-HuhR*), the interrogative word for "which." The handy thing about this word is that it takes the same endings as the definite article. In its base form, *welcher* resembles the nominative masculine *der*; *welcher*. Thus, simply knock off that *-er* ending and apply whichever *der* word ending fits for gender, case, and number! Piece of cake, eh?

Welcher with Singular and Plural Nouns

When *welcher* comes immediately before a noun and introduces a question, it is considered an interrogative pronoun and must agree in number, gender, and case with the noun it precedes. Some common pronouns that follow the same declension patterns as *welcher* are *dieser* ("this"), *jeder* ("each," "every"), *mancher* ("many," "many a"), and *solcher* ("such," "such a"). The following table reviews the declension of *der* words, this time substituting *welch-* into the paradigm.

As a Rule

In conversational German, the definite article, when spoken with heavy stress, functions as the equivalent of the English *this/these* or *that/those: Der Sportwagen ist toll!* ("This/that sports car is neat!"); *Die Autos fahren sehr schnell.* ("These/those cars drive fast.")

The *der* Wort *welch-*

Case	Masculine	Feminine	Neuter	Plural
Nom.	which bus welcher Bus *vel-HuhR boos*	which direction welche Richtung *vel-Huh RiH-toong*	which car welches Auto *vel-Huhs ou-toh*	which cars welche Autos *vel-Huh ou-tohz*
Acc.	welchen Bus *vel-Huhn boos*	welche Richtung *vel-Huh RiH-toong*	welches Auto *vel-Huhs ou-toh*	welche Autos *vel-Huh ou-tohz*
Dat.	welchem Bus *vel-Huhm boos*	welcher Richtung *vel-HuhR RiH-toong*	welchem Auto *vel-Huhm ou-toh*	welchen Autos *vel-Huhn ou-tohz*
Gen.	welches Buses *vel-Huhs boo-suhs*	welcher Richtung *vel-HuhR RiH-toong*	welches Autos *vel-Huhs ou-to*	welcher Autos *vel-HuhR ou-tohz*

The Third Degree

You should be prepared for questions that begin with *welch-* (in its declined form). Here are some common questions you may be asked while traveling around the city. You should recognize a few of the prepositions from Chapter 11, including that tricky two-way preposition *in!*

Welchen Bus nehmen Sie? (m., acc.)
vel-Huhn boos ney-muhn zee
Which bus are you taking?

In welche Richtung fährt der Bus? (f., acc.)
in vel-Huh RiH-toong fähRt deyR boos
In which direction is the bus going?

Welches Auto mieten Sie? (n., acc.)
vel-Huhs ou-toh mee-tuhn zee
Which car are you renting?

Mit welcher Maschine fliegen Sie? (f., dat.)
mit vel-HuhR mah-shee-nuh flee-guhn zee
On which plane are you flying?

Using Which

Have you ever spoken with someone who immediately assumes that you know what he or she is speaking about, no matter what the topic is? See whether you can properly decline the interrogative pronoun *welch-* to find out the specifics of the statements given here. Check your questions in Appendix A.

Example: Ich nehme die U-Bahn. (Welche U-Bahn?)

German	Pronunciation	English
Sie nehmen den Zug.	*zee ney-muhn deyn tsook*	They take the train.
Ich fahre in die Stadt.	*iH fah-Ruh in dee shtAt*	I'm driving into town.
Er mietet ein Auto.	*eR mee-tuht ayn ou-toh*	He rents a car.
Ich besuche einen Freund.	*iH buh-zew-CHuh ay-nuhn fRoynt*	I'm visiting a friend.
Wir gehen in ein Museum.	*veeR gey-uhn in ayn mew-zey-oom*	We're going to a museum.
Sie sucht ein Hotel.	*zee zewCHt ayn hoh-tel*	She's looking for a hotel.
Er nimmt ein Buch mit.	*eR nimt ayn buCH mit*	He's taking along a book.

On the Road

You may want to take a trip with your travel partners around the countryside or go on a castle quest. And the ideal way to do so is to rent a car. The following phrases are useful when renting a car.

Ich möchte ein Auto mieten.
iH möH-tuh ayn ou-toh mee-tuhn
I would like to rent a car.

As a Rule

The very strong verb *empfehlen* changes the *-e* to *-ie* in the second and third person singular, akin to *sehen*, *lesen* ("to read"), and *stehlen* ("to steal"). Having learned the conjugation for *halten* in Chapter 8, you will immediately recognize that *enthalten* contains that stem and will thus change from *-a* to *-ä* with *du* and the *er*, *sie*, and *es* forms.

Wie viel kostet es am Tag (in der Woche)?
vee feel kos-tuht es Am tahk (in deyR vo-CHuh)
How much does it cost per day (per week)?

Welches Auto empfehlen Sie mir?
vel-Huhs ou-toh em-pfey-luhn zee meeR
Which car do you recommend?

Ist das Benzin im Preis enthalten?
ist dAs ben-tseen im pRays ent-hAl-tuhn
Is the gasoline included in the price?

Wie teuer ist die Versicherung?
vee toy-uhR ist dee veR-zi-Huh-Roong
How expensive is the insurance?

Outside the Car

If you decide to rent a car, don't forget to check in the trunk for the regulation jack—in German, *der Wagenheber (deyR vah-guhn-hey-buhR)*—and the spare tire, or *der Ersatzreifen (deyR eR-zAts-Ray-fuhn)*.

Here are a few terms you might find useful when talking about the various features of a car.

German	Pronunciation	English
das Fenster	*dAs fen-stuhR*	window
das Nummernschild	*dAs noo-meRn-shilt*	license plate
das Rad	*dAs Raht*	wheel
das Rücklicht	*dAs Rük-liHt*	tail light
der Auspuff	*deyR ous-poof*	exhaust
der Benzintank	*deyR ben-zeen-tAnk*	gas tank
der Blinker	*deyR blin-kuhR*	turn signal
der Keilriemen	*deyR kayl-Ree-muhn*	fan belt
der Kofferraum	*deyR ko-fe-Roum*	trunk
der Kotflügel	*deyR koht-flü-guhl*	fender
der Kühler	*deyR küh-luhR*	radiator
der Motor	*deyR mo-tohR*	motor
der Scheibenwischer	*deyR shay-buhn-vi-shuhR*	windshield wiper
der Türgriff	*deyR tühR-gRif*	door handle

German	Pronunciation	English
der Vergaser	*deyR feR-gah-suhR*	carburetor
die Antenne	*dee An-te-nuh*	antenna
die Batterie	*dee bA-te-Ree*	battery
die Motorhaube	*dee mo-tohR-hou-buh*	hood
die Reifen	*dee Ray-fuhn*	tires
die Scheinwerfer	*dee shayn-veR-fuhR*	headlights
die Stoßstange	*dee shtoh-shtAn-guh*	bumper
die Windschutzscheibe	*dee vint-shutz-shay-buh*	windshield
die Zündkerzen	*dee tsünt-keR-tsuhn*	sparkplugs

Inside the Car

Here are a few useful terms for things inside a car.

German	Pronunciation	English
das Amaturenbrett	*dAs ah-mA-tew-Ruhn-bRet*	dashboard
das Gaspedal	*dAs gahs-pey-dahl*	accelerator
das Handschuhfach	*dAs hAnt-shew-fACH*	glove compartment
das Lenkrad	*dAs lenk-Raht*	steering wheel
das Radio	*dAs Rah-dee-oh*	radio
der Blinker	*deyR blin-kuhR*	turn signal
der Rückspiegel	*deyR Rük-shpee-guhl*	rear-view mirror
die Bremsen	*dee bRem-suhn*	brakes
die Hupe	*dee hew-puh*	horn
die Kupplung	*dee kup-lung*	clutch
die Schaltung	*dee shAl-tung*	gear shift
die Zündung	*dee tsün-dung*	ignition

You might want to ask someone whether you're heading in the right direction. You never know when you're going to get lost in the woods without your compass.

nach Norden	*nACH noR-duhn*	to the north
nach Süden	*nACH süh-duhn*	to the south
nach Westen	*nACH ves-tuhn*	to the west
nach Osten	*nACH os-tuhn*	to the east

Numbers

Sooner or later you're going to have to learn numbers in German. Numbers are used for telling time, for making dates, for counting, for finding out prices—they're even used to refer to the pages and chapters in this book! So pull out your abacus and start counting.

What's What

Cardinal number   The basic form of a number; numbers used in counting.

Counting

One, two, three, four …. As children, one of the first things we learn to do is count. Numbers that express amounts are known as *cardinal numbers*. The sooner you learn cardinal numbers in German, the better. You're going to need to use numbers for everything from renting a car to locating your gate in an airport. The following table lists the cardinal numbers.

Cardinal Numbers

German	Pronunciation	English
null	*nool*	0
eins	*aynts*	1
zwei	*tsvay*	2
drei	*dRay*	3
vier	*feeR*	4
fünf	*fünf*	5
sechs	*zeks*	6
sieben	*zee-buhn*	7
acht	*ACHt*	8
neun	*noyn*	9
zehn	*tseyn*	10
elf	*elf*	11
zwölf	*tsvölf*	12
dreizehn	*dRay-tseyn*	13
vierzehn	*feeR-tseyn*	14
fünfzehn	*fünf-tseyn*	15
sechzehn	*zeHs-tseyn*	16
siebzehn	*zeep-tseyn*	17

German	Pronunciation	English
achtzehn	*ACH-tseyn*	18
neunzehn	*noyn-tseyn*	19
zwanzig	*tsvAn-tsiH*	20
einundzwanzig	*ayn-oont-tsvAn-tsiH*	21
zweiundzwanzig	*tsvay-oont-tsvAn-tsiH*	22
dreiundzwanzig	*dRay-oont-tsvAn-tsiH*	23
vierundzwanzig	*feeR-oont-tsvAn-tsiH*	24
fünfundzwanzig	*fünf-oont-tsvAn-tsiH*	25
sechsundzwanzig	*zeks-oont-tsvAn-tsiH*	26
siebenundzwanzig	*zee-buhn-oont-tsvAn-tsiH*	27
achtundzwanzig	*ACHt-oont-tsvAn-tsiH*	28
neunundzwanzig	*noyn-oont-tsvAn-tsiH*	29
dreißig	*dRay-siH*	30
vierzig	*feeR-tsiH*	40
fünfzig	*fünf-tsiH*	50
sechzig	*zeH-tsiH*	60
siebzig	*zeep-tsiH*	70
achtzig	*ACH-tsiH*	80
neunzig	*noyn-tsiH*	90
hundert	*hoon-deRt*	100
hunderteins	*hoon-deRt-aynts*	101
hundertzwei	*hoon-deRt-tsvay*	102
zweihundert	*tsvay-hoon-deRt*	200
zweihundereins	*tsvay-hoon-deRt-aynts*	201
zweihunderzwei	*tsvay-hoon-deRt-tsvay*	202
tausend	*tou-zent*	1,000
zweitausend	*tsvay-tou-zent*	2,000
hunderttausend	*hoon-deRt-tou-zent*	100,000
eine Million	*aynuh mee-leeohn*	1,000,000
zwei Millionen	*tsvay mee-leeoh-nuhn*	2,000,000
eine Milliarden	*ayn mee-leeAR-duh*	1,000,000,000
zwei Milliarden	*tsvay mee-leeAR-duhn*	2,000,000,000

After you've learned the basics of counting in German, the main things to remember are …

♦ After the number 20, numbers are expressed in compound words with the 1, 2, 3 … coming first: 1-and-20, 2-and-20, 3-and-20 …. Don't forget to drop the *-s* from *eins* before *einundzwanzig, einunddreißig,* and so on.

♦ *Und* (and) is used to connect the numbers 1 through 9 to the numbers 20, 30, 40, 50, and so on.

♦ The *-s* is dropped from *sechs* to form *sechzehn* (16) and *sechzig* (60). Similarly, the *-en* is dropped from *sieben* to form *siebzehn* (17) and *siebzig* (70).

♦ After 100, *und* is dropped and numbers are expressed the same way they are in English, with 100, 1,000, 1 million, and so on coming first. In German, however, you do not say "one hundred" or "one thousand." You simply say *hundert* (*hoon-deRt*) or *tausend* (*tou-zent*).

♦ Because the sounds of *zwei* (*tsvay*) and *drei* (*dRay*) are so similar, *zwo* (*tsvoh*) is often used for "two" in official language and when giving numbers on the telephone.

> ### We Are Family
>
> Numerous Modern English and Modern German words can be traced back to the word for "one" 1,400 years ago. From the Old English *an,* we have *only, alone,* and *any,* while Old High German *ein* (*en*) spawned the equivalents *einzig, allein,* and *irgendein.*

What Time Is It?

Now that you have familiarized yourself with German numbers, it should be relatively easy for you to tell time. The simplest way to question someone about the time is by saying:

Wie viel Uhr ist es?
vee feel ewR ist es
What time is it?

Wie spät ist es?
vee shpäht ist es
What time is it?

To answer a question about time, start out with *Es ist* …, as in the next example:

Es ist ….
es ist
It is ….

German Culture
In Germany, as in most European countries, colloquial time is given without any reference to A.M. or P.M. Often the 24-hour system—what we call official, or military, time—is used. Accordingly, 1:00 P.M. is 13:00, or *dreizehn Uhr* (*dray-tseyn ewR*); 2:00 P.M. is *vierzehn Uhr* (*feeR-tseyn ewR*); and so on. These may be expressed with a period separating the hour from the minutes 13.00 and 14.00.

Look at the following table for some common phrases to help you tell time.

Telling Time

German	Pronunciation	English
Es ist ein Uhr.	*es ist ayn ewR*	It is 1:00.
Es ist fünf (Minuten) nach zwei.	*es ist fünf (mee-new-tuhn) nACH tsvay*	It is 2:05.
Es ist zehn (Minuten) nach drei.	*es ist tseyn (mee-new-tuhn) nACH dRay*	It is 3:10.
Es ist Viertel nach vier.	*es ist feeR-tuhl nACH feeR*	It is 4:15.
Es ist zwanzig nach fünf.	*es ist tsvAn-tsiH nACH fünf*	It is 5:20.
Es ist fünf vor halb sieben.	*es ist fünf foR hAlp zee-buhn*	It is 6:25.
Es ist halb acht.	*es ist hAlp ACHt*	It is 7:30.
Es ist fünf nach halb acht.	*es ist fünf nACH hAlp ACHt*	It is 7:35.
Es ist zehn nach halb acht.	*es ist tseyn nACH hAlp ACHt*	It is 8:40.
Es ist zwanzig vor neun.	*es ist tsvAn-tsiH foR noyn*	It is 8:40.
Es ist Viertel vor zehn.	*es ist feer-tuhl foR tseyn*	It is 9:45.
Es ist zehn vor elf.	*es ist tseyn foR elf*	It is 10:50.
Es ist fünf vor zwölf.	*es ist fünf foR tsvölf*	It is 11:55.
Es ist Mitternacht.	*es ist mi-tuhR-nACHt*	It is midnight.
Es ist Mittag.	*es ist mi-tahk*	It is noon.

◆ To express the time *after* the hour, give the number of minutes past the hour first, then use *nach*, and then give the hour: *Es ist Viertel nach fünf.* ("It's a quarter past five.")

◆ To express the time before the hour, give the number of minutes before the hour first, then use *vor*; and then give the hour: *Es ist Viertel vor fünf.* ("It's a quarter to five.")

What's What

Um Usually, the preposition *um* means "around," but in time expressions, it means "at." *Um 9 Uhr beginnt das Theaterstück* (*oom noyn ewR buh-gint dAs tey-ah-teR-shtük*) means "The play begins at 9:00."

◆ With all other hours, *halb* is used to express half the way *to* the hour. *Halb sechs* does not mean half past six, but halfway to six (5:30).

◆ To express "at what time" something is occurring, use the preposition *um: Um halb sechs gehen wir.* ("We'll go at 5:30.")

It isn't enough to be able to plod along through numbers and tell people what time it is. You'll need to know more general time expressions. The following table provides some common time expressions.

Time Expressions

German	Pronunciation	English
eine Sekunde	*ay-nuh zey-koon-duh*	a second
eine Minute	*ay-nuh mee-new-tuh*	a minute
eine Stunde	*ay-nuh shtoon-duh*	an hour
morgens	*moR-guhnz*	mornings
am Morgen	*Am moR-guhn*	in the morning
abends	*ah-buhnts*	evenings
am Abend	*Am ah-buhnt*	in the evening (P.M.)
nachmittags	*nACH-mi-tahks*	afternoons (P.M.)
am Nachmittag	*Am nACH-mi-tahk*	in the afternoon
um wie viel Uhr	*oom vee feel ewR*	at what time
genau um Mitternacht	*guh-nou oom mi-tuhR-nACHt*	at exactly midnight
genau um ein Uhr	*guh-nou oom ayn ewR*	at exactly 1:00
um ungefähr/um etwa zwei Uhr	*oom oon-guh-fähR/oom et-vah tsvay ewR*	at about 2:00
ein Viertel	*ayn feeR-tuhl*	a quarter
eine halbe Stunde	*ay-nuh hAl-buh shtoon-duh*	half an hour
in einer Stunde	*in ay-nuhR shtoon-duh*	in an hour
bis zwei Uhr	*bis tsvay ewR*	until 2:00
vor drei Uhr	*foR dRay ewR*	before 3:00
nach drei Uhr	*nACH dRay ewR*	after 3:00
Seit wann?	*zayt vAn*	Since when?
seit sechs Uhr	*zayt zeks ewR*	since 6:00
vor einer Stunde	*foR ay-nuhR shtoon-duh*	an hour ago
jede Stunde	*yey-duh shtoon-duh*	every hour
stündlich	*shtünt-liH*	hourly

German	Pronunciation	English
früh	*fRüh*	early
spät	*shpäht*	late
gestern	*ges-tuhRn*	yesterday
heute	*hoy-tuh*	today
morgen	*moR-guhn*	tomorrow
vorgestern	*foR-ges-tuhRn*	the day before yesterday
übermorgen	*üh-buhR-moR-guhn*	the day after tomorrow

Note that the dative preposition *seit* ("since"), along with the present tense of a verb, is used to express a period of time beginning in the past and extending into the present. To express that you have been living in Berlin for three years, you would say, *Seit drei Jahren wohne ich in Berlin.* Keep this rule in mind to avoid becoming one of the many English speakers who misuse the word *für* ("for") for *seit*.

Wie spät ist es?

Take time now to read the following times aloud. Check your responses in Appendix A.

1. 7.38

2. 3.06

3. 14.00

4. 12.25

5. 19.30

6. 21.50

As a Rule

You can form various kinds of time expressions by combining the adverbs *gestern*, *heute*, *morgen*, *vorgestern*, or *übermorgen* with the nouns *Morgen*, *Vormittag*, *Mittag*, *Nachmittag*, or *Abend* to express things such as "yesterday afternoon": *gestern Nachmittag*. The only two exceptions to this productive permutation are the German expression for "tomorrow morning," *morgen früh* (not *morgen Morgen*), and *übermorgen früh* to indicate "the morning of the day after tomorrow."

The Least You Need to Know

♦ You can use the very strong verb *nehmen* to indicate what transportation you are taking to get from one place to another.

♦ *Welcher* is the interrogative pronoun "which" or "what" and takes the same declination as the definite article.

♦ To rent a car, you might need to know some basic vocabulary for the parts of a car.

♦ Whether you're telling someone the time or listening to the teller count your money at a bank, sooner or later you're going to need to know German cardinal numbers.

Chapter 13

At the Hotel

In This Chapter

- ◆ Checking out hotel facilities
- ◆ Counting with ordinal numbers (an excuse to review adjective endings!)
- ◆ Knowing and *knowing* something
- ◆ Verbs with prefixes, both separable and inseparable
- ◆ Exchanging money and figuring out currency
- ◆ The German equivalent of the English *let's*

You selected the method of transportation that suits your luggage situation and the purchasing power of your wallet. You pay the taxi driver, get off the bus, or exit the subway, to find yourself in front of your hotel.

For some of us, a bed is all we look for in a hotel. For others, cable TV, a telephone, Internet access, a sauna, and a garden-view balcony are the bare necessities. Whatever your personal needs may be, this chapter will help you get comfortable in a German hotel.

What a Hotel! Does It Have ...?

Some people enjoy the adventure of wandering around for hours looking for a hotel they saw online; other people don't feel comfortable unless they've reserved their room a year in advance. Either way, before you hand over your credit card, be sure to verify with the people at *die Hotel Rezeption (dee hoh-tel Rey-tsep-tseeohn)* that they can provide you with whatever it is you need: a quiet room, a wake-up call, or coffee at 4 A.M. The following table will help you get the scoop on just about everything a hotel has to offer.

At the Hotel

German	Pronunciation	English
das Einkaufszentrum	*dAs ayn-koufs-tsen-tRoom*	shopping center
das Fitnesscenter	*dAs fit-nes-sen-tuhR*	fitness center
das Geschäftszentrum	*dAs guh-shäfts-tsen-tRoom*	business center
der Geschenkladen	*deyR guh-shenk-lah-duhn*	gift shop
das Hotel	*dAs hoh-tel*	hotel
das Restaurant	*dAs Re-stou-rohn*	restaurant
das Schwimmbad	*dAs shvim-baht*	swimming pool
das Zimmermädchen	*dAs tsi-muhR-mät-Huhn*	maid service
der Internetzugriff	*deyR in-tuhR-net-tsew-grif*	Internet access
der (Gepäck)Träger	*deyR (guh-päk)tRäh-guhR*	porter
der Aufzug	*deyR ouf-tsewk*	elevator
der Stock	*deyR shtok*	floor, story
die Etage	*dee e-tah-juh*	floor, story
der Kassierer	*deyR kA-see-RuhR*	cashier
der Parkplatz	*deyR pARk-plAts*	parking lot
der Pförtner	*deyR pföRt-nuhR*	concierge
der Portier	*deyR poR-ti-ey*	doorman
der Zimmerservice	*deyR tsi-muhR-suhR-vis*	room service
die Sauna	*dee zou-nah*	sauna
die Reinigung	*dee Ray-ni-goong*	laundry and dry-cleaning service

Whenever you're about to book a room at a hotel, don't let the giddiness you feel at being in a new country prevent you from asking a few important questions about your room. Is it quiet? Does it look out onto the courtyard or onto the street? Is it a smoking room? Are there extra blankets in the cupboard? No matter how luxurious your hotel room, if you forget to ask any of these questions, you may find yourself spending a sleepless night shivering under your thin blanket, listening to the music from the discothek next door, and inhaling the secondhand smoke seeping in under your door. The following table has some words you may find useful when cross-examining hotel receptionists.

German Culture
Travelers interested in cheap, no-frills sleeping can stay at *eine Pension* (*ay-nuh pen-zeeohn*), essentially a boarding house. Depending on whether you want all meals or just breakfast, you can choose *Vollpension* or *Halbpension*. If you want something cozier, try *das Gasthaus* (*dAs gAst-hous*). And finally, there is *das Hotel* (*dAs hoh-tel*).

Hotel Basics

German	Pronunciation	English
das Badezimmer	*dAs bah-duh-tsi-muhR*	bathroom
das Dopplezimmer	*dAs do-pel-tsi-muhR*	double room
das Einzelzimmer	*dAs ayn-tsel-tsi-muhR*	single room
das Telefon	*dAs tey-ley-fon*	telephone
das Zimmer	*dAs tsi-muhR*	room
der Balkon	*deyR bAl-kohn*	balcony
der Farbfernseher	*deyR faRp-feRn-zey-uhR*	color television
das Kabelfernsehen	*dAs feRn-zey-uhn*	cable television
der Safe	*deyR zeyf*	safe
der Schlüssel	*deyR shlü-suhl*	key
der Wecker	*deyR ve-kuhR*	alarm clock
die Badewanne	*dee bah-duh-vA-nuh*	bathtub
die Dusche	*dee dew-shuh*	shower
die Halbpension	*dee hAlp-pen-zee-ohn*	just with breakfast
die Vollpension	*dee fol-pen-zee-ohn*	with meals
die Klimaanlage	*dee klee-mah-An-lah-guh*	air-conditioning
die Toilette	*dee toee-le-tuh*	restroom
die Übernachtung	*dee üh-beR-nACH-toong*	overnight stay
ein Zimmer mit Aussicht	*ayn tsi-muhR mit ous-ziHt*	a room with a view
nach hinten	*nACH hin-tuhn*	at the back
nach vorne	*nACH foR-nuh*	at the front
zum Garten	*tsewm gAR-tuhn*	on the garden
zum Hof	*tsewm hof*	on the courtyard
zur Meerseite	*tsewR meeR-zay-tuh*	on the sea

Now, using the vocabulary you've learned, fill in the blanks of this dialogue between a hotel receptionist (*der Empfangschef*) and a client (*der Gast*). Check your accuracy in Appendix A.

Gast: Guten Tag. Haben Sie ein _____ frei?

Empfangschef: Möchten Sie ein Zimmer mit einem _____? Wir haben ein wunderschönes _____ zur Meerseite.

Gast: Ja, warum nicht? Hat das Zimmer ein _____? Ich erwarte einen wichtigen Anruf.

Empfangschef: Selbstverständlich. Möchten Sie Vollpension oder _____?

Gast: Vollpension, bitte.

Empfangschef: Gut. Die Zimmernummer ist 33. Hier ist Ihr _____. Gute Nacht.

Calling Housekeeping

So what happens if you *do* forget to ask whether there are blankets in the closet and then the temperature drops 20° shortly after you get into bed? Do you shiver all night, or do you call the concierge and ask for more blankets? Here are some expressions that will help you get whatever you need. Because you will usually be asking for *an* object or *a* thing, these nouns are listed with their indefinite articles followed by "m." for masculine nouns, "f." for feminine nouns, "n." for neuter nouns, and "pl." for plural nouns. See the following table.

Necessities

German	Pronunciation	English
die Eiswürfel (m. pl.)	*dee ays-vüR-fuhl*	ice cubes
ein Adapter (m.)	*ayn ah-dAp-tuhR*	an adapter
ein Aschenbecher (m.)	*ayn A-shuhn-be-HuhR*	an ashtray
ein Badetuch (n.)	*ayn bah-duh-tewCH*	a beach towel
ein Handtuch (n.)	*ayn hAn-tewCH*	a towel
ein Kleiderbügel (m.)	*ayn klay-duhR-büh-guhl*	a hanger
ein Kopfkissen (n.)	*ayn kopf-ki-suhn*	a pillow
ein Mineralwasser (n.)	*ayn mi-nuh-Rahl-vA-suhR*	mineral water
ein Stück Seife (n.)	*ayn shtük zay-fuh*	a bar of soap
ein Taschentuch (n.)	*ayn tA-shuhn-tewCH*	a handkerchief

German	Pronunciation	English
eine Bettdecke (f.)	*ay-nuh bet-de-kuh*	a blanket
die Streichhölzer (pl.)	*dee shtRayH-höl-tsuhR*	matches
das Briefpapier (n.)	*dAs bReef-pah-peeR*	stationery
die Ansichtskarkte (f.)	*dee An-ziHts-kAR-tuh*	the postcard
ein Nähkasten (m.)	*ayn näh-kAs-tuhn*	a sewing kit

Complete the following sentences. Keep in mind that the nouns you will be using are direct objects and take the accusative case: The masculine indefinite article *ein* becomes *einen*; the feminine and neuter indefinite articles *eine* and *ein* remain the same in the nominative and accusative cases (see Chapter 7).

> Ich hätte gern …
> *iH hä-tuh geRn*
> I would like …

> Ich brauche …
> *iH brou-CHuh*
> I need …

Achtung

German bathrooms, like many European bathrooms, have what looks like a tiny bathtub, usually next to the toilet, known as a bidet. Non-Europeans sometimes make the mistake of thinking this bathroom fixture is for washing their clothes.

Using these expressions along with the vocabulary you've just learned, try to translate the following sentences into German. Check your translations in Appendix A.

1. I need an adapter.

2. I'd like a mineral water, please.

3. I need stationery.

4. I'd like an ashtray and matches, please.

5. I need a pillow.

6. I would like a beach towel, please.

Going Straight to the Top

Now that you've had a good night's sleep, it's time to explore the hotel a little. To get around, you'll need to know how to get from one floor to another. The numbers used to refer to the floors of a building are known as *ordinal numbers*. An ordinal number refers to a specific number in a series. If your hotel is really fancy, someone in the elevator may ask you, "*Welcher Stock, bitte (vel-HuhR shtok, bi-tuh)?*" Study the ordinal numbers in the following table, and you'll be able to answer this question.

Ordinal Numbers

German Numbers	Pronunciation	English
1. erste	*eRs-tuh*	first
2. zweite	*tsvay-tuh*	second
3. dritte	*dRi-tuh*	third
4. vierte	*feeR-tuh*	fourth
5. fünfte	*fünf-tuh*	fifth
6. sechste	*zeks-tuh*	sixth
7. siebte	*zeep-tuh*	seventh
8. achte	*ACH-tuh*	eighth
9. neunte	*noyn-tuh*	ninth
10. zehnte	*tseyn-tuh*	tenth
11. elfte	*elf-tuh*	eleventh
12. zwölfte	*tsvölf-tuh*	twelfth
20. zwanzigste	*tsvAn-tsiHs-tuh*	twentieth
21. einundzwanzigste	*ayn-oont-tsvan-tsiHs-tuh*	twenty-first
100. hundertste	*hoon-deRt-stuh*	hundredth
1000. tausendste	*tou-zuhnt-stuh*	thousandth

♦ Ordinal numbers are formed by adding *-te* to the numbers 2 through 19 and by adding *-ste* from 20 on. *Erste* ("first"), *dritte* ("third"), *siebte* ("seventh"), and *achte* ("eighth") are exceptions.

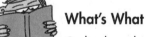

What's What

Ordinal numbers

Numbers that refer to a specific number in a series and answer the question: Which one? They may be preceded by a limiting word and, functioning as an adjective, be declined.

♦ In English, we use letters (1st, 2nd, 3rd) to express ordinal numbers. In German, use a period after the numeral: 1., 2., 3., and so on.

♦ Ordinal numbers are, in fact, adjectives! Hence, they have the desire to agree with the noun they are modifying in gender (masculine, feminine, or neuter), number (singular or plural), and case (nominative, accusative, dative, genitive).

The Declension of Ordinal Numbers

Ordinal numbers are treated as adjectives and can therefore be declined like any other adjective. They take normal adjective endings, as introduced in Chapter 10. In the sentence *Wir nehmen den ersten freien Aufzug zum Restaurant* (*veeR ney-muhn deyn eR-sten fRay-uhn ouf-tsewk tsewm Res-tou-RAn*), "We will take the first available elevator to the restaurant," the ordinal number *ersten* is modifying the singular noun *der Aufzug*.

German Culture

In Germany, as in many European countries, the street-level floor is not numbered. It is referred to as *das Erdgeschoß* (*dAs eRt-guh-shos*). The German first floor is the equivalent of the American second floor.

If you read Chapter 10 carefully, you know that adjectives after a *der* word don't need to "show" much grammar—the *der* word already performs that function! You can surmise by its function in the sentence that *der Aufzug* is the direct object. Thus, it must reflect the masculine accusative, and the adjective *erste* gets an agreeable, weak, and easy *-n*. And what about *frei*? As *ersten* sets the agreeable adjectival precedence, *frei* simply follows suit and becomes *freien*. The three tables that follow give you a quick review of the endings of adjectives—this time ordinal numbers—in the weak, strong, and mixed declension.

Recall that adjectives needn't be burdened with the task of indicating gender, number, or case when they come after *der* words (words such as *dieser, welcher, jeder,* and so on) because the *der* word assumes that responsibility. The weak declension of adjectives illustrated with an ordinal number is shown in the table that follows.

Case	Singular Masculine	Plural Feminine	Neuter	All Genders
Nom.	der erste	die erste	das erste	die ersten
Acc.	den ersten	die erste	das erste	die ersten
Dat.	dem ersten	der ersten	dem ersten	den ersten
Gen.	des ersten	der ersten	des ersten	der ersten

Conversely, adjectives that are not preceded by any type of limiting word have to bear all of the grammar and thus resemble the definite article, also referred to as taking the strong declension: *Zimmer 33, erstes Zimmer auf der rechten Seite* ("room 33, the first room on the right"). Why, you might wonder, is it *erstes* and not *erste* or *erster*? *Zimmer* is a neuter noun (*das*) and is functioning in this phrase as a subject, reflected by the nominative case. Remembering to stretch your mind to allow an *-es* for the *-as* in *das*, only two deviations from your *der* word chart occur when marking adjectives that are not preceded by any type of limiting word (genitive masculine and neuter).

Case	Singular Masculine	Plural Feminine	Neuter	All Genders
Nom.	erst**er**	erst**e**	erst**es**	erst**e**
Acc.	erst**en**	erst**e**	erst**es**	erst**e**
Dat.	erst**em**	erst**er**	erst**em**	erst**en**
Gen.	erst**en**	erst**er**	erst**en**	erst**er**

Adjectives preceded by an *ein* word (words such as *ein, mein, sein, ihr*, and so on) take a weak ending in all but three instances. You might recall that the *ein* in *ein Wagen, ein Auto*, and *Ich habe ein Auto* all look the same yet represent different gender and case. Therefore, given a second chance to reflect a bit of grammatical identity, the adjective following such a word will, indeed, strive to do so. See the table that follows for the mixed declension of adjectives.

Case	Singular Masculine	Plural Feminine	Neuter	All Genders
Nom.	ein erst**er**	eine erst**e**	ein erst**es**	die erst**en**
Acc.	einen erst**en**	eine erst**e**	ein erst**es**	die erst**en**
Dat.	einem erst**en**	einer erst**en**	einem erst**en**	den erst**en**
Gen.	eines erst**en**	einer erst**en**	eines erst**en**	der erst**en**

Ordinal Numbering

Complete the following sentences by supplying an ordinal number and adding the appropriate adjective ending. Check your answers in Appendix A.

Example: Sie hat Angst, ins Flugzeug zu steigen. Es ist ihr erster Flug.

1. Wir haben nicht viel Geld. Wir fahren _____ Klasse.

2. "Erster Stop ist in Marl; zweiter Stop ist in Haltern; _____ Stop ist in Recklinghausen," sagt der Busfahrer.

3. Mein _____ Beruf war Tellerwäscher. Heute bin ich Millionär.

4. Zuerst kommt die Post. Das _____ Gebäude auf der linken Seite ist ein Hotel.

5. Auf der zweiten Etage befindet sich das Restaurant. Auf der _____ Etage ist das Einkaufzentrum.

6. Er hat schon drei Söhne. Sein _____ Kind wird ein Mädchen.

7. Wenn eine Katze schon acht Leben hatte, ist sie jetzt im _____ Lebensjahr!

Clams or Coal? It's All the Same in Money

Just as English has numerous *colloquial* expressions for money—clams, silverbacks, bucks, and so on—similar expressions are used in German, such as *Mäuse* (*moy-zuh*), "mice"; and *Knete* (*kney-tuh*), "dough." Perhaps one of the most culturally specific colloquialisms referring to money in German is *Kohle* (*koh-luh*), "coal." Now that you're wondering how to get your hands on some of that German spending money, you can hit the nearest ATM that is certain to be just around a corner or two, incurring a modest $1–$5 service charge from your home bank. You are guaranteed to get the fairest, most up-to-date exchange rate. Alternatively, you can get your *Euro-Banknoten*, "bank notes," and *Euro-Cent-Münzen*, "coins," at *Wechselstuben* (*vek-suhl-shtew-buhn*), "money exchange booths," at airports and at train stations. The *Deutsche Verkehrs-Kredit Bank* has branches in train stations that stay open until 6 P.M. If all of the ATMs you encounter are out of service (*außer Betrieb*), look to exchange money at one of the larger branches of a bank in cities. The exchange rates at the larger bank branches are higher than at smaller, lesser-known banks, and the commission is lower. Most hotels also exchange money, but their rates are a complete rip-off, really—*ein totaler Nepp*. It's hardly even worth mentioning them.

On the odd chance that you still possess traveler's checks, you may exchange them in the same places you might go to exchange money: banks, money-exchange booths, and post offices. Post offices? Yes, *die Post*. The German post office will change your money for you, which is something you may want to keep in mind if you're cashless in the late afternoon and *still* can't locate a functioning ATM: Post offices stay open until 6 P.M.

What's What

Colloquial Refers to the informal register of a linguistic repertoire. Stemming from the Latin meaning "to speak together," this semitechnical term refers to informal, everyday speech, including slang, as in *He ain't comin'* (He is not coming) or *I'm gonna go* (I am going to go).

Euro?

From 1948 through 2001, Germany's currency was the *Deutsche Mark, DM*. As of January 1, 2002, the *Euro, EUR* or €, replaced the German Mark. Similar to the former *Mark* and *Pfennig* (the breakdown of the Mark into 100 units), the *Euro* is divided into *Euro* and *Cent*. Thus, a book that costs 6,50€ will be read as *sechs Euro fünfzig* (*zeks oy-roh fünf-tsiH*). (Note that the German equivalent of a decimal point is a comma.) The *Euro* may be used in 12 European countries; the *Euro-Banknoten* that come in differently colored and sized 5, 10, 20, 50, 100, 200, and 500 denominations are referred to in German as *die 5-Euro* (*dee fünf oy-roh*), *eine 10-Euro* (*ay-nuh tseyn oy-roh*), and so on. *Euro-Münzen* are produced in every country that accepts them in 1-, 2-, 5-, 10-, 20-, and 50-cent denominations, as well as 1€ and 2€. The German 1- and 2-*Euro-Münzen* depict the *Bundesadler*, "federal eagle"; the 10-, 20-, and 50-*Cent-Stücke*, "cent pieces," show the *Brandenburger Tor*, "Brandenburg Gate"; and the three smallest coins portray an oak branch.

Read the following sentences aloud, checking your number pronunciation in Appendix A. Go on the Internet and find the current exchange rate for the eurodollar. To increase your international financial awareness (and to practice pronouncing your numbers), use these rates to convert the prices in the following exercise to U.S. dollars.

1. Das Buch kostet 13,45€.

2. Die Blumen kosten 7,10€.

3. Die Ansichtskarte kostet 50€.

4. Ein Einzelzimmer kostet 61€.

5. Das Ticket kostet 36,99€.

Approximations and Oddities

In case you don't want to talk exact amounts of money, or anything else that involves counting, you can always use the trusty approximate figures listed in the following table:

Approximate Figures

German	Pronunciation	English
circa	*tseeR-kuh*	about
etwa	*et-vah*	roughly
rund	*Roont*	around, about
ungefähr	*oon-guh-fähR*	approximately
über	*üh-buhR*	over, more than

You might recall from Chapter 12 that a million is a *Million*, but an American billion is a German *Milliarde*, whereas a German *Billion* is an American trillion. Aside from putting commas where we'd place decimals, and vice versa, Germans write the numeral 7 a wee bit differently: They put a line through it so that it looks like a backward capital *F*. Perhaps this feature is to distinguish it from the written 1, which has the initial stroke below the line.

> **We Are Family**
>
> The American usage of "dough" for money or cash began around the 1850s. Dough evolved into the 1960s "bread," used primarily as hippie jargon and by the working class. The German equivalent, *Knete*, developed out of a reference to how people can hold money in their hands for a long time—just like dough!

More Action with Verbs

Do you remember what you learned about verbs in Chapter 8? Verbs are used to express action, motion, or states of being. This section looks at the irregular verb *wissen* and its weak partner, *kennen;* at the meanings of the simple present tense; and at verbs with prefixes.

Expressing Knowledge

The irregular verb *wissen* (*vi-suhn*) states knowledge of something as a fact: *Ich weiß die Adresse von Christoph nicht.* It never refers to persons. You'll recall the other two irregular verbs you've learned, *sein* and *haben.* Why, you might ask, must these verbs be irregular? Interestingly (or not) enough, the verbs *to be, to have, to know,* and *to become* (the fourth irregular verb to be learned later) are high-frequency verbs in most languages and thus mark themselves as meaningful and significant by retaining distinctive forms. In German, distinctiveness translates into changing the consonants, not just the vowels! Observe this behavior in the conjugation of *wissen* in the following table.

The Verb *wissen*

Personal	Singular	Plural
First	ich weiß *iH vays*	wir wissen *veer vis-uhn*
Second	du weißt *dew vayst*	ihr wisst *eer vist*
Third	er, sie, es weiß *er, zee, es, vays*	sie wissen *zee vis-uhn*
Formal	sie wissen *zee vi-suhn*	sie wissen *zee vi-suhn*

There you have it! Not only does a vowel-stem change occur in *all* of the singular conjugations, but you'll observe an ending omission in the *ich* and *er, sie,* and *es* forms.

We told you it was irregular! But take heart: To express knowing, as in indicating familiarity with something or somebody, you can also use a weak verb, *kennen.*

As a Rule _____

There are two German equivalents for the English "to know": *wissen,* which means to know something as a fact, and *kennen,* to be acquainted with a person, place, or thing. *Wissen* is frequently used to form an introductory clause: *Wissen Sie, …? Ich weiß ….* *Kennen* takes only nouns as objects: *Ich kenne Berlin gut. Kennst du diesen Film?* *Kennen* is still used as a verb in Scottish, indicating perception or understanding.

Care to exercise your choice? Try your hand at inserting the correct form of *wissen* or *kennen*! Answers appear in Appendix A.

1. _____ du, wo Kerstin wohnt?

2. Kerstin? Ich _____ niemanden mit dem Namen "Kerstin." Wer ist sie? (*niemand,* "no one"; *wer,* "who")

3. Ich _____, dass sie sehr hübsch und intelligent ist!

4. Na, ja. Vielleicht _____ Ronja sie.

5. _____ wir nicht Kerstins Mann, Frank?

6. Ach ja! Ich _____ ihren Mann vom Bus.

Verbs with Prefixes

The prefixes you're going to learn about here have nothing to do with prices you find on the menu in the restaurant of your fancy hotel. *Pre* means "to come before," and *fix* means "to join onto or with"; thus, a prefix is a series of letters (sometimes a word on its own) that you join to the beginning of another word. Verbs with prefixes, referred to as *two-part* or *compound verbs,* are not a singular German phenomenon. English also has many compound verbs: *to lead* and *to mislead; to rate, to overrate,* and *to underrate; to take, to mistake, to retake, to undertake,* and *to overtake.* In German, as in English, the verb and the compound verb follow the same conjugation; *take* becomes *took* in the past tense, for example, and *mistake* becomes *mistook.*

Coming Apart: Verbs with Separable Prefixes

When you were busy ordering people around and taking directions in Chapter 11, you used verbs with separable prefixes. You sent those prefixes to the end of the command. The rule still holds: Separable prefixes like to get away from their stem verb and go to the end of a clause even in an ordinary statement or question: *Kommst du heute Abend mit? Ja, ich komme um 8 Uhr mit.* Just as the particle helpers in English stand on their own, so can the separable prefixes in German be words on their own, usually adverbs or prepositions. Although in the infinitive form they appear to be one word (as in the verb *weggehen*, which means "to go away"), the prefix functions separately in the sentence *Er geht jetzt weg* ("He's going away now").

What's What

Compound verbs
Verbs that are formed by adding a prefix to the stem verb. German has two types of compound verbs: those with separable prefixes and those with inseparable prefixes.

Some common separable prefixes are *auf-, aus-, an-, bei-, mit-, nach-, vor-, weg-, weiter-, wieder-, zu-, zurück-,* and *zusammen-.*

The following sentences involve separable pre-fix verbs whose meanings you should be able to deduce from your general knowledge of German prepositions and verbs (see Chapter 8). Try to complete the sentences. Recall that a superscript "S" means that the verb is very strong and undergoes a stem-vowel change. The period indicates the separation between the separable prefix and the verb stem. Check your sentences in Appendix A.

Wann _____ wir den Film _____? (an.sehen[S]) When are we viewing the film?

Tina _____ das Buch _____. (vor.lesen[S]) Tina is reading the book out loud.

_____ Sie nie _____! (auf.geben[S]) Never give up!

Gretchen _____ ihr Bier immer _____! (aus.trinken) Gretchen always drinks up all of her beer.

Don't forget that these verbs incur a stem change in the present tense!

Recall how we started noting the *sehr stark* verbs (those verbs undergoing a vowel-stem change in the present tense) in Chapter 8. Also, from now on in this book, separable prefix verbs will be marked in their infinitival form with a period between the prefix and the stem. Although these verbs are not normally represented this way, the period should help you identify them.

As a Rule

When a prefix is separated from a compound verb, the prefix occurs at the end of the clause, which also is often the end of the sentence: *Er geht jeden Morgen um sieben Uhr aus.*

We Are Family
What caused a rift between English and German? When they were still considered Germanic buddies, their common development of stress shifting systematically to a word's first or root syllable helped differentiate them from other Indo-European languages. We still see that predictable stress in German, but not in English. Loss of regular first-syllable stress is just one of the profound effects brought about by the Norman invasion of England in 1066.

Sticking It Out Together: Verbs with Inseparable Prefixes

The German language has one more basic type of verb prefix: the inseparable variety. Inseparable prefixes cannot stand alone and must be attached to a verb. Also noteworthy is the fact that they are not stressed. Compare the separable prefix verb *aus.gehen* with the inseparable *ergeben*[s]. The following prefixes always remain attached to the verb, but if you are creative enough, you can build a "semantic bridge" and link the meaning of the stem with that of the newly formed verb!

Inseparable Prefix	German Verb	English
be- (*buh*)	bekommen	to get, receive
emp- (*emp*)	empfehlen[s]	to recommend
ent- (*ent*)	entdecken	to discover
er- (*eR*)	ergeben[s]	to yield, produce
ge- (*guh*)	gewinnen	to win
miss- (*mis*)	missverstehen	to misunderstand
ver- (*feR*)	vergessen[s]	to forget
zer- (*tseR*)	zerfallen[s]	to decay

From the preceding list, see whether you can fill in the following blanks with the correct verb—correctly conjugated, of course! Read these sentences aloud, remembering *not* to stress the prefix in these verbs. Check your verb choices in Appendix A.

1. Wo _____ Sie das? (Where do you get that?)

2. Ich _____ die Adresse. (I forget the address.)

3. Boris Becker _____ fast immer. (Boris Becker almost always wins.)

4. Welches Restaurant _____ du? (Which restaurant do you recommend?)

Let's ...

The German equivalent of the English *let's* utilizes that nifty imperative, or command form, you were exposed to in Chapter 11 but softens it up with the collective pronoun *wir*. You'll notice that the word order is verb-initial, just as it was in the regular imperative used to order people around. But now we've included ourselves, or "us" in the equation. Have a look:

Essen wir Eis.	Let's eat ice cream.
Kaufen wir ein.	Let's shop.
Finden wir das Museum.	Let's find the museum.

Another way to suggest to a friend that you do something together involves the expression *Lass uns ...* (*lAs oonz*), with the main verb arriving at the end of the suggestion in its infinitival form:

Lass uns ins Restaurant gehen.	Let's go to a restaurant.
Lass uns griechisch essen.	Let's eat Greek.

As a Rule

The use of *doch, mal,* or *doch mal* in imperative constructions adds a subtle but noticeable layer of meaning. *Doch* adds a sense of urgency: *Lass uns doch japanisch essen,* or "Let's do eat Japanese." *Mal* adds a sense of impatience: *Trink mal!* becomes "Come on and drink!" Combining *doch* with *mal* produces a tone that is a little more casual: *Kauf doch mal was,* or "Go ahead and buy something."

Suggest to your friends, using either the *Lass uns ...* or the *Verb + wir* constructions, the following activities. Check your suggestions in Appendix A.

1. Let's travel to Germany. _____

2. Let's go to the garden. _____

3. Let's take the bus. _____

4. Let's visit the city. _____

5. Let's learn German! _____

The Least You Need to Know

◆ If you familiarize yourself with a few basic vocabulary words, you should have no trouble getting what you need in your hotel room.

◆ Form ordinal numbers by adding *-te* to the numbers 2 through 19 and *-ste* to the numbers from 20 on. Memorize the exceptions to this rule: *erste*, *dritte*, *siebte*, and *achte*. Amaze yourself with all the new adjectives you've just acquired!

◆ The verbs *wissen* and *kennen* express knowledge and familiarity.

◆ Many German verbs are compound verbs, or verbs with prefixes. These verbs can be either separable or inseparable.

◆ Use an ubiquitous ATM to get a hold of eurodollars at the best rate.

◆ By beginning a sentence with the verb in its infinitive form followed by a *wir*, you'll be able to make suggestions in the vein of *let's* ….

Part 4

Out and About in Germany

Part 4 comprises chapters for sightseers, shopping addicts, sports fanatics, and gourmets. Once you've learned how to talk about the weather (an important ability in any language, particularly when making small talk), learning how to make suggestions about what you'd like to see, shop for, and eat will keep your outlook sunny!

14

A Date with the Weather

In This Chapter

- ◆ European countries with German-sounding names
- ◆ Describing weather conditions
- ◆ Learning the days of the week
- ◆ Naming the months of the year
- ◆ Breaking up the day

You've been in Germany for a while now, at least within the international borders of this book. You can get around, find a room, spout a few nouns, ask a question or two, tell a little time, and find a room. Now you've arrived in Frankfurt, and you're ready to plan your afternoon. You haven't written a single postcard. If you don't understand the local weather report, a walk to the post office could end up being a soggy sojourn. Weather can make or break your day and provide fodder for endless small talk with strangers.

In this chapter, you'll pick up the vocabulary you need to understand international communication and the weather forecast, and how to make plans in a German city, inside or outside your hotel.

Send Me a Card ... Drop Me a Line!

You're going to Germany, and you want to correspond with some distant relatives, college acquaintances, or the hotel proprietors. How exactly do you address a card?

Achtung

It is not uncommon to find *Straße* abbreviated as *Str.* and to find more than one number for a house address. Never you mind—that is how the *Haus-nummer*, the numerical sign on the street, will read.

Differing from our American system is the ordering of house number followed by street. If you think about it, it really is more logical to know which street you're referring to before knowing exactly where on that street the house lies. In Germany, after the line of the addressee comes the street and then the house number. Conversely, the ZIP code precedes the city in German correspondence. Guess there has to be some leveling out or reciprocation of numeral ordering somewhere! When in Deutschland, you'll want to use Deutsch-style addresses. Here's an example:

German Style	U.S. Style
Bernadette Höfer	Bernadette Höfer
Feldbergstraße 3–7	300 Washington Avenue
55118 Mainz	Mainstreet, MD 21000

Identifying International Abbreviations

International abbreviations are used for the country names. You might have seen stickers on automobiles indicating countries of origin, bearing the same abbreviations. Some abbreviations you might not guess are listed here:

- CH for Switzerland (Confederatio Helvetica)
- SK for Slovakia (die Slowakei)
- PL for Poland (Polen)
- E for Spain (Spanien)

What is Germany's abbreviation? Why, *D* for *Deutschland*, of course!

Call Me ...

Reading a German business card, advertisement, or brochure, you're likely to encounter more than an address—most likely, a telephone number. Unlike American telephone numbers, which consist of a three-digit area code followed by a seven-digit number, the exact length of telephone numbers in Germany is variable. Most phone numbers have a city prefix consisting of three or four digits, and the actual phone number may be four to seven digits long. Go ahead and tack on another digit, a zero in front of the city code, if phoning from within Germany. Not to worry if you dial a wrong number or can't write as fast as directory assistance would assume—the post office (*die Post*) sells phone cards. Once you get your paws on one of these colorful cards, you can experiment and frustrate at your own pace. Now do you feel the need to really learn your numbers? As an aid, the following table lists some useful communication terms. (For more in-depth information on telephone etiquette, cell phone usage, and that trip to the post office, see Chapter 23.)

> **German Culture**
>
> The postal service in Germany also provides phone service. Tell the postal worker behind the counter that you want to make a long-distance call, and he or she will indicate which phone booth is available. You pay (cash only) after your call. Long-distance calls made from the post office are considerably cheaper than those placed from a hotel.

Communication Terms

German	Pronunciation	English
die Adresse	*dee A-dRe-suh*	the address
die Ansichtskarte	*dee An-ziHts-kAR-tuh*	the postcard
der Brief	*deyR bReef*	the letter
die Hausnummer	*dee hous-noo-muhR*	the house number
das Land	*dAs lAnt*	the country
die Post	*dee post*	the post office
die Postkarte	*dee post-kAR-tuh*	the postcard
die Postleitzahl	*dee post-layt-tsahl*	the ZIP code
die Stadt	*dee shtAt*	the city
die Straße	*dee shtrA-suh*	the street
die Telefonnummer	*dee tey-ley-fo-noo-muhR*	the telephone number
der Wohnort	*deyR von-oRt*	the town of residence
Was bedeutet …?	*vAs buh-doy-tuht*	What does _____ mean?
Wie bitte?	*vee bi-tuh*	Excuse me?
Wie ist deine/ Ihre Telefonnummer?	*vee ist day-nuh/ee-Ruh tey-ley-fo-noo-muhR*	What is your telephone number?
Wie schreibt man …?	*vee shraypt mAn*	How does one write …?

Using the information-gathering vocabulary you've just acquired, try to fill in the following blanks. Check your accuracy in Appendix A.

1. Ich kenne die Straße, aber nicht die _____.

2. Die _____ kommt vor der Stadt in der Adresse.

3. Ich habe ein Telefon. Meine _____ ist 03-45-60.

4. Du schickst eine _____ an deine Mutter.

5. Sein Name ist sehr lang! _____ das?

Now try to fill in the information requested in German.

Name _____

Wohnort _____

Straße und Hausnummer _____

Postleitzahl und Stadt _____

Telefonnummer _____

European Countries, According to Germans

As an American (if you are), you come from America and speak *American*. Okay, maybe you speak *English* or some other variety. The point is that every language personalizes other countries' names to suit their language's sound systems. German names for countries should be fairly recognizable to you, but the pronunciation may be challenging. The following table lists some European countries:

Country Names

German	Pronunciation	English
Albanien	*Al-bah-neeuhn*	Albania
Belgien	*bel-geeuhn*	Belgium
Bulgarien	*bool-gah-Reeuhn*	Bulgaria
Dänemark	*däh-nuh-mARk*	Denmark
Deutschland	*doytch-lAnt*	Germany
Finnland	*fin-lAnt*	Finland
Frankreich	*frAnk-rayH*	France
Griechenland	*gree-Huhn-lAnt*	Greece

German	Pronunciation	English
Großbritannien	*gros-bRi-tah-neeuhn*	Great Britain
Irland	*eer-lAnt*	Ireland
Italien	*ee-tah-leeuhn*	Italy
Lettland	*let-lAnt*	Latvia
Litauen	*lee-tou-uhn*	Lithuania
Liechtenstein	*leeH-tuhn-shtayn*	Liechtenstein
Luxemburg	*look-suhm-buHRk*	Luxembourg
die Niederlande	*dee nee-duhR-lAn-duh*	the Netherlands
Norwegen	*noR-vey-guhn*	Norway
Österreich	*ös-tuh-RayH*	Austria
Polen	*poh-luhn*	Poland
Portugal	*poR-too-gAl*	Portugal
Russland	*roos-lAnt*	Russia
die Schweiz	*dee shvayts*	Switzerland
Schweden	*schvey-duhn*	Sweden
die Slowakei	*dee sloh-vah-kay*	Slovakia
Spanien	*shpah-neeuhn*	Spain
Tschechien	*tshe-Hee uhn*	Czech Republic
Ungarn	*ewn-gARn*	Hungary

Try your hand now at the international abbreviations, indicating which country the following postcards are from using the dative case (because *aus* always requires the dative) if the country appears with a definite article. Check your answers in Appendix A.

1. CH aus _____

2. D aus _____

3. I aus _____

4. A aus _____

5. GB aus _____

6. F aus _____

And don't forget the good old United States: *die Vereinigten Staaten (dee feR-ayn-ik-tuh shtah-tuhn)*!

It's 20°, But They're Wearing Sandals!

Americans in Germany catch the amusement of native Germans for leaving their hotels in 20° weather in heavy winter jackets. Why? The answer is simple: The Americans misunderstood the weather forecast. Remember, Germans use Celsius (or centigrade), not Fahrenheit, the way we do in the United States. Twenty degrees in German weather terminology is actually 68° Fahrenheit!

The phrases in the following table will come in handy when the topic is weather.

Weather Expressions

German	Pronunciation	English
Wie ist das Wetter?	*vee ist dAs ve-tuhR*	How is the weather?
Das Wetter ist herrlich.	*dAs ve-tuhR ist heR-liH*	The weather is wonderful.
Das Wetter ist furchtbar.	*dAs ve-tuhR ist fooRHt-bahR*	The weather is awful.
Das Wetter ist schlecht.	*dAs ve-tuhR ist shleHt*	The weather is bad.
Das Wetter ist schön.	*dAs ve-tuhR ist shöhn*	The weather is beautiful.
Das Wetter ist schrecklich.	*dAs ve-tuhR ist shRek-liH*	The weather is horrible.
Die Sonne scheint.	*dee zo-nuh shaynt*	The sun is shining.
Es blitzt und donnert.	*es blitst oont do-nuhRt*	There is lightning and thunder.
Es gibt Regenschauer.	*es gipt Rey-guhn-shou-uhR*	There are rain showers.
Es ist bewölkt.	*es ist buh-völkt*	It is cloudy.
Es ist feucht.	*es ist foyHt*	It is humid.
Es ist heiß.	*es ist hays*	It is hot.
Es ist heiter.	*es ist hay-tuhR*	It is clear.
Es ist kalt.	*es ist kAlt*	It is cold.
Es ist kühl.	*es ist kühl*	It is cool.
Es ist nebelig.	*es ist ney-buh-liH*	It is foggy.
Es ist regnerisch.	*es ist Rek-nuh-Rish*	It is rainy.
Es ist sonnig.	*es ist zo-niH*	It is sunny.
Es ist stürmisch.	*es ist shtüR-mish*	It is stormy.
Es ist windig.	*es ist vin-diH*	It is windy.
Es regnet.	*es Rek-nuht*	It is raining.
Es schneit.	*es shnayt*	It is snowing.
Es ist warm.	*es ist vARm*	It is warm.
Es regnet in Strömen.	*es Rek-nuht in shtRöh-muhn*	It is pouring.

How's the Weather?

Look at the weather map of Germany. Use complete sentences to describe the weather in the following cities. Check your weather predictions in Appendix A.

1. Erfurt

2. München

3. Schwerin

4. Kiel

5. Düsseldorf

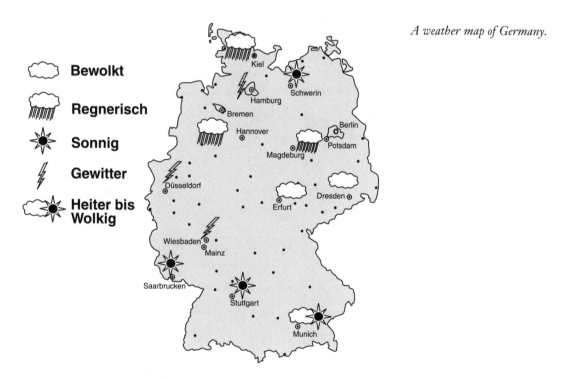

A weather map of Germany.

What's the Temperature?

The following phrases will enable you to talk about and understand simple conversations about the weather.

Welche Temperatur ist es?
vel-Huh tem-puh-Rah-tewR ist es
What's the temperature?

German Culture

To convert Fahrenheit to Celsius, subtract 32 from the Fahrenheit temperature and multiply the remaining number by .5. To convert Celsius to Fahrenheit, multiply the Celsius temperature by 1.8 and then add 32.

Es sind minus zehn Grad.
es zint mee-noos tseyn gRaht
It's -10°.

Es sind zehn Grad unter Null.
es zint tseyn gRaht oon-tuhR nool
It's 10° below zero.

Es sind (plus) zwanzig Grad.
es zint (ploos) tsvAn-tsiH gRaht
It's 20°.

But the Weather's Supposed to Be ...

German newspapers and Internet sites contain information on the weather, just as American ones do. The maps often include Germany and Western Europe. Look at the table for the German terms commonly used to describe weather.

der Nebel	*deyR ney-buhl*	fog
bewölkt	*buh-völkt*	cloudy
der Hagel	*deyR hah-guhl*	hail
der Regen	*deyR Rey-guhn*	rain
der Schnee	*deyR shney*	snow
der Schneeregen	*deyR shney-Rey-guhn*	sleet
der Sprühregen	*deyR shpRüh-Rey-guhn*	drizzle
der Regenschauer	*dee Rey-guhn-shou-uhR*	shower
die Sonne	*dee zo-nuh*	sun
der Sturm	*deyR shtuRm*	storm
der Wind	*deyR vint*	wind
frisch	*fRish*	chilly
der klare Himmel	*deyR klah-Ruh hi-muhl*	clear sky
leicht	*layHt*	weak
leicht bewölkt	*layHt buh-völkt*	slightly cloudy
mäßig	*mäh-siH*	moderate
neblig	*ney-bliH*	foggy

stark bewölkt	*shtARk buh-völkt*	very cloudy
stark	*shtARk*	strong
wechselhaft	*vek-suhl-hAft*	changeable

Days, Months, Seasons!

Remember sitting in kindergarten (a German word, by the way, which means "child garden") and learning the days of the week, the months of the year, and the seasons? This section focuses on precisely those elementary things: days, months, dates, and seasons.

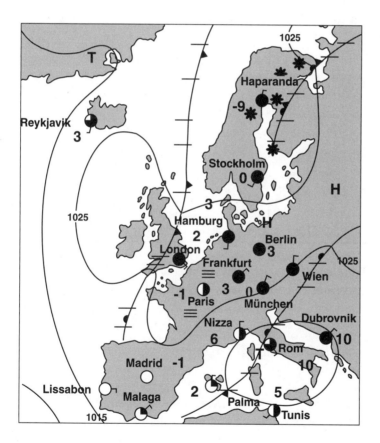

A weather map of Europe.

What Day Is It?

You've really been enjoying the great weather on your vacation, and now you've completely lost track of time. The days melt together like a dream. One day you wake up and leave your hotel to go shopping, only to find that all the stores are closed. It's early in the afternoon, the sun is shining, and cars are driving up and down the avenue. Is it a holiday? You stop a passerby and ask what day it is. "*Sonntag,*" he says. If you don't know the days of the week, you may think this *Sonntag* is some important date in German history or that he's talking about his favorite author. Of course, *Sonntag* is "Sunday," the day when, in Germany, almost all stores are closed. Study the German names for the days of the week in the following table.

Days of the Week

German	Pronunciation	English
der Tag	*deyR tahk*	day
die Woche	*dee vo-CHuh*	week
die Wochentage	*dee vo-CHuhn-tah-guh*	days of the week
Montag	*mon-tahk*	Monday
Dienstag	*deenz-tahk*	Tuesday
Mittwoch	*mit-voCH*	Wednesday
Donnerstag	*deenz-tahk*	Thursday
Freitag	*fRay-tahk*	Friday
Samstag	*zAmz-tahk*	Saturday
Sonnabend	*zon-ah-bent*	Saturday
Sonntag	*zon-tahk*	Sunday
am Wochenende	*Am vo-CHuhn-en-duh*	on the weekend
Welcher Tag ist heute?	*vel-CHuhr tahk ist hoy-tuh*	What day is today?

To express *on* when talking about a specific day, Germans use the contraction *am*, a combination of the preposition *an* and *dem* (*dem* being the dative form of the masculine definite article, *der*).

> Am Montag gehe ich in die Stadt.
> *Am mohn-tahk gey-uh iH in dee shtAt*
> On Monday I go downtown.

To express that you do something on a specific day every week, simply add an *-s*, just as you do in English, to the end of the day, but don't capitalize it unless it begins the sentence:

> Ich gehe dienstags in die Stadt.
> *iH gey-uh deenz-tahks in dee shtAt*
> I go downtown on Tuesdays.

Try responding to the following questions in simple sentences:

1. Welcher Tag ist heute?
   vel-CHuhr tahk ist hoy-tuh
   What day is today?

2. Was machen Sie montags?
   vas mA-CHuhn zee mon-taks
   What do you do on Mondays?

3. Was machen Sie am Wochenende?
   vas mA-CHuhn zee Am vo-CHuhn-en-duh
   What do you do on the weekend?

4. Welcher Tag ist morgen?
   vel-CHuhR tahk ist moR-gen
   What day is tomorrow?

Achtung

According to traditional German law, all stores (with the exception of bakeries that opted to open for two hours) had to close on Sunday. Train stations could always have an open grocery store, florist, or card shop because train stations were *Touristenzone*, a tourist zone. However, Berlin and several formerly East German cities declared themselves to be *Touristenzonen*.

As a Rule

Remember, the days of the week, the months of the year, and the four seasons are masculine. So when you place them after either an accusative *or* a dative preposition, such as *an*, *in*, and *vor*, they take the dative case. Although you might recognize these prepositions as taking either the accusative or the dative case, when they appear in conjunction with time, they always take the dative case.

A Mouthful of Months

Now that you know how to chat about the weather, you can ask friendly natives what the weather will be like in April, September, or even next month. The following table lists the months of the year.

Months of the Year

German	Pronunciation	English
der Monat	*deyR moh-nAt*	month
das Jahr	*dAs yahR*	year
Januar	*yah-new-ahR*	January
Februar	*feb-Rew-ahR*	February
März	*mäRts*	March

continues

Months of the Year (continued)

German	Pronunciation	English
April	*ah-pRil*	April
Mai	*mahee*	May
Juni	*yew-nee*	June
Juli	*yew-lee*	July
August	*ou-goost*	August
September	*zep-tem-buhR*	September
Oktober	*ok-toh-buhR*	October
November	*noh-vem-buhR*	November
Dezember	*dey-tsem-buhR*	December
Geburtstag	*guh-booRts-tahk*	birthday
der Urlaub	*deyr ewR-loup*	vacation

To make clear that something is expected to happen in a particular month, use the contraction *im*, a combination of the preposition *in* + *dem* expressing masculine dative case.

> Mein Freund hat im Oktober Geburtstag.
> *mayn froynt hAt im ok-toh-buhR guh-booRts-tahk*
> My boyfriend's birthday is in October.

Now answer the following questions using *im* + *Monat*. Check your sentence structure in Appendix A.

German Culture

Every February before Lent, cities in Germany "go crazy." These days are referred to as the *Tolle Tage* (*to-luh tah-guh*), "crazy days." *Karneval* (*kAR-ne-vAl*), otherwise known down south as *Fasching* (*fah-sheeng*), is a major event in Catholic parts of the country. If you're in Köln, Mainz, or München during the final days before Lent, expect parades, partying, and costumes everywhere!

1. Wann ist Ihr Geburtstag?
   vAn ist eeR guh-booRts-tahk
   When is your birthday?

2. Wann machen Sie in diesem Jahr Urlaub?
   vAn mA-CHuhn zee in dee-zuhm yahR ewR-loup
   When are you taking your vacation this year?

3. Welcher ist Ihr Lieblingsmonat?
   vel-CHuhR ist eeR leep-leenks-mon-nAt
   What's your favorite month?

4. Wann beginnt die Schule?
   van buh-gint dee shew-luh
   When does school begin?

The Four Seasons

As you engage in German conversations, you'll probably want to talk about the seasons. The information you need is in the following table. Notice how logical and concise the German for "season of the year" is: *Jahres* (*of the year*) + *Zeit* (*time*).

The Seasons of the Year

German	Pronunciation	English
die Jahreszeit	*dee yah-Ruhs-tsayt*	season
der Winter	*deyR vin-tuhR*	winter
der Frühling	*deyR fRüh-ling*	spring
das Frühjahr	*das fRüh-yahR*	spring
der Sommer	*deyR zo-muhR*	summer
der Herbst	*deyR heRpst*	autumn, fall

Because seasons are comprised of months, it makes sense to use the same dative prepositional contraction, *im*, to express seasons:

Ich fahre im Winter in die Alpen.
iH fah-Ruh im vin-tuhR in dee Al-puhn
I'm going in the winter to the Alps.

German Culture

Overall, the weather in many German-speaking countries is moderate: Your sweat won't evaporate off your brow in summer, and in winter, your breath won't condense into ice cubes that fall clinking to the ground. If you're visiting Munich, pack a raincoat; it has more rainfall than other cities in Germany. In the mountainous regions of Switzerland and Austria, where glaciers keep the snow from melting all year round, you can get the best of both worlds—summer skiing in a T-shirt!

Try to answer the following questions concerning *die Jahreszeiten*. Responses are in Appendix A.

1. Wann schneit es viel?
   van shnayt es feel
   When does it snow lots?

2. Wann fallen die Blätter von den Bäumen?
   van fA-luhn dee blä-tuhR fon deyn boy-muhn
   When do the leaves fall from the trees?

3. Wann blühen die Blumen?
   van blüh-uhn dee blew-muhn
   When do the flowers bloom?

4. Wann scheint die Sonne oft?
   van shaynt dee zo-nuh oft
   When does the sun shine often?

Measures of Time

The Fourth of July, your own birthday, and the year you were first kissed: What do these things have in common? Well, if you want to chat about them, you have to learn a few words that deal with dates. You can start with some general terms that deal with chunks of time.

German	Pronunciation	English
eine Stunde	*ay-nuh shtoon-duh*	an hour
ein Tag	*ayn tahk*	a day
eine Woche	*ay-nuh vo-CHuh*	a week
ein Monat	*ayn moh-nAt*	a month
ein Jahr	*ayn yahR*	a year
zwei Jahre	*tsvay yah-Ruh*	two years
einige Jahre	*ay-ni-guh yah-Ruh*	some years
nächstes Jahr	*näH-stuhs yahR*	next year
letztes Jahr	*lets-tuhs yahR*	last year

Making a Date

Whether you have a dentist appointment or a romantic rendezvous, you will have to express the date of the appointment differently than you do in English. Here is a formula for expressing the date correctly in German:

day of the week + *der* (ordinal) number + month + year

Freitag, der fünfundzwanzigste April 2003
fray-tahk, deyR tsvay-oont-tsvAn-stiH-stuh ah-pRil tsvay-tau-zuhnt dray
Friday, the 25th of April 2003

You write and punctuate dates in German differently than you do in English. Compare the following date (May 6, 2003) in English and in German.

> May 6, 2003 (5/6/03)
> der 6. Mai 2003 (6.5.03)

When writing letters in German, the place from which you are writing is given first, followed by the date. Note that the accusative *den* is used when expressing a definite time when no preposition is present.

> Annapolis, den 25.4.2003

Days of the month are expressed with ordinal numbers: *der erste Januar, der zweite Februar, der dritte März*, and so on.

At first glance, the way you express the year in German looks like it could take a year to say. If you were to express the year 2003, for example, you would say this:

> zweitausenddrei
> *tsvay-tau-zuhnt-dray*

We Are Family

Any language borrows lexical material from other languages. Some languages borrow more than others and borrow more from some sources than others. While nouns make up the highest proportion of transfers followed by adjectives, along the way, English has borrowed a few grammatical words, as the borrowing of the Old Norse pronoun *they* into Old English. More modern English borrowings from Germanic languages include; from Dutch: *cookie, golf, landscape*; German: *waltz, yodel*; Icelandic: *geyser, saga*; Norse: *creek, muggy, sky, squall*; Swedish: *ombudsman, glogg*; Norwegian: *lemming, ski, slalom*.

To get information about the date, you should be able to ask the following questions:

> Welcher Tag ist heute?
> *vel-CHuhR tahk ist hoy-tuh*
> What day is today?

> Der wievielte ist heute?
> *deyR vee-feel-tuh ist hoy-tuh*
> What's today's date?

Someone who answers your question will probably begin his or her response with one of the following phrases:

> Heute ist der ....
> *hoy-tuh ist deyR...*
> Today is the ....

Do you constantly forget important dates? Practice what you've just learned by listing the following dates in German. Check your sentences in Appendix A.

Example: Weihnachten

Answer: Weihnachten ist am 25. Dezember.

1. Valentinstag

2. Ihr Geburtstag

3. Der Hochzeitstag Ihrer Eltern

4. Neujahr

Time Expressions

You don't always speak in terms of exact dates—sometimes "in a week" or "a few days ago" will do. The expressions in the following table will help you schedule events, make plans, and arrange trysts. (Some of these expressions should already be familiar to you from Chapter 12.)

Time Expressions

German	Pronunciation	English
in	*in*	in
vor	*foR*	ago
nächste Woche	*näH-stuh vo-CHuh*	next week
letzte Woche	*lets-tuh vo-CHuh*	last week
der Abend	*deyR ah-buhnd*	evening
vorgestern	*foR-ges-tuhRn*	day before yesterday
gestern	*ges-tuhRn*	yesterday
heute	*hoy-tuh*	today
morgen	*moR-guhn*	tomorrow
übermorgen	*üh-buhR-moR-guhn*	day after tomorrow
am nächsten Tag	*Am näH-stuhn tahk*	the next day

German	Pronunciation	English
heute in einer Woche	*hoy-tuh in ay-nuhR vo-CHuh*	a week from today
heute in zwei Wochen	*hoy-tuh in tsvay vo-CHuhn*	two weeks from today
der Morgen	*deyR moR-guhn*	morning
der Nachmittag	*deyR nACH-mi-tahk*	afternoon

Now translate the following sentences into English. Check your translations in Appendix A.

1. Heute in einer Woche habe ich Geburtstag.

2. Gestern war schönes Wetter.

3. Samstags spiele ich Tennis.

4. Übermorgen reisen wir nach Deutschland.

5. Am nächsten Tag essen wir im Restaurant.

The Least You Need to Know

♦ German addresses list the street first, followed by the house number. The ZIP code precedes the city. Phone numbers vary in length.

♦ The German word for Germany is *Deutschland*, Austria is *Österreich*, and Switzerland is *die Schweiz*.

♦ Learning a few weather expressions will help you figure out whether you should leave your umbrella in the closet.

♦ The days of the week in German are *Montag, Dienstag, Mittwoch, Donnerstag, Freitag, Samstag* (but *Sonnabend* in northern Germany), and *Sonntag*.

♦ The months of the year in German are *Januar, Februar, März, April, Mai, Juni, Juli, August, September, Oktober, November,* and *Dezember.*

♦ The four seasons are *Frühling, Sommer, Herbst,* and *Winter.*

Let's Sightsee

In This Chapter

♦ Enjoying the pleasures of sightseeing

♦ Expressing your attitude with modals

♦ Expressing your reactions to suggestions

♦ Making suggestions in an inclusive way

You turn on the radio in your hotel room, and a voice says that today will be a warm, sunny day. If you're in Berlin, it's the perfect weather to see *das Brandenburger Tor* (the Brandenburg Gate), which stood as a symbol for the division of Germany after the Berlin Wall was built. If you're in Köln, you can visit the famous Dom and then sit down for a few hours at an outdoor café.

You look through your guidebook to see which museums are open and where they are located. Then you take the elevator downstairs and get a map of the city from the receptionist at the front desk. Now you are ready to venture out into a German, Swiss, or Austrian city to explore the parks, the streets, or the shopping districts. After reading this chapter, not only will you be able to find your way around, but you'll be well on your way to giving your opinions in German.

What Do You Want to See?

What's it going to be? The ancient rooms of a castle, the remains of the Berlin Wall, or the paintings in a museum? To express what you can see in a given place, you will need to use *man sieht* (*mAn zeet*), "one sees," which is colloquially expressed in English as "you see." Remember that *sehen* is a very strong verb. The complete conjugation for the present tense is given in Chapter 8.

The expression *man sieht* is quite versatile—you can use it to talk about practically anything. Practice the following expressions.

> In Berlin sieht man das Brandenburger Tor.
> *in beR-leen zeet mAn dAs bRAn-duhn-booR-guhR toR*
> In Berlin you see the Brandenburg Gate.

> Im Zirkus sieht man Elefanten.
> *im tsiR-koos zeet mAn ey-ley-fAn-tuhn*
> In the circus you see elephants.

> Im Kino sieht man einen Film.
> *im kee-non zeet mAn ay-nuhn film*
> In the cinema you see a movie.

 As a Rule

The basic word order rule for German can be expressed by the pseudomathematical expression XV_2, which translates to the verb always coming in the second position in the sentence (unless you're commanding or posing a yes/no question). X is the subject, an adverb, or a prepositional phrase, as in *Morgen gehe ich ins Kino*. In other words, if the subject does not begin the sentence, the subject will follow the verb. Either way, you end up with the verb in the second position!

Use the phrase *man sieht* to complete the following items. Because you'll be discussing "where" something is seen, and *in* is either an accusative or dative preposition (depending on whether there is motion), you'll be using the dative case and contractions for ease. Remember that the masculine *der* and neuter *das* become *dem* in the dative case, contracting with the preposition *in* to become *im*. The feminine *die* becomes *der* in the dative case. Check your sentences in Appendix A.

Example: das Aquarium/die Fische (the aquarium/the fish)

Answer: Im Aquarium sieht man die Fische.

1. der Nachtclub/eine Vorstellung (the nightclub/the show)

2. die Kathedrale/die Glasmalerei (the cathedral/the stained glass)

3. das Schloß/die Wandteppiche (the castle/the tapestries)

4. der Zoo/die Tiere (the zoo/the animals)

5. das Museum/die Bilder und Skulpturen (the museum/the paintings and sculptures)

6. das Kino/der Film (the cinema/the movies)

7. die Disco/die Tänzer (the disco/the dancers)

8. die Bibliothek/alte Bücher (the library/old books)

May, Must, Can—What Kind of Mode Are You In?

To make suggestions or express attitudes in German, you will need to use *modal verbs*—helping verbs used with other verbs. In the sentence *Wir müssen nach Hause gehen*, for example, the modal verb *müssen* modifies the act of the main verb, *gehen*, expressing the attitude of the speaker toward an action—the equivalent of *must*. Adding a modal to another verb is like having a puppy: Life is never the same again. Modals modify the action of the main verb (just like Sparky turns everything upside down) and significantly alter the meanings of sentences. For example, "We must go home" is much different from "We go home."

When a modal is used with another verb, the modal expresses the attitude of the agent (the subject of the sentence) to the main verb's meaning. The six principal modal auxiliary verbs in German and what they express are as follows:

What's What

Modal verb A verb used with another verb (in its infinitival form) to signal contrasts in speaker attitude. The six principal modal verbs in German are *sollen, müssen, dürfen, können, wollen,* and *mögen.*

♦ *sollen* (*zo-luhn*), ought to: obligation, expectation

♦ *müssen* (*mü-suhn*), to have to: necessity, probability

♦ *dürfen* (*düR-fuhn*), to be allowed to: permission, politeness

♦ *können* (*kö-nuhn*), to be able to: ability, possibility

- *wollen* (*vo-luhn*), to want to: wish, desire, intention

- *mögen* (*möh-guhn*), to like (something): liking, wish

Because the present tense of modal auxiliary verbs is irregular, the best thing for you to do is to grit your teeth and memorize the conjugations (see the following six tables). A long time ago, the original present-tense forms of modals fell into disuse, and the original strong (vowel-changing) past tense assumed present tense meaning. This accounts linguistically for why all modals except *sollen* take a stem change in the singular. As you'll see, the first person and third person singular have the same form. Again, this phenomenon is related to the usage of the past-tense form. Simply put, learn the infinitive and the singular stem, and you'll have it made!

Conjugation of a Modal Auxiliary Verb: *sollen*

Person	Singular	English	Plural	English
First	ich soll *iH zol*	I ought to	wir sollen *veeR zo-luhn*	we ought to
Second	du sollst *dew zolst*	you ought to	ihr sollt *eeR zolt*	
Third	er, sie, es soll *eR, zee, es zol*	he, she, it ought to	sie sollen *zee zo-luhn*	they ought to
Formal	Sie sollen *zee zo-luhn*	you ought to	Sie sollen *zee zo-luhn*	you ought to

Did you notice that the first and third person singular are identical? These are also the only forms with modals that don't take the regular ending you've come to associate with present-tense verb conjugations. And did you pick up on how the first person and third person plural exactly resemble the infinitive?

Conjugation of a Modal Auxiliary Verb: *mögen*

Person	Singular	English	Plural	English
First	ich mag *iH mahk*	I like to	wir mögen *veeR möh-guhn*	we like to
Second	du magst *dew mahkst*	you like to	ihr mögt *eeR möhkt*	you like to
Third	er, sie, es mag *eR, zee, es mahk*	he, she, it likes to	sie mögen *zee möh-guhn*	they like to
Formal	Sie mögen *zee möh-guhn*	you like to	Sie mögen *zee möh-guhn*	you like to

Conjugation of a Modal Auxiliary Verb: *dürfen*

Person	Singular	English	Plural	English
First	ich darf *iH dARf*	I am allowed to	wir dürfen *veeR* *düR-fuhn*	we are allowed to
Second	du darfst *dew dARfst*	you are allowed to	ihr dürft *eeR düRft*	you are allowed to
Third	er, sie, es darf *er, zee, es dARf*	he, she, it is *allowed to*	sie dürfen *zee düR-fuhn*	they are allowed to
Formal	Sie dürfen *zee düR-fuhn*	you are allowed to	Sie dürfen *zee düR-fuhn*	you are allowed to

Conjugation of a Modal Auxiliary Verb: *können*

Person	Singular	English	Plural	English
First	ich kann *iH kAn*	I am able to	wir können *veeR kö-nuhn*	we are able to
Second	du kannst *dew kAnst*	you are able to	ihr könnt *eeR könt*	you are able to
Third	er, sie, es kann *er, zee, es, kAn*	he, she, it is able to	sie können *zee kö-nuhn*	they are able to
Formal	Sie können *zee kö-nuhn*	you are able to	Sie können *zee kö-nuhn*	you are able to

Conjugation of a Modal Auxiliary Verb: *müssen*

Person	Singular	English	Plural	English
First	ich muss *iH moos*	I have to	wir müssen *veeR mü-suhn*	we have to
Second	du musst *dew moost*	you have to	ihr müsst *eeR müst*	you have to
Third	er, sie, es muss *er, zee, es moos*	he, she, it has to	sie müssen *zee mü-suhn*	they have to
Formal	Sie müssen *zee mü-suhn*	you have to	Sie müssen *zee mü-suhn*	you have to

Conjugation of a Modal Auxiliary Verb: *wollen*

Person	Singular	English	Plural	English
First	ich will *iH vil*	I want to	wir wollen *veeR vo-luhn*	we want to
Second	du willst *dew vilst*	you want to	ihr wollt *eeR volt*	you want to
Third	er, sie, es will *er, zee, es vil*	he, she, it wants to	sie wollen *zee vo-luhn*	they want to
(Formal)	Sie wollen *zee vo-luhn*	you want to	Sie wollen *zee vo-luhn*	you want to

The Power of Suggestion

Imagine that you are in a group traveling through Germany. A friend of yours who visited Hamburg a year ago has told you to be sure to visit the St. Pauli's Fischmarkt after going out dancing and reveling on a Saturday night. She says that people who don't feel like sleeping gather there in the early hours of Sunday morning with the market workers and eat breakfast. You don't know how others in your group would feel about going to St. Pauli's seafood fest, but you do know that there's only one way to find out: by suggesting it! To make suggestions in German, use the modals *sollen*, *dürfen*, *können*, or *wollen* plus the infinitive.

If your suggestions don't seem to have the desired effect, use the modal *müssen* to express "must." Use *mögen* to express the things you like to do (on a regular basis).

> ### We Are Family
>
> While both the *can* of English and the *können* of German may be used in the contemporary sense of "receive permission," did you know that the Old English *cunnan* meant "know"? This meaning was retained until the sixteenth or seventeenth centuries (Early Modern English) and is still retained in German: *Ich kann Deutsch*, "I know German."

Note that the modal is the conjugated verb and, hence, is in the second position in the sentence. The verb carrying the main meaning and action is placed in infinitival form at the end of the sentence. You're inflecting the modal to show agreement with the subject (person, number); the accompanying verb is referred to as a *dependent infinitive*—unvarying in form and always sent to the end of the sentence. After all, why stack verbs if you can separate them?

Remember that five out of the six modal auxiliary verbs (*dürfen, können, mögen, müssen,* and *wollen*) change their stem vowel in the first, second, and third person singular forms.

sollen + gehen

German	Pronunciation	English
Sollen wir zum Fischmarkt gehen?	*zo-luhn veeR tsewm fish-mARkt gey-uhn*	Should we go to the fish market?
Wir sollen zum Fischmarkt gehen.	*veeR zo-luhn tsewm fish-mARkt gey-uhn*	We are supposed to go to the fish market.

wollen + gehen

German	Pronunciation	English
Wollt ihr zum Fischmarkt gehen?	*volt eeR tsewm fish-mARkt gey-uhn*	Do you want to go to the fish market?
Wir wollen zum Fischmarkt gehen.	*veeR vo-luhn tsewm fish-mARkt gey-uhn*	We want to go to the fish market.

mögen + gehen

German	Pronunciation	English
Magst du zum Fischmarkt gehen?	*mahkst dew tsewm fish-mARkt gey-uhn*	Do you like to go to the fish market?
Ich mag zum Fischmarkt gehen.	*iH mahk tsewm fish-mARkt gey-uhn*	I like to go to the fish market.

müssen + gehen

German	Pronunciation	English
Müssen sie zum Fischmarkt gehen?	*mü-suhn zee tsewm fish-mARkt gey-uhn*	Must they go to the fish market?
Sie müssen zum Fischmarkt gehen.	*zee mü-suhn tsewm fish-mARkt gey-uhn*	They must go to the fish market.

dürfen + gehen

German	Pronunciation	English
Darf ich zum Fischmarkt gehen?	*dARf iH tsewm fish-mARkt gey-uhn*	Am I allowed to go to the fish market?
Ich darf zum Fischmarkt gehen.	*iH dARf tsewm fish-mARkt gey-uhn*	I'm allowed to go to the fish market.

können + gehen

German	Pronunciation	English
Können wir nach Hause gehen?	*kö-nuhn veeR nACH hou-zuh gey-uhn*	Can we go home?
Wir können nach Hause gehen.	*veeR kö-nuhn nACH hou-zuh gey-uhn*	We can go home.

Making Suggestions

It's summertime ... and the living is easy. Suggest five things you and your group of travelers can do together, and express each suggestion in three different ways.

Try your hand at inserting the correct form of the modal (and sending the dependent infinitive to the end) in the following sentences. Check your sentences in Appendix A.

1. Ich komme später. (können)

2. Was machst du? (wollen)

3. Christina lernt viel. (müssen)

4. Dieser Film ist sehr gut. (sollen)

5. Wolfram kommt nicht mit. (dürfen)

Responding to Suggestions

You don't want to be someone who is always telling everyone else what you should do, what you must do, and what you can do all the time, do you? You'll probably want to give other people a chance to make suggestions, and when they do, you'll want to respond. In the following sections, you'll learn some common ways of responding to suggestions.

Just Say Yes, No, Absolutely Not

If you're irritated with whomever is making a given suggestion, by all means answer with a brusque "yes" or "no." Otherwise, you may want to take a somewhat gentler approach and decline a suggestion with, "Yes, but ...."

Ja, ich bin daran interessiert.
yah, iH bin dah-RAn in-tuh-Re-seeRt
Yes, I'm interested in that.

Ja, es interessiert mich(sehr), aber ….
yah, es in-tuh-Re-seeRt miH (zeeR), ah-buhR
Yes, I'm (very) interested, but ….

Nein, leider interessiert es mich (überhaupt) nicht.
nayn, lay-duhR in-tuh-Re-seeRt es miH (üh-buhR-houpt) niHt
No, unfortunately, I'm not (at all) interested.

Nein, ich bin nicht daran interessiert.
nayn, iH bin niHt dah-RAn in-tuh-Re-seeRt
No, I'm not interested in that.

Achtung

Don't confuse the first- and third-person singular forms of the modal *wollen* ("want to") with the English look-alike "will." *Beka will eine Radtour machen* means "Beka wants to go on a bike ride"—not that she will go on one!

Das macht mir Spaß.
das maCHt meeR shpahs
That's fun.

Ich möchte lieber ….
iH möH-tuh lee-buhR
I would rather ….

To express boredom, dislike, or disgust, say:

German	Pronunciation	English
Ich mag … nicht.	*iH mahk … niHt*	I don't like ….
Ich habe keine Lust.	*iH hah-buh kay-nuh loost*	I don't feel like it.
Es ist langweilig.	*es ist lAng-vay-liH*	It's boring.
Das ist grauenhaft.	*das ist gRou-uhn-hAft*	That is horrible.

As a Rule

When used in the sense of "to like," *mögen* usually stands by itself, without a dependent infinitive. *Ich mag den Film nicht. Magst du Schokolade? Möchte* is the polite, subjunctive form of the modal *mögen*. The meaning of *mögen* is "to like"; the meaning of *möchte* is "would like (to)." *Ich möchte Musik hören* means "I would like to listen to music."

What Do You Think?

When someone suggests that the two of you go to the opera, and the suggestion appeals to you, answer with *Ich finde die Oper toll*. If you begin your answers with *Ich finde*, you can be pretty much assured that you're going to be saying something that makes sense. Here are some alternative ways to show your enthusiasm:

Ich liebe die Oper!
iH lee-buh dee oh-puhR
I love opera!

Ich mag die Oper.
iH mahk dee oh-puhR
I like opera.

To express joy, excitement, or anticipation at doing something, give your positive opinion by saying this:

Es ist ….
es ist
It is ….

Das ist ….
dAs ist
That is ….

Ich finde es ….
iH fin-duh es
I find it ….

Here are some common German superlatives:

German	Pronunciation	English
fantastisch!	*fAn-tAs-tish*	fantastic!
schön!	*shöhn*	beautiful!
wunderschön!	*voon-deR-shöhn*	wonderful!
super!	*zew-puhR*	super!
unglaublich!	*oon-gloup-liH*	unbelievable!
sensationell!	*zen-zah-tseeon-el*	sensational!

More Suggestions

Once again, it's time to put what you know to work. Imagine that you are planning a trip with a close friend. Your friend is a bit of a dreamer and keeps suggesting a million different things for the two of you to do. Practice letting your friend down gently by giving an affirmative answer and then a negative answer to his or her suggestions. Check possible responses in Appendix A.

Example: Lass uns nach Berlin reisen!

Answer: Super! Ich mag Berlin.

    Nein, ich will nicht nach Berlin reisen.

1. Lass uns eine Kirche besichtigen!

2. Lass uns eine Ausstellung sehen!

3. Lass uns nach Europa reisen!

4. Lass uns Bilder anschauen!

5. Lass uns in die Oper gehen!

6. Lass uns Norwegisch lernen!

7. Lass uns ein Auto mieten!

> **German Culture**
>
> The German language is rich in slang and colloquialisms. The many ways of saying "great" or "cool" include *klasse*, *prima*, *spitze*, *toll*, *geil*, *riesig* (literally, "gigantic"), and *elefantös*. (Turn *elephant* into an adjective, and this is what you get!)

The Least You Need to Know

◆ You can get around a city by knowing a few basic German words for sightseeing attractions and the phrases that describe what you plan to do there.

◆ After you've memorized the irregular conjugation of the six modal auxiliary verbs (*sollen, müssen, dürfen, können, wollen*, and *mögen*), making suggestions is easy: Use the modal auxiliary verb + the dependent infinitive at the end of the sentence.

◆ You can begin your response to virtually any suggestion with the expression *Ich finde es ....*

◆ To make a suggestion, use the expression *Lass uns* and finish it with an infinitive, as in *Lass uns nach München fahren.*

Chapter 16

Shop Till You Drop

In This Chapter

♦ Stores and what they sell

♦ Clothing, colors, sizes, materials, and designs

♦ Accusative and dative personal pronouns

♦ Demonstrative adjectives: this, that, these, and those

Once you've seen the sights and been to the restaurants, you may want to spend a day or two shopping. Do you like to buy souvenirs for your friends? Do you enjoy shopping for yourself, or do you really dislike trying to locate the right size, color, material, and design in a jungle of hangers, racks, salespeople, and merchandise? Whether you love it or hate it, this chapter will help you prepare to shop.

Store-Bought Pleasures

One of the least expensive (and, for some, most enjoyable) ways to shop is with your eyes. The following table will start you on your way to guilt-free browsing by helping you identify stores and their offerings. Words that may form compounds with the meaning of "store" include *das Geschäft, der Laden, and die Handlung*. Hence, you might find a book (*Buch*) in a *Buchgeschäft*, in a *Buchladen*, or in a *Buchhandlung*. In the table, items that one might find in each store are listed in their plural form followed by their gender (m., f., or n.).

Stores

Store	What You Can Buy There
das Bekleidungsgeschäft (*dAs buh-klay-doorgz-guh-shäft*) clothing store	die Bekleidung, f., (*dee buh-klay-doong*): clothes
die Boutique (*dee boo-teek*) boutique	
das Blumengeschäft (*dAs blew-muhn-guh-shäft*) florist	die Blumen, f., (*dee blew-muhn*): flowers
das Lederwarengeschäft (*dAs ley-deR-vah-Ren-guh-shäft*) leather goods store	die Gürtel, m., (*dee güR-tuhl*); die Lederjacken, f., (*dee ley-duhR-yA-kuhn*); die Portemonnaies, n., (*dee poRt-mo-neyz*): belts, leather jackets, wallets
das Musikgeschäft (*dAs mew-zik-guh-shäft*) music store	die CDs, f., (*dee tse-dez*); die Kassetten, f., (*dee kA-se-tuhn*): CDs, tapes
das Sportgeschäft (*dAs shpoRt-guh-shäft*) sport shop	die Sportbekleidung, f., (*dee shpoRt-buh-klay-doong*); die Turnschuhe, m., (*dee tooRn-shew-uh*); die Sportgeräte, n., (*dee shpoRt-guh-Räh-tuh*): sports clothing, sneakers, sports equipment
der Geschenkartikelladen (*deyR guh-shenk-AR-ti-kuhl-lah-duhn*) gift shop	die Miniaturdenkmäler, n., (*dee mee-nee-ah-tooR-denk-mäh-luhR*); die Souvenirs, n., (*dee sew-vuh-neeRz*); die T-shirts, n., (*dee tee-shiRts*); die Stadtpläne, m., (*dee shtAt-pläh-nuh*): miniature monuments, souvenirs, T-shirts, maps
der Kiosk (*deyR kee-osk*) newsstand	die Zeitungen, f., (*dee tsay-toon-guhn*); die Zeitschriften, f., (*dee tsayt-shRif-tuhn*): newspapers, magazines
der Tabakladen (*deyR tA-bAk-lah-duhn*) tobacconist	die Zigaretten, f., (*dee tsee-gah-Re-tuhn*); die Zigarren, f., (*dee tsee-gA-Ruhn*); die Feuerzeuge, n., (*dee foy-uhR-tsoy-guh*): cigarettes, cigars, lighters
die Apotheke (*dee ah-po-tey-kuh*) pharmacy	die Medikamente, n., (*dee me-dee-kah-men-tuh*): medicine
die Buchhandlung (*dee bewCH-hAnt-loong*) bookstore	die Bücher, n., (*dee bü-CHuhR*): books

Store	What You Can Buy There
die Drogerie (*dee dRoh-guh-Ree*) drug store	die Schönheitsartikel, m., (*dee shön-hayts-AR-tee-kuhl*): beauty articles
die Papierwarenhandlung (*dee pah-peeR-wah-Ruhn- hAn-dloong*) stationery store	die Stifte, m., (*dee shtif-tuh*); die Schreibwaren, f., (*dee shRayp-vah-Ruhn*): pens, stationery
die Parfümerie (*dee pAR-fü-muh-Ree*) perfume store	das Parfüm (*dAs paR-füm*): perfume
das Schmuckgeschäft (*dAs shmook-guh-shäft*) or der Juwelier (*deyR yoo-vey-lee-uhR*) jewelry store	der Schmuck (*deyR shmook*): jewelry

---

German Culture

Large department stores, *Kaufhäuser* (*kouf-hoy-zuhR*), may be found in German cities. Aside from tendering the same goods and services as American department stores, they typically include a supermarket, indicated on the store directory as *Lebensmittel* (*ley-benz-mi-tuhl*), in the basement, or *Untergeschoß* (*oon-tuhR-guh-shos*).

The Clothes Make the Mann

If you packed too little or want to check out European fashions, the vocabulary in the following table will help you identify something in the latest fashion, or *in der neusten Mode* (*in deyR noy-stuhn moh-duh*). Articles of clothing that occur in the plural are noted by a following (pl.). Note that *die Hose* (pair of pants or trousers) is singular, unlike its English equivalent.

Clothing

German	Pronunciation	English
die Größe	*dee gröh-suh*	size
das Hemd	*dAs hemt*	shirt
die Bluse	*dee blew-zuh*	blouse
das Kleid	*dAs klayt*	dress

continues

Clothing   (continued)

German	Pronunciation	English
das T-shirt	*dAs tee-shiRt*	T-shirt
der Anzug	*deyR An-tsewk*	suit
der Badeanzug	*deyR bah-duh-An-tsewk*	bathing suit
der Büstenhalter	*deyR bü-stuhn-hAl-tuhR*	bra
or der BH	*deyR bey-hah*	abbreviation for "bra"
der Gürtel	*deyR güR-tuhl*	belt
der Hut	*deyR hewt*	hat
der Pullover	*deyR pool-oh-vuhR*	pullover
der Regenmantel	*deyR Rey-guhn-mAn-tuhl*	raincoat
der Rock	*deyR Rok*	skirt
der Schal	*deyR shahl*	scarf
der Schlafanzug	*deyR shlahf-An-tsook*	pajamas
die Handschuhe (pl.)	*dee hAnt-schew-uh*	gloves
die Hose	*dee hoh-zuh*	pair of pants
die Jacke	*dee yA-kuh*	jacket
die Jeans	*dee jeens*	jeans
die Krawatte	*dee kRah-vA-tuh*	necktie
der Mantel	*deyR mAn-tuhl*	coat
der Schlips	*deyR schlips*	necktie
die Shorts (pl.)	*dee shoRts*	shorts
die Mütze	*dee mü-tsuh*	cap
das Sakko	*dAs za-ko*	sports jacket
die Schuhe (pl.)	*dee shew-uh*	shoes
die Socken (pl.)	*dee zo-kuhn*	socks
die Strumpfhose	*dee shtRoompf-hoh-zuh*	tights, stockings
die Turnschuhe (pl.)	*dee tooRn-shew-uh*	sneakers
die Tennisschuhe (pl.)	*dee te-nis-shew-uh*	tennis shoes
die Unterwäsche	*dee oon-tuhR-vä-shuh*	underwear

Wear It Well

Now that you've bought it, you can finally wear it. The following table helps you express the concept of wearing clothing with the very strong verb *tragen* (*tRah-guhn*), "to wear" or "to carry."

The Verb *tragen*

Person	Singular	English	Plural	English
First	ich trage *iH tRah-guh*	I wear	wir tragen *veeR tRah-guhn*	we wear
Second	du trägst *dew tRähkst*	you wear	ihr tragt *eeR tRahkt*	you wear
Third	er, sie, es trägt *eR, zee, es tRäkt*	he, she, it wears	sie tragen *zee tRah-guhn*	they wear
Formal	Sie tragen *zee tRah-guhn*	you wear	Sie tragen *zee tRah-guhn*	you wear

What do you normally wear on your feet before you put on your shoes? What do you normally wear on your head when it's cold out? See whether you can fill in the blanks with the correct form of the verb *tragen* and appropriate vocabulary. Check your conjugations in Appendix A.

Example: Zum Sport _____ ich _____.

Answer: Zum Sport trage ich Turnschuhe.

1. Unter (under) unseren Schuhen _____ wir _____.

2. Wenn (when) ich schlafe, _____ ich einen _____.

3. Unter deiner Hose _____ du _____.

4. Wenn es regnet, _____ ich einen _____.

5. Im Winter _____ ihr warme _____.

6. Wenn man in die Oper (to the opera) geht, _____ man einen _____ mit einem _____.

7. Im Sommer _____ viele Leute (people) _____ und ein _____.

Colors

Certain colors are associated with certain moods or states of being. Don't be too quick to use the colors in the following table figuratively—at least, not in the same way you would use them in English. *Er ist blau* (*eR ist blou*), which translates into "he is blue," does not mean "he is sad." Germans use this phrase to indicate that someone has had too much to drink. However you use them, the colors (*die Farben*) in the following table will help you describe people, places, and things.

Colors

German	Pronunciation	English
beige	*beyj*	beige
blau	*blou*	blue
braun	*bRoun*	brown
gelb	*gelp*	yellow
grau	*gRou*	gray
grün	*gRün*	green
lila	*lee-lah*	purple
orange	*oR-An-juh*	orange
rosa	*Roh-zah*	pink
rot	*Rot*	red
schwarz	*shvaRts*	black
weiß	*vays*	white

To describe any color as light, simply add the word *hell* (*hel*) as a prefix to the color to form a compound adjective:

hellrot	hellgrün	hellblau
hel-Rot	*hel-gRün*	*hel-blou*
light red	light green	light blue

To describe a color as dark, add the word *dunkel* (*doon-kuhl*) as a prefix to the color to form a compound adjective:

dunkelrot	dunkelgrün	dunkelblau
doon-kuhl-Rot	*doon-kuhl-gRün*	*doon-kuhl-blou*
dark red	dark green	dark blue

The following table offers some additional adjectives that are useful when describing clothing.

Fashionable Adjectives

German	Pronunciation	English
breit	*brayt*	wide
eng	*eng*	narrow
gemustert	*guh-moos-tuhRt*	patterned
gepunktet	*guh-poonk-tuht*	polka-dotted

German	Pronunciation	English
gestreift	*guh-shtRayft*	striped
kariert	*kah-ReeRt*	plaid
modisch	*moh-dish*	fashionable

To express need or desire, you can use *möchten*, which, although it is the subjunctive form of the modal verb *mögen*, is often used as a present-tense verb on its own. *Ich möchte* is the equivalent of "I would like." Don't confuse it with *mögen*, which means "to like (something)." You can make a big mistake by confusing the two. If you're in a clothing store and you say, *"Ich möchte Kleider"* ("I would like some dresses") instead of *"Ich mag Kleider"* ("I like dresses"), you might end up with an armful of dresses and be expected to try them on, whether you're in the mood for trying on dresses or not. Now try to translate the following sentences into German. Remember that colors and patterns are adjectives, so they are declined according to what type of word precedes the adjective and the following noun (see Chapter 10). Also, the item that you "like" functions as the direct object in the sentence and thus takes the accusative case. Check your translations in Appendix A.

Example: I'd like a green dress.

Answer: Ich möchte ein grünes Kleid.

1. I'd like a light red skirt.
2. I'd like a dark blue suit.
3. I'd like a light yellow hat.
4. I'd like a gray jacket.
5. I'd like a polka-dotted tie.
6. I'd like a plaid pair of pants.
7. I'd like a fashionable bathing suit.
8. I'd like a striped shirt.

Fabric Preferences

Some people can't tolerate polyester, others find silk pretentious, and others won't wear anything that isn't at least 95 percent cotton. The following table will help you pick the material (*die Materialien*) you prefer when you shop.

Materials

German	Pronunciation	English
das Leder	*dAs ley-deR*	leather
das Leinen	*dAs lay-nuhn*	linen

continues

Materials (continued)

German	Pronunciation	English
das Nylon	*dAs nay-lon*	nylon
das Polyester	*dAs poh-lee-es-tuhR*	polyester
das Wildleder, *or,* Veloursleder	*dAs vilt-ley-duhR, dAs vuh-looRz-ley-duhR*	suede
der Flanell	*deyR flah-nel*	flannel
der Kaschmir	*deyR kAsh-meeR*	cashmere
der Kord	*deyR koRt*	corduroy
die Baumwolle	*dee boum-wo-luh*	cotton
die Seide	*dee zay-duh*	silk
die Wolle	*dee vo-luh*	wool

To explain that you want something made out of a certain material, use the dative preposition *aus* followed by only the noun.

> Ich möchte ein Kleid aus Seide.
> *iH möH-tuh ayn klayt ous zay-duh*
> I'd like a silk dress.

What's the Object?

In Chapter 7, you learned about the accusative (*direct object*) case and the dative (*indirect object*) case relative to nouns. Now you're going to see how these cases affect pronouns.

If a friend tells you that she loves her favorite pair of shoes and that she wears her favorite pair of shoes all the time and that she takes off her favorite pair of shoes only when she gets blisters from dancing too much, you would probably want to take off one of *your* shoes and hit her over the head with it. She could be less long-winded if she stopped repeating *favorite pair of shoes* (a direct object noun in English) and replaced it with *them* (a direct object pronoun in English). In German, the direct object is in the accusative case and is often called the accusative object. The animate object that is receiving the action of the verb is the indirect object and is marked in the dative case in German, also called the dative object. If you've forgotten what you learned about cases in Chapter 7, this summary should refresh your memory.

What's What

Direct object The noun or pronoun that receives the action of the verb. The verb assigns this object the accusative case.

Nouns or pronouns in the accusative case answer the question of whom or what the subject is acting on and can refer to people, places, things, or ideas.

	Nominative (Subj.)	Verb	Accusative (Direct Obj.)
With noun	Ich (I)	trage (wear)	meine Lieblingsschuhe. (my favorite shoes)
With pronoun	Ich (I)	trage (wear)	sie. (them)
With noun	Sie (they)	lieben (love)	das Leben. (life)
With pronoun	Sie (they)	lieben (love)	es. (it)

Indirect object nouns or pronouns (in German, nouns or pronouns in the dative case) answer the question of to whom or to what the action of the verb is being directed.

	Nominative (Subj.)	Verb	Dative (Indirect Obj.)	Accusative (Direct Obj.)
With noun	Ich (I)	kaufe (buy)	meinem Freund (my friend)	eine Mütze. (a cap)
With pronoun	Ich (I)	kaufe (buy)	ihm (him)	eine Mütze. (a cap)
With noun	Sie (she)	gibt (gives)	ihrer Schwester (her sister)	ein Geschenk. (a gift)
With pronoun	Sie (she)	gibt (gives)	ihr (her sister)	ein Geschenk. (a gift)

The English language uses direct and indirect pronouns to avoid repeating the same nouns over and over again. In German, direct object pronouns are in the accusative case, and indirect object pronouns are in the dative case. The following table provides a comprehensive chart of accusative personal pronouns in German. We've already used this paradigm to show subject (personal) pronouns and to conjugate verbs.

Accusative Personal Pronouns (Object Pronouns)

	Singular	English	Plural	English
First	mich (*miH*)	me	uns (*oonz*)	us
Second	dich (*diH*)	you	euch (*oyH*)	you
Third	ihn (*een*)	him	sie (*zee*)	them
	sie (*zee*)	her		
	es (*es*)	it		
Formal	Sie (*zee*)	you	Sie (*zee*)	you

The accusative case of the direct object should be easy enough to learn if you remember that the German *mich* has the same initial sounds as the English *me* (the object of a sentence or the object of a prepositional phrase). Then *dich* rhymes with *mich* but borrows the *d* sound from *du*. As far as third person singular masculine is concerned, it ends in an *n*, just like the accusative masculine *den* or *einen*. The German *uns* closely resembles the English *us*.

Try your hand at replacing the accusative noun phrases, indicated in boldface, with the appropriate accusative personal pronouns. Check your pronouns in Appendix A.

1. Ich trage **eine enge Hose.**

2. Du trägst **einen schönen Hut.**

3. Kerstin trägt **ein breites Hemd.**

4. Frank trägt **weiße Tennisschuhe.**

What's What

Indirect object   The person, animal, or other animate object to whom/which something is given or something is done. The dative case marks the indirect object in German.

Es is used as a direct object pronoun for neuter nouns, most of which are things. There are, however, a few exceptions. *Es* means "her," for example, in the sentence *Ich liebe es*, when *es* refers to *das Mädchen*.

Because English relies on prepositions to express the function of someone receiving something (indirect object) and German relies on the dative case to indicate this function, we've included that little English helper preposition for dative personal pronouns in the following table.

Dative Personal Pronouns (Indirect Object Pronouns)

	Singular	English	Plural	English
First	mir (*meeR*)	(to) me	uns (*oonz*)	(to) us
Second	dir (*diH*)	(to) you	euch (*oyH*)	(to) you
Third	ihm (*eem*)	(to) him	ihnen (*ee-nuhn*)	(to) them
	ihr (*eeR*)	(to) her		
	ihm (*eem*)	(to) it		
Formal	Ihnen (*ee-nuhn*)	(to) you	Ihnen (*ee-nuhn*)	(to) you

Egads! How to assimilate this information? Again, recall the dative definite articles: masculine = *dem*, feminine = *der*, neuter = *dem*, plural = *den*. You'll notice that the ends of *ihm*, *ihr*, *ihm*, and *ihnen* share similarities in their final sounds. Latch on to your English *him* and *her* for another reminder.

And now for a little practice substituting the economical dative personal pronouns for the long-winded indirect object noun phrases, indicated in boldface. Check your pronouns in Appendix A.

1. Ich gebe **meinen lieben Studenten** Schokolade.

2. Bernadette **schenkt ihrer toleranten** Schwester Blumen.

3. Thomas dankt **seinem nervösen Freund** für den Kaffee.

4. Wir geben **dem freundlichen Kind** eine Olive.

As a Rule

When dealing with neuter nouns ending in *-chen* or *-lein*, you can use either the pronoun *es* (following the grammatical gender) or the pronouns *er* or *sie*, depending on the logical gender of the noun.

◆ Was macht Ihr Söhnchen?

◆ Es (or er) geht ....

◆ Das Mädchen will nicht mehr singen.

◆ Es (or Sie) ist müde.

Position of Object Pronouns

In swank social circles, position is everything. It's the same with direct and indirect objects in German. If we're dealing with noun phrases, the indirect (dative) object precedes the direct object (accusative):

> Ich schreibe dem Vater eine Postkarte.
> *iH shRay-buh deym fah-tuhR ay-nuh post-kAR-tuh*
> I write a postcard to the father.

> **Achtung** _____
>
> Remember, *ihn* and *ihm* are used for nouns with the masculine noun marker *der*, *sie* and *ihr* are used for nouns with the feminine noun marker *die*, and *es* and *ihm* are used for nouns with the neuter noun marker *das*. For masculine, feminine, and neuter nouns with the plural noun marker *die*, use *sie* for direct object pronouns and *ihnen* for indirect object pronouns.

However, if the direct object of a sentence is a pronoun, it precedes the indirect object:

> Ich schreibe sie ihm. Ich schreibe sie dem Vater.
> *iH shRay-buh zee eem iH shRay-buh zee deym fah-tuhR*
> I write it to him. I write it to the father.

Note that *eine Postkarte* is replaced with the feminine pronoun *sie*, not with the ubiquitous inanimate neuter English "it" equivalent (*es*).

Using Direct Object Pronouns

A German friend invites you to accompany her shopping in Düsseldorf. She won't buy anything unless she receives an affirmative second opinion. Use direct object pronouns to answer the questions she asks you in the dressing room. Check your answers in Appendix A.

Example:

Magst du die graue Bluse?

Ja, ich mag sie.

Nein, ich mag sie nicht.

1. Magst du den schwarzen Schal?

2. Magst du die dunkelgrünen Schuhe?

3. Magst du die hellrote Hose?

4. Magst du das blaue Hemd?

Using Indirect Object Pronouns

When she finishes shopping for herself, your friend wants to buy a few presents for certain members of her family. Unfortunately, she can't think of anything interesting to buy them. Offer her suggestions (in the form of commands), replacing the indirect object (dative noun phrase) with a pronoun and expressing the direct object in the accusative case according to the following example. Remember that *ein* in the accusative masculine becomes *einen*. Check your sentences in Appendix A.

Example:

Hans/ ein Hut (m., der Hut) Schenke ihm einen Hut.

1. die Eltern/ ein Schal (m., der Schal)

2. die Schwester/ ein Kleid (n., das Kleid)

3. der Bruder/ eine kurze Hose (f., die kurze Hose)

4. die Oma/ eine Strumpfhose (f., die Strumpfhose)

> **German Culture**
>
> European sizes (*Größen*) vary greatly from American sizes. While with clothing you might find S, M, L, and XL, you'll more than likely encounter numbered sizes such as 34–44 for women (*Damen*) and 36–54 for men (*Herren*). Shoe sizes for both men and women range from 36 upwards.

Now rewrite these four commands using *only* pronouns. Because the direct object will be a pronoun, the direct object pronoun will precede the indirect object. Verify your pronouns in the appendix.

Example:

Schenke ihm einen Hut. = Schenke ihn ihm.

Asking for Something

Here are some phrases to help you through the most common in-store shopping situations:

Kann ich Ihnen helfen?
kAn iH ee-nuhn hel-fuhn
May I help you?

Nein danke, ich schaue mich nur um.
nayn dAn-kuh, iH shou-uh miH nooR oom
No, thank you, I am (just) looking.

Ja, ich würde gern (+ accusative object) sehen.
yah, iH vüR-duh geRn ... zey-uhn
Yes, I would like to see …

Was wünschen Sie?
vAs vün-shuhn zee
What would you like?

Ich suche (+ accusative object).
iH zew-CHuh
I'm looking for ….

Welche Größe brauchen Sie?
vel-Huh gröh-suh brou-CHuhn zee
What size do you need?

Größe …
gröh-suh
Size …

Was ist im Sonderangebot?
vAs ist im zon-duhR-An-guh-bot
What's on sale?

I'll Take This

To ask your salesperson (or the cashier, or anyone else within asking distance) for his or her opinion about a suit, tie, hat, or skirt, you'll need to use a *demonstrative adjective*.

What's What

Demonstrative adjectives Adjectives such as *dieser* ("this") that point out someone or something specific—a particular noun.

The demonstrative adjective *dieser* ("this") allows you to be specific about an item. You encountered these types of *der* words in Chapter 12. The important thing to remember is that, in German, demonstrative adjectives must agree in number, gender, and case with the noun they modify. Because demonstrative adjectives inflect like definite articles, the following table reviews the declension of *dieser*, a *der Wort*, in all four cases.

Demonstrative Adjectives: *This, That, These, Those*

Case	Masculine	Feminine	Neuter	Plural
Nom.	dies**er** Hut	diese Hose	dies**es** Kleid	diese
	dee-zuhR hewt	*dee-zuh hoh-zuh*	*dee-zuhs klayt*	*dee-zuh*
Acc.	dies**en** Hut	diese Hose	dies**es** Kleid	diese
	dee-zuhn hewt	*dee-zuh hoh-zuh*	*dee-zuhs klayt*	*dee-zuh*

Case	Masculine	Feminine	Neuter	Plural
Dat.	dies**em** Hut	dies**er** Hose	dies**em** Kleid	dies**en**
	dee-zuhm hewt	*dee-zuhR hoh-zuh*	*de-zuhm klayt*	*dee-zuhn*
Gen.	dies**es** Hutes	dies**er** Hose	dies**es** Kleides	dies**er**
	dee-zuhs hewts	*dee-zuhR hoh-zuh*	*dee-zuhs klayts*	*dee-zuhR*

Expressing Opinions

You've tried on a million hats, and not one of them is right. Just when you're about to give up, you find the perfect hat. If you're happy with an item, you may want to express your pleasure. On the other hand, perhaps you are dissatisfied with the fit or style of something. You may express your opinion with the phrases in the following table. Note that *gefallen* and *stehen* use the dative case to express the person whom (indirect object) something (the direct, accusative object) pleases or fits.

German	Pronunciation	English
Das gefällt mir.	*dAs guh-fält miR*	I like it. (literally: It is pleasing to me.)
Das steht mir gut.	*dAs shteyt miR gewt*	That suits me well.
Es ist angenehm.	*es ist An-guh-neym*	It is nice.
Es ist elegant.	*es ist ey-ley-gAnt*	It's elegant.
Es ist praktisch.	*es ist pRAk-tish*	It's practical.
Es gefällt mir nicht.	*es guh-fält miR niHt*	I don't like it.
Das steht mir nicht.	*dAs shteyt miR niHt*	That doesn't suit me.
Es ist schrecklich.	*es ist shRek-liH*	It is horrible.
Es ist zu klein.	*es ist tsew klayn*	It's too small.
Es ist zu groß.	*es ist tsew gRohs*	It's too big.
Es ist zu eng.	*es ist tsew eng*	It's too tight.
Es ist zu lang.	*es ist tsew lAng*	It's too long.
Es ist zu kurz.	*es ist tsew kooRts*	It's too short.

What's Your Preference?

Many questions concerning style and size begin with the interrogative pronoun *welcher*, another *der* word introduced in Chapter 12. *Welcher* follows the same declension as the demonstrative pronoun *dieser*, shown in the demonstrative adjectives table.

Sample question:

Welches Hemd gefällt Ihnen am besten?
vel-Huhs hemt guh-fält ee-nuhn Am bes-tuhn
Which shirt do you like best?

Answer:

Dieses Hemd dort gefällt mir am besten.
dee-suhs hemt doRt guh-fält meeR Am bes-tuhn
I like that shirt there best.

Now it's time to practice what you've learned about the interrogative pronoun *welcher*. Respond to the questions in the following exercise with the correctly declined form of *welcher*. Check your questions in Appendix A.

Example: Ich suche ein Geschäft.

Answer: Welches Geschäft?

1. Diese Krawatte gefällt uns.

2. Der Anzug steht dir gut.

3. Das T-shirt schenke ich meinem Bruder.

4. Ich suche meine Schuhe.

5. Ich mag dieses Kleid.

6. Sie möchte diesen Schlafanzug dort.

Did you figure out that the article of clothing in the first three sentences was the subject and, hence, in the nominative case? And what about the final three sentences? Yup, direct objects, thus expressed in the accusative case.

The Least You Need to Know

◆ You should be able to recognize the German names of stores and what they sell.

◆ You can use the verb *tragen* to talk about what you are wearing.

◆ In German, direct object pronouns are in the accusative case, and indirect object pronouns are in the dative case.

◆ The demonstrative adjective *dieser* helps you to indicate someone or something by expressing this or that (and, in the plural form, these or those). Its interrogative partner, *welcher*, can help you clarify which one.

Chapter 17

Auf dem Markt: Eating on the Go

In This Chapter

- ◆ Where to buy various kinds of food
- ◆ How to read a wine label
- ◆ How to express quantity
- ◆ Identifying what you want and asking for it

In Chapter 16, you learned how to shop for fashion items. You told the salespeople what you wanted and answered their questions. You learned about colors, patterns, and preferences. Now your wallet is a little lighter, your suitcase is a little heavier, and your stomach feels a little emptier than it did when you set out earlier in the day. It's too early for dinner, so you decide to stop for a snack.

What do you feel like eating? You could get a sandwich (ein belegtes Brot, *ayn buh-lek-tuhs bRoht*) at a Café (*dAs kah-fey*) or a Bäckerei (*ay-nuh bä-kuh-Ray*), or stop in a Supermarkt (*deyR zew-peR-mARkt*) for bread (das Brot, *dAs bRoht*) and cheese (der Käse, *deyR käh-zuh*) and make your own. This chapter will help you get the food you want in just the right amount.

Shopping Around

One way to save money when you're traveling is to buy the fixings to make your own lunches and snacks, or learn where to eat cheaply and easily. The list of foods and food shops in the following table should help you keep your appetite sated while you shop and sightsee. Bear in mind that the supermarket and an open-air market are the only two establishments where you are likely to find exclusively foodstuff.

Foods and Food Shops

German	Pronunciation	English
der Fisch	*deyR fish*	fish
das Fischgeschäft	*dAs fish-guh-shäft*	fish store
das Lebensmittelgeschäft	*dAs ley-buhnz-mi-tuhl-guh-shäft*	grocery store
der Nachtisch	*deyR nACH-tish*	dessert
der Proviant	*deyR pRoh-vee-Ant*	provisions
der Supermarkt	*deyR zew-peR-mARkt*	supermarket
das Brot	*dAs bRoht*	bread
die Bäckerei	*dee bä-kuh-Ray*	bakery
der Bäcker	*deyR bä-kuhR*	baker
die Früchte	*dee fRüH-tuh*	fruits
das Gebäck	*dAs guh-bäk*	pastry (sweet)
die Konditorei	*dee kon-dee-toR-ay*	café, pastry shop
die Meeresfrüchte	*dee mee-Ruhs-fRüH-tuh*	seafood
das Obst	*dAs opst*	fruit
das Gemüse	*dAs guh-müh-zuh*	vegetables
die Obst- und Gemüsehandlung	*dAs opst oont guh-müh-zuh-hAnt-loong*	produce shop
das Fleisch	*dAs flaysh*	meat
die Metzgerei	*dee mets-guh-Ray*	butcher shop
der Metzger	*deyR mets-guhR*	butcher
die Spirituosen	*dee Spee-Ree-too-oh-zuhn*	liquors
die Süßigkeiten	*dee züh-siH-kay-tuhn*	candies
der Wein	*deyR vayn*	wine
die Weinhandlung	*dee vayn-hAnt-loong*	wine store

Getting There

You've familiarized yourself with all the food and pastry shops near your hotel. You're armed with nothing but your appetite and some euros! When it's time to go out into the world for supplies to stock your miniature hotel refrigerator or your backpack, use the verb *gehen* and the preposition *zu* + the correctly declined definite article to identify the store you're about to visit. Keep in mind that the preposition *zu* is always followed by the dative case. Of course, once you're there, you are *in* + dative case!

Dative Preposition and Article	Contraction	Example	English
zu + dem = (masc. and neut.)	zum	Ich gehe zum Supermarkt. *iH gey-uh tsoom zew-peR-mARkt*	I go to the supermarket.
zu + der = (fem.)	zur	Ich gehe zur Weinhandlung. *iH gey-uh tsooR vayn-hant-loong*	I go to the liquor store.

You know what you want—now figure out where to go to get those items! Check your responses in Appendix A.

Example: Gemüse: Ich gehe zur Obst- und Gemüsehandlung.

1. Gebäck

2. Fleish

3. Brot

4. Fisch

Alright! So you've figured out where to go for certain items. Of course, there is more than one alternative and source for food. Some cities have a daily open-air market; in other cities, these markets might be open just one or two days a week. You can always go to a supermarket, but don't overlook the smaller stores and produce handlers proudly displaying their offerings along the sidewalk underneath awnings. Because most produce is labeled in the plural (think "tomatoes"), the following charts list most items in their plural forms, providing the singular gender afterward.

German Culture

To grab a quick bite to eat, stop at *the* German fast-food option—*der Imbiss* or *Schnellimbiss.* Located on virtually every busy corner, this is a small booth or stand where you can get a variety of sausages (*eine Curry-, Weiß-, or Knackwurst*) served on a small hard roll with mustard, French fries, and *Pommes frites* (*po-mes*) to eat with a small plastic fork. Or, you can get *einen Hamburger* or *eine Frickadelle,* a hamburger without a roll.

Vegetables

German	Pronunciation	English
das Gemüse	*dAs guh-müh-zuh*	vegetables
die Aubergine	*dee oh-beR-jee-nuh*	eggplant
der Blumenkohl	*deyR blew-muhn-kohl*	cauliflower
die Bohnen, f.	*dee boh-nuhn*	beans
der Brokkoli, m.	*dee bRo-koh-lee*	broccoli
die Erbsen, f.	*dee eRp-suhn*	peas
eingelete Gurken, f.	*ayn-gu-leyk-tuh gooR-kuhn*	pickles
die Gurken, f.	*dee gooR-kuhn*	cucumbers
die Karotten, f.	*dee kah-Ro-tuhn*	carrots
die Kartoffeln, f,	*dee kAR-to-fuhln*	potatoes
der Kohl	*deyR kohl*	cabbage
der Kopfsalat	*deyR Kopf-zah-laht*	lettuce
der Mais	*deyR mays*	corn
die Pilze (pl.)	*dee pil-tsuh*	mushrooms
das Sauerkraut	*dAs zou-uhR-kRout*	pickled cabbage
der Sellerie	*deyR ze-luh-Ree*	celery
der Spargel	*deyR shpAR-guhl*	asparagus
der Spinat	*deyR spee-naht*	spinach
die Tomaten, f.	*dee toh-mah-tuhn*	tomatoes
die Zwiebeln, f.	*dee zvee-buhln*	onions

Auf dem Markt is the way to express being at the open-air market. While there, you can find almost anything: fresh flowers, produce, eggs, cheese, meat, sausage, fish, bread, and so on. Because most items are labeled by name along with a price, the market is also an opportune place to learn vocabulary.

Fruits and Nuts

German	Pronunciation	English
das Obst	*dAs opst*	fruit
die Ananas	*dee A-nah-nAs*	pineapple
die Äpfel, m.	*dee Âp-fel*	apples
die Aprikosen, f.	*dee Ap-Ree-koh-zuhn*	apricots
die Pfirsiche, m.	*dee pfeeR-ziH-uh*	peaches
die Bananen, f.	*dee bah-nah-nuhn*	bananas
die Birnen, f.	*dee beeR-nuhn*	pears
die Blaubeeren, f.	*dee blou-bey-Ruhn*	blueberries
die Erdbeeren, f.	*dee eRt-bey-Ruhn*	strawberries
die Haselnüsse, f.	*dee hah-zuhl-nüh-suh*	hazelnuts
die Himmbeeren, f.	*dee him-bey-Ruhn*	raspberries
die Johannisbeeren, f.	*dee yoh-hA-nis-bey-Ruhn*	currants
die Kastanien, f. *or* die Maronen, f.	*dee kAs-tah-nee-uhn,* *dee mah-Roh-nuhn*	chestnuts
die Kirschen, f.	*dee keeR-shuhn*	cherries
die Mandeln, f.	*dee mAn-duhln*	almonds
die Melone, f.	*dee mey-loh-nuh*	melon
die Nüsse, f.	*dee nü-suh*	nuts
die Orangen, f. or die Apfelsinen, f.	*dee oh-RAn-juhn or* *dee Ap-fel-zee-nuhn*	oranges
die Pflaumen, f.	*dee pflou-muhn*	plums
die Preiselbeeren, f.	*dee pRay-zuhl-bey-Ruhn*	cranberries
die Trauben, f.	*dee trou-buhn*	grapes
die Walnüsse, f.	*dee vAl-nüh-suh*	walnuts
die Wassermelone	*dee vA-suhR-mey-loh-nuh*	watermelon
die Rosinen, f.	*dee Roh-zee-nuhn*	raisins
die Zitronen, f.	*dee tsee-tRoh-nuhn*	lemons

At the Butcher or Delicatessen (*beim Metzger*)

German	Pronunciation	English
das Fleisch	*dAs flaysh*	meat
das Kalbfleisch	*dAs kAlp-flaysh*	veal
das Schweinefleisch	*dAs shvay-nuh-flaysh*	pork

continues

At the Butcher or Delicatessen (*beim Metzger*)   (continued)

German	Pronunciation	English
das Lamm	*dAs lAm*	lamb
das Rindfleisch	*dAs Rint-flaysh*	beef
das Rippensteak	*dAs Ri-puhn-steyk*	rib steak
das Rumpfsteak	*dAs Roompf-steyk*	rump steak
das Schnitzel	*dAs shnit-suhl*	cutlet
das Wienerschnitzel	*dAs vee-nuhR-shnit-suhl*	breaded veal cutlet
der Hammelbraten	*deyR hA-mel-bRah-tuhn*	roast mutton
der Rinderbraten	*deyR Rin-deR-bRah-tuhn*	roast beef
der Aufschnitt	*deyR ouf-shnit*	sliced cold meat
der Schinken	*deyR shin-kuhn*	ham
der Speck	*deyR shpek*	bacon
die Bratwurst	*dee bRaht-vooRst*	fried sausage
die Leber	*dee ley-buhR*	liver
die Leberwurst	*dee ley-buhR-vooRst*	liver sausage
die Wurst	*dee vooRst*	sausage
das Huhn or das Hähnchen	*dAs hewn, dAs hähn-Hen*	chicken

Most fishmongers at the market offer sandwiches of pickled herring, smoked salmon, shrimp salad, or fried fish on crusty rolls at quite a reasonable price.

At the Fish Store (*auf dem Markt*)

German	Pronunciation	English
der Fisch	*deyR fish*	fish
die Meeresfrüchte (pl.)	*dee mey-Ruhs-früH-tuh*	seafood
der Hummer	*deyR hoo-muhR*	lobster
der Kabeljau	*deyR kah-bel-you*	cod
der Krebs	*deyR kReyps*	crab
der Lachs	*deyR lAks*	salmon
der Tintenfish	*deyR tin-tuhn-fish*	squid
der Thunfisch	*deyR tewn-fish*	tuna
die Auster	*dee ous-tuhR*	oyster
die Flunder/der Rochen	*dee floon-duhR/deyR Ro-CHuhn*	flounder
die Forelle	*dee foh-Re-luh*	trout
die Garnele	*dee gahR-ney-luh*	shrimp

German	Pronunciation	English
die Krabben (f.)	*dee kRA-buhn*	shrimp, prawns
der Matjes	*deyR mAt-yeyz*	young herring
der Hering	*deyR hey-ring*	herring
die Seezunge	*dee zey-tsoon-guh*	sole

At the Dairy (*auf dem Markt*)

German	Pronunciation	English
das Ei/die Eier (pl.)	*dAs ay/dee ay-eR*	eggs
der Käse	*deyR käh-zuh*	cheese
der Joghurt/Jogurt	*deyR yoh-gooRt*	yogurt
die Butter	*dee boo-tuhR*	butter
die Magermilch	*dee mah-guhR-milH*	skim milk
der Quark	*deyR kvaRk*	soft curd cheese
die Sahne	*dee zah-nuh*	cream
die saure Sahne	*dee zou-Ruh zah-nuh*	sour cream
die Schlagsahne	*dee shlAk-zah-nuh*	whipped cream
die Vollmilch	*dee fol-milH*	whole milk

Although many supermarkets offer a combined bakery and pastry shop, selling both bread items and pastries, outside of that setting you will most likely encounter *eine Bäckerei* that sells only bread items and flat coffee cakes, probably some to-go type sandwiches, and coffee for drinking at a stand-up table in the bakery. If you desire a torte, piece of cake, or other delectable pastry, frequent *eine Konditorei*, where you may point to the type of pastry you'd like to savor in the establishment or get the sweet *zum Mitnehmen* to take with you. These sandwiches are typically open-faced, so you can see what you get.

At the Bakery and Pastry Shop (*in der Bäckerei und in der Konditorei*)

German	Pronunciation	English
das Brot	*dAs bRoht*	bread
das Brötchen *or* die Semmel	*dAs bRöht-Huhn or deyR ze-muhl*	roll
das Plätzchen *or* die Kekse (pl.)	*dAs pläts-Huhn or dee kek-suh*	cookie
das Roggenbrot	*dAs Ro-guhn-bRoht*	rye bread

continues

At the Bakery and Pastry Shop (*in der Bäckerei und in der Konditorei*) (continued)

German	Pronunciation	English
das Toastbrot *or* der Toast	*dAs tohst-bRoht*	white bread (toast)
das Vollkornbrot	*dAs fol-koRn-bRoht*	whole-grain bread
das Weißbrot	*dAs vays-bRoht*	white bread
der Apfelstrudel	*deyR Ap-fuhl-shtRew-duhl*	apple strudel
der Berliner	*deyR beR-lee-nuhR*	jelly doughnut
der Kuchen	*deyR kew-CHuhn*	cake
die Schwarzwälder-kirschtorte	*dee shvARts-väl-duhR-keeRsh-toR-tuh*	Black Forest (cake)
Kirschtorte	*kiRsh-toR-tuh*	cherry pie
die Torte	*dee toR-tuh*	tart

At the Supermarket (*im Supermarkt*)

German	Pronunciation	English
die Getränke	*dee guh-tRän-kuh*	drinks
das Bier	*dAs beeR*	beer
das Mineralwasser	*dAs mi-nuh-Rahl-vA-suhR*	mineral water
der Kaffee	*deyR kA-fey*	coffee
der Saft	*deyR zAft*	juice
der Tee	*deyR tey*	tea
der Wein	*deyR vayn*	wine
die Limonade	*dee lee-moh-nah-duh*	lemonade, or a type of soft drink
die Cola	*dee koh-luh*	cola
die Cola Light	*dee koh-luh layt*	diet cola
die Milch	*dee milH*	milk
kohlensäurehaltig	*koh-len-zoy-Ruh-hAl-tiH*	carbonated
nicht kohlensäurehaltig	*niHt koh-len-zoy-Ruh-hAl-tiH*	noncarbonated

When you go into a grocery store, be prepared to either bring your own reusable cloth bags or pay a small fee for the shop's sturdy plastic bags. At discount grocery stores like *Aldi*, you'll also need to put a deposit on the cart. Expect the checker to push the items into your cart, after which you'll bag them at another counter. Also bear in mind that Germany is environment friendly (*umweltfreundlich*), and you'll be charged for a deposit on most glass containers.

Prost! ("Cheers!")

On wine labels in Germany, you will come across four different categories of grapes used for wines: *Spätlese* (*shpät-ley-zuh*), indicating a dry wine; *Auslese* (*ous-ley-zuh*), indicating a fairly dry wine made from ripe grapes; *Beerenauslese* (*beyR-uhn-ous-ley-zuh*), indicating a sweet wine made from a special kind of very ripe grape; and *Trockenbeerenauslese* (*tRo-kuhn-bey-Ruhn-ous-ley-zuh*), indicating a very sweet (usually quite expensive) wine. Here are some terms you should know if you're a wine lover:

German	Pronunciation	English
(sehr) trocken	(*zeyR*) *tRo-kuhn*	(very) dry
lieblich	*leep-liH*	sweet
mild	*milt*	mild
leicht	*layHt*	light

If you're a beer drinker, put down this book, go to your local brew pub, and take a sip of a good German beer. Your taste buds will tell you more about German beer than we possibly can. Here are a few terms and phrases that might help you in a German *Kneipe* (*knay-puh*, f.), or pub:

German	Pronunciation	English
ein Altbier	*ayn Alt-beeR*	a bitter ale
ein Bier vom Faß	*ayn beeR fom fAs*	a draft beer
ein dunkles Bier	*ayn doon-kluhs beeR*	a dark beer
Ein Bier, bitte.	*ayn beeR, bi-tuh*	A beer, please.
ein helles Bier	*ayn he-luhs beeR*	a light beer
ein Pils	*ayn pilts*	a bitter (light beer)

German Culture

Terms for beer and wine differ in different parts of Germany. In Southern Germany, where most of the wine is produced, *ein Schoppen* refers to a glass of wine. Thus, to order a glass of Riesling, you would say, *Einen Schoppen Riesling, bitte!* Depending where the *Kneipe* or *Biergarten* is in Germany, you might be able to sample *eine Berliner Weiße*, beer with raspberry syrup; *ein Alsterwasser*, half beer and half Sprite; *einen Radler*, the Southern Germany equivalent of beer and Sprite; or *einen Diesel*, a mixture of beer and cola.

You can use the verb *trinken* to order a beer or that special glass of wine. The following table is not quite complete. Because *trinken* is a normal strong verb (incurring no stem-vowel change in the present tense), you can go ahead and prove your mastery of present tense verb endings by applying them to the stem here so conveniently provided!

Conjugation of the Verb *trinken*

Person	Singular	English	Plural	English
First	ich trinke	I drink	wir trinken	we drink
Second	du trink**st**	you drink	ihr trink**t**	you drink
Third	er, sie, es trink**t**	he, she, it drinks	sie trink**en**	they drink
Formal	Sie trink**en**	you drink	Sie trink**en**	you drink

Worked up a thirst, have you? Picture yourself in a *Biergarten* in München. How would you ask someone what he or she wants to drink? How would you answer someone if you were asked? How would you explain to someone what the people around you are imbibing? Fill in the blanks with the correct form of *trinken*. Check your conjugations in Appendix A.

Example: Der Mann an der Theke _____ ein Bier vom Faß.

Answer: Der Mann an der Theke trinkt ein Bier vom Faß.

1. Was möchten Sie _____?

2. Ich möchte ein Bier _____.

3. Die beiden Frauen am Nachbartisch _____ Kaffee.

4. Mattias und ich _____ gern lieblichen Wein.

5. Am liebsten _____ ich Limonade.

6. Was _____ du am liebsten?

It's the Quantity That Counts

You've been invited to an outdoor buffet in the countryside. The hostess has asked you to bring cheese and meat. The hostess has invited just a few other people, so you figure a pound each of cheese and meat ought to be enough. When you go to *der Supermarkt*, however, the man behind the counter does not understand how much cheese or meat you want. In Germany, the metric system is used for measuring quantities of food. Liquids are measured in liters. Let the following table help you order the right amounts of meat and cheese so you don't have any leftovers.

Getting the Right Amount

German	Pronunciation	Amount
zwei Pfund (ein Kilo)	*tsvay pfoont (ayn kee-loh)*	2 pounds of
ein Sack eine Tüte	*ayn zAk ay-nuh tüh-tuh*	a bag of
eine Flasche	*ay-nuh flA-shuh*	a bottle of
eine Schachtel	*ay-nuh shACH-tuhl*	a box of
eine Dose	*ay-nuh doh-zuh*	a can of
ein Becher	*ayn be-HuhR*	a container of
eine Kiste	*ay-nuh kis-tuh*	a case of
ein Liter	*ayn lee-tuhR*	a liter of
ein Dutzend	*ayn doo-tsent*	a dozen
ein halbes Pfund (250 Gramm)	*ayn hAl-buhs pfoont (250 gRAm)*	a half pound of
ein Gefäß ein (Einmach) Glas	*ayn guh-fähs ayn (ayn-mACH) glAs*	a jar of
ein Packet	*ayn pA-keyt*	a package of
ein Pfund (ein halbes Kilo) (500 Gramm)	*ayn pfoont (ayn hAl-buhs kee-loh) (500 gRAm)*	a pound of
ein Stück	*ayn shtük*	a piece of
ein Viertel	*ayn feeR-tuhl*	a quarter of
eine Scheibe	*ay-nuh shay-buh*	a slice of

What if you want to try a bit of something before buying it, or if you simply want to have a taste or a bite of someone else's dessert after dinner? Here are a few expressions you may find useful.

As a Rule

You'll notice that the German measurements and weights are in the singular. That's rather economical, if you consider it. The *zwei* in front of *Pfund* already conveys the idea of more than 1 pound! Speaking of pounds, *ein Pfund* is approximately *ein halbes Kilo* (half a kilogram). Naturally, any rule of the fist (*Faustregel*) has exceptions—the feminine measurement quantities take the plural: *two Flaschen Mineralwasser.*

German	Pronunciation	English
ein bisschen	*ayn bis-Huhn*	a little bit of
etwas	*et-vAs*	some
genug	*guh-newk*	enough
mehr	*meyR*	more
viel	*feel*	a lot of
wenig	*vey-niH*	little/not much
weniger	*vey-nee-guhR*	less/fewer
zu viel	*tsew feel*	too much
zu wenig	*tsew vey-niH*	too little/not enough

A Trip to the Market

You have written a list of foods you will need for a picnic (*ein Picknick*) with a group of friends. As you approach the outdoor farmer's market where you want to do your shopping, however, you realize that your English list of ingredients will be of little use to you. As you pass by the stands, someone calls out: "Frische Âpfel!" Someone else calls out: "Zwölf Eier für nur ein Euro!" To make yourself understood, you must translate everything on your list into German and politely request the items. Check your translations in Appendix A.

Example: (a jar of pickles)

Answer: Ich möchte ein glas eingelete Gurken, bitte.

Achtung

To ask for a slice of cheese in German, you say, *Ich möchte eine Scheibe Käse* (*iH möH-tuh ay-nuh shay-buh käh-zuh*). To ask for a specific kind of cheese, however, you say (pointing at the cheese), *Ich möchte eine Scheibe von diesem Käse dort* (*iH möH-tuh ay-nuh shay-buh fon dee-zuhm käh-zuh doRt*), or, "I want a slice of that cheese there."

1. Three bottles of wine

2. A half pound of shrimp

3. One fourth of a pound of cheese

4. A bag of cherries

5. A dozen eggs

6. One kilogram of salmon

7. Three pounds of potatoes

8. A half kilogram of sausage

9. A liter of cream

10. A case of beer

Getting What You Want

Are you tired of the crowds in supermarkets? Go to one of the smaller neighborhood stores on a less frequented side street near your hotel. These are sometimes referred to as a *Tante-Emma-Laden* (literally, an "Aunt Emma Store"). Although the selection is less extensive than at a supermarket, you'll find most everything you desire. Someone there will probably be happy to help you with your shopping. Be prepared for the following questions:

> Was möchten Sie?
> *vAs möH-tuhn zee*
> What would you like?

> Was wünschen Sie?
> *vAs vün-shuhn zee*
> What can I do for you?

> Kann ich Ihnen helfen?
> *kAn iH ee-nuhn hel-fuhn?*
> May I help you?

You might begin your answer with one of the following phrases:

> Ich möchte ….
> *iH möH-tuh*
> I would like ….

> Können Sie mir … geben?
> *kö-nuhn zee meeR … gey-buhn*
> Could you give me …?

> bitte
> *bi-tuh*
> please

You might then be asked:

> Sonst noch etwas?
> *zonst noH et-vAs*
> Something else?

> Ist das alles?
> *ist dAs A-luhs*
> Is that all?

We Are Family

German and English did drift apart during the Middle English period, 1100–1500, when many Old English words—those in fashion from 450 to 1100—were supplanted primarily by French vocabulary. French food-oriented loanwords that over-shadowed the previous Germanic lexicon include *dinner, supper, taste, broil, fry, serve, beverage, sauce, salad, gravy, fruit, grape, beef, pork, mutton, salmon, sugar,* and *mustard.*

An appropriate response would be to give additional items you need or to answer:

Ja (Danke), das ist alles.
ya (dAn-kuh), dAs ist ah-luhs
Yes (thank you), that's all.

You are *auf dem Markt*. Construct a dialogue between you and a clerk. Are you prepared to state specific amounts and to respond to the clerk's questions?

The Least You Need to Know

◆ You should know the names of German foods and types of stores.

◆ *Ich möchte* followed by the desired item (and amount) will get you almost anything you want.

◆ The best German wines are white.

◆ Don't forget your "please" and "thank you" with *bitte* and *danke schön*.

Chapter 18

Restaurant Hopping

In This Chapter

- ◆ Figuring out the gastronomic possibilities
- ◆ How to order in a restaurant, bar, or café
- ◆ How to figure out exactly what you want
- ◆ Dietary preferences

You're in München and you're starving. As you take the crowded elevator down from your hotel room to the lobby, your stomach starts to growl. You've been so busy using your brilliant mind to figure out where to go and what to buy that you've neglected a humbler, but just as important, part of your body: your stomach.

Germany is a country well known for hearty, satisfying repasts. Of course, before you can even begin to satisfy your hunger by venturing into an eating venue, you must know how to order whatever you want in German (it wouldn't hurt to be able to understand the specials when the waiter recites them, either). By the end of this chapter, you will be able to order meals in German and make specific requests.

Where Can I Get Something to Eat Around Here? (*Wo kann ich denn hier etwas zu essen bekommen?*)

You'll be happy to know that when hunger strikes, many types of eating establishments are waiting to feed you. The one you choose depends on the following factors: the kind of meal you want, the kind of service you want, and the size of your budget. Are you looking for breakfast, *das Frühstück* (*dAs fRüh-shtük*); for lunch, *das Mittagessen* (*dAs mi-tahk-e-suhn*); or for dinner, *das Abendessen* (*dAs ah-buhnt-e-suhn*)? Germany has many different words for places where one can eat or drink something. Try one of these:

- ◆ *der Imbiss* (*deyR im-bis*), fast-food stand or snack counter

- ◆ *das Café* (*dAs kA-fey*), coffee house serving mainly desserts and light dishes such as open-faced sandwiches

- ◆ *das Restaurant* (*dAs Res-tou-Rohn*), general word for "restaurant"

- ◆ *das Lokal* (*dAs loh-kAl*), general word for an establishment that serves food and drinks

- ◆ *die Gaststätte* (*dee gAst-shtä-tuh*), full-service restaurant

- ◆ *der Gasthof/das Gasthaus* (*deyR gAst-hof, dAs gAst-hous*), small inn with pub or restaurant

- ◆ *die Kneipe* (*dee knay-puh*), small, simple pub or bar

- ◆ *die Studentenkneipe* (*dee shtew-den-tuhn-knay-puh*), typical place where students gather, serving drinks and simple food

- ◆ *das Wirtshaus* (*dAs veeRts-hous*), pub serving mainly alcoholic beverages and some food

German Culture
Water, water everywhere and not a drop to drink! In Germany, you won't find the obligatory glass of water on your table. A word of caution: If you ask for water in a restaurant (*ein Glas Wasser, bitte*), you will most likely get a glass of mineral water—and a bubbly one, at that. If you really want just plain tap water, ask for *Leitungswasser* (*lay-tungz-vA-suhr*).

I Could Eat a Horse (*Ich habe einen Mordshunger*)

When you do finally pick a restaurant, you'll probably have to know how to do a few things before you get there. You may have to call to find out the exact location of the restaurant. If the restaurant is a good one and it's the weekend, you'll need to make a reservation. But never forgo the opportunity to stumble across a wonderful *Lokal* by strolling around, perusing the menu posted outside, and sneaking in for a peek. You'll also get an idea of what time a restaurant serves until by finding the phrase *warme Küche bis …*—literally, "warm cuisine until …." The following list contains some phrases you may find useful when dining out:

German	Pronunciation	English
Ich möchte einen Tisch reservieren.	*iH möH-tuh ay-nuhn tish Re-zuhR-vee-Ruhn*	I would like to reserve a table.
für heute Abend	*führ hoy-tuh ah-bent*	for this evening
für morgen Abend	*führ moR-guhn ah-bent*	for tomorrow evening
für Samstag Abend	*führ zAmz-tahk ah-bent*	for Saturday night
für zwei Personen	*führ tsvay peR-zoh-nuhn*	for two people
auf der Terrasse, bitte	*ouf deyR te-RA-suh, bi-tuh*	on the terrace, please
im Biergarten	*im beeR-gAR-tuhn*	in the beergarden
am Fenster	*Am fen-stuhR*	at the window
im Raucherbereich	*im Rou-CHuhR-buh-RayH*	in the smoking section
im Nich-raucherbereich	*im niHt-Rou-HuhR-buh-RayH*	in the nonsmoking section
an der Theke	*An deyR tey-kuh*	at the bar

Remember that when you use one of these prepositional phrases in a sentence after the conjugated modal verb *möchte*, the dependent infinitive, *reservieren*, should come at the end of the sentence, as in the following examples:

Ich möchte einen Tisch für heute Abend reservieren.
iH möH-tuh ay-nuhn tish führ hoy-tuh ah-bent Re-zuhR-vee-Ruhn
I'd like to reserve a table for this evening.

Ich möchte einen Tisch für Samstag Abend für zwei Personen auf der Terasse reservieren.
iH möH-tuh ay-nuhn tish führ zAmz-tahk ah-bent führ tsvay peR-zoh-nuhn ouf deyR te-RA-suh Re-zuhR-vee-Ruhn
I'd like to reserve a table for two on the terrace for Saturday evening.

Dining Out

It's Saturday night, and you want to try the fare at one of the fanciest restaurants in Berlin. Call and make a reservation in the nonsmoking section. Be aware that smoking is more accepted and much more widely tolerated in Germany than in the United States. Hence, there may not be a nonsmoking section, or it may, in actuality, be non-existent. The person on the other end of the line may ask you this question:

> Einen Tisch für wie viele Personen?
> *ay-nuhn tish fühR vee fee-luh peR-zoh-nuhn*
> A table for how many people?

Answer this way:

> Einen Tisch für vier Personen, bitte.
> *ay-nuhn tish fühR feeR peR-zoh-nuhn, bi-tuh*
> A table for four, please.

You've arrived at the restaurant, and the hostess has seated you. Now what? Bear in mind that German restaurant service is different from American service. Your wait-person in Germany will not rush you. In fact, you may have to assert yourself to get certain things done. Not to say that you have to be pushy, but you are in control of your dining experience—you own that table until you are ready to depart. But before you depart, did you hold your utensils in the European fashion? Germans hold the knife in the right hand and the fork in the left, and don't switch them around. They also tend to keep their hands on the table at all times rather than resting a hand in their laps. Regardless of *how* you eat, the next chart provides some useful phrases *im Restaurant:*

Eating Out

German	Pronunciation	English
Wir/ich möchten/möchte bestellen.	*veer/iH möH-tuhn/ möH-tuh buh-shte-luhn*	We/I would like to order.
Bitte schön. Was darf's sein?	*bi-tuh shön, vAs dARfs zayn*	What would you like?
Was bekommen Sie?	*vas buh-ko-muhn zee*	What would you like?
Ich möchte gern …	*iH möH-tuh geRn*	I would like …
Ich nehme …	*iH ney-muh*	I'll take …
Was empfehlen Sie?	*vAs em-pfey-luhn zee*	What do you recommend?
Und zu trinken?	*oont tsew trin-kuhn*	And to drink?
Bringen Sie mir bitte …	*brin-guhn zee meer bi-tuh*	Please bring me …
Hat's geschmeckt?	*hAts guh-shmekt*	Did it taste good?

German	Pronunciation	English
Ja, es hat sehr gut geschmeckt.	*ya, es hAt zeyR gewt guh-shmekt*	Yes, it was very tasty.
Ja, sehr.	*ya, zehR*	Yes, very good.
Zahlen bitte!	*tsah-luhn bi-tuh*	Check, please.
die Speisekarte	*dee shpay-zuh-kAR-tuh*	menu
kalte Teller	*kAl-tuh te-luhR*	cold dishes
warme Telle	*wAR-muh te-luhR*	warm dishes
die Vorspeise	*dee foR-shpay-zuh*	appetizer
das Gericht	*dAs guh-riHt*	dish (of food)
das Hauptgericht	*dAs houpt-guh-RiHt*	main dish
die Beilage	*dee bay-lah-guh*	side dish
die Nachspeise *or* der Nachtisch	*dee nACH-shpay-zuh deyR nACH-tish*	dessert

As a Rule

In all but the most exclusive restaurants in German-speaking countries, if the restaurant is very crowded, it is acceptable and quite normal for people to ask to share a table. In fact, there might not be a host for seating, so simply ask an occupied table: *Ist hier noch frei?* "Is this seat taken?" If it is still available, you'll hear, *Ja, hier ist noch frei.* If it's already taken, listen for the word *besetzt* (*buh-zetst*), as in *Nein, hier ist besetzt,* telling you that the seat is taken.

Unfortunately, when your appetizer comes, you have no cutlery with which to eat. Also, you're thirsty; you need a glass of something. The terms in the following table should be of use to you when you are in a restaurant and want to identify and label everything on your table.

A Table Setting

German	Pronunciation	English
das Besteck	*dAs buh-stek*	cutlery
das Geschirr	*dAs guh-sheeR*	tableware
die Gabel	*dee gah-buhl*	fork
das Glas	*dAs glAs*	glass
der Löffel	*deyR lö-fuhl*	spoon
die Kellnerin	*dee kel-nuh-Rin*	waitress

continues

A Table Setting (continued)

German	Pronunciation	English
der Kellner	*deyR kel-nuhR*	waiter
das Messer	*dAs me-suhR*	knife
die Pfeffermühle	*dee pfe-fuhR-müh-luh*	pepper mill
der Salzstreuer	*deyR zAlts-shtRoy-uhR*	salt shaker
die Serviette	*dee zeR-vee-e-tuh*	napkin
der Suppenlöffel	*deyR zoo-puhn-lö-fuhl*	soup spoon
der Suppenteller	*deyR zoo-puhn-te-luhR*	soup dish
die Tasse	*dee tA-suh*	cup
der Teelöffel	*deyR tey-lö-fuhl*	teaspoon
der Teller	*deyR te-luhR*	dinner plate
die Tischdecke	*dee tish-de-kuh*	tablecloth
die Untertasse	*dee oon-teR-tA-suh*	saucer

Something's Missing

If something is missing from your table setting and you need to ask the waiter or bus-boy for it, the verb *fehlen (fey-luhn)* will empower you to state what is missing; *fehlen* takes the dative case. The great thing about dative verbs in general is that they allow the subject (focus) of the utterance to be on the item being discussed. For instance, your fork is missing: *Mir fehlt die Gabel* translates literally into "To me is missing the fork." But isn't this what you really mean? And doesn't this give you a chance to practice all the dative personal pronouns you learned in Chapter 16?

Try your hand at describing what's missing from the table by using the dative verb *fehlen*. Begin with the dative pronoun for the person who's missing the item.

Example: Your napkin is missing, thus, *Dir fehlt die Serviette*. Note that the form of the verb is in the third person singular because the subject of the sentence is *die Serviette*, the napkin. You will begin each statement with the dative personal pronoun which reflects who is missing something, followed by the verb that is conjugated to agree with the subject—the thing which is missing! Check your command of dative pronouns with the verb *fehlen* in Appendix A.

1. My cup is missing.

2. His spoon is missing.

3. Her knife is missing.

4. Our salt shaker is missing.

You Need What?

Suppose that the table isn't already set, and you *need* something. Remember how to express a need? In Chapter 12, you learned how to ask for extra amenities for your hotel room. Now tell your waiter what you need by using those items from the preceding table and the verb *brauchen*. Remember, the items following the verb will be in the accusative case and must be declined correctly.
Check your sentences in Appendix A.

Example: How would you say you need a plate?

Ich brauche einen Teller.

1. How would you ask for a menu?

2. How would you ask for a glass?

3. How would you ask for a napkin?

4. How would you ask for a saucer?

> **CAUTION**
>
> **Achtung** _____
>
> Do not confuse *das Menü (dAs mey-nüh)* with the printed menu, *die Speisekarte (dee shpay-zuh-kAR-tuh)*. *Das Menü* is a set combination of items from the menu at a specific price. There may be several offered each day.

Waiter, I'd Like ...

If you want a waiter and want to behave in an antiquated way, you could shout *Herr Ober (heR oh-buhR)*, and there he'd be. If you prefer to be more modern, simply signal with your hand, or say *Bedienung*, which covers both male and female servers. Your waiter tonight asks whether you want to start with something to drink. Use the phrase *ich hätte gern (iH hä-tuh geRn)* followed by whatever you would like (in the accusative case). To tell the waiter that you want mineral water, for example, you would say: *Ich hätte gern ein Mineralwasser, bitte*. The following table lists popular German dishes for a hearty appetite, *für den großen Hunger*.

Meat or Fish as a Main Course (*Fleisch oder Fisch als Hauptgericht*)

German	Pronunciation	English
das Bündnerfleisch	*dAs bünt-nuhR-flaysh*	thinly sliced, air-dried beef
das deutsche Beefsteak	*dAs doy-tshuh beef-steyk*	Salisbury steak
das Gulasch	*dAs goo-lAsh*	beef stew with spicy paprika
das Lammkotelett	*dAs lAm-kot-let*	lamb chop
das Spanferkel	*dAs shpAn-feR-kuhl*	suckling pig/pig roast
die Leber	*dee ley-buhR*	liver
das Naturschnitzel	*dAs nah-tooR-shnit-suhl*	unbreaded veal cutlet

continues

Meat or Fish as a Main Course (*Fleisch oder Fisch als Hauptgericht*)
(continued)

German	Pronunciation	English
das Schweinskotlett	*dAs shvaynz-kot-let*	pork chop
das Wienerschnitzel	*dAs vee-nuhR-shnit-suhl*	breaded veal cutlet
das Jägerschnitzel	*dAs yäh-guhR-shnit-suhl*	veal/pork cutlet with mushrooms and peppers
das Zigeunerschnitzel	*dAs tsi-goy-nuhR-shnit-suhl*	cutlet with a spicy sauce of red and green peppers
der Bauernschmaus	*deyR bou-uhRn-shmous*	smoked pork, sausages, dumpling, tomato, and sauerkraut
der Hackbraten	*deyR hAk-bRah-tuhn*	meatloaf
der Kalbsbraten	*deyR kAlps-bRah-tuhn*	roast veal
der Rinderbraten	*deyR Rin-duhR-bRah-tuhn*	roast beef
der Sauerbraten	*deyR zou-uhR-bRah-tuhn*	marinated pot roast
Hühnerbrust	*dee hüh-nuhR-broost*	chicken breast
der Huhn vom Rost	*deyR hewn fom Rost*	grilled chicken
die Ente mit Rotkohl	*dee en-tuh mit Rot-kohl*	duckling with red cabbage
der Leberkäs	*deyR ley-buhR-kähs*	a type of meatloaf in Southern Germany
Matjes nach Hausfrauenart	*mA-tyeyz nACH hous-frou-uhn-ARt*	young herring in cream with apples and onions
der Stockfisch in Rahmsauce	*deyR shtok-fish in Rahm-Zos*	salt cod in cream
die geräucherte Forelle	*dee guh-Roy-HuhR-tuh fo-Re-luh*	smoked trout

That's the Way I Like It

With certain dishes, you have a choice about how they're served or cooked. For example, if you order eggs, you'll want to let the waiter know how you like them cooked. Your waiter may ask you something like this:

> Wie wollen (möchten) Sie sie (ihn, es)?
> *vee vo-luhn (möH-tuhn) zee zee (een, es)*
> How do you want them (it)?

The adjectives and egg items in the following table provide you with possibilities.

How Would You Like It Prepared?

German	Pronunciation	English
angebräunt	*An-guh-bRoynt*	browned
blutig/halb durch	*blew-tiH/hAlp dooRCH*	rare
gut durchgebraten	*gewt dooRCH-guh-bRA-tuhn*	well-done
gedünstet	*guh-düns-tuht*	steamed
gebraten	*guh-bRA-tuhn*	roasted
gebacken	*guh-bA-kuhn*	baked
paniert	*pah-neeRt*	breaded
püriert	*püh-ReeRt*	pureed
das Omelett	*dAs om-let*	omelet
das Spiegelei	*dAs shpee-guhl-ay*	fried eggs
die Rühreier	*dee RühR-ay-uhR*	scrambled eggs
hartgekocht	*hARt-guh-koCHt*	hard-boiled
pochiert	*po-sheeRt*	poached
weichgekocht	*vayH-guh-koCHt*	soft-boiled

Is anything more frustrating in a restaurant than having your favorite food arrive at your table overcooked, undercooked, too greasy, or over easy instead of scrambled? Practice expressing what you want the way you want it. These words may come in handy when someone else is doing the cooking. Check your orders in Appendix A.

Example: Ich möchte meine Eier _____ (soft-boiled).

Answer: Ich möchte meine Eier weichgekocht.

1. Sie möchte ihr Steak _____ (well-done).

2. Hans möchte seinen Fisch _____ (breaded).

3. Wir möchten unsere Kartoffeln _____ (pureed).

4. Ich möchte mein Gemüse _____ (steamed).

5. Ich hätte gern _____ (fried eggs).

German Culture

You'll find loads of international cuisine in Germany. You can eat *griechisch* (Greek), *chinesisch* (Chinese), *indisch* (Indian), *japanisch* (Japanese), and so on. If you opt for *italienisch* (Italian), expect *eine Pizza* to be individual sized. And do not order a *Pizza mit Peperoni* unless you want a pizza with hot chili peppers. If you want something closer to the American "pepperoni pizza," order a *Pizza mit Salami*.

Spice It Up

If your tongue's idea of heaven is hot chilies and spicy salsa, German food might seem a little bland. Spice things up with seasonings. The following table provides a list of some common herbs, spices, and condiments.

Herbs, Spices, and Condiments

German	Pronunciation	English
das Basilikum	*dAs bah-zee-lee-koom*	basil
die Butter	*dee boo-tuhR*	butter
der Dill	*deyR dil*	dill
der Essig	*deyR e-siH*	vinegar
der Honig	*deyR hoh-niH*	honey
der Knoblauch	*deyR knohb-louCH*	garlic
die Konfitüre	*dee kon-fi-tüh-Ruh*	jam
die Kräuter (pl.)	*dee kroy-tuhR*	herbs
die Marmelade	*dee mAR-muh-lah-duh*	jam
die Mayonnaise	*dee mah-yoh-nay-zuh*	mayonnaise
der Meerrettich	*deyR mey-Re-tiH*	horseradish
das Öl	*dAs öhl*	oil
der Oregano	*deyR oh-Rey-gah-no*	oregano
der Pfeffer	*deyR pfe-fuhR*	pepper
das Salz	*dAs zAlts*	salt
der Senf	*deyR zenf*	mustard
der Zucker	*deyR tsoo-kuhR*	sugar

Special Diets

Do you get little red spots all over your face when you eat strawberries? Are you on a restricted diet? Be prepared to use the following phrases to express your special needs.

German	Pronunciation	English
Ich bin auf (einer) Diät.	*iH bin ouf (ay-nuhR) dee-eyt*	I am on a diet.
Ich bin Vegetarier.	*iH bin vey-gey-tah-Ree-uhR*	I'm a vegetarian.
Ich kann nichts essen, was ... enthält.	*iH kAn niHst e-suhn, vAs ... ent-hält*	I can't eat anything with ... in it.

German	Pronunciation	English
Ich kann kein (e, -en) … essen (trinken).	*iH kAn kayn (uh, -uhn) e-suhn (tRin-Kuhn)*	I can't have …
die Meeresfrüchte	*dee mey-Ruhs-fRüH-tuh*	seafood
die gesättigten Fette	*dee guh-zä-tiH-tuhn fe-tuh*	saturated fats
Ich suche nach einem Gericht mit—niedrigem Cholesteringehalt.	*iH zew-CHuh nACH ay-nuhm guh-RiHt mit nee-dRee-guhm ko-les-tey-Reen-guh-hAlt*	I'm looking for a dish (that is) low in cholesterol.
niedrigem Fettgehalt	*nee-dRee-guhm fet-guh-hAlt*	low in fat
niedrigem Natriumgehalt	*nee-dRee-guhm nA-tRee-oom-guh-hAlt*	low in sodium
keine Milchprodukte	*kay-nuh milH-pRo-duk-tuh*	nondairy
salzfrei	*zAlts-fRay*	salt-free
zuckerfrei	*tsoo-kuhR-fRay*	sugar-free

As a Rule

An important way to express negation is to use the negative article, *kein*. The declination of *kein* mirrors that of *ein*. It may be used to negate a noun that would be preceded by the indefinite article *ein* or no article. *Wir haben keine Speisekarte* means "We don't have a menu." The negative of *Ich habe Hunger*, "I am hungry," is *Ich habe keinen Hunger*, "I am not hungry."

Something Light

If you're not a big eater or you aren't very hungry, tell the server *Ich habe keinen großen Hunger*—literally, "I don't have a big hunger" or "I'm not very hungry." Or, state that you want something small: *Ich möchte eine Kleinigkeit essen.* Numerous soups, potato dishes, and salads will fit the bill. You might find the following items on a menu listed under the heading *für den kleinen Hunger* (for a small appetite).

Soups, Potatoes, and Salads (*Suppen, Kartoffeln, und Salate*)

German	Pronunciation	English
die Bauernsuppe	*dee bou-uhRn-zoo-puh*	cabbage and sausage soup
die Bohnensuppe	*dee boh-nuhn-zoo-puh*	bean soup
die Frühlingssuppe	*dee fRüh-links-zoo-puh*	spring vegetable soup
die Kraftbrühe mit Ei	*dee kRAft-bRüh-huh mit ay*	beef broth with raw egg
die Linsensuppe	*dee lin-zuhn-zoo-puh*	lentil soup

continues

Soups, Potatoes, and Salads (*Suppen, Kartoffeln, und Salate*) (continued)

German	Pronunciation	English
die Ochsenschwanzsuppe	*dee ok-suhn-shvAnts-zoo-puh*	oxtail soup
die Tomatensuppe	*dee toh-mah-tuhn-zoo-puh*	tomato soup
das Bauernfrühstück	*dAs bou-uhRn-früh-shtük*	bacon and potato omelet
die Bratkartoffeln	*dee bRAt-kAR-to-fuhln*	hash browns, roasted potatoes
Kartoffel-puffer/brei/püree	*kAR-to-fuhl poo-fuhR/bray/püh-rey*	whipped potatoes
die Ofenkartoffel	*dee oh-fuhn-kAR-to-fuhl*	baked potato
die Salzkartoffeln	*dee zAlts-kAr-to-fuhln*	salted boiled potatoes
eine kleine Portion	*ay-nuh klay-nuh poR-tseeon*	a small portion
eine große Portion	*ay-nuh gro-suh poR-tseeon*	a large portion
ein kleiner Salat	*ayn klay-nuhR zah-lAt*	a small salad
der Bauernsalat	*deyR bou-uhRn-zah-lAt*	green salad with cheese, tomatoes, onions, and olives in a vinaigrette
der Bohnensalat	*deyR boh-nuhn-zah-lAt*	pickled bean salad
ein gemischter Salat	*ayn guh-mish-tuhR zah-lAt*	a green salad with pickled vegetables
der Gurkensalat	*deyR gooR-kuhn-zah-lAt*	pickled cucumber salad
der Geflügelsalat	*deyR guh-flüh-guhl-zah-lAt*	chicken salad

And now you're done. Where's the check (*die Rechnung*)? In the server's mind and pocket, of course. Unlike in the United States, where the server places the bill on the table fairly soon after you put down your fork, the Germans let you take your time. You pay the bill when you're ready by telling your *Bedienung, Zahlen, bitte*. The server will calculate the bill at the table and expect you to pay on the spot. Separate checks are the norm.

How About Some Strudel, Sweetie?

Do you have a sweet tooth? Then your favorite part of the meal is probably the end of it. In Germany, your sweet tooth will be satisfied (your other teeth may acquire a few extra cavities, if you're not careful). Cake is normally eaten around 4:00 in the afternoon for *Kaffee* (*kA-fey*), an early afternoon coffee break. The following table lists some of the most delicious desserts.

Delectable Desserts (*leckere Nachspeisen*)

German	Pronunciation	English
der Apfelstrudel	*deyR ap-fuhl-shtrew-duhl*	apple strudel
der Kuchen	*deyR kew-CHuhn*	coffee-cake type of cake, often including fruit or poppyseeds
der Obstsalat	*deyR opst-zah-laht*	fruit salad
der Pfirsich Melba	*deyR pfeeR-ziH mel-bah*	peach Melba
der Schokoladenpudding	*deyR shoh-koh-lah-duhn-poo-ding*	chocolate pudding
die Pfannkuchen (pl.)	*dee pfAn-kew-CHuhn*	crepes (pl.)
die Rote Grütze	*dee Roh-tuh gRü-tsuh*	berry compote
die Sachertorte	*dee zA-CHuhR-toR-tuh*	chocolate cake
die Schwarzwälder Kirschtorte	*dee shvARts-väl-duhR keeRsh-toR-tuh*	Black Forest cake
die Torte	*dee toR-tuh*	layered cake or fruit tart

If you're an ice cream lover, of course, you'll want to go to an ice cream vendor—just look for anything containing the word *Eis.* You'll find ice cream parlors where you can sit and relax for a long while at cute little tables. Or, if you prefer eating on the run, find an ice cream vendor who sells ice cream by the very small scoop—*eine Kugel.* You'll want to try at least three varieties! The following terms will help you get the amount and flavor you want.

German	Pronunciation	English
das Eis	*dAs ays*	ice cream
das Erdbeereis	*dAs eRt-beyR-ays*	strawberry ice cream
das Haselnußeis	*dAs hah-zuhl-noos-ays*	hazelnut ice cream
das Schokoladeneis	*dAs shoh-koh-lah-den-ays*	chocolate ice cream
das Vanilleeis	*dAs vah-ni-lee-uh-ays*	vanilla ice cream
das Pistazieneis	*dAs pi-stah-tsee-uhn-ays*	pistachio ice cream
der Eisbecher	*deyR ays-be-HuhR*	dish of ice cream
mit Schlagsahne	*mit shlAk-zah-nuh*	with whipped cream
mit Schokoladensoße	*mit shoh-koh-lah-den-zoh-suh*	with chocolate sauce
in einer Waffel	*in ay-nuhR vA-fuh*	in a waffle cone

Are You Thirsty? (*Hast du Durst?*)

If you're not a wine or beer drinker, you may want to know how to order certain non-alcoholic beverages with your dinner. The following table provides a list of drinks you might enjoy at any time before, during, or after dinner or at the *Eiscafé* in the late afternoon.

Beverages (*Getränke*)

German	Pronunciation	English
der Kaffee	*deyR kA-fey*	coffee
einen Kaffee mit Milch	*ay-nuhn kA-fey mit milH*	a coffee with milk
einen Kaffee mit Zucker	*ay-nuhn kA-fey mit tsoo-kuhR*	a coffee with sugar
einen schwarzen Kaffee	*ay-nuhn shvAr-tsuhn kA-fey*	a black coffee
einen entkoffinierten Kaffee	*ay-nuhn ent-ko-fi-neeR-tuhn kA-fey*	a decaffeinated coffee
einen Eiskaffee	*ay-nuhn ays-kA-fey*	an iced coffee
der Capuccino	*deyR ka-poo-chee-no*	cappuccino, often served with whipped cream
mit Schlagsahne	*mit shlAk-zah-nuh*	with whipped cream
eine Cola	*ay-nuh ko-lA*	a coke
eine Cola Light	*ay-nuh ko-lA layt*	a diet coke
der Tee	*deyR tey*	tea
einen Tee mit Zitrone	*ay-nuhn tey mit tsee-tRoh-nuh*	a tea with lemon
das Mineralwasser	*dAs mi-nuh-Rahl-vA-suhR*	mineral water

Good Morning, Say Cheese

In Germany, cheese often accompanies *Wurst* as a part of a fortifying breakfast. Yogurt, coffee, tea, juice, fresh rolls, cereal, butter, jam, honey, fresh fruit, and other yummy things help round out the typical German breakfast. Here are some expressions that will help you determine the cheese that is most to your liking.

German	Pronunciation	English
der Käse	*deyR käh-zuh*	cheese
mild	*milt*	mild
scharf	*shARf*	sharp

German	Pronunciation	English
hart	*hARt*	hard
weich	*vayH*	soft
würzig	*vüR-tsiH*	spicy

As for the rest of breakfast, most places where you might stay overnight offer a buffet-style breakfast. You merely choose between *Kaffee oder Tee* and select whatever else you desire. You danced till dawn, and now you are hungry. You think, *Ich habe Hunger!* Go over to that *Frühstücksbuffet* and describe what you would like to eat, remembering to place whatever it is that you are desiring in the accusative case.

Ich möchte ….

Ich nehme ….

Ich hätte gern ….

We Are Family

German word-building strategy (derivational morphology) is rather similar to that of English, so knowledge of one part of a German word often allows you to guess the meaning of the entire word. Old English (OE) suffixes were directly related to those in older Germanic dialects: the OE *-nes*, recognized in Modern English as *-ness*, as in *smallness* or *happiness*, is comparable to the Germanic *-keit*, observable in *Kleinigkeit* or *Fröhlichkeit*.

It Was Delicious

Don't keep your satisfaction to yourself when you like what you've eaten. To express joy, pleasure, amazement, and wonder when a meal has been exceptional, use the following superlative phrases.

Das Essen war ausgezeichnet!
dAs e-suhn vahR ous-guh-tsayH-nuht
The meal was great!

Das Steak war vorzüglich!
dAs steyk vahR foR-tsühk-liH
The steak was excellent!

German Culture

In most German restaurants, *das Trinkgeld* (*tRink-gelt*)—the tip—is included in the price of the meal (generally 15 percent). Still, it is common practice to round up the bill. If your bill is 10,50€, for example, you might give the waiter 11€ or 12€ and say, (*Es*) *stimmt so*, the equivalent of "Keep the change."

Die Bedienung ist großartig!
dee buh-dee-nung ist gRohs-AR-tiH
The service is great!

This chapter ends with the very last thing you need to know in a restaurant: how to ask for your bill. Remember, *Zahlen, bitte!* Well, there's another way of expressing yourself. Take your pick!

Die Rechnung bitte.
dee ReH-noong bi-tuh
The check, please.

The Least You Need to Know

♦ You can find someplace to eat by asking, *Wo kann ich denn hier etwas zu essen bekommen?*

♦ In Germany, the customer controls the pace of service in a restaurant.

♦ You can read a German menu with very little difficulty and satiate a large or a small appetite.

♦ You can express dietary preferences and pleasures.

Chapter 19

What Do *You* Feel Like Doing?

In This Chapter

◆ Having fun in Germany

◆ Extending, accepting, and refusing invitations

◆ Using adverbs to describe abilities

You've visited tourist attractions, you've strolled through quiet parks, and you've bought souvenirs for your friends back home. The meals you've eaten have been delicious. Now that both your appetite and your curiosity have been satisfied, you want to have a little fun.

It's up to you. Do you feel like going to the movies, playing some tennis, shooting a little pool, or hearing some live jazz? Perhaps you want to dress up, find a casino, and try your luck at fortune's wheel. After reading this chapter, you'll be ready to try almost anything, to brag about your talents and skills, and to invite someone to join you for a drink, a stroll, or a night on the town.

Are You a Sports Fan?

Whatever your sport, you will probably be able to participate in it while in Germany (if your favorite sports are spectator sports, you're in luck—soccer is the national favorite). In the following sections, you will learn the terms for many sports, where these sports are played, and how to tell someone which games you enjoy.

What's Your Game?

Even those who claim to detest spectator sports have a game they play or used to play that is close to their hearts. No doubt you can find at least one game you enjoy playing out of those listed in the following table.

Sports (*Sportarten*)

German	Pronunciation	English
Sport treiben	*shpoRt tRay-buhn*	to play sports
Billiard spielen	*bee-lee-ahRt shpee-luhn*	to play billiards
Tennis spielen	*te-nis shpee-luhn*	to play tennis
Tischtennis spielen	*tish-te-nis shpee-luhn*	to play table-tennis
Federball spielen	*feh-duhR-bAl shpee-luhn*	to play badminton
Basketball spielen	*bAs-ket-bAl shpee-luhn*	to play basketball
Schach spielen	*shACH shpee-luhn*	to play chess
berg.steigen	*beRk-shtay-guhn*	to climb mountains
spazieren gehen	*spA-tsee-Ruhngey-uhn*	to go for a walk
Rad fahren	*Rat fah-Ruhn*	to bicycle
angeln	*An-geln*	to fish
Handball spielen	*hant-bAl shpee-luhn*	to play team handball
wandern	*vAn-duhRn*	to hike
reiten	*Ray-tuhn*	to ride horseback
Ski fahren	*skee fah-Ruhn*	to ski
Wasserski laufen	*vA-suhR-skee lou-fuhn*	to water-ski
Schlittschuh laufen	*shlit-shew lou-fuhn*	to go ice skating
segeln	*zey-guhln*	to sail
schwimmen	*shvi-muhn*	to swim
Aerobic machen	*eh-Roh-bik mA-CHuhn*	to do aerobics
Bodybuilding machen	*bo-dee bil-ding mA-CHuhn*	to do weight training

Welchen Sport treibst du gern? What sport do *you* like to play? To say that you enjoy a sport, use this construction:

   Ich + conjugated verb + *gern*

Ich schwimme gern.
iH shvi-muh geRn
I like to swim.

For sports that are made up of a noun and a verb (*Rad fahren, Wasserski laufen*), use the following construction:

Ich + conjugated verb + *gern* + noun

Ich laufe gern Wasserski.
iH lou-fuh geRn vA-suhR-skee
I like to water-ski.

As a Rule

Saying how often you do something involves the accusative case with a time expression. If you go for a walk every day, the "every day" will be declined in the accusative: *Ich gehe jeden Tag spazieren.* If you like to walk the entire day, you would say, *Ich gehe den ganzen Tag spazieren.*

Where to Play

Have you ever tried to play a game of basketball on a soccer field? Or a game of tennis in a boxing ring? Can you imagine water-skiing in a swimming pool? If you're stranded in a German-speaking country and are determined to play your game, you can probably figure out a way to play it anywhere—or you can make life easy on yourself and memorize the expressions in the following table.

Where to Go for Sports

German	Pronunciation	English
das Eisstadion	*dAs ays-shtah-deeon*	ice-skating rink
der Fußballplatz	*deyR fews-bAl-plAts*	soccer field
der Sportplatz	*deyR shpoRt-plAts*	playing field
der Basketballplatz	*deyR bAs-ket-bAl-plAts*	basketball court
das Gebirge	*dAs guh-beeR-guh*	mountain
das Sportstadion	*dAs shpoRt-shtah-dee-on*	sports stadium
das Swimmbad	*dAs shvim-baht*	swimming pool
das Hallenbad	*dAs hA-luhn-baht*	indoor swimming pool
das Freibad	*dAs fray-baht*	outdoor swimming pool
der Tennisplatz	*deyR te-nis-plAts*	tennis court
der Boxring	*deyR box-Ring*	boxing arena
die Skipiste	*dee skee-pis-tuh*	ski slope

continues

Where to Go for Sports   (continued)

German	Pronunciation	English
die Sporthalle	*dee shpoRt-hA-luh*	gymnasium
die Autorennbahn	*dee ou-toh-Ren-bahn*	car-racing track
der See	*deyR zey*	lake
der Fluss	*deyR floos*	river
die Wiese	*dee vee-zuh*	meadow

Now put what you've learned to use by filling in the blanks with the appropriate vocabulary. Notice that if you're talking about *where* you can engage in these sports, the construction involves a two-way preposition—those that take either the accusative case indicating motion or the dative case indicating position. When discussing *where* something occurs, you use the dative case. But if you're going there, the construction is accusative. Here we've provided the appropriate prepositions and articles for you. Check your responses in Appendix A.

Example: Tennis spiele ich auf dem _____.

Answer: Tennis spiele ich auf dem Tennisplatz.

1. Ich wandere am liebsten im _____.

2. Fußball spielen wir auf dem _____.

3. Zum Skifahren gehe ich auf die _____.

4. Anna schwimmt gern im _____.

5. Wir segeln gern auf dem _____.

6. Schlittschuh lauft ihr im _____.

Express Your Desire with *Mögen*

In Chapter 15, you learned to use modals in the present tense to express your attitude. To tell someone that you would like to do something, use the verb *mögen* (*möh-guhn*) "to like" in the *subjunctive* mood—that is, make it sound a little politer and more inviting: *ich möchte* (*iH möH-tuh*), or "I would like." Of course, you end the sentence with a dependent infinitive; otherwise, no one will know what you would like to do. You'll notice that the first and third person singular have the same ending, which is consistent with what you already know about modals. Naturally, the plural forms are as you would expect. *Mögen* is conjugated in the following table.

German Culture
Although Germans are tennis *fans*, they are soccer *fanatics*. No single U.S. game can compete with it in popularity. Few Germans are immune to the excitement of the matches played among the country's 18 best first-division teams, *Fußball-Budesliga*. But when they're not watching *Fußball*, Germans can be found engaging in leisure activities at sport clubs, *Sportvereine*, where healthful exercise is balanced with social interaction.

The Verb *Mögen* in the Subjunctive ("Would Like To")

Person	Singular	English	Plural	English
First	ich möchte *iH möH-tuh*	I would like	wir möchten *veeR möH-tuhn*	we would like
Second	du möchtest *dew möH-test*	you would like	ihr möchtet *eeR möH-thut*	you would like
Third	er, sie, es möchte *eR, zee, es möH-tuh*	he, she, it would like	sie möchten *zee möH-tuhn*	they would like
Formal	Sie möchten *zee möH-tuhn*	you would like	Sie möchten *zee möH-tuhn*	you would like

Now fill in the blanks with the appropriate form of *möchten*. Check your verb conjugations in Appendix A.

Example: Ich _____ Fußball spielen.

Answer: Ich möchte Fußball spielen.

1. Anne _____ bergsteigen.

2. Wir _____ wandern.

3. Franz und Klara _____ reiten.

4. Ihr _____ in der Sporthalle Federball spielen.

5. Hans und Franz _____ am Fluss angeln.

What's What

Subjunctive   A type of mood, grammatically speaking, that marks speakers' attitudes toward the truth of their assertions or obligation, permission, or suggestion. The verb form in the subjunctive mood indicates that something is relatively unlikely or contrary to fact, which is where we leave off with *möchten* because expressing politeness is often something extraordinary and unreal!

Extending an Invitation

If you are traveling alone, or if your traveling companion starts to snore in his or her chair after lunch, you may need to find someone with whom to play your favorite sport.

Use the verb *mögen* in the subjunctive (*möchten*), followed by the subject and whatever verb you choose, as illustrated in the following construction:

Möchten Sie or *möchtest du* + (sport) verb

Möchten Sie Bergsteigen gehen?
möH-tuhn zee beRk-shtay-guhn
Would you like to go mountain climbing?

Möchtest du Tennis spielen?
möH-test dew te-nis shpee-luhn
Would you like to play tennis?

Accepting an Invitation

Not only is accepting an invitation a way of showing the natives that you're friendly, but you'll probably end up having a great time if you do! Whether it's a romantic dinner, a doubles tennis match, or simply a walk in the park, the following phrases will help you gracefully accept any invitation.

German	Pronunciation	English
Selbstverständlich	*zelpst-feR-shtänt-liH*	Of course
Natürlich	*nah-tüR-liH*	Naturally
Warum nicht?	*vah-Room niHt*	Why not?
Ja, das ist eine gute Idee.	*yah, dAs ist ay-nuh gew-tuh ee-dey*	Yes, that's a good idea.
Wenn du (Sie) willst (wollen)	*ven dew (zee) vilst (vo-luhn)*	If you like
Fantastisch	*fAn-tAs-tish*	Fantastic

Refusing an Invitation

Of course, if you always say yes to invitations, you probably won't have any time left for yourself. In fact, if you love traveling, chances are good that you also enjoy spending time alone in museums, cathedrals, cafés, airports, and sleeping compartments on trains. It may be just as important for you to learn how to gracefully refuse an invitation as it is for you to learn how to gracefully accept one. Sooner or later, you'll probably find the following phrases useful.

German	Pronunciation	English
Das ist unmöglich.	*dAs ist oon-mök-liH*	That's impossible.
Nein, ich habe keine Lust.	*nayn, iH hah-buh kay-nuh loost*	No, I don't feel like it.
Nein, ich habe keine Zeit.	*nayn, iH hah-buh kay-nuh tsayt*	No, I have no time.
Es tut mir leid.	*es toot meeR layt*	I'm sorry.
Ich bin müde.	*iH bin müh-duh*	I'm tired.
Ich bin beschäftigt.	*iH bin buh-shäf-tiHt*	I'm busy.

Showing Indecision and Indifference

Your best buddy asks you to go ice skating. You haven't been ice skating since you were nine, and you figure you'll look like a jerk trying, but you're a good sport. So you shrug and let him know it's all the same to you. Try a few of these useful phrases to show your indifference.

German	Pronunciation	English
Das ist mir egal.	*dAs ist meeR ey-gahl*	It makes no difference to me.
Was du willst.	*vAs dew vilst*	Whatever you'd like.
Ich weiß nicht.	*iH vays niHt*	I don't know.
Vielleicht	*fee-layHt*	Maybe
Mal sehen.	*mahl zeh-uhn*	We'll see.

Do You Accept or Refuse?

If you know how to tell someone which sports you like, chances are good that you'll be asked to play sooner or later. Practice what you've learned in this chapter to accept and refuse invitations. Give the German for the following sentences. Questions and possible responses appear in Appendix A.

Example: Would you like to play tennis? No, I don't feel like it.

Answer: Möchten Sie Tennis spielen? Nein, ich habe keine Lust.

1. Would you like to play basketball? Yes, that's a good idea.

2. Would you like to hike? No, I'm tired.

3. Would you like to play soccer? Why not?

4. Would you like to fish? No, I don't have the time.

5. Would you like to play badminton? No, I'm tired.

6. Would you like to ride bikes? Naturally.

Let's Do Something Else

There are many reliable ways of having a good time, and new ways are being invented every day. If sports aren't your thing, you may want to suggest some other kind of activity. To tell someone that you would like to go to the opera, you might say this:

Ich möchte in die Oper gehen.
iH möH-tuh in dee oh-puhR gey-uhn
I would like to go to the opera.

If you'd like to go to the movies, you could say this:

Ich möchte ins Kino gehen.
iH möH-tuh ins kee-noh gey-uhn
I'd like to go to the movies.

Use the phrases in the following table to make creative suggestions.

Places to Go and Things to Do

Place	English	Activity	English
in die Oper gehen *in dee oh-puhR gey-uhn*	to go to the opera	die Musik hören *dee mew-zeek höh-Ruhn*	to listen to music
zum Strand gehen *tsewm stRAnt gey-uhn*	to go to the beach	schwimmen, sich sonnen *shvi-muhn, siH zo-nuhn*	to swim, to lie in the sun
in die Disko gehen *in dee dis-ko gey-uhn*	to go to the discotheque	tanzen *tAn-tsuhn*	to dance
ins Ballett gehen *ins bA-let gey-uhn*	to go to the ballet	die Tänzer anschauen *dee tän-tsuhR An-shou-uhn*	to watch
ins Kasino gehen *ins kah-zee-noh gey-uhn*	to go to the casino	spielen *shpee-luhn*	to play
ins Kino gehen *ins kee-noh gey-uhn*	to go to the movies	einen Film sehen *ay-nuhn film zey-uhn*	to see a movie
ins Theater gehen *ins tey-ah-tuhR gey-uhn*	to go to the theater	ein Theaterstück sehen *ayn tey-ah-tuhR-shtük zey-uhn*	to see a play

Place	English	Activity	English
ins Konzert gehen *ins kon-tseRt gey-uhn*	to go to a concert	ein Orchester hören *ayn oR-kes-tuhR höh-Ruhn*	to hear a concert
zu Hause bleiben *tsew hou-zuh blay-buhn*	to stay at home	meditieren *me-dee-tee-Ruhn*	to meditate
		faulenzen *fou-len-tsuhn*	to lie around

Entertaining Options

Sometimes, after the shops and the restaurants, the sightseeing and the sweating, there's nothing better than sitting in front of the television and chilling out. You could cozy up with the *Fernsehzeitung (feRn-zey-tsay-toong,* the German *TV Guide)* and settle in for a pleasant evening. Alternatively, you might go to the local movie theater (if it's not too far away). In the following sections, you will learn some important entertainment vocabulary.

At the Movies and on TV

Go ahead and switch on the set. One great thing about German television is that the commercials are all lumped together at the end of a program or halfway through. And television advertisements are a great way to test your knowledge of German because they use relatively simple language, speak in the present tense, and rely on visuals. If you flip through the *Ferhnsehzeitung,* you'll discover that movie listings contain not only a synopsis of the plot, but also a category or genre. The different kinds of movies and shows are listed for you in the following table. But some useful phrases to pose to your companion follow:

Was gibt es im Fernsehen?
vAs gipt es im feRn-zey-uhn
What's on TV?

Welche Art von Film gibt es?
vel-Huh Art fon film geept es
What kind of film is it?

Television Programs and Movies (*Fernsehprogramme und Filme*)

German	Pronunciation	English
der Abenteuerfilm	*deyR ah-ben-toy-uhR-film*	adventure film
die Komödie	*dee koh-möh-dee-uh*	comedy
der Dokumentarfilm	*deyR doh-kew-men-tAR-film*	documentary
das Drama	*dAs dRah-mah*	drama
der Horrorfilm	*deyR ho-Ror-film*	horror movie
der Krimi	*deyR kRee-mee*	thriller
die Liebesgeschichte	*dee lee-buhs-guh-shiH-tuh*	love story
die Nachrichten	*dee nACH-RiH-tuhn*	news
die Seifenoper	*dee zay-fuhn-oh-puhR*	soap opera
die Serie	*dee zeyR-eeyuh*	series
der Spielfilm	*deyR shpeel-film*	feature film
der Wetterbericht	*deyR ve-tuhR-buh-RiHt*	weather
der Trickfilm	*deyR tRik-film*	cartoon

At a Concert

If you go to a concert in Germany, you'll certainly want to tell your friends about it. In Germany, as in America, when referring to the cellist or to the pianist, you can simply refer to the instrument: "The cello was exceptional," or *Das Cello war außergewöhnlich* (*dAs che-loh vAR ou-suhR-guh-vöhn-liH*). The following table lists the most common musical instruments.

Musical Instruments (*Musikinstrumente*)

German	Pronunciation	English
das Akkordeon	*dAs A-koR-de-ohn*	accordion
das Cello	*dAs che-loh*	cello
die Flöte	*dee flöh-tuh*	flute
die Geige	*dee gay-guh*	violin
die Gitarre	*dee gee-tA-Ruh*	guitar
die Harfe	*dee hAR-fuh*	harp
das Horn	*dAs hoRn*	horn
die Klarinette	*dee klah-Ree-ne-tuh*	clarinet
das Klavier	*dAs klA-veeR*	piano

German	Pronunciation	English
die Oboe	*dee oh-boh-uh*	oboe
die Pauke	*dee pou-kuh*	bass drum
die Posaune	*dee po-zou-nuh*	trombone
das Saxophon	*dAs zak-soh-fohn*	saxophone
das Schlagzeug	*dAs shlAk-tsoyk*	drums
die Trommel	*dee tRo-muhl*	drum
die Trompete	*dee tRom-pey-tuh*	trumpet

Expressing Your Enjoyment or Disappointment

When you enjoy a film or a concert, you can express your enjoyment by using the following phrases. When referring to a movie (*der Film*), use the masculine pronoun *er*. Likewise, use the neuter *es* when referring to a *Konzert* (*das*):

German	Pronunciation	English
Ich liebe den Film/ das Konzert!	*iH lee-buh deyn film/ dAs kon-tseRt*	I love the film/ the concert!
Es ist ein guter Film/ein gutes Konzert.	*es ist ayn gew-tuhR film/ayn gew-tuhs kon-tseRt*	It is a good film/a good concert.
Er/es ist orginell.	*eR/es ist o-Ri-gee-nel*	It is original.
Er/es ist interessant.	*eR/es ist in-tey-Re-sAnt*	It is interesting.
Es ist amüsant.	*es ist ah-müh-zAnt*	It is amusing.
Es ist spannend.	*es ist shpA-nuhnt*	It is suspenseful.
Es ist bewegend.	*es ist buh-vey-guhnt*	It is moving.

If you found the film or show disappointing, use any of these phrases to show your disapproval:

German	Pronunciation	English
Ich hasse den Film/das Konzert.	*iH hA-suh deyn film/dAs kon-tseRt*	I hate the film/the concert.
Er/es ist schlecht.	*eR/es ist shleHt*	It is bad.
Er/es ist absoluter Schrott.	*eR/es ist ap-soh-lew-tuhR shRot*	It is total garbage.
Es ist immer wieder das gleiche.	*es ist i-muhR vee-duhr dAs glay-Huh duhR*	It is always the same thing.

Adverbs: Modifying Verbs

Adverbs are used to modify verbs or adjectives. You can use adverbs to describe how well, how badly, or in what way something is done, as in "He plays the piano wonderfully" or "I swim amazingly well." English adverbs are formed by adding the ending *-ly* to adjectives, resulting in words like *happily, quickly, slowly, moderately,* and so on.

We Are Family

In Old English (450–111 C.E.), the most productive category of adverbs was that of qualitative adverbs formed from adjectives simply by adding *-e* or *-lic* to the adjective stem. Although the Old English *-lic* (now *-ly*) was originally an adjective suffix (as in *homely* or *friendly*), it has since become the standard way of forming an adverb. The Old High German (500–1050) adjectival equivalent, *–lich,* is still evident in adjectives (such as *freundlich* and *sportlich*) and adverbs such as *endlich.*

In German, almost all adjectives can be used as adverbs. In addition, many words are adverbs only. They express location relevant to the speaker, such as *dort* (*doRt*), or "there," and *hier* (*heeR*), or "here." The only adverbs with endings are words that express a higher degree—that is, adverbs that appear in the comparative and superlative forms. To form the comparative of adverbs, add *-er* to the adverb: *Der Abenteuerfilm ist spannender als* (more suspenseful than) *der Dokumentafilm.* To compare two things, simply insert *als* between the items to be compared. To form the superlative, add *am* before the superlative and *-sten* to the adverb: *Der Abenteuerfilm ist am spannendsten* (the most suspenseful). Naturally, something that is best/worst/most does not need a comparison: *Kalte Suppe ist am schlechtesten* (the worst)!

What's What

Adverbs Words used to modify verbs or adjectives.

The best way to understand the difference between adverbs and adjectives is to know that adjectives modify nouns (and, therefore, take an ending if they precede a noun), whereas adverbs modify verbs, in the sense of specifying the time, manner, or place. Compare the use of *gut* and *laut* as adjectives and adverbs in the following sentences.

Boris Becker ist ein guter Tennisspieler. (adj.)
bo-Ris be-keR ist ayn gew-tuhR te-nis-shpee-luhR
Boris Becker is a good tennis player.

Ich kann auch gut spielen. (adv.)
iH kAn ouH gewt shpee-luhn
I can also play well.

In der Disko hört man nur laute Musik. (adj.)
in deyR dis-koh höRt mAn newR lou-tuh mew-zeek
In the disco, you hear only loud music.

Das Orchester spielt das Stück viel zu laut. (adv.)
dAs oR-kes-tuhR shpeelt dAs shtük feel tsew lout
The orchestra plays the piece far too loudly.

As a Rule

The word *adverb* implies its principal function, which is to be added to, or to modify, a verb. But don't let the name fool you. Adverbs can also modify adjectives, as they do in the following sentences:

Das Frühstück war sehr gut.
dAs fRüH-shtük vAR zeyR gewt
The breakfast was very good.

Seine Geschichte war höchst langweilig.
zay-nuh guh-shiH-tuh vAR höHst lAng-vay-liH
His story was very boring.

Exclusively Adverbs

Although most adjectives can be used as adverbs, many words can be used only as adverbs. The following table lists common adverbs that do not double as adjectives.

Plain Old Adverbs

German	Pronunciation	English
anschließend	*An-shlee-suhnt*	then, afterward
bald	*bAlt*	soon
da	*dA*	there
danach	*dA-nACH*	then/after that
dort	*doRt*	there
endlich	*ent-liH*	at last
früh	*fRüh*	early
ganz	*gAnts*	quite, entirely
gelegentlich	*guh-ley-guhnt-liH*	occasionally
gestern	*ges-tuhRn*	yesterday
heute	*hoy-tuh*	today

continues

Plain Old Adverbs   (continued)

German	Pronunciation	English
hier	*heeR*	here
immer	*i-muhR*	always
jetzt	*yetst*	now
manchmal	*mAnH-mahl*	sometimes
nie	*nee*	never
noch	*noCH*	still
nur	*nuR*	only
oft	*oft*	often
plötzlich	*plöts-liH*	suddenly
sehr	*zeyR*	very
sofort	*zoh-foRt*	immediately
spät	*shpäht*	late
zusammen	*tsew-zA-muhn*	together

Here are some sample sentences that use these adverbs:

> Heute spielen wir Fußball.
> *hoy-tuh shpee-luhn veeR fews-bAl*
> Today we play soccer.

> Ich möchte sofort ins Schwimbad gehen.
> *iH möH-tuh zo-foRt ins shvim-bAt gey-uhn*
> I'd like to go into the swimming pool immediately.

Position of Adverbs

Brace yourself: You're not finished with adverbs yet. Adverbs can be divided into categories. The most common categories of adverbs are time, manner, and place. *Heute* in *Sie geht heute ins Kino (zee geyt hoy-tuh ins kee-noh)*, or "Today she goes to the movies," uses an adverb of time; *langsam* in the sentence *Er läuft langsam (eR loyft lang-zahm)*, or "He runs slowly," is an adverb of manner; and *hier* in *Hier fühle ich mich wie zu Hause (heeR füh-luh iH miH vee tsew hou-zuh)*, or "I feel at home here," is an adverb of place.

So what happens when you stack adverbs in one sentence? How do you know which adverb to put where? In English, it's a matter of topicalization—whatever you want to stress occurs first. But in German, there are rules. And these rules are easily learned.

Simply remember this clue: TeMPo. Adverbs of *time* come first. Adverbs of *manner* come next. Then come adverbs of *place*. Or, if you prefer, use the German acronym *ZAP: Zeit, Art, Platz.* Note that the English word order does not correspond to this.

> Er fährt heute mit dem Fahrrad dort(hin). (time, manner, place)
> *eR fähRt hoy-tuh mit deym fah-RAt doRt-(hin)*
> He drives (to) there today on his bicycle.

If two adverbs of the same type occur in a sentence, the more general adverb precedes the more specific adverb. After all, isn't it more logical to know the broad span of time before narrowing it down?

> Er fährt morgen um 8 Uhr dorthin. (general time, specific time)
> *eR fähRt moR-guhn oom ACHt ewR*
> He is driving at 8:00 tomorrow morning.

Achtung

The adverb of time *morgen* means "tomorrow." *Der Morgen,* however, means "the morning." To say "tomorrow morning," use *morgen früh*, not *morgen Morgen*. For example, you would say, *Wir gehen morgen früh nach Hause* ("We're going home tomorrow morning").

How Well Do You Do Things?

Now you're ready to use adverbs to describe your stunning abilities. The following table contains some common adverbs (all of which, incidentally, can be used as adjectives) that you can use to tell someone how well (or poorly) you can do something.

Common Adverbs for Describing Abilities

German	Pronunciation	English
schnell	*shnel*	fast
langsam	*lAng-zahm*	slow
gut	*gewt*	good
schlecht	*shleHt*	bad
ausgezeichnet	*ous-guh-tsayH-nuht*	excellent
schrecklich	*shRek-liH*	terribly
grauenhaft	*gRou-uhn-hAft*	horribly
wunderbar	*voon-duhR-bAR*	wonderfully

Adverbs in Action

Are you a good golfer? How well do you sing? Can you run for miles, or are you a good sprinter? How well do you dance? Use adverbs to tell how well you perform the following activities. Remember to conjugate the verb to agree with *ich*. Check your accuracy in Appendix A.

As a Rule _____

Nicht is the German negative particle. It follows the inflected verb (*Mein Bruder raucht nicht*), pronouns, and most noun objects (*Du kennst meinen Bruder [ihn] nicht*). *Nicht* precedes most other elements, such as adjectives, adverbs, and prepositional phrases: *Ich bin nicht nervös. Ich fahre nicht gern. Dieses Bier ist nicht für mich.*

Example: (Deutsch sprechen) Ich spreche Deutsch langsam.

1. tanzen

2. Klavier spielen

3. kochen

4. Golf spielen

5. laufen

6. singen

7. Tennis spielen

8. wandern

The Least You Need to Know

◆ *Sport treiben* is the expression for playing sports, but the verb *spielen* is used to express participation in a specific sport: *Ich treibe viel Sport. Jeden Tag spiele ich Tennis.*

◆ If you like to do something, use the adverb *gern* + a noun or a verb.

◆ The verb *möchten* can be used to politely extend, accept, and refuse invitations.

◆ Adverbs are words that modify both verbs and adjectives. Most German adverbs can also function as adjectives.

Part 5

Angst: Solving Problems on the Go

All the fun and games you've been enjoying have left you frazzled and worn out. Part 5 introduces many useful terms you'll need to confront and remedy some problems concerning repair of your beauty, health, clothing, and other possessions. Better yet, you'll also learn how to ask for the kind of haircut you want and to express various kinds of aches and pains (along with their locations on your body).

Chapter **20**

Dealing with Disaster

In This Chapter

◆ Personal services

◆ Problems and solutions

◆ Comparing and contrasting

You've been eating, buying things, watching TV—to put it mildly, having a good old time. And then, all of a sudden, the problems start. You've stained your favorite silk shirt, you have an ingrown toenail, and your shoes have worn down so much that you can actually feel the city streets through the soles when you walk! And that's not all. Yesterday you sat on your glasses and broke one of the lenses, you ripped the hem of your jacket on a door handle, and you lost your address book. Don't worry. Everything you need to repair yourself is just a few blocks—or perhaps even just a phone call—away. By the end of this chapter, all your problems will be under control.

My Hair Needs Help, Now!

Is your perm coming out? Are your roots showing? Maybe you just want to return to your native land with a new do. Whatever your reasons for wanting to venture into a hair salon, you will need to have the basic vocabulary to get your hair styled just so.

Beautify Yourself

In Germany, *der Friseursalon* (*deyR fRee-zühR-zah-lon*), or hairdresser, is generally for both men and women. When a woman goes to get her hair done, she says, *Ich gehe zum Friseur* (*iH gey-uh tsewm fRee-zühR*). If you want special services such as pedicures, manicures, or facials, you go to a beauty salon: *Ich gehe zum Kosmetiksalon* (*iH gey-uh tsewm kos-mey-tik-zah-lon*).

To get what you want, begin your requests to the beauty consultant with the following phrase:

> Ich hätte gern ….
> *iH hä-tuh geRn*
> I would like ….

Most salons provide the services listed in the following table.

Hair Care

German	Pronunciation	English
eine Tönung (f.)	*ay-nuh töh-noong*	a tint
ein Haarschnitt (m.)	*ayn hahR-shnit*	a haircut
eine Dauerwelle (f.)	*ay-nuh dou-uhR-ve-luh*	a perm
eine Färbung (f.)	*ay-nuh fäR-boong*	a coloring
eine Pediküre (f.)	*ay-nuh pey-dee-küh-Ruh*	a pedicure
eine Gesichtsmassage (f.)	*ay-nuh guh-ziHts-mA-sah-juh*	a facial
eine Haarwäsche (f.)	*ay-nuh hahR-vä-shuh*	a shampoo
eine Maniküre (f.)	*ay-nuh mA-nee-küh-Ruh*	a manicure

The article following the phrase *ich hätte gern* should be in the accusative case. To let someone know you'd like a haircut, say this:

> Ich hätte gern einen Haarschnitt.
> *iH hä-tuh geRn ay-nuhn hahR-shnit*
> I'd like a haircut.

Another way of getting services in a beauty salon is to use the subjunctive mood of the modal verb *können*. The following table contains some phrases that use *können* in the subjunctive to help you make polite requests.

Other Services

German	Pronunciation	English
Könnten Sie mir bitte den Pony zurechtschneiden?	*kön-tuhn zee meeR bi-tuh deyn po-nee tsew-ReHt-shnay-duhn*	Could you please cut my bangs?
Könnten Sie mir bitte die Haare nachschneiden?	*kön-tuhn zee meeR bi-tuh dee hah-Ruh nACH-shnay-duhn*	Could you please trim my hair?
Könnten Sie mir bitte die Haare glätten?	*kön-tuhn zee meeR bi-tuh dee hah-Ruh glä-tuhn*	Could you please straighten my hair?
Könnten Sie mir bitte die Haare fönen?	*kön-tuhn zee meeR bi-tuh dee hah-Ruh föh-nuhn*	Could you please blow-dry my hair?

As a Rule

Unlike English, which uses the possessive adjective when referring to body parts (*my* hair, *my* finger), German makes use of the handy dative case to refer to the person whose appendage something is, and the simple definite article: *Könnten Sie mir bitte die Haare fönen?* You used a similar concept when you were missing a fork back in Chapter 18: *Mir fehlt die Gabel.* Also, unlike in English, *hair* is used in German in the plural: *die Haare.*

Expressing Your Preferences

Getting a haircut in a foreign country is truly a brave thing to do because, let's face it, it's hard enough to get the kind of haircut you want when both you and your hairdresser speak the same language. The phrases in the following table might help.

Hairstyles

German	Pronunciation	English
lang	*lAng*	long
mittellang	*mi-tuhl-lAng*	medium length
kurz	*kooRts*	short
gewellt	*guh-velt*	wavy
lockig	*lo-kiH*	curly
glatt	*glAt*	straight
stufig	*shtew-fiH*	layered
geflochten	*guh-floCH-tuhn*	braided
schwarz	*shvARts*	black

continues

Hairstyles

German	Pronunciation	English
kastanienbraun	*kAs-tah-nee-uhn-bRoun*	auburn
rot	*Rot*	red
in einer dunkleren Farbe	*in ay-nuhR doonk-luh-Ruhn fAR-buh*	in a darker color
in einer helleren Farbe	*in ay-nuh he-luh-Ruhn fAR-buh*	in a lighter color
in der gleichen Farbe	*in deyR glay-Huhn fAR-buh*	in the same color

German Culture

Speaking of hair and heads, a few German idioms use these images: *um ein Haar* (by a whisker) and *ein Haar in der Suppe finden* (to find fault with something). These idioms are fairly literal in their interpretation. *Jemandem den Kopf waschen,* however, does not mean to wash someone's (expressed in the dative) head, but rather "to give someone a piece of one's mind."

Suppose you are allergic to particular beauty products, chemicals, or lotions. Or perhaps you can't abide certain smells. Do you detest the way most hairspray leaves your hair feeling like straw? If you don't like certain hair-care products, speak up. Begin your request to the hairdresser with either of the following phrases:

Ich möchte kein(-e, -en) ….
iH möH-tuh kayn(-uh, -uhn)
I don't want any ….

Bitte, benutzen Sie kein(-e, -en) ….
bi-tuh, buh-noot-tsuhn zee kayn(-uh, -uhn)
Please, don't use ….

German	Pronunciation	English
das Haargel	*dAs hahR-geyl*	gel
das Haarspray	*dAs hahR-shpRey*	hairspray
das Shampoo	*dAs shAm-pew*	shampoo
der Haarschaum	*deyR hahR-shoum*	mousse
die Haarlotion	*dee hahR-loh-tseeohn*	lotion
die Pflegespülung	*dee pfley-guh-shpüh-loong*	conditioner

I Need Help

There will undoubtedly be times, particularly if you take what you've learned of the German language and venture into a German-speaking country, when you will find yourself in need of a helping hand. The problem is, how do you get this helping hand to help you? The sections that follow will help you prepare for an encounter at the dry-cleaner's, at the Laundromat, at the shoemaker's, and so on.

Help!

When you have minor problems—a stain, a broken shoelace, a ripped contact lens—that occur in a universe where chaos seems to dispel what little order there is, you will find the following phrases useful.

> Um wie viel Uhr öffnen Sie?
> *oom vee feel ewR öf-nuhn zee*
> What time do you open?

> Um wie viel Uhr schließen Sie?
> *oom vee feel ewR shlee-suhn zee*
> What time do you close?

> An welchen Tagen haben Sie geöffnet (geschlossen)?
> *An vel-Huhn tah-guhn hah-buhn zee guh-öf-net (guh-shlo-suhn)*
> What days are you open (closed)?

> Können Sie mein(-e, -en) … reparieren?
> *kö-nuhn zee mayn(-uh, -uhn) … Re-pah-Ree-Ruhn*
> Can you fix my … for me?

> Können Sie ihn (es, sie) heute reparieren?
> *kö-nuhn zee een (es, zee) hoy-tuh Re-pah-Ree-Ruhn*
> Can you fix it (them) today?

> Kann ich bitte eine Quittung bekommen?
> *kAn iH bi-tuh ay-nuh kvi-toong buh-ko-muhn*
> Can I have a receipt, please?

At the Dry-Cleaner—*in die Reinifung*

Stains, spills, and tears happen to clothing no matter how careful you are or where you are. Why not take your shirt to the cleaner and remedy the unsightliness? The person helping you will probably ask you something like, "*Wo liegt das Problem?*" (*vo leekt dAs pRo-blem*). Knowing how to explain your problem and ask for the necessary type of service is crucial.

> Das Hemd ist schmutzig.
> *dAs hemt ist shmoot-siH*
> The shirt is dirty.

> Mir fehlt ein Knopf.
> *meeR feylt ayn knopf*
> I'm missing a button.

Ich habe ein Loch in meiner Hose.
iH hah-buh ayn loCH in may-nuhR hoh-zuh
I have a hole in my pants.

Da ist ein Flecken.
dA ist ayn fle-kuhn
There's a stain.

You've explained the problem. Now you must be clear about what you want done to correct it. Try these phrases, inserting the appropriate form of *dies-* in the accusative with the following clothing items (refer back to Chapter 16 to brush up on articles of clothing vocabulary). Check your accuracy in Appendix A.

Können Sie diese(-s, -n) … für mich reinigen, bitte?
kö-nuhn zee dee-zuh(-s, -n) … fühR miH ray-ni-guhn, bi-tuh
Can you clean this (these) for me, please (blouse, sports jacket, tie)?

Können Sie diese(-s, -n) … für mich bügeln, bitte?
kö-nuhn zee dee-zuh(-s, -n) … fühR miH büh-guhln, bi-tuh
Can you iron this (these) for me, please (jacket, shorts, scarf)?

Können Sie diese(-s, -n) … für mich stärken, bitte?
kö-nuhn zee dee-zuh(-s, -n) … fühR miH shtäR-kuhn, bi-tuh
Can you starch this (these) for me, please (pair of pants, shirt, skirt)?

Können Sie diese(-s, -n) … für mich nähen bitte?
kö-nuhn zee dee-zuh(-s, -n) … fühR miH näh-uhn, bi-tuh
Can you sew this (these) for me, please (dress, suit, socks)?

At the Laundromat—*im Waschsalon*

If the laundry that has piled up in the corner of your hotel room is made up of basic, run-of-the-mill dirty clothes, you may want to stuff everything into a bag and wander the city streets in search of the nearest Laundromat. These phrases will be of use to you in your search:

Ich suche einen Waschsalon.
iH zew-CHuh ay-nuhn vAsh-zah-lohn
I'm looking for a Laundromat.

Ich habe viel dreckige Wäsche.
iH hah-buh feel dRe-ki-guh vä-shuh
I have a lot of dirty clothes.

Ich möchte meine Wäsche waschen lassen.
iH möH-tuh may-nuh vä-shuh vA-shuhn lA-suhn
I want to have my clothes washed.

Welche Waschmaschine kann ich benutzen?
vel-Huh vAsh-mA-shee-nuh kAn iH buh-noo-tsuhn
Which washing machine can I use?

Welcher Trockner ist frei?
vel-HuhR tRok-nuhR ist fRay
Which dryer is free to use?

Wo kann ich Waschpulver kaufen?
vo kAn iH vAsh-pool-vuhR kou-fuhn
Where can I buy laundry soap?

Now create your own vocabulary list from the previous phrases and check your vocabulary in Appendix A.

1. laundry = die Wäsche

2. dryer =

3. Laundromat =

4. washing machine =

5. laundry soap =

6. to wash =

7. to look for =

8. to buy =

9. to use =

10. dirty =

At the Shoemaker—*beim Schuster*

Did both heels snap off your favorite leather boots? Have you been walking so much that you have worn away the soles of your shoes? Perhaps you simply want to be able to see your smiling face reflected in your polished patent leather dress shoes. Whatever your reasons for visiting your local shoemaker, the following phrases will help you make your desires clear.

Können Sie ... für mich reparieren?
kö-nuhn zee ... führR miH re-pah-ree-Ruhn
Can you fix ... for me?

diese Schuhe
dee-zuh shew-uh
these shoes

diese Stiefel
dee-zuh shtee-fuhl
these boots

diesen Absatz
dee-zuhn ap-zAts
this heel

diese Sohle
dee-zuh zoh-luh
this sole

Haben Sie Schnürsenkel?
hah-buhn zee shnüR-zen-kuhl
Do you have shoelaces?

Können Sie meine Schuhe putzen, bitte?
kö-nuhn zee may-nuh shew-uh poot-zuhn, bi-tuh
Can you polish my shoes, please?

I Need These Shoes

Your clothes are filthy. Your best dress is ripped. Your shoes are a wreck. The heels are worn down, and the shoes themselves are encrusted with mud. You have a party to go to later in the evening! What should you do? You can start by using what you've learned to translate the following sentences into German. Check your translation in Appendix A.

Example: Can you fix these shoes for me?

Answer: Können Sie diese Schuhe für mich reparieren?

1. I'm looking for a Laundromat.

2. Can you dry-clean this dress for me?

3. What time do you close?

4. Can you polish my shoes, please?

5. I have lots of dirty clothes.

6. Where can I polish these shoes?

At the Optometrist–*beim Optiker*

Almost everyone with less than perfect vision has had the unfortunate experience of looking for hours for a favorite (and only) pair of glasses. Finally, you plop yourself down on a chair, frustrated and exhausted, to the muffled sound of breaking glass. If you happen to sit on your glasses while in Deutschland, these phrases may come in handy:

Können Sie diese Brille reparieren, bitte?
Kö-nuhn zee dee-zuh bRi-luh Re-pah-Ree-Ruhn, bi-tuh
Can you repair these glasses for me, please?

Das Glass (das Gestell) ist zerbrochen.
dAs glAs (dAs guh-shtel) ist tseR-bRo-CHuhn
The lens (the frame) is broken.

Können Sie diese Kontaktlinsen ersetzen.
kö-nuhn zee dee-zuh kon-tAkt-lin-zuhn eR-ze-tsuhn
Can you replace these contact lenses?

Verkaufen Sie Sonnenbrillen?
feR-kou-fuhn zee zo-nuhn-bRi-luhn
Do you sell sunglasses?

As a Rule

Word order   To form a yes/no question in German, place the inflected verb first, as you do in English: Are you looking for a laundromat? *Suchen Sie einen Waschsalon?* If the question begins with a question word, such as *wann* (when), *warum* (why), *wo* (where), or *wie viel* (how much), the inflected verb comes in second position, followed by the subject: *Wo finde ich einen Waschsalon?*

At the Jeweler–*beim Juwelier*

Has your watch stopped? If you want to catch your train or plane on time, you may want to have your watch repaired. Try these phrases when you're at the jewelry store:

Meine Armbanduhr ist kaputt.
may-nuh ARm-bAnt-ewR ist kA-poot
My watch is broken.

Können Sie diese Armbanduhr reparieren?
kö-nuhn zee dee-zuh ARm-bAnt-ewR Re-pah-Ree-Ruhn
Can you repair this watch?

Meine Armbanduhr läuft zu schnell (langsam).
may-nuh ARm-bAnt-ewR loyft tsew shnel (lAng-zAm)
My watch is fast (slow).

Verkaufen Sie Batterien?
feR-kou-fuhn zee bA-tuh-Ree-uhn
Do you sell batteries?

Your watch is broken, and you are due to meet a friend later in the day. You stop by a jewelry store in Zürich with the following problems. Formulate questions for the jeweler. Check your accuracy in Appendix A.

Ich habe keine Batterien.

Ich brauche eine Armbanduhr.

Meine Armbanduhr läuft nicht.

At the Camera Shop—*beim Fotogeschäft*

If you lost or forgot your camera, or if you simply need to buy some film, you will probably want to stop at a camera shop. Here are some phrases that may come in handy:

Ich brauche einen Fotoapparat.
iH bRou-CHuh ayn foh-toh-A-pA-Raht
I need a camera.

Ich brauche eine Videokamera.
iH bRou-CHuh ayn vee-dee-oh-kA-muhRA
I need a video camera.

Haben Sie Farbfilme (Schwarzweißfilm) mit 20 (36) Bildern?
hah-buhn zee fARp-fil-muh (shvARts-vays-film) mit 20 (36) foh-toz
Do you have color (black-and-white) film with 20 (36) photos?

Können Sie diesen Film entwickeln, bitte?
kö-nuhn zee dee-zuhn film ent-vi-kuhln, bi-tuh
Can you develop this film, please?

If the sun has been shining for weeks and you're looking gorgeous, and the photographs that your wife, husband, friend, or companion have been taking of you just aren't coming out right, you may need a new camera. Walk into the nearest camera shop and tell the photo assistant what you need. Don't forget to order a few rolls of film.

Help, I Lost My Passport!

Here are the phrases you will need to get through some common angst-inducing situations.

Wo ist …?
vo ist
Where is …?

das Polizeiamt
dAs po-li-tsay-Amt
the police station

das amerikanische Konsulat
dAs ah-mey-Ree-kah-ni-shuh kon-zew-laht
the American consulate

die amerikanische Botschaft
dee ah-mey-Ree-kah-ni-shuh bot-shAft
the American Embassy

Ich habe … verloren.
iH hah-buh … feR-loh-Ruhn
I have lost ….

meinen Pass (m., acc.)
may-nuhn pAs
my passport

mein Portemonnaie (n., acc.)
mayn poRt-moh-ney
my wallet

meine Handtasche (f., acc.)
may-nuh hAn-tA-shuh
my purse

Helfen Sie mir, bitte.
hel-fuhn zee meeR, bi-tuh
Help me, please.

Ich brauche einen Dolmetscher.
iH bRou-CHuh ay-nuhn dol-met-chuhR
I need an interpreter.

Spricht jemand hier Englisch?
shpRiHt yeh-mAnt heeR eng-lish
Does anyone here speak English?

Comparison Shopping

Just because you're in a foreign country doesn't mean you shouldn't shop around. Whether it's a hotel, a jewelry store, a clothing store, or a train station, ask about prices. Then go to other hotels, stores, and so on and ask about their prices. Find the best deal and take it!

Adverbs and Adjectives Compared

When you are explaining to someone why you bought this here and that there, you will have to know how to use adjectives and adverbs to compare things. Adverbs and adjectives have three forms: the *positive* form, *billig* (*bi-liH*, "cheap"); the *comparative* form, *billiger* (*bi-li-guhR*, "cheaper"); and the *superlative* form, *der/die/das billigste* (*deyR/dee/dAs bi-lik-stuh*) or *am billigsten* (*Am bi-lik-stuhn*). All of these mean "the cheapest." The form of the definite article and the ending on the adjective vary according to case and gender.

Adjectives and adverbs show levels of degree in English either by adding *-er* (or modifying the adjective with *more*) to form the comparative or by adding *-est* (or using *most*) to form the superlative. The process is quite similar and even simpler in German: The ending *-er* is used to form the comparative for both adjectives and adverbs of any length (*intelligenter*), and *-(e)st* is used to form the superlative (*der intelligenteste*). An *-e* is added to the *-st* superlative inflection when the adjective or adverb ends in *t, ß, ss,* or *z,* so that there aren't numerous *s* sounds piling up on each other.

Notice that, when used attributively, adjectives in the superlative take adjective endings. For example, in "the tastiest cheese," *der leckerste Käse, lecker* precedes a nominative masculine noun. Thus, the superlative ending for that adjective is *-ste* because it takes an inflection to agree with the noun it's modifying. For adverbs, the superlative ending becomes *-(e)sten* because the preposition/article contraction *am* precedes it (*an + dem*).

What's What

Positive form Simple adverbs or adjectives.

Comparative form The *more* form that adjectives and adverbs take when compared.

Superlative form The *most* form that adjectives and adverbs take when they are compared.

We Are Family

In present-day German, most monosyllabic adjectives and adverbs incur a sound change in the comparative and superlative forms. This sound change can be traced back to the days of Old High German (500–1050 C.E.), when adjectives and adverbs took an ending that promoted the shifting in sounds. The endings have been lost, but the sound change remains: *alt* becomes *älter*. Hmm … is there a similarity between that German comparison for *old* and the English *old* and *elder*?

The following list gives you the adjective *stark* (*shtARk*, or "strong") in the base, comparative, and superlative forms. Notice the addition of an umlaut in the comparative and superlative forms. This sound mutation occurs quite frequently with adjectives and adverbs of one syllable with the vowels *a*, *o*, or *u*.

Adjective Degree	German	Pronunciation	English
Positive	der stark**e** Regen	*deyR shtahR-kuh rey-guhn*	the heavy rain
Comparative	der stärk**ere** Regen	*deyR shtäR-kuh-Ruh rey-guhn*	the heavier rain
Superlative	der stärk**ste** Regen	*deyR shtäRk-stuh rey-guhn*	the heaviest rain

The following list gives you the adverb *stark* in the positive, comparative, and superlative forms.

Adjective Degree	German	Pronunciation	English
Positive	Es regnet stark.	*es Reyg-nuht shtARk*	It rains hard.
Comparative	Es regnet stärk**er**.	*es Reyg-nuht shtäR-kuhR*	It rains harder.
Superlative	Es regnet **am** stärk**sten**.	*es Reyg-nuht Am shtäRk-stuhn*	It rains the hardest.

As a Rule

The superlative of an adjective is formed by adding *-st* to the positive form. The *-st* is expanded to *-est* if the adjective stem ends in *-d*, *-t*, or a silibant such as *-s*, *-st*, *-ß*, or *-z*, as in *Im Winter sind die Tage am kürzesten*. Remember that if the adjective precedes a noun, it is attributive in function and takes an adjective ending to agree in number, gender, and case: *Trier ist die älteste Stadt in Deutschland*. The one exception to this rule of adding an *-e* before the *-st* is the superlative of *groß*: *größt-*, as in *Bayern ist das größte Land Deutschlands*.

The following two tables list the adjectives you will need (in their comparative and superlative forms) to be a good comparison shopper.

Adjectives Used to Compare

Positive	English	Comparative	Superlative
billig *bi-liH*	cheap	billiger *bi-li-guhR*	am billigsten *Am bi-liH-stuhn*
schön *shöhn*	beautiful	schöner *shöh-nuhR*	am schönsten *Am shöhn-stuhn*
groß *gRoß*	big	größer *gRöß-suhR*	am größten *Am gRös-tuhn*
klein *klayn*	small	kleiner *klay-nuhR*	am kleinsten *Am klayn-stuhn*
bunt *boont*	colorful	bunter *boon-tuhR*	am buntesten *Am boon-tuhs-tuhn*
weich *vayH*	soft	weicher *vay-HuhR*	am weichesten *Am vay-Huhs-tuhn*
warm *vARm*	warm	wärmer *väR-muhR*	am wärmsten *Am väRm-stuhn*
teuer *toy-uhR*	expensive	teurer *toy-RuhR*	am teuersten *Am toy-uhR-stuhn*

Remember, when forming the comparative with adverbs, add the ending -*er* to the positive form of the adverb. To form the superlative, use the formula *am* + positive form of adverb + the ending -(*e*)*sten*.

Achtung

To express that someone or something is "more and more so" in German, the adverb *immer* is used with a comparative form, a base adjective followed by the comparative suffix -*er*. *Die Autos fahren immer schneller* means "Cars are going faster and faster."

Irregular Comparisons

Some adjectives and adverbs have irregular comparative and superlative forms. You should be able to discern the similarities between some of the irregular German degree forms and their irregular English counterparts. And, yes, you guessed it: You're simply going to have to commit these to memory.

Positive	English	Comparative	English	Superlative	English
gern *geRn*	gladly	lieber *lee-buhR*	more gladly	am liebsten *Am leep-stuhn*	most gladly
gut *gewt*	good	besser *be-suhR*	better	am besten *Am be-stuhn*	the best
hoch *hoCH*	high	höher *höh-uhR*	higher	am höchsten *Am höH-stuhn*	the highest
nah *nah*	close	näher *näh-uhR*	closer	am nächsten *Am näH-stuhn*	the closest
oft *oft*	often	öfter *öft-uhR*	more often	am öftesten *Am of-tuh-stuhn*	the most often
viel *feel*	much	mehr *meyR*	more	am meisten *Am may-stuhn*	the most

Make a Degree Evaluations

Try your hand at applying comparative and superlative judgments to hair, laundry, and jewelry—topics covered in this chapter—and translate the following English phrases into German. Don't forget to add adjective endings where appropriate! Check your mastery in Appendix A.

Example: the prettiest hair coloring die schönste Färbung

1. the shortest haircut

2. the curliest perm

3. a darker color

4. the dirtiest shirt

5. the cheapest Laundromat

6. This dryer is bigger.

7. the nearest jeweler (masc.)

8. My watch runs the slowest.

The Least You Need to Know

◆ You can get the services you need and put your angst-ridden hours to an end with a few simple phrases.

◆ You will be able to recognize the locations offering these services because the German expressions *Wäscherei* and *Waschsalon* contain the English cognate *wash;* *Schuster* sounds like *shoe;* and *Optiker* resembles the English *optician.*

◆ The comparative and superlative forms in German are formed in much the same way as they are in English: by adding *-er* and *-(e)st.*

◆ The irregular forms of *gut, besser,* and *am besten* and *viel, mehr,* and *am meisten* also mirror their English equivalents.

Chapter **21**

Doctor, Doctor: *"Ich bin krank"*

In This Chapter

- ♦ Your body

- ♦ Symptoms, illnesses, and cures

- ♦ The irregular verb *tun* in the expression *weh tun*

- ♦ Expressing how long

- ♦ How to use reflexive verbs

Now you know from Chapter 20 how to take care of all those little things that go wrong when you're traveling. But what about slightly bigger problems? What happens if you get sick? Unfortunately, many travelers have minor aches, pains, headaches, and upset stomachs. Time differences, foreign food and water, air-conditioned airplanes, and hot hotel rooms, on top of trying to adjust to constantly changing conditions, can do a number on your body. In this chapter, you'll learn the key words and phrases you need to complain in German about everything from a headache to a not-so-happy tummy.

Where Does It Hurt?

The first thing you need to know is how to tell the doctor where, specifically, you're experiencing pain or discomfort. Try some of the words in the following table.

Parts of the Body

German	Pronunciation	Plural	Pronunciation	English
das Auge	*dAs ou-guh*	die Augen	*dee ou-guhn*	eye(s)
das Bein	*dAs bayn*	die Beine	*dee bay-nuh*	leg(s)
das Gehirn	*dAs guh-hiRn*	die Gehirne	*dee guh-hiR-nuh*	brain(s)
das Gesicht	*dAs guh-ziHt*	die Gesichter	*dee guh-ziH-tuhR*	face(s)
das Handgelenk	*dAs hAnt-guh-lenk*	die Handgelenke	*dee hAnt-guh-len-kuh*	wrist(s)
das Herz	*dAs heRts*	die Herzen	*dee heR-tsuhn*	heart(s)
das Knie	*dAs knee*	die Knie	*dee knee-uh*	knee(s)
das Ohr	*dAs ohR*	die Ohren	*dee oh-Ruhn*	ear(s)
der Arm	*deyR ARm*	die Arme	*dee Ar-muh*	arm(s)
der Busen	*deyR bew-zuhn*	die Busen	*dee bew-zuhn*	breast(s)
der Finger	*deyR fin-guhR*	die Finger	*dee fin-guhR*	finger(s)
der Fingernagel	*deyR fin-guR-ney-guhl*	die Fingernägel	*dee fin-guR-ney-guhl*	fingernails
der Fuß	*deyR fews*	die Füsse	*dee fü-suh*	foot (feet)
der Fußknöchel	*deyR fews-nö-Huhl*	dieFußknöchel	*dee fews-knö-Huhl*	ankle(s)
der Hals	*deyR hals*	die Hälse	*dee häl-zuh*	neck(s)
der Kopf	*deyR kopf*	die Köpfe	*dee köp-fuhf*	head(s)
der Körper	*deyR köR-puhR*	die Körper	*dee köR-puhR*	body(ies)
der Magen	*deyR mah-guhn*	die Mägen	*dee mä-guhn*	stomach(s)
der Mund	*deyR moont*	die Münder	*dee Mün-duhR*	mouth(s)
der Rücken	*deyR Rü-kuhn*	die Rücken	*dee Rü-kuhn*	back(s)
der Zahn	*deyR tsahn*	die Zähne	*dee tsäh-nuh*	tooth (teeth)
der Zeh	*deyR tsey*	die Zehen	*dee tsey-hun*	toe(s)
die Brust	*dee bRoost*	die Brüste	*dee bRüs-tuh*	chest(s)
die Hand	*dee hAnt*	die Hände	*dee hän-duh*	hand(s)
die Haut	*dee hout*	die Häute	*dee hoy-tuh*	skin(s)
die Kehle	*dee key-luh*	die Kehlen	*dee key-luhn*	throat(s)
die Nase	*dee nah-zuh*	die Nasen	*dee nah-zuhn*	nose(s)
die Schulter	*dee shool-tuhR*	die Schultern	*dee shool-tuhRn*	shoulder(s)

German	Pronunciation	Plural	Pronunciation	English
die Wirbelsäule	*dee viR-buhl-zoy-luh*	spine		
die Zunge	*dee tsoon-guh*	die Zungen	*dee tsoon-guhn*	tongue(s)
die Lippe	*dee li-puh*	die Lippen	*dee li-puhn*	lip(s)

Pain

How would you tell a German that you have a headache? a sore throat? a stomachache? You could point to your head, your throat, or your stomach and contort your face in agony, perhaps grunting or yowling for emphasis. Or, you could learn how to express these things in German. In the following sections, you will learn how to express pains, aches, and illnesses in German.

What Seems to Be the Problem?

When you go to the doctor, the first question will probably be *Was haben Sie? (vAs hah-buhn zee)*, or "What's troubling you?" Use the following formula to answer:

> *Ich habe* + body part that hurts + *-schmerzen*

Examples:

Ich habe Bauchschmerzen.	*iH hah-buh bouCH-shmeR-tsuhn*	I have a stomachache.
Ich habe Zahnschmerzen.	*iH hah-buh tsahn-shmeR-tsuhn*	I have a toothache.
Ich habe Kopfschmerzen.	*iH hah-buh kopf-shmeR-tsuhn*	I have a headache.

Maybe your traveling companion was crazy enough to stay out all night trying to carry on a conversation over the music at a *Disko*. To speak about someone else's pains, conjugate the verb *haben*:

Er hat Halsschmerzen.	*eR hAt hAlz-shmeR-tsuhn*	He has a sore throat.

Another way of talking about your symptoms is to use the expression *weh tun (vey tewn)*, "to hurt," which is a dative expression that requires an indirect object pronoun (dative personal pronoun). Before you learn how to use this expression, familiarize yourself with the very strong verb *tun (toon)*, "to do."

Person	Singular	English	Plural	English
First	ich tue *iH tew-uh*	I do	wir tun *veeR tewn*	we do
Second	du tust *dew tewst*	you do	ihr tut *eeR tewt*	you do
Third	er, sie, es tut *eR, zee, es tewt*	he, she, it does	sie tun *zee tewn*	they do
Formal	Sie tun *zee tewn*	you do	Sie tun *zee tewn*	you do

The basic formula you will need to create a sentence using the expression *weh tun* is as follows:

> Body part + conjugated form of *tun* + indirect object pronoun + *weh*

Your indirect object pronoun must agree with the subject. Here's a review of the indirect object pronouns you learned in Chapter 16.

Dative Pronouns	English	Dative Pronouns	English
mir	to me	uns	to us
dir	to you	euch	to you
ihm, ihr, ihm	to him, to her, to it	ihnen	to them
Ihnen	to you		

Examples:

> Der Fuß tut mir weh.
> *deyR fews tewt meeR vey*
> My foot hurts me.

As a Rule

The order of the words in sentences that use *weh tun* can change without altering the meaning of the sentence. The subject remains "marked" as such in the nominative case:

Mir tut der Fuß weh.

Der Fuß tut mir weh.

More Symptoms

You may need to come up with something more specific than a vague ache or pain to give your doctor a shot at curing you. You'll then want to be able to understand, or at least anticipate, some of the questions the doctor might pose you. Consult the following table for specific symptoms.

Other Symptoms

German	Pronunciation	English
das Fieber	*dAs fee-buhR*	fever
der Schüttelfrost	*deyR shü-tuhl-fRost*	chills
der (Haut)Ausschlag	*deyR (hout)ous-shlahk*	rash
der Absess	*deyR Ap-ses*	abscess
der blaue Fleck	*deyR blou-uh flek*	bruise
der Durchfall	*deyR dooRCH-fAl*	diarrhea
der gebrochene Knochen	*deyR ge-bRo-CHuh-nuh kno-CHuhn*	broken bone
der Husten	*deyR hew-stuhn*	cough
der Knoten	*deyR knoh-tuhn*	lump
der Krampf	*deyR kRAmpf*	cramps
der Schmerz	*deyR shmeRts*	pain
die Beule	*dee boy-luh*	bump
die Blase	*dee blah-zuh*	blister
die Magenverstimmung	*dee mah-guhn-feR-shti-moong*	indigestion

Hatten Sie jemals ...?
hA-tuhn zee yey-mAlz
Have you ever had ...?

Haben Sie eine Krankenversicherung?
hah-buhn zee ay-nuh kRAn-kuhn-feR-zi-Huh-Roong
Do you have health insurance?

Leiden Sie unter ...?
lay-duhn zee oon-tuhR
Do you suffer from ...?

What's Wrong?

After your visit to the doctor, you may want to call your friends and relatives and give them a detailed description of your illness. Most maladies can be expressed with the verb *haben*. Here's the basic formula:

Subject pronoun + conjugated form of *haben* + (indefinite article) noun

Common Nouns Used for Expressing Sicknesses

German	Pronunciation	English
das Asthma	*dAs Ast-mah*	asthma
der Herzinfarkt	*deyR heRts-in-fARkt*	heart attack
der Krebs	*deyR kReyps*	cancer
der Schlaganfall	*deyR shlahk-An-fAl*	stroke
der Sonnenstich	*deyR zo-nuhn-shtiH*	sunstroke
die Angina	*dee An-gee-nah*	angina
die Bauchschmerzen	*dee bouCH-shmeR-tsuhn*	stomachache
die Blinddarmentzündung	*dee blint-dahRm-ent-tsün-doong*	appendicitis
die Bronchitis	*dee bRon-Hee-tis*	bronchitis
die Erkältung	*dee eR-käl-toong*	cold
die Erschöpfung	*dee eR-shö-pfoong*	exhaustion
die Gicht	*dee giHt*	gout
die Grippe	*dee gRi-puh*	flu
die Kinderlähmung	*dee kin-deR-ley-moong*	poliomyelitis
die Kopfschmerzen	*dee kopf-shmeR-tsuhn*	headache
die Leberentzündung	*dee ley-buhR-ent-tsün-doong*	hepatitis
die Lungenentzündung	*dee loon-guhn-ent-tsün-doong*	pneumonia
die Masern (pl.)	*dee mah-zuhRn*	measles
die Windpocken	*dee vint-po-kuhn*	chicken pox
die Röteln	*dee Röh-tuhln*	German measles

You may also hear the following expressions. They take the verb *sein*, followed by an adjective.

German	Pronunciation	English
Ich bin erkältet.	*iH bin eR-käl-tuht*	I have a cold.
Ich bin krank.	*iH bin kRAnk*	I'm sick.

Doctor, Doctor

You've been beleaguered by a series of illnesses. Use what you've learned to express your symptoms to a doctor. Check your complaints in Appendix A.

Example: A toothache

Answer: Ich habe Zahnschmerzen.

1. A cold
2. A cough
3. A headache
4. A stomachache
5. A blister
6. A fever

German Culture

When you travel in Germany, try to get sick during business hours weekdays. You will find that Pharmacies, *die Apotheken* (*dee ah-poh-tey-kuhn*), are open anywhere from 8:00 A.M. to 7:00 P.M. Monday through Friday and until 2:00 P.M. on Saturday, depending on the region and the size of the city. Don't confuse pharmacies with *die Drogerien* (*dee dRoh-guhR-eeuhn*), which are similar to American drugstores. German pharmacists will give you helpful advice (free!) and often refer you to a doctor.

How Long Have You Felt This Way?

One question a nurse or doctor will ask is, *Seit wann haben Sie diese Krankheit?* (*zayt vAn hah-buhn zee dee-zuh kRAnk-hayt*), or "How long have you had this illness?" The doctor may also ask, *Wie lange haben Sie diese Beschwerden schon?* (*vee lAn-guh hah-buhn zee dee-zuh buh-shveR-duhn shon*), or "How long have you had these problems?" Answer either of these questions with the following construction:

> *Seit* + amount of time you've been sick

Don't forget that the prepositional phrase following the preposition *seit* is a dative preposition and always requires the dative case.

> Example:
>
> Seit einer Woche
> *zayt ay-nuhR vo-CHuh*
> For a week
>
> Seit einem Tag
> *zayt ay-nuhm tahk*
> For a day
>
> Seit zwei Tagen
> *zayt tsvay tah-guhn*
> For two days

If the aches and pains you're experiencing are too minor to merit the attention of a doctor—let's say you have a headache or a sore throat—you'll probably want to try a little self-care. Why not visit your local pharmacy, *Apotheke (ah-poh-tey-kuh)*?

From Finding Drugs to Finding Toothpaste

Whether you're looking for medication or a can of hairspray, you want to be sure you're looking in the right place. You can find most of the items listed in the following table in either a *Drogerie*, drugstore, or one of the smaller supermarkets in Germany.

Drugstore Items

German	Pronunciation	English
das (milde) Abführmittel	*dAs (mil-duh) Ap-fühR-mi-tuhl*	laxative (mild)
das Asperin	*dAs As-pey-Reen*	aspirin
das Deodorant	*dAs dey-oh-doh-RAnt*	deodorant
das Enthaarungswachs	*dAs ent-hah-Roongz-vAks*	depilatory wax
das Heizkissen	*dAs hayts-ki-suhn*	heating pad
das Körperpuder	*dAs köR-peR-pew-duhR*	talcum powder
das Mundwasser	*dAs moont-vA-suhR*	mouthwash
das Shampoo	*dAS shAm-pew*	shampoo
das Thermometer	*dAs teR-moh-mey-tuhR*	thermometer
der (elektrische) Rasierer	*deyR (ey-lek-tRi-shuh) Rah-zee-RuhR*	razor (electric)
der Alkohol	*deyR Al-koh-hohl*	alcohol
der Eisbeutel	*deyR ays-boy-tuhl*	ice pack
der Erste-Hilfe-Kasten	*deyR eR-stuh-hil-fuh-kA-stuhn*	first-aid kit
der Hustensaft	*deyR hew-stuhn-sAft*	cough syrup
der Kamm	*deyR kAm*	brush
der Schnuller	*deyR shnoo-luhR*	pacifier
der Spiegel	*deyR shpee-guhl*	mirror
die Aknemedizin	*dee Ak-nuh-mey-dee-tseen*	acne medicine
die Augentropfen	*dee ou-guhn-tRo-pfuhn*	eye drops
die Enthaarungscreme	*dee ent-hah-Roongz-kReym*	depilatory cream
die Feuchtigkeitscreme	*dee foyH-tiH-kayts-kreym*	moisturizer
die Flasche	*dee flA-shuh*	bottle
die Heftpflaster	*dee heft-pflA-stuhR*	Band-Aids
die Hustenbonbons	*dee hew-stuhn-bon-bonz*	cough drops
die Kondome	*dee kon-doh-muh*	condoms

German	Pronunciation	English
ein (Magen) Säure/ein neutralisierendes Mittel	*ayn (mah-guhn) zoy-Ruh/ayn noy-tRah-lee-zee-Ren-duhs mi-tuhl*	an antacid
die Mullbinde	*dee mool-bin-duh*	gauze bandage
die Nagelfeile	*dee nah-guhl-fay-luh*	nail file
die Nasentropfen	*dee nah-zuhn-tRo-pfuhn*	nose drops
die Pinzette	*dee pin-tse-tuh*	tweezers
die Rasiercreme	*dee Rah-zeeR-kReym*	shaving cream
die Rasierklinge	*dee Rah-zeeR-klin-guh*	razor blade
die Schere	*dee shey-Ruh*	scissors
die Schlaftabletten	*dee shlahf-tA-ble-tuhn*	sleeping pills
die Sicherheitsnadeln	*dee zi-HuhR-hayts-nah-duhln*	safety pins
die Taschentücher	*dee tA-shuhn-tüh-HuhR*	tissues
die Vitamine	*dee vee-tah-mee-nuh*	vitamins
die Watte	*dee vA-tuh*	cotton
die Wattestäbchen	*dee vA-tuh-shtäp-Huhn*	cotton swabs
die Windeln	*dee vin-duhln*	diapers
die Zahnbürste	*dee tsahn-büR-stuh*	toothbrush

Special Needs

Did you break your leg skiing? Do you need a wheelchair? Many pharmacies in Germany specialize in medical appliances. The following table details items you may need if you are temporarily or permanently physically challenged. Start by asking the pharmacist this:

> Wo kann ich ein(-e, -en) … bekommen?
> *vo kAn iH ayn(-uh, -uhn) … buh-ko-muhn*
> Where can I get …?

> **German Culture**
>
> *Das Rezept* means both a prescription for medication and a recipe. Stemming from the Latin meaning "to receive," *das Rezept* was initially used by pharmacists referring to instructions for medication from doctors. Its meaning became more generalized to refer to instructions in the kitchen.

Special Needs

German	Pronunciation	English
der (Spazier) Stock	*deyR (shpah-tseeR) shtok*	cane
die Krücken	*dee kRü-kuhn*	crutches

continues

Special Needs (continued)

German	Pronunciation	English
das Hörgerät	*dAs höR-guh-Räht*	hearing aid
der Rollstuhl	*deyR Rol-shtewl*	wheelchair
die Gehhilfe	*dee gey-hil-fuh*	walker

Have It on Hand

Imagine that you rent a small apartment in Düsseldorf. Which items do you need to ensure that you have a well-stocked medicine cabinet? Use a form of *brauchen* and check your translations in Appendix A.

Example: to freshen breath

Answer: Ich brauche Mundwasser.

1. For headaches

2. When you break your foot

3. For minor cuts and burns

4. To blow your nose

5. When you can't sleep

6. When you have a cough

7. When you need to shave

8. When you can't sleep

9. When you get a hangnail

What's What

Reflexive verb A verb that always takes a reflexive pronoun because the action of the verb reflects back on the subject of the sentence. The subject and the object relate to the same entity.

Reflexive pronoun A pronoun that forms a part of a reflexive verb in which the action refers back to the subject. These are identical to personal pronouns except for the third person singular and plural, and the formal *Sie*-form, all of which are *sich*. Reflexive pronouns must agree in terms of number and gender with the subject.

What Are You Doing to Yourself?

To express how you feel, use the *reflexive verb sich fühlen*. The *sich* in front of this verb is known as a *reflexive pronoun* because it refers back to the subject. In other words, the action performed "reflects back" onto the subject performing the action. The following table shows you how to conjugate the reflexive verb *sich fühlen* using the correct reflexive pronouns (remember, in the infinitive form, reflexive verbs are marked as reflexive with the preceding reflexive pronoun *sich*).

The Verb: *sich fühlen*

Person	Singular	English	Plural	English
First	ich fühle mich *iH füh-luh miH*	I feel	wir fühlen uns *veeR füh-luhn oonz*	we feel
Second	du fühlst dich *dew fühlst diH*	you feel	ihr fühlt euch *eeR fühlt oyH*	you feel
Third	er, sie, es fühlt sich *eR, zee, es fühlt ziH*	he, she, it feels	sie fühlen sich *zee füh-luhn ziH*	they feel
Formal	Sie fühlen sich *zee füh-luhn ziH*	you feel	Sie fühlen sich *zee füh-luhn ziH*	you feel

Reflexive Verbs

Reflexive pronouns show that a subject is performing the action of the verb on itself. In other words, the subject and the reflexive pronoun both refer to the same person(s) or thing(s); for example, "he hurt himself" and "we enjoyed ourselves." The following table shows reflexive pronouns as they should appear with their reflexive verbs in both the dative and the accusative. You'll notice that the only thing new under the sun is the appearance of *sich*, which actually simplifies matters because the third person singular and plural (and formal, of course) in both the accusative and the dative is the same: *sich!*

Accusative and Dative Reflexive Pronouns

Accusative Pronouns	Pronunciation	English	Dative Pronouns	Pronunciation	English
mich	*miH*	myself	mir	*meeR*	for myself
dich	*diH*	yourself	dir	*deeR*	for yourself
sich	*ziH*	himself herself itself	sich	*ziH*	for himself for herself for itself
uns	*oonz*	ourselves	uns	*oonz*	for ourselves
euch	*oyH*	yourselves	euch	*oyH*	for yourselves
sich	*ziH*	themselves	sich	*ziH*	for themselves
sich formal	*ziH*	yourself/ yourselves (formal)	sich (formal)	*ziH*	for yourself/ yourselves (formal)

Compare the pronouns in the following sentences:

1. Du fühlst dich schlecht.
   dew fühlst diH shleHt
   You feel bad.

2. Du kaufst dir ein Medikament.
   dew koufst deeR ayn me-dee-kah-ment
   You buy yourself medicine.

Do you see the difference? The second-person singular reflexive pronoun (it's a mouthful, but there's no other way of putting it) in the first sentence appears in the accusative case. Why? Because in the first sentence, the reflexive pronoun serves as a direct object. The second-person singular reflexive pronoun in the second sentence appears in the dative case. In the second sentence, the pronoun serves as an indirect object because the reflexive pronoun, *dir*, is receiving a direct object, *ein Medikament*.

Now, using what you've learned about reflexive pronouns and about the verb *sich fühlen*, you should be able to express how you and others feel:

Ich fühle mich schlecht.   Ihr fühlt euch gut.
iH füh-luh miH shleHt   *eeR fühlt oyH gewt*
I feel bad.   You all feel good.

Reflexive or Not?

You can't always tell from the English verb whether the German verb will be reflexive. So your best bet is simply to learn the common reflexive verbs in German.

Common Reflexive Verbs

German	Pronunciation	English
sich entspannen	*ziH ent-shpA-nuhn*	to relax (oneself)
sich erholen	*ziH eR-hoh-luhn*	to recuperate (oneself)
sich verletzen	*ziH feR-le-tsuhn*	to injure (oneself)
sich waschen[S]	*ziH vA-shuhn*	to wash (oneself)
sich setzen	*ziH ze-tsuhn*	to sit (oneself) down
sich treffen[S]	*ziH tRe-fuhn*	to meet (each other)
sich anmelden*	*ziH An-mel-duhn*	to sign (oneself) up
sich anziehen*	*ziH An-tsee-uhn*	to dress (oneself)
sich ankleiden*	*ziH An-klay-duhn*	to dress (oneself)

German	Pronunciation	English
sich ausziehen*	*ziH ous-tsee-uhn*	to undress (oneself)
sich umziehen*	*ziH oom-tsee-uhn*	to change (oneself)
sich rasieren	*ziH Rah-zee-Ruhn*	to shave (oneself)
sich schminken	*ziH shmin-kuhn*	to put make-up on (oneself)
sich fertig machen	*ziH fer-tiH mah-CHuhn*	to get (oneself) ready
sich fit halten ˢ	*ziH fit hAl-tuhn*	to keep (oneself) fit
sich kämmen	*ziH kä-muhn*	to comb (oneself)
sich erkälten	*ziH eR-käl-tuhn*	to catch a cold
sich duschen	*ziH doo-shun*	to take a shower
sich strecken	*ziH shtre-kuhn*	to stretch (oneself)
sich die Zähne putzen	*ziH dee tsäh-nuh poo-tsuhn*	to brush one's teeth

ˢ*denotes a very strong verb, incurring a stem-vowel change in the present tense: waschen → wäscht; treffen → trifft.*

denotes a separable prefix verb.

Reflexive Verbs in Action

Use what you've learned about reflexive verbs to describe all the different things you must do to get ready before leaving your hotel room in the morning. Then talk about the things you do before going to bed at night. Check your sentences in Appendix A.

1. sich waschen
2. sich rasieren
3. sich anziehen
4. sich fertig machen
5. sich strecken
6. sich ausziehen
7. sich hinlegen

> ### We Are Family
>
> Forming reflexive pronouns by combining *-self* with the personal pronoun began in Middle English (1110–1500 C.E.) and became more frequent subsequently. However, the older (Germanic) practice of using the simple object form of the pronoun as a reflexive also continued for quite a while.

Commanding Reflexively

When you use reflexive verbs to tell your husband to shave or to tell your children to wash their hands before dinner, the reflexive pronoun usually comes at the end of the sentence unless the reflexive verb has a separable prefix or you have an object or adverb in the command. Remember, when you use the formal second person singular or plural, you must always include *Sie* as part of the command:

Verletz dich nicht!	*feR-letst diH niHt*	Don't hurt yourself!
Waschen Sie sich!	*vA-shun zee ziH*	Wash yourself!
Wascht euch!	*vAsht oyH*	Wash yourselves!
Zieh(e) dich an!	*tsee(-uh) diH An*	Get dressed!

As a Rule

The reflexive pronoun follows the conjugated verb except in a question, when the subject must first frame the verb, followed by the reflexive pronoun:

Ich wasche mich. I wash myself.

Warum fühlst du dich schlecht? Why are you feeling poorly?

Be Bossy

You're traveling with a group of friends, and you're all getting ready to go out. Practice using reflexive verbs by telling a friend to do and then not to do the following. Check your imperatives in Appendix A.

Achtung

When reflexive verbs are used in German, the reflexive pronoun must be stated. (In many cases the reflexive pronoun can be omitted in English, as in the sentence "I shaved before going to the wedding.")

1. To wash oneself

2. To change clothing

3. To shave

4. To get ready

5. To sit down

6. To relax

The Least You Need to Know

◆ If you become ill in a German-speaking country, your recovery will be a lot easier if you know how to express your symptoms correctly.

◆ You can express illness in various ways. For starters, use the conjugated form of the verb *haben* + the body part that hurts + the ending *-schmerzen*. Alternatively, use the expression *weh tun*.

◆ Reflexive pronouns show that the action of reflexive verbs reflects back on the subject of the sentence.

Die Vergangenheit: In the Past

In This Chapter

- ◆ Using the present perfect
- ◆ All about the helping verbs *haben* and *sein*
- ◆ Asking questions and giving answers in the past tense

So far, you've been navigating through Deutschland in the present tense. Imagine now that, after purchasing the items you need for a well-stocked medicine cabinet in Chapter 21, you walk out of the pharmacy without taking the bag filled with items you've already paid for. You don't realize that the bag is missing until a taxi has driven you halfway home. What do you do now?

Talking About the Past

You must, of course, go back to the pharmacy and tell the person behind the counter (someone new—the person who was there earlier has stepped out for lunch) what happened. To do so, you will have to talk about the past, known in German as *die Vergangenheit* (*dee feR-gAn-guhn-hayt*).

You can speak in the past tense in various ways. In English, for example, you can say, "I went to the store." In German, this tense is referred to as *das Präteritum* (*dAs pRä-tey-Ree-toom*), or the simple past—so simple that it needs only one verb form to express it. You also can say, "I have gone to the store." This tense is referred to as *das Perfekt* (*dAs peR-fekt*), or the present-perfect tense. When you say "I had gone to the store," you are speaking in the past in yet another way, referred to as *das Plusquamperfekt* (*dAs ploos-kvahm-peR-fekt*), or the past-perfect tense. This chapter focuses on the formation of *das Perfekt*, the most common way of speaking in the past in German.

Strong Verbs

You already have a head start on the formation of the perfect tense in German. English and German form the perfect tense in much the same way. Both languages use an *auxiliary* or helping verb (have/*haben*) with the past participle to form the present-perfect tense: "I have bought"/*ich habe gekauft*. The only hitch is that some verbs in German use the verb *to be* (*sein*) as an auxiliary: *Ich bin gegangen* ("I have gone"). Here's the basic formula for forming the *Perfekt*:

Subject + the conjugated form of *sein* or *haben* in the present + past participle

The important thing to remember is that after you learn how to form the past participle, you won't have any trouble speaking in the past. The past participle never changes. Only the auxiliary verbs *haben* and *sein* change to agree with the subject. So how is the past participle formed? Most past participles take *ge-* at the beginning of the verb (when you're dealing with verbs with separable prefixes, however, the *ge-* comes after the separable prefix in the formation of the past participle).

All strong verbs have a past participle ending in *-en*, as do some in English, such as *taken*, *eaten*, and *spoken*. Do you remember strong verbs from Chapter 8? The main difference between strong and weak verbs is that strong verbs have a vowel change in one of their principal parts. If they're very strong (*sehr stark*), they incur a change already in the third person singular, present; if they're merely *stark*, the change comes out in the simple past and the past participle forms. English verbs follow this pattern, too: *sing*, *sang*, *sung* (in German, *singen*, *sang*, *gesungen*). Think of strong verbs as verbs so stubborn that they insist on having their own way. Although these verbs follow certain patterns of vowel changes, it would probably take you longer to memorize the patterns than to memorize the past participle for the strong verbs you use. Our advice? Start memorizing. In the following list, *hat* means that the auxiliary verb is *haben*, and *ist* means that it is *sein*.

What's What

Auxiliary verb   A verb that serves as the specifier of the main verb—it *helps* the main verb. In the case of the German *Perfekt* tense, the auxiliary verb enables the main verb to pop up in its past participial form at the end of the phrase: *Paul hat mich geliebt.*

Infinitive	Third Person Singular + Past Participle	Pronunciation	English Past Participle
backen[s]	hat gebacken	*hAt guh-bA-kuhn*	to bake
bleiben	ist geblieben	*ist guh-blee-buhn*	to stay
essen	hat gegessen	*hAt guh-ge-suhn*	to eat
fahren[s]	ist gefahren	*ist guh-fah-Ruhn*	to drive
geben[s]	hat gegeben	*hAt guh-gey-buhn*	to give
gehen	ist gegangen	*ist guh-gAn-guhn*	to go
genießen	hat genossen	*hAt guh-no-suhn*	to enjoy
heben	hat gehoben	*hAt guh-hoh-buhn*	to lift, to raise
laufen[s]	ist gelaufen	*ist guh-lou-fuhn*	to run, to walk
nehmen[s]	hat genommen	*hAt guh-no-muhn*	to take
schlafen[s]	hat geschlafen	*hAt guh-shlah-fuhn*	to sleep
singen	hat gesungen	*hAt guh-zoon-guhn*	to sing
sprechen	hat gesprochen	*hAt guh-shpRo-CHuhn*	to speak
stehen	hat gestanden	*hAt guh-shtAn-duhn*	to stand
trinken	hat getrunken	*hAt guh-tRoon-kuhn*	to drink
tun	hat getan	*hAt guh-tahn*	to do
waschen[s]	hat gewaschen	*hAt guh-vA-shuhn*	to wash
ziehen	hat gezogen	*hAt guh-tsoh-guhn*	to pull

[s] *denotes a very strong verb that takes a vowel change in the second and third person singular.*

In the following sentences, two verbs from the list are used along with the conjugated auxiliary verbs *haben* or *sein* to form sentences in the *Perfekt*.

> Sie hat ihre Schlaftabletten genommen.
> *zee hAt ee-Ruh shlahf-tAb-le-tuhn guh-no-muhn*
> She took her sleeping pills.

> Du bist zur Drogerie gegangen.
> *dew bist tsewR dRoh-guh-Ree guh-gAn-guhn*
> You have gone to the drugstore.

As you can see, to form the *Perfekt* with strong verbs, all you have to do is conjugate *haben/sein* correctly and add *ge-* to the beginning of the strong verb in its altered past-participle form. Yes, that form is not highly predicable and needs to be learned by rote. At least you can anticipate that the past participle form of a strong verb will end in *-en!*

> ### We Are Family
>
> Believe it or not, all stem-vowel changes in both English and German can be traced to a stage in Germanic that had seven distinct verb "classes." Verbs within each class followed a pattern of ablaut-vowel sound change according to their phonetic properties. As an example, let's consider the present-day German verb *nehmen* ("to take"). This verb was part of verb class IV because it contained (and still does) a simple *l, r,* or *m* sound. Hence, its sound-change pattern was *e, i, a, o,* resulting in *nehmen, nimmt, nahm, hat genommen.*

Forming the Past Participle with Weak Verbs

The difference between the formation of the *Perfekt* with strong and weak verbs is that the past participles of weak verbs end in *-t,* resembling the English dental suffix *-ed.* For this reason, when you are forming a past participle, you need to know whether the verb is weak or strong. *Gegangen* is a strong verb. Giving it the weak verb ending *-t* in the past participle (resulting in the unfortunately ungrammatical *Ich habe gegangt*) would be as incorrect as saying "I have goed" in English.

Weak verbs were discussed in Chapter 8. When conjugated, weak verbs follow a set pattern of rules and retain the same stem vowel throughout the conjugation. That is, add a *ge-* prefix to the *stem* (infinitive minus final *-en*) and a *-t* suffix. After you come up with the past participle, just plug it into the same formula:

> Subject (noun or pronoun) + the conjugated form of *sein* or *haben* in the present tense + past participle

Here are some common weak verbs and their past participles:

Infinitive	Third Person Singular + Past Participle	Pronunciation	English Past Participle
antworten	hat geantwortet	*hAt guh-Ant-voR-tuht*	to answer
arbeiten	hat gearbeitet	*hAt guh-AR-bay-tuht*	to work
benutzen (NS)	hat benutzt	*hAt buh-nootst*	to use
brauchen	hat gebraucht	*hAt guh-bRouCHt*	to need
kaufen	hat gekauft	*hAt guh-kouft*	to buy
kochen	hat gekocht	*hAt guh-koCHt*	to cook
kosten	hat gekostet	*hAt guh-kos-tuht*	to cost, to taste
kratzen	hat gekratzt	*hAt guh-krA-tsuhn*	to scratch
lehren	hat gelehrt	*hAt guh-leyRt*	to teach

Infinitive	Third Person Singular + Past Participle	Pronunciation	English Past Participle
lernen	hat gelernt	*hAt guh-leRnt*	to learn
rauchen	hat geraucht	*hAt guh-rouCHt*	to smoke
sagen	hat gesagt	*hAt guh-zAkt*	to say
spazieren	ist spaziert	*ist shpA-tseeRt*	to walk
studieren (oh-la-la)	hat studiert	*hAt shtew-deeRt*	to study
trauen	hat getraut	*hAt guh-tRout*	to trust, to dare, to marry
träumen	hat geträumt	*hAt guh-tRoymt*	to dream
versuchen (NS)	hat versucht	*hAt feR-zooCHt*	to try

What in the world does "oh-la-la" after the verb *studieren* mean? Why, that German verbs that end in *-ieren* are of French origin, of course! Thus, they are a bit resistant to totally resembling a German past participle, and although they will accept the *-t* suffix, they will not accept the *ge-* prefix. Oh! And what does "NS" after *benutzen* and *versuchen* mean? Only that *be-* and *ver-* are inseparable prefixes and, thus, will not tolerate a *ge-* prefix, either.

Forming the Past Participle with Mixed Verbs

The final German verb type is known as "mixed" because, like a codependent couple, these verbs share both strong and weak tendencies. Mixed verbs add the *-t* ending to form their past participle, just as weak verbs do. However, like strong verbs, the stem vowel of the infinitive changes in the past tense. Here is a list of the infinitives and past participles of some common mixed verbs.

Infinitive	Third Person Singular + Past Participle	Pronunciation	English Past Participle
brennen	hat gebrannt	*hAt guh-bRAnt*	to burn
bringen	hat gebracht	*hAt guh-bRACHt*	to bring
denken	hat gedacht	*hAt guh-dACHt*	to think
kennen	hat gekannt	*hAt guh-kAnt*	to know
nennen	hat genannt	*hAt guh-nAnt*	to name
rennen	ist gerannt	*ist guh-RAnt*	to run
senden	hat gesandt	*hAt guh-zAnt*	to send
wenden	hat gewandt	*hAt guh-vAnt*	to turn
wissen	hat gewußt	*hAt guh-voost*	to know

As a Rule

Although it may seem as if most verbs are strong (and, therefore, must be memorized by rote), less than 20 percent of German verbs fall into this category. Bear in mind that you need memorize a strong verb only one time. Once you establish the paradigm for the very strong verb "to eat"—*essen/isst/hat gegessen*—you can automatically conjugate "to forget": *vergessen, vergisst, hat vergessen.*

Using *sein* in the *Perfekt*

The present-perfect tense in German is made up of the present tense of the auxiliary *haben* or *sein* and the past participle of the verb. Because most verbs are *transitive*—that is, they can take a direct object—*haben* is used very frequently in the formation of the *Perfekt*. Some verbs, however, use *sein* instead of *haben* as an auxiliary in the present perfect (you are already familiar with some of them). Verbs that take *sein* are *intransitive verbs* that almost always express motion or a change of condition. Familiarize yourself with the past participles of the most commonly used of these verbs.

What's What

Intransitive verbs   The category of verbs that do not take a direct object.

Transitive verbs   The category of verbs that can take a direct object.

Past Participle	Third Person Singular	Pronunciation	English Past Infinitive+ Participle
sein	ist gewesen .	*ist guh-vey-zuhn*	to be
werden	ist geworden	*ist guh-voR-duhn*	to become
bleiben	ist geblieben	*ist guh-blee-buhn*	to stay
kommen	ist gekommen	*ist guh-ko-muhn*	to come
gehen	ist gegangen	*ist guh-gAn-guhn*	to go
reisen	ist gereist	*ist guh-Rayst*	to travel
fliegen	ist geflogen	*ist guh-flo-guhn*	to fly
wandern	ist gewandert	*ist guh-vAn-duhRt*	to hike, to wander
laufen[s]	ist gelaufen	*ist guh-lou-fuhn*	to run
sterben[s]	ist gestorben	*ist guh-shtoR-buhn*	to die
steigen	ist gestiegen	*ist guh-shtee-guhn*	to climb

[s] *denotes a very strong verb that incurs a sound change in the second and third person singular present tense.*

Producing the *Perfekt*

Now try to explain to someone how you happened to leave your purchases behind. English translations are provided so that you know exactly what happened in the past. Check your production in Appendix A.

Example: Ich _____ zur Drogerie _____ (kommen).

Answer: Ich bin zur Drogerie gekommen. (I came to the drugstore.)

1. Ich _____ in die Drogerie _____ (gehen). (I went into the drugstore.)

2. Ich _____ Aspirin und Rasierschaum aus dem Regal _____ (nehmen). (I took aspirin and shaving cream from the shelf.)

3. Ich _____ meine Einkäufe zur Kasse _____ (bringen). (I brought my purchases to the cash register.)

4. Sie _____ nicht viel _____ (kosten). (They didn't cost much.)

5. Ich _____ der Kassiererin _____ (antworten). (I answered the sales clerk.)

6. Ich _____ nicht an meine Einkaufstasche _____ (denken). (I didn't think about my shopping bag.)

7. Ich _____ sie nicht _____ (mitnehmen*). (I didn't take it with me.)

Achtung

Make sure you send that past participle (your *ge-* form) to the end of the sentence. Make them wait for the verb! After all, you've already given your listener a conjugated helping verb next to the subject. And patience is a virtue! *Ich habe von einem Elefant mit einer Maus auf seinem Rücken geträumt.*

Position of *nicht*

As a general rule, when you say "no" in the past, *nicht* comes after the auxiliary verb *sein*. With verbs that take *haben*, *nicht* comes after the direct object. *Nicht* always precedes the past participle.

> Ich bin nicht in die Drogerie gegangen.
> *iH bin niHt in dee dRoh-guh-Ree guh-gAn-guhn*
> I did not go to the drugstore.

Ich habe meine Vitamine nicht genommen.
iH hah-buh may-nuh vee-tah-mee-nuh niHt guh-no-muhn
I did not take my vitamins.

Sie hat das Rezept nicht gelesen.
zee hAt dAs Rey-tsept niHt guh-ley-zuhn
She did not read the prescription.

Er ist nicht nach Hause gefahren.
eR ist niHt nACH hou-zuh guh-fah-Ruhn
He did not drive home.

All You Did

Sometimes it seems like there just aren't enough hours in the day! But look at all that your friends accomplished. Explain in the past tense what you and your friends managed to get done today in the following exercise. Check your sentences in Appendix A.

Example: (ich/die Blumen kaufen)

Answer: Ich habe die Blumen gekauft.

1. du/ins Museum gehen

2. er/die Einkäufe vergessen

3. sie (sg.)/ zum Friseur fahren

4. Sie/den Anruf machen

5. wir/den Film sehen

6. ihr/an eure Eltern denken

7. ich/Toast machen

8. du/in den Bergen wandern

9. sie (pl.)/die Oper genießen

10. ich/ein Glas Wein trinken

Forming a Question in the Past

In case you're afraid that you are going to have to learn something entirely new to form questions in the past tense, don't be: You can use intonation. To ask a question, just speak with a rising inflection.

Du hast an die Reise gedacht?
Dew hAst An dee Ray-zuh guh-dACHt
Have you thought about the trip?

Another way of asking questions is to add the word *oder* (*oh-duhR*) or the phrase *nicht wahr* (*niHt vahR*) to the end of your statements:

Du hast an die Reise gedacht, oder?
Dew hAst An dee Ray-zuh gu-dACHt, oh-duhR
You have thought about the trip, right?

Du hast an die Reise gedacht, nicht wahr?
Dew hAst An dee Ray-zuh gu-dACHt, niHt vahR
You have thought about the trip, haven't you?

The most common way of forming questions is to reverse the word order of the subject nouns or pronouns and the conjugated form of the verb (this change is called *inversion*):

Du bist nach Hause gegangen.
Bist du nach Hause gegangen?

Answering a Question Negatively in the Past

Are you in a disagreeable mood? To answer negatively, use *nein* (*nayn*) at the beginning of the statement and then follow the auxiliary verb with *nicht* (*niHt*). Remember, both questions and answers in the past usually end with the past participle.

Haben Sie geraucht?
hah-buhn zee guh-RouCHt

Nein, ich habe nicht geraucht.
nayn, iH hah-buh niHt guh-RouCHt

When the action of the verb is referring to a thing not preceded by a definite article, you can use the expression *kein* to give a negative answer in the past: *Ich habe kein Fleisch gegessen* ("I ate no meat").

Ask Questions

Why was the party so bad? Why did the plane refuel? Why did your mother say what she said? Why did so-and-so lose his job? Never mind that it's none of your business.

Form negative and affirmative questions in the past out of the following sentences. Check your questions in Appendix A.

Example: Du bist nach Berlin gefahren.

Answers: Bist du nach Berlin gefahren?

Bist du nicht nach Berlin gefahren?

1. Ihr seid zum Friseur gegangen.

2. Sie haben den Hustensaft getrunken.

3. Du hast an die Einkaufstasche gedacht.

4. Almut hat geraucht.

The Least You Need to Know

◆ You can form the past tense by using the auxiliary verbs *haben* or *sein* and a past participle.

◆ To speak in the present-perfect tense (in German, *das Perfekt*), use the following formula: subject + conjugated present tense (*das Präsens*) of *haben* or *sein* + past participle.

◆ To ask questions in the past tense in German, use intonation, add the tags *oder* or *nicht wahr* to the end of the statement, or use inversion.

Part **6**

When in Germany, Do As the Germans Do

You may decide that the German life is for you. Learn how to communicate in the twenty-first century or via old, reliable snail mail and telephone. You can even find a place to live—be it a room in a boardinghouse or a castle in the Alps—and learn how to pay for it!

Chapter 23

Communicating: Phone, Mail, and Internet

In This Chapter

- ◆ Figuring out phones
- ◆ How to use reflexive verbs in the past tense
- ◆ Internet access in Germany
- ◆ Sending snail mail
- ◆ All about the verbs *schreiben* ("to write") and *lesen* ("to read")

You're feeling better than you have in a long time. Your headache is gone, thanks to the aspirin you retrieved in the preceding chapter. Now you're ready to do the one thing you've been postponing since you arrived at your hotel: call the folks back home.

Readers used to the American phone system will find calling home from Germany a challenge. There is the confusion of incompatible standards for cellular, wireless, or mobile phones similar to the mixture of conflicting television standards between countries. Dealing with traditional pay phones, first you'll have to purchase a phone card from a post office (which means finding a post office) because most phone booths (small yellow glass booths every few blocks on city streets) no longer accept coins. More modern telecommunicators may opt to use either their own or a rented cell phone. And then there's the luxury of electronic communication. This chapter teaches you how to place a local or international call from Germany, Switzerland, or Austria, and offers cell phone solutions and Internet options. Along the communicative way, you'll also learn about using reflexive verbs in the past tense.

Phoning the Hotel or Home

Before you even get near a Deutsche Telekom phone booth, be prepared for something new. Expect the procedure you will use to make local and long-distance calls to be a challenge. The best-case scenario really would be for you to find someone to show you how, but if you are truly alone, read the instructions in the phone booth carefully. If you need to make an operator-assisted call, you'll have to learn to identify the type of call you're trying to make. The following table lists your options.

Types of Phone Calls

German	Pronunciation	English
das Auslandsgespräch	*dAs ous-lAnts-guh-shpRähH*	out-of-the-country call
das Ferngespräch	*dAs feRn-guh-shpRähH*	long-distance call
das Ortsgespräch	*dAs oRts-guh-shpRähH*	local call
das R-Gespräch	*dAs eR-guh-shpRähH*	collect call

Your Basic German Telephone

Perhaps you're lucky enough to have a German friend explain the whole procedure of making a long-distance call to you before you even step into a phone booth. To be able to understand what she's saying, you'll have to familiarize yourself with the parts of a German phone and these other helpful words.

The Telephone (*das Telefon*)

German	Pronunciation	English
das öffentliche Telefon	*dAs ö-fent-li-Huh tey-ley-fohn*	public phone
der Fernsprechautomat or die Telefonkabine	*deyR feRn-shpRähH-ou-toh-mAt* or *dee tey-ley-fohn-kah-bee-nuh*	phone booth
das Telefon	*dAs tey-ley-fohn*	telephone

German	Pronunciation	English
das Telefonbuch	*dAs tey-ley-fohn-bewCH*	telephone book
das tragbare (schnurlose)	*dAs tRahk-bah-Ruh (shnooR-loh-zuh)*	cordless phone
Telefon	*tey-ley-fohn*	portable phone
das Freizeichen or der Wahlton	*dAs fray-tsay-Huhn or deyR vahl-tohn*	dial tone
der Anrufbeantworter	*deyR An-Rewf-buh-Ant-vohR-tuhR*	answering machine
der Lautsprecher	*deyR lout-shpRe-HuhR*	speaker telephone
der Telefonhörer	*deyR tey-ley-fohn-höh-RuhR*	receiver
die Auskunft	*dee ous-koonft*	information
die Tastatur	*dee tA-stah-tewR*	keypad
die Telefonkarte	*dee tey-ley-fohn-kAR-tuh*	phone card
die Telefonnummer	*dee tey-ley-fohn-noo-muhR*	telephone number
die Telefonzelle	*dee tey-ley-fohn-tse-luh*	booth
die Vermittlung	*dee feR-mit-loong*	operator
die Wählscheibe	*dee vähl-shay-buh*	dial
die Wähltaste	*dee vähl-tA-stuh*	button

Making a Call

The majority of public phone booths in Germany (85 percent) and Austria take only phone cards, or *Telefonkarten* (*tey-ley-fohn-kAR-tuhn*), that you can get from the post office in various denominations. In Germany, information for calls is 11833 (Deutsche Telekom) or on the Internet at www.teleauskunft.de. Remember, it's cheaper to make calls on weekends and after 8 P.M.

Now that you know a little bit about placing a phone call in a German-speaking country, a few more vocabulary items might come in handy if an automated recording speaks to you or an answering machine picks up on the other end. At the very least, it would be to your advantage to understand that you are being asked to leave a message!

Phoning Vocabulary

German	Pronunciation	English
anrufen*ˢ	*An-Rew-fuhn*	to call
der Anrufbeantworter	*deyR An-rewf-buh-Ant-voR-tuhR*	answering machine
auf ein Freizeichen warten	*ouf ayn fray-tsay-Huhn vAR-tuhn*	to wait for the dial tone

continues

Phoning Vocabulary   (continued)

German	Pronunciation	English
auflegen*	*ouf-ley-guhn*	to hang up (the receiver)
den Hörer abnehmen*ˢ	*deyn höh-RuhR Ap-ney-muhn*	to pick up the receiver
die (Telefon) leitung	*dee (tey-ley-fohn) lay-toong*	the (telephone) line
die Leitung ist besetzt	*dee lay-toong ist buh-zetst*	the line is busy
die Vorwahl kennen	*dee fohR-vahl ke-nuhn*	to know the area code
eine Nachricht hinterlassen*ˢ	*ay-nuh nACH-RiHt hin-tuhR-lA-suhn*	to leave a message
eine Telefonkarte (f.) einführen*	*ay-nuh tey-ley-fohn-kAR-tuh ayn-füh-Ruhn*	to insert the card
mit der Vermittlung sprechenˢ	*mit deyR feR-mit-loong shpRe-Huhn*	to speak to the operator
telefonieren (mit.)	*tey-ley-foh-nee-Ruhn*	to telephone
wählen	*väh-luhn*	to dial
verwählen	*feR-väh-luhn*	to misdial
zurückrufen*ˢ	*tsew-Rük-Rew-fuhn*	to call back
das Telefon klingelt	*dAs tey-ley-fohn klin-guhlt*	the phone rings
Auf Wiederhören	*ouf-vee-duhR-höh-Ruhn*	good-bye (on the phone)
außer Betrieb	*ou-suhR buh-tReep*	out of order

*The verbs with an * have separable prefixes, while the verbs with an ˢ are strong—the past participles end in -en and may incur a stem change.*

Phoning Home

You've been trying to make a long-distance call via Deutsche Telekom, and you can't get through. The operator asks you what you've been doing, and you explain the problem. Fill in the blanks of the following sentences using the correctly conjugated verb (use what you learned in Chapter 22 about the *Perfekt* to use verbs in the past tense—auxiliary verb + past participle). To form the past participle with verbs with separable prefixes, add *ge-* after the prefix before the stem: *Ich habe meinen Freund angerufen.* Check your answers in Appendix A.

Example: Das Telefon _____ oft _____ (klingeln).

Answer: Das Telefon hat oft geklingelt.

1. Ich _____ den Hörer _____ (abnehmen*ˢ).

2. Ich _____ die Telefonkarte _____ (einführen*).

3. Dann _____ ich die Telefonnummer _____ (wählen).

4. Ich _____ eine Nachricht _____ (hinterlassen*ˢ)

5. Danach _____ ich den Hörer _____ (auflegen*).

An Actual Phone Conversation

You've read the lists, you've memorized the verbs, and you've studied the vocabulary. Now, can you put what you've learned into practice? See whether you understand this telephone dialogue between Johannes and Frau Gehring. Check your comprehension with a translation in Appendix A.

Frau Gehring: Gehring, Guten Tag.

Johannes: Hallo, hier ist Johannes. Kann ich bitte Tanja sprechen?

Frau Gehring: Einen Moment, bitte. Es tut mir leid. Sie ist nicht zu Hause.

Johannes: Wann kann ich sie erreichen?

Frau Gehring: Ich weiß nicht, wann sie wiederkommt. Möchtest du eine Nachricht hinterlassen?

Johannes: Nein, danke. Ich rufe später nochmal an. Auf Wiederhören.

Gehring: Auf Wiederhören.

Did you notice how a German answers the phone? Not with the American "Hello," but rather with his or her last name (*der Familienname*). Also, the caller immediately identifies herself after the greeting. Instead of "Is so-and-so there?", you'll say, "*Kann ich so-und-so sprechen?*" How about the closing salutation? It's rather logical to say that you'll hear from someone again, "*Auf Wiederhören,*" rather than see someone because, after all, you *are* speaking to them.

German Culture

Calling long distance from a hotel is much more expensive than calling from a phone booth. Long-distance phone calls can be made from most phone booths in Germany, Switzerland, and Austria (you should look for the sign Ausland/International near the phone). The most economical way to make a call is to purchase a phone card (these can be purchased at a post office). The magnetic strip, similar to the strip on credit cards, enables you to use phone booths all over Europe. To make an international call, dial 00 + the country code + the area code + the phone number of the person you are trying to reach. You'll see the area codes for local numbers on the sign next to the phone.

Operator ...

You can run into many problems when you're making a phone call. You may dial the wrong number, get a never-ending busy signal, or get an answering machine instead of a person. Here are some phrases you may hear (or need to say) when you run into rough times on the phone.

Welche Nummer haben sie gewählt?
vel-Huh noo-muhR hah-buhn zee guh-vählt
What number did you dial?

Es tut mir leid. Ich muss mich verwählt haben.
es toot miR layt. iH moos miH feR-vählt hah-buhn
I'm sorry. I must have dialed the wrong number.

Wir wurden unterbrochen.
veeR vooR-duhn oon-tuhR-bRo-CHuhn
We got disconnected.

Bitte wählen Sie die Nummer noch einmal.
bi-tuh väh-luhn zee dee noo-muhR noCH ayn-mahl
Please redial the number.

Diese Telefonleitung wurde abgestellt.
dee-zuh tey-ley-fohn-lay-toong vooR-duh ap-guh-shtelt
This telephone number has been disconnected.

Das Telefon ist defekt (außer Betrieb).
dAs tey-ley-fohn ist dey-fekt (ou-suhR be-tReep)
The telephone is out of order.

German Culture

The postal service in Germany also provides phone service. Tell the postal worker behind the counter that you would like to make a long-distance call, and he or she will indicate which phone booth is available. You pay (cash only) after your call. Long-distance calls made from the post office are considerably cheaper than calls made from your hotel or from one of the yellow or more modern gray phone booths you'll see along city streets.

Rufen Sie mich später zurück.
Rew-fuhn zee miH shpäh-tuhR tsew-Rük
Call me back later.

Ich kann Sie akustisch nicht verstehen.
iH kAn zee A-koos-tish niHt feR-shtey-uhn
I can't hear you.

Es meldet sich niemand.
es mel-det ziH nee-mAnt
There's no answer.

Melden (melde) Sie sich (dich) wieder!
mel-duhn (mel-duh) zee ziH (diH) vee-duhR
Keep in touch!

Ich muss auflegen.
iH moos ouf-ley-guhn
I have to hang up.

Relying on American Phone Companies

Another noncellular option remains: to use an international phone card service. Sprint, MCI WorldCom, and AT&T all have toll-free numbers in Germany, Austria, and Switzerland. You simply dial that number to reach a U.S. operator or to direct dial anywhere you want to call. You can charge the call to your American phone card or call collect. The downside to this is that you may arrive home to a phone bill much larger than you anticipated. These toll-free numbers are subject to change, so be sure to verify the latest access numbers before heading abroad:

Germany: Sprint 0800-888-0013, MCI WorldCom 0800-888-8000, AT&T 0800-2255-288;

Austria: Sprint 022-903-014, MCI WorldCom 022-903-012, AT&T 0800-200-288;

Switzerland: Sprint 0800-899-777, MCI WorldCom 0800-89-0222, AT&T 0800-89-0011.

Und ein Handy/Mobiltelefon/Funktelefon?

You can obtain cellular service for overseas use in various ways. You can purchase or rent a handset from your current cell phone provider, sign up for the service and then roam internationally, or rent a cell phone from a cell phone rental company. The obvious advantage to using your current cell phone provider is that this allows you to retain your U.S. phone number: People can call your regular cell phone number and reach you in Germany. Although this is convenient for people calling from the United States, it is expensive for those calling within Germany. Also, roaming rates tend to be very expensive. Carriers such as Cingular and T-Mobile have switched to the worldwide cellular platform called GSM and can provide you with a triband phone that works everywhere in the world where there is cell phone service.

To rent a phone through a cellular rental company, find an online vendor who will send you a handset that is compatible for overseas use, along with a foreign cell phone number (*die Handynummer*). You are billed for the handset rental plus minute usage, generally with a minimum per-day usage quota. You mail back the rental once you return from your trip and are billed for airtime use and the handset rental. Again, your bill could be more than you expected. Another option is to rent a cell phone directly at an international airport. Having this last-minute option is convenient, although you won't have the luxury of comparison shopping online. Bear in mind that phone rental rates are expensive, and the per-minute airtime costs are based on the roaming rates of your provider.

If you're willing to make the effort, your best bet is to obtain two items: a cell phone that works overseas and a Subscriber Information Module (SIM) card, a small chip that easily slips into the phone and stores important information. Rates vary, but domestic calls are, on average, less than 25¢ per minute and about 50¢ per minute to call the United States. More important, perhaps, is that incoming calls from anywhere in the world are always free. You simply purchase a prepaid SIM card for Germany that allows for pay-as-you-go cellular communication. After you slip it into the phone and phone away, you can purchase reload vouchers to add more talk time if you run out of call credit. You may purchase one by simply walking into a cell phone store in Germany.

CellularAbroad.com offers country-specific SIM cards. If you are traveling to more than one country, you can purchase a prepaid international SIM card that works in nearly all countries. You retain one phone number internationally, but the rates are not as good as those with country-specific cards, and you won't get free incoming calls.

What Did You Do to Yourself? Reflexive Verbs in the Past

Were you unable to phone someone who was expecting your call? You'll probably have to give the person a reason. To explain your situation, you may need to use reflexive verbs in the *Perfekt*. All reflexive verbs use *haben* as an auxiliary verb in the present-perfect. Here are the various conjugations for "I have misdialed—I dialed the wrong number":

Ich habe mich verwählt.	Wir haben uns verwählt.
Du hast dich verwählt.	Ihr habt euch verwählt.
Er/Sie/Es hat sich verwählt.	Sie haben sich verwählt.
Sie haben sich verwählt. (formal)	

To form the negative with reflexive verbs, *nicht* follows the reflexive pronoun.

Er hat sich nicht gemeldet. (He didn't answer.)

You can form negative questions in the past with reflexive verbs in several ways:

- Through inversion: *Hat er sich nicht gemeldet?*
- Through intonation: *Er hat sich nicht gemeldet?*
- By using the tag *oder* or *nicht wahr: Er hat sich nicht gemeldet, nicht wahr?*

They're Busy

Tell what these people were doing when the phone was ringing, replacing the proper noun with a personal pronoun. Remember that the form of *haben* must agree with the subject and that the past participle appears at the end. Strong verbs (those whose past participles end in an *–en* and may incur a stem-vowel mutation) are indicated with an [s], while separable ones are followed by an asterisk. Check your sentences in Appendix A.

Example: (Anna/ sich die Haare waschen[s])

Answer: Sie hat sich die Haare gewaschen.

1. Maria/ sich anziehen[s]*
2. Stefan/ sich rasieren
3. Mark und ich/ sich waschen[s]
4. Ben und Uli/ sich die Zähne putzen
5. Christoph/ sich umziehen[s]*
6. Karl/ sich kämmen
7. Theresa/ sich schminken
8. Heinz-Friedrich/ sich fertig machen

Hey, It's the Twenty-First Century!

Faxes, modems, e-mail, and the Internet have spread their tentacles far and wide. If you need to send a fax or e-mail from Germany, you'll want to know the following terms:

German	Pronunciation	English
das Faxgerät	*dAs fax-guh-Rät*	fax machine
die Faxnummer	*dAs fax-noo-muhR*	fax number
ein Fax senden	*ayn fax zen-duhn*	to send a fax
etwas faxen	*et-vAs fak-suhn*	to fax something
das Fax-Modem	*dAs fax-moh-dem*	fax modem
das Internet	*dAs in-teR-net*	Internet
die E-Mail	*dee ee-meyl*	e-mail
eine Nachricht senden	*dee nACH-RiHt zen-duhn*	to send a message
die E-Mail Adresse	*dee ee-meyl A-dRe-suh*	e-mail address
der Drucker	*deyR dRü-kuhr*	printer
der Computer	*deyR kom-pyew-tuhR*	computer
die Taste	*dee tAs-tuh*	key
die Tastatur	*dee tAs-tuh-tewR*	keyboard
der Bildschirm	*deyR bilt-sheeRm*	computer screen

If you depend on e-mail to stay connected to your friends, family, work, you name it, you'll be relieved to learn that most computer jargon, even in Germany, is in English. Take, for example, the idiomatic expression *auf die Tasten hämmern (ouf dee tAs-tuhn hä-muhRn)*. Can you guess what noun the verb *hämmern* comes from, in both English and German? If you figured out that *auf die Tasten hämmern* is the equivalent of the English "to hammer on the keyboard," you might be good enough to *hämmern*.

Do you want to chat? (*Wollen Sie chatten?*) Join a German *Chat-Raum* and investigate the local *Chat-Events*. One of the many German search engines to start you off is www.lycos.de. Next to English, the most popular language of the Internet is German. From a German website (often ending with the letters *de*), you'll be able to keep abreast of the current weather and news, order a pizza, read a magazine, plan your next destination, or cyberconnect with real Germans!

> **We Are Family**
>
> German is becoming more like English, believe it or not! Take into consideration some new verbs entering German, such as *emailen*, "to e-mail," and *faxen*, "to fax." Seems simple enough, eh? Simply add the German infinitive ending of *–en*. But it gets better! The past tense of *emailen* is *geemailt*!

Do You Need Your PC in Germany?

The biggest difference between Internet access in Europe and in the United States is that local calls are charged by the minute in Europe. That means that even if your ISP has a local dial-up connection, you still have to pay for each minute that you're online. German telecom rates are lower in the late evening or on holidays, but still more expensive than you might be accustomed to. The largest German Internet service provider is Deutsch Telekom's T-Online. AOL Germany and CompuServe Germany are next in line. AOL Germany can be accessed by members at the country-wide number 0-19-14 from anywhere in Germany.

To get a phone plug converter for your modem, go to a department store or telephone shop—anywhere mobile phones are sold. Ask for a connection cable with the RJ-11 connector for your laptop/notebook modem on one end and the German connector on the other. A phone line tester that comes with plug adapters could save your computer. Beware! Many German hotels charge very high telephone fees even for local calls. Always check the rates before you go online from your hotel room. Some American hotel chains do have RJ-11 phone plugs in their rooms.

Cybercafés are located throughout the larger cities in individual cafés or in the technology section in department stores. This provides you with the opportunity to stay online while traveling without a computer. Get into the universal access offered by having a web-based e-mail account, offered at no charge by services like Verizon or Yahoo. Web cafés charge from $6 to $16(US) per hour of online time, usually determined by the half hour.

Snail Mail

You've spent the whole day in a museum just a few inches away from the oils Albrecht Dürer pushed around on a canvas to create his masterpieces. Now you're dying to get to a café where you can sit down and whip off a few postcards telling friends and family what you've done.

You spend a couple of hours writing your own postal masterpieces. Now you want to be sure that everything you've written reaches its destination. Whatever you send by the *Deutsche Bundespost* (*doy-tchuh boon-duhs-post*) will, of course, get to wherever it's going (the German postal system is famous worldwide for its efficiency). The question is, how soon will it get there? Before you do any letter or postcard writing, you're going to want to know how to ask for paper, envelopes, and other items. The following table will help you.

Alles über die Post: **Mail and the Post Office**

German	Pronunciation	English
das Paket	*dAs pah-keyt*	package, parcel
das Porto	*dAs poR-toh*	postage
das Postfach	*dAs post-fACH*	post office box
das Telegramm	*dAs tey-ley-gRAm*	telegram
der Brief	*deyR bReef*	letter
der Briefkasten	*deyR bReef-kAs-tuhn*	mailbox
der Briefträger	*deyR bReef-tRäh-guhR*	mailman
der Briefumschlag	*deyR bReef-oom-shlahk*	envelope
der Empfänger	*deyR emp-fän-guhR*	addressee
das Postamt	*dAs post-amt*	post office
der Postbeamte	*deyR post-be-Am-tuh*	postal worker
der Absender	*deyR Ap-zen-duhR*	sender
der Telefondienst	*deyR tey-ley-fohn-deenst*	telephone service
die Briefmarke	*dee bReef-maR-kuh*	stamp
der Briefmarkenautomat	*deyR bReef-maR-kuhn-ou-to-mat*	stamp machine
der Briefwechsel	*deyR bReef-vek-suhl*	correspondence
die Bundespost	*dee boon-duhs-post*	federal postal service
die Luftpost	*dee looft-post*	air letter
die Postanweisung	*dee post-An-vay-zoong*	postal order
die Postkarte	*dee post-kAR-tuh*	postcard
ein Bogen (m.) Briefmarken	*ayn boh-guhn bReef-mAR-kuhn*	a sheet of stamps

As a Rule

When you're in the post office requesting stamps, use the counting term *mal* to tell the clerk how many of a certain stamp you need: *Sechsmal ein Euro Briefmarken* (*zeks-mAl ayn oy-Roh bReef-maR-kuhn*) indicates that you want six 1€ stamps. Of course, the use of *mal* is not limited to the purchasing of postage; it can be used with cardinal numbers, as in *zweimal die Woche*, "two times per week"; or *hundertmal im Monat*, "a hundred times per month." And "ten times"? *zehnmal*. Just remember to combine the particle for "times" and the number.

Getting Service at the Post Office

You've written your letter, folded it, doused it with perfume, and scribbled your return address and the address of your beloved on the envelope. Now all you have to do is find a mailbox. If you don't know where one is, ask this:

> Wo ist das nächste Postamt?
> *voh ist dAs näH-stuh post-Amt*
> Where is the nearest post office?

> Wo finde ich den nächsten Briefkasten?
> *voh fin-duh iH deyn näH-stuhn bReef-kA-stuhn*
> Where do I find the nearest mailbox?

Of course, different kinds of letters and packages require different kinds of forms and have different postal rates. Once you've found a post office (it has a yellow sign with black letters that say "BP Post"), you should know how to ask for the type of service you need:

> Was kostet das Porto?
> *vAs kos-tuht dAs poR-toh*
> What's the postal rate?

German	Pronunciation	English
für das Ausland	*fühR dAs ous-lAnt*	for a foreign country
für die Vereinigten Staaten	*fühR dee feR-ay-nik-tuhn shtah-tuhn*	for the United States
für einen Luftpostbrief	*fühR ay-nuhn looft-post-bReef*	for an air-mail letter
für einen Einschreibebrief	*fühR ay-nuhn ayn-shRay-buh-bReef*	for a registered letter
für eine Eilpost	*fühR ay-nuh ayl-post*	for a special delivery
für einen Eilbrief	*fühR ay-nuhn ayl-bReef*	for an express letter

Here are a few more useful phrases:

> Ich möchte diesen Brief (per Luftpost, per Eilpost) verschicken.
> *iH möH-tuh dee-zuhn bReef (peR looft-post, peR ayl-post) feR-shi-kuhn*
> I would like to send this letter (by air mail, special delivery).

> Ich möchte dieses Paket per Nachnahme schicken.
> *iH möH-tuh dee-zuhs pah-keyt peR nACH-nah-muh shi-kuhn*
> I would like to send this package COD.

German Culture

You'd better check your calendar before heading off to the *Postamt* because Germany celebrates many holidays, many of them religious. The most important are Christmas (*Weihnachten*), New Year (*Neujahr*), and Easter (*Ostern*), which are celebrated for two days each. The various German states also observe regional holidays, especially around Easter. An important nonreligious holiday in Germany is the Day of German Unity (*Tag der deutschen Einheit*) on October 3.

Wie viel wiegt dieser Brief?
vee-feel veekt dee-zuhR bReef
How much does this letter weigh?

Wann wird der Brief ankommen?
vAn viRt deyR bReef An-ko-muhn
When will the letter arrive?

Wie lange dauert es, bis der Brief ankommt?
vee lAn-guh dou-eRt es, bis deyR bReef An-komt
How long will it take for the letter to arrive?

Readin' and Writin'

When you're filling out forms at the post office, you may have some trouble figuring out what goes into which tiny bureaucratic-looking box. To ask a postal worker where you should write what information, use the strong verb *schreiben* (*shRay-buhn*), "to write." *Schreiben* is a normal strong verb, so its conjugation in the present tense is thoroughly predictable. What you need to learn is its past participle, the equivalent of the English "written": *hat geschrieben*. Now you are equipped to talk about what you wrote yesterday!

Speaking of writing, you'll also be doing a lot reading—of signs, of forms, of your own letters, and of other people's letters. The very strong verb *lesen* (*ley-zuhn*), "to read," will help you express exactly what kind of reading you are doing. The stem vowel *e* changes to *ie* in the second and third person singular, as illustrated in the following table. Incidentally, the past-tense form for *lesen* is *hat gelesen*.

The Verb *lesen*

Person	Singular	English	Plural	English
First	ich lese *iH ley-zuh, iH ley-zuh*	I read	wir lesen *veeR ley-zuhn*	we read
Second	du liest *dew leest*	you read	ihr lest *eeR leyst*	you read
Third	er, sie, es liest *eR, zee, es leest*	he, she, it reads	sie lesen *zee ley-zuhn*	they read
Formal	Sie lesen *zee ley-zuhn*	you read	Sie lesen *zee ley-zuhn*	you read

Can You Read This?

Have you been glancing at German magazines and newspapers whenever you pass a newsstand? Why don't you buy something that looks interesting? One of the best ways to improve your reading skills is to read. The following table lists some of the things you can read when you are in Germany.

Things to Read

German	Pronunciation	English
die Anzeige	*dee an-tsay-guh*	ad
die Werbung	*dee ver-boong*	ad
das Buch	*dAs bewCH*	book
das Kinderbuch	*dAs kin-duhR-bewCH*	children's book
das Tagebuch	*dAs tah-guh-bewCH*	journal/diary
der Fahrplan	*deyR fahR-plAn*	train/bus schedule
die Zeitschrift	*dee tsayt-shRift*	news magazine
die Illustrierte	*dee i-lew-stReeR-tuh*	magazine
die Speisekarte	*dee shpay-zuh-kAR-tuh*	menu
die Zeitung	*dee tsay-toong*	newspaper
der Roman	*deyR Roh-mahn*	novel
die Quittung	*dee kvi-toong*	receipt
das Schild	*dAs shilt*	sign
die Warnung	*dee vAR-noong*	warning

Getting It Right

Now that you're familiar with reading and writing in German, see whether you can fill in the blanks with the correct forms of *lesen* and *schreiben*. Check your conjugations in Appendix A.

Example: Er _____ eine Zeitung.

Answer: Er <u>liest</u> eine Zeitung.

1. Ich _____ meinem Freund einen Brief.

2. Wir _____ ein Buch.

3. Sie _____ ihren Eltern eine Postkarte.

4. Du _____ die Wohnungsanzeigen.

5. Ich _____ eine Illustrierte.

6. Wolfram _____ gern Kinderbücher.

7. Ihr _____ uns jede Woche.

The Least You Need to Know

- Use the information next to the public phone in Germany or on the front page of the German Yellow Pages to guide you through most of your phone calls.

- Even though spoken German might seem more difficult to understand over the phone, the protocol of telephoning will be familiar to you. If you feel utterly bewildered, you can always respond with, "Wie, bitte?" to request repetition or explanation.

- Reflexive verbs use *haben* as an auxiliary verb in the past perfect.

- A few key phrases will help you when you need to send a fax or e-mail. The German expressions are generally cognates of the English—of course, you'll need to add an *-en* to the verb *fax* to make it a German infinitive.

- Getting and sending mail in Germany is easy once you figure out where the nearest post office is and master the polite phrase for "I would like": *Ich möchte.*

- Knowing the conjugations for *schreiben* ("to write") and *lesen* ("to read") will help you fill out forms at the post office and will aid in your exploration of a large selection of newspapers, magazines, and various books and maps at a train station.

Chapter 24

Going to the Bank

In This Chapter

- ◆ Understanding banking terms
- ◆ Expressing polite requests or wishes
- ◆ Giving advice
- ◆ Speaking in the subjunctive mood

Chances are, you've already cashed a significant portion of your traveler's checks and have nearly reached the limit on all your credit cards. Now it's time for you to learn how to deal with money in a foreign country. You may need to use the long-distance phone skills you learned in Chapter 23 to call home and have one of your loved ones prove his or her love by sending cash.

Or perhaps you have a lot of money in a Swiss bank account, and you'd like to invest it in some German business deals your friends have been telling you about. If you're involved in business, many of the new terms in this chapter will be of use to you.

To the Bank!

Hotels, restaurants, and banks—these are the places where you will probably spend a good deal of your time when you travel. Banks are of particular importance because, sooner or later, you'll probably need to locate an ATM, exchange money, or cash traveler's checks. If you're planning to reside for an extended period of time in a German-speaking country, you may even want to take out a loan to set up a business, purchase real estate, play the stock market, or open a checking account.

> **Achtung**
>
> Although many establishments in Germany accept credit cards, plastic is a less widespread phenomenon in Germany than it is in the United States. Be sure that you see the imprimatur of your credit card company on the window or menu of the establishment where you're about to eat—otherwise, you may be washing dishes until the banks open at 9:00 A.M.

Learning Banking Lingo

If you need to do anything involving your friendly local banker, you'll have to acquaint yourself with the banking terms in the following table. Much of this vocabulary is useful outside of the financial institution realm.

Banking Terms

German	Pronunciation	English
abheben*	*Ap-hey-buhn*	withdraw
ausfüllen*	*ous-fü-luhn*	fill out
leihen	*lay-uhn*	borrow
das Bankkonto	*dAs bAnk-kon-toh*	bank account
das Bargeld	*dAs bahR-gelt*	cash
das Darlehen	*dAs dahR-ley-uhn*	loan
das Einkommen	*dAs ayn-ko-muhn*	revenue
das Geldwechselbüro	*dAs gelt-vek-suhl-büh-Roh*	money-exchange bureau
das Kontobuch	*dAs kon-toh-bewCH*	bankbook
das Scheckbuch	*dAs shek-bewCH*	checkbook
das Sparkonto	*dAs shpAR-kon-toh*	savings account
das Wechselgeld	*dAs vek-suhl-gelt*	change (coins)
der (Kassen) Schalter	*deyR (kA-suhn) shAl-tuhR*	(teller's) window
der Angestellte	*deyR An-guh-shtel-tuh*	employee

German	Pronunciation	English
der Ankauf	*deyR An-kouf*	purchase
der Bankautomat	*deyR bAnk-ou-toh-maht*	automatic teller machine
der Bankdirektor	*deyR bAnk-dee-Rek-tohR*	bank manager
der Einzahlungsbeleg	*deyR ayn-tsah-loongz-bey-leyk*	deposit slip
der Geldfluss	*deyR gelt-floos*	cash flow
der Geldschein	*deyR gelt-shayn*	bill
der Kassierer/die Kassiererin	*deyR kA-see-RuhR/dee kA-see-Ruh-Rin*	teller
der Kontostand	*deyR kon-toh-shtAnt*	balance
der Reisescheck	*deyR Ray-zuh-shek*	traveler's check
der Verkauf	*deyR feR-kouf*	sale
der Wechselkurs	*deyR vek-suhl-kooRs*	exchange rate
die Abhebung	*dee Ap-hey-boong*	withdrawal
die Abzahlung	*dee Ap-tsah-loong*	installment payment
die Anzahlung	*dee An-tsah-loong*	down payment
die Einzahlung	*dee ayn-tsah-loong*	deposit
die Filiale	*dee fi-lee-ah-luh*	branch
die Hypothek	*dee hüh-poh-teyk*	mortgage
die Münze	*dee mün-tsuh*	coin
die Quittung	*dee kvi-toong*	receipt
die Ratenzahlung	*dee Rah-tuhn-tsah-loong*	installment plan
die Restzahlung	*dee Rest-tsah-loong*	final payment
die Schulden	*dee shool-duhn*	debt
die Überweisung	*dee üh-buhR-vay-zoong*	transfer
die Überziehung	*dee üh-buhR-tsee-oong*	overdraft
die Unterschrift	*dee oon-tuhR-shRift*	signature
die Zahlung	*dee tsah-loong*	payment
ein überzogener Scheck (m.)	*ayn üh-buhR-tsoh-guh-nuhR shek*	an overdrawn check
einzahlen*	*ayn-tsah-luhn*	to deposit
kurzfristig	*kooRts-fRis-tiH*	short term
langfristig	*lAng-fRis-tiH*	long term
das Konto überziehen	*dAs kon-toh üh-buhR-tsee-uhn*	to overdraft
sparen	*shpah-Ruhn*	save
überweisen	*üh-buhR-vay-zuhn*	transfer
unterschreiben	*oon-tuhR-shRay-buhn*	sign (to)
verleihen	*feR-lay-uhn*	to loan
wechseln	*vek-suhln*	change (transaction)

* indicates that these are separable-prefix verbs.

Transactions You Need to Make

If you plan to settle down in Germany, you'll probably need to use some of the following phrases that relate to exchanging money, making a deposit or a withdrawal, opening a checking or savings account, or applying for a loan.

Wie sind Ihre Öffnungszeiten?
vee zint ee-Ruh öf-noongz-tsay-tuhn
What are the banking hours?

German Culture

Most German banks are open Monday through Friday from approximately 8 or 9 A.M. to 4 or 5 P.M. Open hours of German banks *do* differ; some of them close for a lunch break, while others may remain open longer on Thursdays but close earlier on Fridays. Still others may take a certain weekday afternoon off. Your best bet is to consult the posted open hours. The largest banks are the Commerzbank, the Deutsche Bank, the Dresdner Bank, and the Volksbank.

Ich möchte …
iH möH-tuh
I would like …

eine Einzahlung machen
ay-nuh ayn-tsah-loong mA-CHuhn
to make a deposit

eine Abhebung machen
ay-nuh ap-hey-boong mA-CHuhn
to make a withdrawal

eine Zahlung machen
ay-nuh tsah-loong mA-CHuhn
to make a payment

ein Darlehen aufnehmen
ayn dAR-ley-uhn ouf-ney-muhn
to take out a loan

einen Scheck einlösen
ay-nuhn shek ayn-löh-zuhn
to cash a check

ein Konto eröffnen
ayn kon-toh eR-öf-nuhn
to open an account

ein Konto schließen
ayn kon-toh shlee-suhn
to close an account

etwas Geld wechseln
et-vAs gelt vek-suhln
to change some money

> **CAUTION**   **Achtung** _____
>
> German officials require your documents to be translated into German and stamped. Official stamps are *sehr* important in Germany and must occasionally be supplemented by a seal—perhaps a throwback to the fifteenth to nineteenth centuries! In the case of translation, only state-approved translators can give valid stamps. Where to find one? Check the Internet, the Yellow Pages, and newspapers—and be prepared to pay!

Werde ich einen monatlichen Kontoauszug bekommen?
veR-duh iH ay-nuhn mo-nAt-li-Huhn kon-toh-ous-tsewk buh-ko-muhn
Will I get a monthly statement?

Wie hoch ist der heutige Wechselkurs?
vee hoCH ist deyR hoy-ti-guh vek-suhl-kooRs
How high is today's exchange rate?

Haben Sie einen Bankautomaten?
hah-buhn zee ay-nuhn bAnk-ou-toh-mah-tuhn
Do you have an automatic teller machine?

Wie benutzt man ihn?
vee buh-nootst mAn een
How does one use it?

Ich möchte eine Hypothek aufnehmen.
iH möH-tuh ay-nuh hüh-poh-teyk ouf-ney-muhn
I'd like to take out a mortgage.

Wie hoch sind die monatlichen Zahlungen?
vee hoCH zint dee moh-nAt-li-Huhn tsah-loon-guhn
How much are the monthly payments?

Wie hoch ist die Zinsrate?
vee hoCH ist dee tsinz-Rah-tuh
What is the interest rate?

Wie groß ist der Zeitraum für das Darlehen?
vee gRohs ist deyR tsayt-Roum fühR dAs dAR-ley-uhn
What's the time period of the loan?

Would You Please ...

Remember that prodding, kind of sweet-sounding form of the modal *mögen (möchten)* and the polite form of *können (könnten)*? Well, those were the modals in the subjunctive mood. How about a surefire way to be able to express any verb, sentiment, or thought in a more tentative, modest, or polite way? Pay attention! In German, the subjunctive is frequently used to make statements and pose questions in such a manner. Compare these:

Gib mir mein Geld zurück!
gep meeR mayn gelt tsuh-Rük
Give me back my money!

With the subjunctive:

Würden Sie mir bitte mein Geld zurückgeben?
vüR-duhn zee meeR bi-tuh mayn gelt tsuh-Rük-gey-buhn
Would you please give me back my money?

The Subjunctive Verb *würden*

Person	Singular	English	Plural	English
First	ich würde *iH vüR-duh*	I would	wir würden *veeR vüR-duhn*	we would
Second	du würdest *dew vüR-duhst*	you would	ihr würdet *eeR vüR-duht*	you would
Third	er, sie, es würde *eR, zee, es vüR-duh*	he, she, it would	sie würden *zee vüR-duhn*	they would
Formal	Sie würden *zee vüR-duhn*	you would	Sie würden *zee vüR-duhn*	you would

In spoken German, like the English *would*, a form of *würde* can be used with almost any infinitive to express polite requests or wishes, or to give advice. As with any verb phrase, the unconjugated verb (infinitive/past participle) goes at the end of the sentence. Observe:

Würdest du mir helfen?
vüR-duhst dew meer hel-fuhn
Would you help me?

Ich würde gern mitkommen.
iH vüR-duh geRn mit-ko-muhn
I would like to come along.

Ich würde nicht so viel essen.
iH vür-duh niHt zo feel e-suhn
I wouldn't eat so much.

We Are Family

How global we are! Although using the actual subjunctive form of a verb (taking an ending and an umlaut, if a strong verb) used to be considered "good German," it has become customary to use the English-like form of *würde* + infinitive, practically mirroring the English construction of *would*. In Early Modern English (1500–1800 C.E.), the English modals were already infused with a subjunctive flavor—much like they exist today—regularly used with present or future meaning, implying speculation or politeness.

Now it's your turn to express yourself politely to your friends and family (informally). Rather than blurting out commands, seduce your audience into doing what you want them to do. Check your polite requests in Appendix A.

Example: Komm schnell! → *Würdest du bitte schnell kommen?*

1. Schreib oft!

2. Lies gute Zeitungen!

3. Nimm dein Medikament!

Instead of stating what you want to do (*ich will*), suggest it coyly.

Example: Ich will griechisch essen.→ *Ich würde gern griechish essen.*

1. Ich will nach Spanien fahren.

2. Ich will lang schlafen.

3. Ich will nur tanzen.

Finally, rather than telling someone what to or not to do, go ahead and give gentle advice:

Example: Studier mehr!→ *Ich würde mehr studieren.*

1. Geh in die Oper!

2. Trink mehr Milch!

3. Kauf nicht alles!

What Would You Do?

If you're not sure whether you're going to get everything done, you will probably want to use the subjunctive mood. In an ideal world, you would never have to use this mood—you would make a list of things to do and do them. Unfortunately, as much as you would like to do things and as much as you should do them, you don't always get them done. Thank goodness for the *subjunctive mood.*

I'm in a Subjunctive Mood

German has separate forms for verbs that are in the subjunctive mood, forms that are used to express wishes or contrary-to-fact statements. It's worth learning the subjunctive of certain high-frequency German verbs because it is very useful to be able to express yourself politely, or hope and long for something that is not. Because we're nearing the end of the book and you've already been exposed to the subjunctive form of *haben* (when you ordered food or requested other items), let's look at it. The entire subjunctive conjugation of *haben* appears in the following table.

The Subjunctive Forms for *haben*

Person	Singular	Plural
First	ich hätte	wir hätten
	iH hä-tuh	*veeR hä-tuhn*
Second	du hättest	ihr hättet
	dew hä-tuhst	*eeR hä-tuht*
Third	er, sie, es hätte	sie hätten
	eR, zee, es hä-tuh	*zee hä-tuhn*
Formal	Sie hätten	Sie hätten
	see hä-tuhn	*see hä-tuhn*

That's all fine and dandy, but what does it mean? Well, the German subjunctive can be translated into English a couple of ways. The way we have been understanding the subjunctive employs the adverb *gern* as a crutch:

> Ich hätte gern zwei Brötchen.
> *iH hä-tuh geRn tsvay bRöt-Huhn*
> I would like to have two rolls.

In this utterance, the *gern* helps to express the "like" part of the equation. The *hätte* expresses "would have." Nice and neat to have one sound-adulterated word express two English words, huh?

What's What

Subjunctive mood The verb form that indicates that something is relatively unlikely, conjectural, implausible, or contrary to fact.

You Have Three Wishes

You are walking along a path in the woods when you come upon a pear-shaped blue bottle. You try to twist the cork free, and, finally, it comes loose. You are surrounded by smoke, and a genie in *Lederhosen* and suspenders and a long beard is floating in the air before you. "*Sie haben drei Wünsche frei,*" the genie says. "*Was würden Sie am liebsten haben?*" ("You have three wishes. What would you most like to have?") Come up with a list of things you'd like to have, using the following suggestions. Check your wishes in Appendix A.

Example: einen BMW

Answer: Ich hätte am liebsten einen BMW.

1. ein Schloß

2. ein Stück Schwarzwälder Kirschtorte

3. viel Geld

4. ein Haus in den Alpen

5. ein großes Bier

6. viele schöne Blumen

The Least You Need to Know

◆ Familiarity with the appropriate banking terms will be your greatest asset when you are in a German bank.

◆ To express yourself politely with any verb, supply a form of the subjunctive *würde* plus an infinitive at the end. (*Ich würde …*)

◆ With the subjunctive mood of *haben* (*hätten*), you can express what you would like to have, be it food, cars, castles, or a good cup of coffee.

Chapter 25

Seeing Into the Future

In This Chapter

- ◆ Apartments and houses
- ◆ Rooms, furnishings, amenities, and appliances
- ◆ Speaking in the future tense
- ◆ Bureaucracy of residence and car registration

Are you tired of the hassles of a hotel? Is too much noise reaching your room from the street? Why not consider some modest alternative, like renting an apartment?

In this chapter, you'll learn how to get furnishings and appliances in case you decide to stay a while and explore the country in greater depth. You'll also learn how to express your plans for the future.

Lodgings

More people are becoming either temporary or permanent expatriates. Some of these adventurous folk migrate to Germany. You never know when you may decide that you want to start a new life in the *Bundesrepublik* and rent an apartment or even buy a house of your own.

In any case, you should be prepared to read and understand the apartments-for-rent and houses-for-sale sections of the *Zeitung* and be able to speak with real estate agents about properties to rent or to buy. The following table has the vocabulary you'll need to describe your ideal dwelling.

The House, the Apartment, the Rooms

German	Pronunciation	English
das Arbeitszimmer	*dAs AR-bayts-tsi-muhR*	study
das Badezimmer	*dAs bah-duh-tsi-muhR*	bathroom
das Dach	*dAs dACH*	roof
das Dachgeschoss	*dAs dACH-guh-shos*	attic
das Erdgeschoss	*dAs eRt-guh-shos*	ground floor
das Esszimmer	*dAs es-tsi-muhR*	dining room
das Fenster	*dAs fen-stuhR*	window
der Stock	*deyR shtok*	floor (story)
das Schlafzimmer	*dAs shlahf-tsi-muhR*	bedroom
das Treppenhaus	*dAs tRe-puhn-hous*	staircase
das Wohnzimmer	*dAs vohn-tsi-muhR*	living room
der Abstellraum	*deyR Ap-shtel-Roum*	storage room
der Aufzug	*deyR ouf-tsewk*	elevator
der Besitzer	*deyR buh-zi-tsuhR*	owner
der Fußboden	*deyR fews-boh-duhn*	floor
der Hinterhof	*deyR hin-tuhR-hohf*	backyard
der Innenhof	*deyR i-nuhn-hohf*	courtyard
der Kamin	*deyR kah-meen*	fireplace
der Keller	*deyR ke-luhR*	basement
der Mieter	*deyR mee-tuhR*	tenant
der Mietvertrag	*deyR meet-feR-tRahk*	lease
der Portier	*deyR poR-tee-eR*	doorman
der Vermieter	*deyR feR-mee-tuhR*	landlord
der Wandschrank	*deyR vAnt-shRAnk*	closet
die Decke	*dee de-kuh*	ceiling
die Dusche	*dee dew-shuh*	shower
die elektrische Heizung	*dee ey-lek-tRi-shuh hay-tsoong*	electric heating
die Gasheizung	*dee gahs-hay-tsoong*	gas heating
die Instandhaltung	*dee in-shtAnt-hAl-toong*	maintenance

German	Pronunciation	English
die Klimaanlage	*dee klee-mah-An-lah-guh*	air-conditioning
die Küche	*dee küh-Huh*	kitchen
die Miete	*dee mee-tuh*	rent
die Sauna	*dee zou-nah*	sauna
die Terrasse	*dee te-RA-suh*	terrace
der Balkon	*deyR bAl-kon*	balcony
die Wand	*dee vAnt*	wall
die Waschküche	*dee vAsh-küh-Huh*	laundry room
die Wohnung	*dee voh-noong*	apartment

Buying or Renting

Do you want to rent an apartment? Would you prefer to buy a house? Whether you're buying or renting, these phrases will serve you well.

Ich suche ….
iH zew-CHuh
I'm looking for ….

einen Immobilienmakler (m.)
ay-nuhn i-moh-bee-lee-uhn-mAk-luhR
a real estate agency

den Anzeigenteil
den An-tsay-guhn-tayl
the advertisement section

den Anzeigenteil für Immobilien
deyn An-tsay-guhn-tayl fühR i-moh-bee-lee-uhn
the real estate advertising section

Ich möchte … mieten (kaufen)
iH möH-tuh … mee-tuhn (kou-fuhn)
I would like to rent (buy) ….

eine Wohnung
ay-nuh voh-noong
an apartment

eine Eigentumswohnung
ay-nuh ay-guhn-tewmz-voh-noong
a condominium

Wie hoch ist die Miete?
vee hohCH ist dee mee-tuh
What is the rent?

Gibt es Einbrüche?
gipt es ayn-bRü-Huh
Are there break-ins?

Wie teuer ist die Instandhaltung der Wohnung (des Hauses)?
vee toy-uhR ist dee in-shtAnt-hAl-toong deyR voh-noong (des hou-zuhs)
How much is the maintenance of the apartment (house)?

Wie hoch sind die monatlichen Zahlungen?
vee hohCH zint dee moh-nAt-li-Huhn tsah-loon-guhn
How much are the monthly payments?

Ich möchte eine Hypothek aufnehmen.
iH möH-tuh ay-nuh hüh-poh-teyk ouf-ney-muhn
I'd like to apply for a mortgage.

Muss ich eine Kaution hinterlassen?
moos iH ay-nuh kou-tsee-ohn hin-tuhR-lA-suhn
Do I have to leave a deposit?

All the Comforts of Home

Start living in your new home; soon enough your needs become clear. When you go to close the curtains, you'll realize that they're missing. When you walk across the living room floor, the echo of your footsteps against the wood reminds you that a carpet would come in mighty handy. As evening falls and the rooms grow dark, you'll wish you had a lamp. The following table gives you a head start on the furniture and accessories you may not know you need until you really start to miss them.

Furniture and Accessories

German	Pronunciation	English
das Bett	*dAs bet*	bed
das Bücherregal	*dAs bü-HuhR-Rey-gahl*	bookshelf
das Eisfach	*dAs ays-fACH*	freezer
der Fernseher	*deyR feRn-zey-uhR*	television
der Kühlschrank	*deyR kühl-shRAnk*	refrigerator
der Ofen	*deyR o-fuhn*	oven

German	Pronunciation	English
der Sessel	*deyR ze-suhl*	armchair
der Stuhl	*deyR shtewl*	chair
der Teppich	*deyR te-piH*	carpet
das Sofa	*dAs zoh-fuh*	sofa
der Tisch	*deyR tish*	table
der Couchtisch	*deyR coutch-tish*	coffee table
der Schreibtisch	*deyR shRayp-tish*	desk
der Trockner	*deyR tRok-nuhR*	dryer
die elektrischen Küchengeräte	*dee ey-leyk-tRi-shuhn küh-Huhn-guh-Räh-tuh*	kitchen appliances
die Gardinen	*dee gAR-dee-nuhn*	curtains
die Kommode	*dee ko-moh-duh*	dresser
die Möbel (pl.)	*dee möh-buhl*	furniture
die Spülmaschine	*dee shpühl-mA-shee-nuh*	dishwasher
die Uhr	*dee ewR*	clock
möbliert	*möh-bleeRt*	furnished
unmöbliert	*oon-möh-bleeRt*	unfurnished
ruhig	*Ru-iH*	calm
hell	*hel*	bright
bequem	*buh-kveym*	comfortable

Auf Möbelsuche (on the Search for Furniture)

Suppose you've found an unfurnished house or apartment. What kinds of furniture do you need? Formulate sentences (using the accusative case for the direct object) saying that you need the following items. Refer to Chapter 10 if you need some adjectival adjustment. Check your sentences in Appendix A.

> Example: a big bed   Ich brauche ein großes Bett.

1. A comfortable sofa

2. A small chair

3. A stylish clock

4. A bright lamp

5. An inexpensive table

Read this advertisement and then try to describe in English what you can expect if you shop at this particular furniture store. Check your comprehension in Appendix A.

German Culture

In Germany, the kitchen and bathroom are not counted as "rooms" when describing the number of rooms in an apartment. Thus, a *Zweizimmerwohunung* has one bedroom and a living room. An *Appartement* is just as quaint and cozy as it sounds: it's a studio or efficiency apartment.

Möbelhaus Müller

Absolute Qualitätsgarantie

Wir garantieren kostenlose Reparatur der Möbel innerhalb der ersten zwei Jahre.

Wir liefern Ihnen Ihre Möbel kostenlos nach Hause.

Wir kaufen Ihre alten Möbel zurück.

Wir versichern Ihnen absolute Preis- und Qualitätsgarantie.

There's Hope for the Future

If you're planning to stay in Germany longer than anticipated, or you even acquire some property, the first thing you're going to have to do is learn how to express your plans in the *future tense*.

Expressing the Future

To express the future in German colloquial speech, the present tense is often used in reference to the future, utilizing adverbs such as *soon* and *next week*. This also is done in English, though not as commonly. Another way of speaking in the future is to use the future tense. To form the future tense, use the present tense of the auxiliary verb *werden* (veR-duhn) along with the infinitive of the main verb. *Werden* literally means "to become," but it loses this meaning when utilized as a helping verb to form the future tense. Earlier you learned that German has four irregular verbs. Well, *werden* is the fourth! You'll observe that it is, indeed, irregular: It not only changes the stem vowel, but it also goofs around with consonants and endings.

The following table conjugates the auxiliary verb *werden* to produce the future tense of *kaufen*.

What's What

Future tense To form the future tense, use the present tense of the auxiliary verb *werden* with the infinitive of the verb.

Here is the formula to produce the future tense:

Subject + conjugated present tense of *werden* + the infinitive of the verb

---

werden + kaufen = Future Tense of *kaufen*

Person	Singular	English	Plural	English
First	ich werde kaufen *iH veR-duh kou-fuhn*	I will buy	wir werden kaufen *veeR veR-duhn kou-fuhn*	we will buy
Second	du wirst kaufen *dew virst kou-fuhn*	you will buy	ihr werdet kaufen *eeR veR-duht kou-fuhn*	you will buy
Third	er, sie, es wird kaufen *eR, zee, es virt kou-fuhn*	he, she, it will buy	sie werden kaufen *zee ver-duhn kou-fuhn*	they will buy
Formal	Sie werden kaufen *zee veR-duhn kou-fuhn*	you will buy	Sie werden kaufen *zee veR-duhn kou-fuhn*	you will buy

Tomorrow's Plans

Make a list of all the things you and your friends are going to do tomorrow, using subject pronouns and verbal phrases. Check your sentences in Appendix A.

Example: ich/ein Auto kaufen

Answer: Ich werde ein Auto kaufen.

1. Christa und Inge/ins Kino gehen

2. Klaus/Brot backen

3. Ingo und ich/Tennis spielen

4. Meine Mutter/zum Zahnarzt gehen

5. ich/Norbert anrufen

6. Liesel und ich/ein Buch lesen

7. ihr/Rad fahren

8. Wolfram und Catharine/viel Deutsch sprechen

We Are Family

Old English verbs were inflected for only two tenses: present and past. Without a future conjugation, the present was used to express future time, with adverbs added to avoid ambiguity. Whereas English relies on *will* plus an infinitive to express the future ("She will call him tomorrow"), German can express the future with the present tense and an adverb: *Sie ruft ihn morgen an* ("She'll call him tomorrow").

So You Want to Live in Germany?

If you want to live and work in Germany (and you're not a citizen of the European Union), be prepared for *sehr viel:* red tape. You'll need to acquire a residence permit at the residents' registration office (*Einwohnermeldeamt*) within two weeks of moving to a new community. This rule applies to everyone, even students living in a community temporarily. (In addition, you must notify the same *Einwohnermeldeamt* when you move out of a community.) You'll also need a work permit, which itself requires a written offer of employment sufficient to convince the bureaucracy that only you—and no European with the right to work in Germany—can do the job. Hey, the United States subjects all foreign workers to this routine, after all.

Sound like a lot? Well, you might make it easier by contacting your local German diplomatic representative before you leave home. That way, you'll find out in advance where you stand, which documents and photos to take along, whether you'll have to take a physical at the public health department, and various other bureaucratic sundries. Once you get to Germany, you'll have ample time to try out your German because you'll be skipping from one permit-issuing office to another and back again, if you get something wrong. Just think of it as a board game—if you're very fortunate, you won't have to return to Go too many times. Oh! Did we mention that permits need to be renewed at set intervals? Ah! The fun never ends!

German Culture

Be forewarned that the way many Germans drive might require you, as a passenger or a driver, to have nerves of steel. Most stretches of the *Autobahn* do not have a speed limit, and drivers generally tend to ignore the "recommended" speed of 130 kilometers per hour—around 80 miles per hour. Slower traffic is not only supposed to keep to the right, but it does, as those in the left lane overtake at breakneck speed. If you are in that left lane and see a faint flash of headlights behind you, figure that you have two seconds, tops, to get the heck over to the right, lest you become a hood ornament.

I Need My Wheels!

Alright, so you figured out you're in it for the long haul, and you just can't bear waiting for the trains to run. You desire the freedom and independence that an automobile can provide. Well, by now you're accustomed to searching out various governmental agencies and standing in line. Thus, you won't be surprised to learn that registering a car is about the same (and perhaps as bothersome) as registering yourself. Naturally, if you change your address during your car's lifetime, you have to re-register the car, in person, after you have re-registered yourself. Of course, you'll need to clear your car through the motor vehicle inspection department (*TÜV*) before you can register it—and thereafter once every two years. If your car passes that inspection, you can feel pretty proud to be driving in Germany and can rest assured that your car is in pretty good shape.

The Least You Need to Know

♦ After you learn a few basic phrases, you should have no trouble buying or renting an apartment, house, or castle (you never know!) from a German real estate agent.

♦ To furnish specific rooms, you will have to know the vocabulary for furnishings, amenities, and appliances.

♦ To speak of something you plan to do in the future, use the perfect tense with an implication of future action, or use the future tense, which is formed with the helping verb *werden* conjugated in the present + the verb in the infinitive.

♦ If you intend to stay in Germany somewhat permanently, you'll need to register yourself and, if you'll be working, obtain a work permit.

♦ A car, if you have one, adheres to the same rules of registration as you do!

Answer Key

You will find the answers to the exercises in this book arranged here by chapter and heading.

Chapter 1

Your Turn at Inside Information

1. Wir sind <u>innerhalb</u> <u>von</u> zwei Stunden zu Hause.

2. Er hatte <u>direkte</u> Informationen über das Pferderennen.

3. Wir gehen ins <u>Innere</u> der Höhle.

4. Er versteckt den Schlüssel im <u>Innern</u> der Schachtel.

5. Der <u>Magen</u> des Mannes schmertz.

Chapter 4

How Much Do You Understand Already?

1. Der Bandit ist blond.

2. Die Bank ist modern.

3. Die Olive ist parallel.

4. Der Wind ist warm.

5. Das Chaos ist irrational.

Cognate Conversation

1. Das Wetter ist gut.

2. Ist das Buch interessant?

3. Der Autor ist populär.

4. Das Parfüm ist attraktiv.

5. Der Wind ist warm.

6. Der Charakter ist primitiv.

7. Das Herz ist wild.

8. Das Salz ist weiß.

Putting It All Together

1. The president and the bandit bake tomatoes.

2. The uncle drinks wine.

3. The tiger and the elephant swim in the ocean.

4. The film begins in a supermarket.

5. "Religion or chaos? A modern problem," said the young, intelligent author.

6. The doctor and the detective find the lamp interesting.

7. My brother has a guitar.

8. The alligator costs $10,000.

Chapter 5

Describing Travel

1. Ich fahre <u>mit dem Zug/mit dem Flugzeug</u> von Wisconsin nach Vancouver.

2. Ich fahre <u>mit dem Auto/mit dem Bus</u> vom Flughafen zum See.

3. Ich fahre <u>mit dem Schiff</u> über den See.

4. Ich fahre <u>mit der Straßenbahn/mit der U-bahn/mit dem Bus</u> in einer Großstadt.

5. Ich gehe <u>zu Fuß</u> an die Uni.

Expressing Time

1. bis bald/auf Wiedersehen

2. bis später/bis heute Abend

3. pünktlich

4. (zu) spät

5. (zu) früh

6. von Zeit zu Zeit

7. regelmäßig/täglich/jeden Tag

8. wöchentlich

Stating Location

1. Gegenüber der Post ist der Bahnhof.

2. Vor dem Museum ist der Parkplatz.

3. Links neben dem Hotel ist der Bahnhof.

4. Hinter dem Café ist der Spielplatz.

5. Gegenüber der Bäckerei ist der Parkplatz.

What's Your Opinion?

1. <u>Ich habe keine Ahnung.</u> Ich habe den Wetterbericht nicht gelesen.

2. <u>Das ist eine tolle Idee.</u> Ich schwimme sehr gern!

3. <u>Du hast recht.</u> Das ist mir schon oft passiert.

4. <u>Das ist mir egal.</u> Ich glaube, in jeder Zeitung finden wir einen Wetterbericht.

5. <u>Klar!</u> Ich will den neusten Arnold Schwarzenegger Film sehen.

How Are You?

1. Ich bin <u>müde.</u>

2. Mir ist <u>kalt.</u>

3. Sie weint. Sie ist <u>traurig.</u>

4. Ich bin <u>glücklich,</u> dass das Wetter gut ist.

5. Mein Magen knurrt. Ich bin <u>hungrig.</u>

6. Ich bin <u>verliebt.</u>

7. Ich kann nicht mehr! Ich bin <u>fertig.</u>

8. Ich bin <u>fit.</u>

9. Ich bin <u>gut gelaunt.</u>

Chapter 6

Compound Nouns

1. die Hotelkette

2. das Musikgeschäft

3. das Geschenkpapier

4. die Telefonnummer

5. der Briefkasten

6. die Schwerkraft

7. der Treffpunkt

Im Zimmer Sind ...

1. die Zimmer

2. die Gärten

3. die Wände

4. die Bilder

5. die Bücher

6. die Schüsseln

7. die Briefe

8. die Zeitungen

Chapter 7

Identifying Function

1. (Den Studenten) findet <u>der Detektiv</u> intelligent.

2. [Dem Vater] schicken <u>die Kinder</u> (den Kaffee).

3. <u>Die Menschen</u> helfen [den Kindern].

4. (Das Paket) packt <u>der Lehrer.</u>

5. Die Mütter bringen [den Vätern] (die Blumen).

Du, Ihr, or Sie?

1. Wie finden <u>Sie</u> Amerika?

2. Was machen <u>Sie</u>?

3. Was bringt <u>ihr</u>?

4. Was trinkst <u>du</u>?

5. Warum stinkst <u>du</u>?

6. Was planen <u>Sie</u>?

Er, Sie, Es?

1. <u>Sie</u> tanzten.

2. <u>Sie</u> war heiter.

3. <u>Sie</u> weinte.

4. <u>Er</u> war betrunken.

5. <u>Es</u> ist groß.

Chapter 8

Painless Conjugation

1. Ich <u>suche</u> das Museum.

2. Klaus <u>reserviert</u> ein Hotelzimmer.

3. Sie <u>warten</u> auf den Bus.

4. Ihr <u>mietet</u> ein Auto.

5. Wir <u>fragen</u> nach der Adresse.

6. Ich <u>lerne</u> Deutsch.

7. Ich <u>reise</u> nach Hamburg.

8. Er <u>braucht</u> ein Taxi.

9. Du <u>telefonierst</u> mit deiner Mutter.

10. Tina <u>bestellt</u> ein Glas Wein.

11. Christoph, du <u>tanzt</u> gut.

12. Der Professor <u>arbeitet</u> jeden Tag.

13. Die Professorin <u>öffnet</u> das Fenster.

14. Die Pizza <u>kostet</u> nur 7 Euro.

Bear the Sound Change and Conjugate

1. Hans <u>isst</u> gern Bratwurst.

2. Er <u>gibt</u> mir einen guten Tip.

3. Christoph <u>sieht</u> einen Biergarten.

4. Petra <u>trifft</u> ihre deutsche Brieffreundin.

5. Du <u>sprichst</u> sehr gut Englisch.

6. Karl <u>liest</u> die Süddeutsche Zeitung.

7. Almut <u>fährt</u> nach Berlin.

8. Der Bus <u>hält</u> vor der Kirche.

9. Der Bayer <u>bläst</u> das Horn.

10. Meine Freundin <u>empfiehlt</u> das Restaurant.

11. Die Sonne <u>scheint</u> sehr hell.

12. Du <u>wäschst</u> die Wäsche jede Woche.

13. Paul <u>läuft</u> sehr schnell und oft.

14. Er <u>genießt</u> sein Bier.

15. Die Professorin <u>trägt</u> einen Mikro-Rock.

Ask Me If You Can

1. Kostet das Ticket 200 Euro?
2. Ist das Terminal für internationale Flüge?
3. Steht die Flugnummer auf dem Ticket?
4. Gibt es Toiletten auf dieser Etage?
5. Dauert der Flug zwei Stunden?
6. Ist das Abendessen inklusiv?

Chapter 9

Professions

1. Ich bin Kellner (Kellnerin).
2. Er ist Krankenpfleger.
3. Sie ist Ärztin.
4. Ich bin Rechtsanwalt (Rechtsanwältin).
5. Du bist Student (Studentin).
6. Er ist Polizist.
7. Sie ist Geschäftsführerin.
8. Sie sind Schriftsteller (schriftstellerin).

Ask Away

A: Sample Questions

1. Woher kommst du?
2. Mit wem reist du?
3. Wohin reist du?
4. Was trinkst du?
5. Wo trinkst du?
6. Wie lang(e) trinkst du?

B: Sample Questions

1. Wie heißt sie?
2. Woher kommt sie?
3. Wie lang(e) reist sie?
4. Wo reist sie?
5. Gefällt ihr die Schweiz?
6. Wann reist sie zurück?

Chapter 10

Mine, All Mine

1. seine Schwester
2. mein Onkel
3. unsere Familie
4. eure Kinder
5. der Bruder des Mädchens
6. die Mutter des Mannes
7. die Eltern des Kindes
8. der Ehemann meiner Schwester
9. die Eltern seiner Frau
10. die Tante deines Cousins

Using Possessive Adjectives to Show Your Preference

1. Mein Lieblingsfilm ist ....
2. Meine Lieblingsschriftstellerin ist ....
3. Mein Lieblingsbuch ist ....
4. Meine Lieblingsstadt ist ....
5. Mein Lieblingssänger ist ....

Breaking the Ice

1. Darf ich mich vorstellen? Mein Name ist ....
2. Ich komme aus ....
3. Ich bin ....
4. Woher kommen Sie?
5. Kennen Sie (meinen Bruder, meine Schwester, meine Mutter, meinen Vater ...)?
6. Das ist ....
7. Mein Name ist .... Es freut mich, Sie kennenzulernen.

Using Idioms with *haben*

1. Er <u>hat keine Lust</u> mitzukommen.
2. Sie <u>hat den Mut</u>, Bungy-Jumping zu machen.
3. Er <u>hat die Absicht</u> zu heiraten.
4. Anne und Mark <u>haben die Zeit</u>, eine Reise nach Deutschland zu machen.
5. Ihr <u>habt Glück</u> im Spiel.

Applying Adjectives

A. 1. Wo spielt dieser interessant<u>e</u> Film?

2. Ich nehme das kalt<u>e</u> Bier.

3. Jedes rot<u>e</u> T-Shirt ist billig.

4. Wir besuchen die klein<u>e</u> Stadt.

5. Sie lesen den best<u>en</u> Autor.

B. 1. Das ist warm<u>es</u> Brot.

2. Sie hat klug<u>e</u> Ideen.

3. Frisch<u>er</u> Salat ist gesund.

4. Haben Sie schön<u>e</u> Blumen?

5. Lieb<u>e</u> Kerstin, ….

C. 1. Mainz ist eine schön<u>e</u>, alt<u>e</u> Stadt.

2. Er ist mein best<u>er</u> Freund.

3. Ich sehe seine jung<u>e</u> Schwester.

4. Wo ist ein gut<u>es</u> Restaurant?

5. Wir kaufen ein neu<u>es</u> Auto.

Chapter 11

Signs Everywhere

1. D   4. C
2. B   5. A
3. E

Giving Commands

A. Sie (formal)

B. ihr (informal, pl.)

C. du (informal, sg.)

Giving Orders

Verb	du	ihr	Sie	English
abbiegen	Biege ab!	Biegt ab!	Biegen Sie ab!	Turn!
weiter-gehen	Geh(e) weiter!	Geht weiter!	Gehen Sie weiter!	Go on!
laufen	Lauf(e)!	Lauft!	Laufen Sie!	Walk!
mitfahren	Fahr(e) mit!	Fahrt mit!	Fahren Sie mit!	Ride along!

Dative Prepositions

1. aus <u>dem</u> Flugzeug
2. bei <u>dem</u> (beim) Flughafen
3. von sein<u>er</u> Arbeit
4. zu <u>die</u> (zum) Hotel

Accusative Prepositions

1. durch <u>das</u> (durchs) Land
2. ohne <u>das</u> Ticket
3. um <u>den</u> Sitz
4. bis <u>die</u> Sicherheitskontrolle

Two-Way Prepositions

1. auf dein<u>en</u> Sitz
2. an <u>der</u> Grenze
3. in <u>der</u> Toilette
4. neben <u>das</u> Bett
5. unter dein<u>em</u> Handgepäck

Chapter 12

A Means to an End

1. Ich nehme ein Taxi, um zum Geschäft zu kommen.

2. Wir nehmen die Straßenbahn, um in die Innenstadt zu kommen.

3. Er nimmt das Auto, um zur Kirche zu fahren.

4. Du nimmst das Fahrrad, um aufs Land zu fahren.

Using Which

1. Welchen Zug nehmen Sie?

2. In welche Stadt fährst du?

3. Welches Auto mietet er?

4. Welchen Freund besuchst du?

5. In welches Museum geht ihr?

6. Welches Hotel sucht sie?

7. Welches Buch nimmt er mit?

Wie spat ist es?

1. sieben Uhr achtunddreißig

2. drei Uhr sechs/sechs (Minuten) nach drei

3. vierzehn Uhr

4. zwölf Uhr fünfundzwanzig/ fünf vor halb eins

5. neunzehn Uhr dreißig/halb zwanzig

6. einundzwanzig Uhr fünfzig/fünf vor zweiundzwanzig

Chapter 13

What a Hotel! Does It Have ...?

Gast: Guten Tag. Haben Sie ein Zimmer frei?

Empfangschef: Möchten Sie ein Zimmer mit einem Balkon? Wir haben ein wunderschönes Zimmer mit Aussicht zur Meerseite.

Gast: Ja, warum nicht? Hat das Zimmer ein Telefon? Ich erwarte einen wichtigen Anruf.

Empfangschef: Selbstverständlich. Möchten Sie Vollpension oder Halbpension?

Gast: Vollpension, bitte.

Empfangschef: Gut. Die Zimmernummer ist 33. Hier ist Ihr Schlüssel. Gute Nacht.

Calling Housekeeping

1. Ich brauche einen Adapter.

2. Ich hätte gern ein Mineralwasser.

3. Ich brauche Briefpapier.

4. Ich hätte gern einen Aschenbecher und Streichhölzer.

5. Ich brauche ein Kopfkissen.

6. Ich möchte ein Badetuch, bitte.

The Declension of Ordinal Numbers

1. Wir haben nicht viel Geld. Wir fahren zweiter Klasse.

2. "Erster Stop ist Marl; zweiter Stop ist Haltern; dritter Stop ist Recklinghausen," sagt der Busfahrer.

3. Mein erster Beruf war Tellerwäscher. Heute bin ich Millionär.

4. Zuerst kommt die Post. Das zweite Gebäude auf der linken Seite ist ein Hotel.

5. Auf der zweiten Etage befindet sich das Restaurant. Auf der dritten Etage ist das Einkaufszentrum.

6. Er hat schon drei Söhne. Sein viertes wird ein Mädchen.

7. Wenn eine Katze schon acht Leben gehabt hatte, ist sie jetzt im neunten Lebensjahr.

Euro

1. Das Buch kostet dreizehn (Euro) fünf-undvierzig.

2. Die Blumen kosten sieben Euro zehn.

3. Die Ansichtskarte kostet fünfzig Cents.

4. Ein Einzelzimmer kostet einundsechzig Euro.

5. Das Ticket kostet sechsunddreißig (Euro) neunundneunzig.

wissen or *kennen?*

1. <u>Weißt</u> du, wo Kerstin wohnt?

2. Ich <u>kenne</u> niemanden mit dem Namen "Kerstin."

3. Ich <u>weiß</u>, dass sie sehr hübsch und intelligent ist!

4. Vielleicht <u>kennt</u> Ronja sie.

5. <u>Kennen</u> wir nicht Kerstins Mann, Frank?

6. Ich <u>kenne</u> ihren Mann vom Bus.

Coming Apart: Verbs with Separable Prefixes

1. Wann <u>sehen</u> wir den Film <u>an</u>?

2. Tina <u>liest</u> das Buch <u>vor</u>.

3. <u>Geben</u> Sie nie <u>auf</u>!

4. Gretchen <u>trinkt</u> ihr Bier immer <u>aus</u>!

Sticking It Out Together: Verbs with Inseparable Prefixes

1. Wo <u>bekommen</u> Sie das?

2. Ich <u>vergesse</u> die Adresse.

3. Boris Becker <u>gewinnt</u> fast immer.

4. Welches Restaurant <u>empfiehlst</u> du?

Let's ...

1. Lass uns nach Deutschland reisen!/ Reisen wir nach Deutschland!

2. Lass uns in den Garten gehen!/Gehen wir in den Garten!

3. Lass uns den Bus nehmen!/Nehmen wir den Bus!

4. Lass uns die Stadt besuchen!/Besuchen wir die Stadt!

5. Lass uns Deutsch lernen!/Lernen wir Deutsch!

Chapter 14

Call Me ...

1. Ich kenne die Straße, aber nicht die <u>Hausnummer</u>.

2. Die <u>Postleitzahl</u> kommt vor der Stadt in der Adresse.

3. Ich habe ein Telefon. Meine <u>Telefonnummer</u> ist 03-45-60.

4. Du schickst eine <u>Postkarte/Ansichtskarte</u> an deine Mutter.

5. Sein Name ist sehr lang! <u>Wie buchstabiert man</u> das?

European Countries, According to Germans

1. aus der Schweiz

2. aus Deutschland

3. aus Italien

4. aus Österreich

5. aus Großbritanien

6. aus Frankreich

How's the Weather?

1. Erfurt: bewölkt

2. München: heiter bis wolkig

3. Schwerin: sonnig

4. Kiel: regnerisch

5. Düsseldorf: gewitter

A Mouthful of Months

1. Mein Geburtstag ist im …
2. Ich mache Urlaub im …
3. Mein Lieblingsmonat ist der …
4. Die Schule beginnt im …

The Four Seasons

1. Es schneit viel im Winter.
2. Die Blätter fallen von den Bäumen im Herbst.
3. Die Blumen blühen im Frühling.
4. Die Sonne scheint oft im Sommer.

Dates

1. Valentinstag ist am 14. Februar.
2. Mein Geburtstag ist am ….
3. Der Hochzeitstag meiner Eltern ist am ….
4. Neujahr ist am 1. Januar.

Time Expressions

1. My birthday is a week from today.
2. Yesterday, the weather was good.
3. Saturdays I play tennis.
4. We travel to Germany the day after tomorrow.
5. We are eating in a restaurant the next day.

Chapter 15

What Do You Want to See?

1. Im Nachtclub sieht man eine Vorstellung.
2. In der Kathedrale sieht man die Glasmalerei.
3. Im Schloß sieht man (die) Wandteppiche.
4. Im Zoo sieht man (die) Tiere.
5. Im Museum sieht man (die) Bilder und Skulpturen.
6. Im Kino sieht man den Film.
7. In der Disco sieht man (die) Tänzer.
8. In der Bibliothek sieht man (die) Bücher.

Making Suggestions

1. Ich kann später kommen.
2. Was willst du machen?
3. Christina muss viel lernen.
4. Dieser Film soll sehr gut sein.
5. Wolfram darf nicht mitkommen.

More Suggestions

1. Lass uns eine Kirche besichtigen!

   Fantastisch! Ich liebe Kirchen.

   Nein, das interessiert mich nicht.

2. Lass uns eine Ausstellung sehen!

   Ja, das interessiert mich.

   Nein, das ist langweilig.

3. Lass uns nach Europa reisen!

   Ja, ich liebe Europa.

   Nein, ich mag Europa nicht.

4. Lass uns Bilder anschauen!

   Ja, das interessiert mich.

   Nein, ich habe keine Lust.

5. Las uns in die Oper gehen!

   Ja, das interessiert mich.

   Nein, das interessiert mich nicht.

6. Lass uns mit der U-bahn fahren!

   Ja, ich mag das.

   Nein, ich mag das nicht.

7. Lass uns ein Auto mieten!

   Wunderschön! Das macht mir Spaß!

   Nein, ich kann nicht Auto fahren!

Chapter 16

Wear It Well

1. Unter unseren Schuhen tragen wir Socken.
2. Wenn ich schlafe, trage ich einen Schalfanzug.
3. Unter deiner Hose trägst du Unterwäsche.
4. Wenn es regnet, trage ich einen Regenmantel.
5. Im Winter tragt ihr warme Handschuhe.
6. Wenn man in die Oper geht, trägt man einen Anzug mit einem Schlips.
7. Im Sommer tragen viele Leute Shorts und ein T-shirt.

Colors

1. Ich möchte einen hellroten Rock.
2. Ich möchte einen dunkelblauen Anzug.
3. Ich möchte einen hellgelben Hut.
4. Ich möchte eine graue Jacke.
5. Ich möchte eine/einen gepunktete/gepunkteten Krawatte/Schlips.
6. Ich möchte eine karierte Hose.
7. Ich möchte einen modischen Badeanzug.
8. Ich möchte ein gestreiftes Hemd.

Accusative Pronouns

1. Ich trage sie.
2. Du trägst ihn.
3. Kerstin trägt es.
4. Frank trägt sie.

Dative Pronouns

1. Ich gebe ihnen Schokolade.
2. Bernadette schenkt ihr Blumen.
3. Thomas dankt ihm für den Kaffee.
4. Wir geben ihm eine Olive.

Using Direct Object Pronouns

1. Ja, ich mag ihn./Nein, ich mag ihn nicht.
2. Ja, ich mag sie./Nein, ich mag sie nicht.
3. Ja, ich mag sie./Nein, ich mag sie nicht.
4. Ja, ich mag es./Nein, ich mag es nicht.

Using Indirect Object Pronouns

1. Schenk ihnen einen Schal!
2. Schenk ihr ein Kleid!
3. Schenk ihm eine kurze Hose!
4. Schenk ihr eine Strumpfhose!
5. Schenke ihn ihnen!
6. Schenke es ihr!
7. Schenke sie ihm!
8. Schenke sie ihr!

What's Your Preference?

1. Welche Krawatte?
2. Welcher Anzug?
3. Welches T-shirt?
4. Welche Schuhe?
5. Welches Kleid?
6. Welchen Schlafanzug?

Chapter 17

Getting There

1. Ich gehe zur Konditorei.
2. Ich gehe zum Metzger/zur Metzgerei.
3. Ich gehe zur Bäckerei/zum Bäcker.
4. Ich gehe zum Fischgeschäft.

Trinken

1. Was möchten Sie trinken?
2. Ich möchte ein Bier trinken.

3. Die beiden Frauen am Nachbartisch <u>trinken</u> Kaffee.

4. Mattias und ich <u>trinken</u> gern milden Wein.

5. Am liebsten <u>trinke</u> ich Limonade.

6. Was <u>trinkst</u> du am liebsten?

A Trip to the Market

1. Ich möchte drei Flaschen Wein.

2. Ich möchte ein halbes Pfund Garnelen.

3. Ich möchte ein Viertel Pfund Käse.

4. Ich möchte eine Tüte Kirschen.

5. Ich möchte ein Dutzend Eier.

6. Ich möchte ein Kilo Lachs.

7. Ich möchte drei Pfund Kartoffeln.

8. Ich möchte ein halbes Kilo/ein Pfund Wurst.

9. Ich möchte einen Liter Sahne.

10. Ich möchte eine Kiste Bier.

Chapter 18

Something's Missing

1. Mir fehlt die Tasse.

2. Ihm fehlt der Löffel.

3. Ihr fehlt das Messer.

4. Uns fehlt der Salzstreuer.

You Need What?

1. Ich brauche eine Speisekarte.

2. Ich brauche ein Glas.

3. Ich brauche eine Serviette.

4. Ich brauche eine Untertasse.

That's the Way I Like It

1. Sie möchte ihr Steak <u>gut durchgebraten</u>.

2. Hans möchte seinen Fisch <u>paniert</u>.

3. Wir möchten unsere Kartoffeln <u>püriert</u>.

4. Ich möchte mein Gemüse <u>gedünstet</u>.

5. Ich hätte gern ein <u>Spiegelei</u>.

Chapter 19

Where to Play

1. Ich wandere am liebsten im <u>Gebirge</u>.

2. Fußball spielen wir auf dem <u>Fußballplatz</u>.

3. Zum Ski fahren gehe ich auf die <u>Skipiste</u>.

4. Anna schwimmt gern im <u>Schwimmbad</u>.

5. Wir segeln gern auf dem <u>Meer</u>.

6. Schlittschuh lauft ihr im <u>Eisstadion</u>.

Express Your Desire with Mögen

1. Anne <u>möchte</u> bergsteigen.

2. Wir <u>möchten</u> wandern.

3. Franz und Klara <u>möchten</u> reiten.

4. Ihr <u>möchtet</u> in der Sporthalle Federball spielen.

5. Hans und Franz <u>möchten</u> am Fluss angeln.

Do You Accept or Refuse?

1. Möchten Sie Basketball spielen? Ja, das ist eine gute Idee.

2. Möchten Sie wandern? Nein, ich bin müde.

3. Möchten Sie Fußball spielen? Warum nicht?

4. Möchten Sie angeln? Nein, ich habe keine Zeit.

5. Möchten Sie Federball spielen? Nein, ich bin müde.

6. Möchten Sie Radfahren? Natürlich.

Just How Good Are You at Adverbs?

1. Ich tanze ….
2. Ich spiele … Klavier.
3. Ich koche ….
4. Ich spiele … Golf.
5. Ich laufe ….
6. Ich singe ….
7. Ich spiele … Tennis.
8. Ich wandere ….

Chapter 20

At the Dry Cleaner

1. diese Bluse, dieses Sakko, diese Krawatte/diesen Schlips
2. diese Jacke, diese Shorts, diesen Schal
3. diese Hose, dieses Hemd, diesen Rock
4. dieses Kleid, diesen Anzug, diese Socken

At the Laundromat

1. dryer = der Trockner
2. laundromat = der Waschsalon
3. washing machine = die Waschmaschine
4. laundry soap = der Waschpulver
5. to wash = waschen (sehr stark)
6. to look for = suchen
7. to buy = kaufen
8. to use = benutzen
9. dirty = dreckig/schmutzig

I Need These Shoes

1. Ich suche einen Waschsalon.
2. Können Sie dieses Kleid für mich reinigen?
3. Um wie viel Uhr schließen Sie?

4. Können Sie mir meine Schuhe putzen, bitte?
5. Ich habe viel dreckige Wäsche.
6. Wo kann ich diese Schuhe putzen?

At the Jeweler—beim Juwelier

1. Verkaufen Sie Batterien?
2. Verkaufen Sie Armbanduhren?
3. Können Sie meine/diese Armbanduhr reparieren?

Make Degree Evaluations

1. der kürzeste Haarschnitt
2. die lockigste Dauerwelle
3. eine dunklere Farbe
4. das schmutzigste/dreckigste Hemd
5. der billigste Waschsalon
6. Dieser Trockner ist größer.
7. der nächste Juwelier
8. Meine Armbanduhr läuft am langsamsten.

Chapter 21

Doctor, Doctor

1. Ich habe eine Erkältung.
2. Ich habe Husten.
3. Ich habe Kopfschmerzen.
4. Ich habe Bauchschmerzen.
5. Ich habe eine Blase.
6. Ich habe Fieber.

Have It on Hand

1. Ich brauche Aspirin.
2. Ich brauche Krücken.
3. Ich brauche Heftpflaster.

4. Ich brauche Taschentücher.

5. Ich brauche Schlaftabletten.

6. Ich brauche Hustenbonbons.

7. Ich brauche Rasierschaum.

8. Ich brauche eine Wärmflasche.

9. Ich brauche eine Nagelfeile.

Reflexive Verbs in Action

1. Ich wasche mich.

2. Ich rasiere mich.

3. Ich ziehe mich an.

4. Ich mache mich fertig.

5. Ich strecke mich.

6. Ich ziehe mich aus.

7. Ich lege mich hin.

Be Bossy

1. Wasch(e) dich! Wasch(e) dich nicht!

2. Zieh dich um! Zieh dich nicht um!

3. Rasier dich! Rasier dich nicht!

4. Mach(e) dich fertig! Mach(e) dich nicht fertig!

5. Setz dich! Setz dich nicht!

6. Entspann dich! Entspann dich nicht!

Chapter 22

Producing the Perfekt

1. Ich <u>bin</u> in die Drogerie <u>gegangen</u>.

2. Ich <u>habe</u> Aspirin und Rasierschaum aus dem Regal <u>genommen</u>.

3. Ich <u>habe</u> meine Einkäufe zur Kasse <u>gebracht</u>.

4. Sie <u>haben</u> nicht viel <u>gekostet</u>.

5. Ich <u>habe</u> der Kassiererin <u>geantwortet</u>.

6. Ich <u>habe</u> nicht an meine Einkaufstasche <u>gedacht</u>.

7. Ich <u>habe</u> sie nicht <u>mitgenommen</u>.

All You Did

1. Du bist ins Museum gegangen.

2. Er hat die Einkäufe vergessen.

3. Sie ist zum Friseur gefahren.

4. Sie hat den Anruf gemacht.

5. Wir haben den Film gesehen.

6. Ihr habt an eure Eltern gedacht.

7. Ich habe Toast gemacht.

8. Du bist in den Bergen gewandert.

9. Sie haben die Oper genossen.

10. Ich habe ein Glas Wein getrunken.

Ask Questions

1. Seid ihr zum Friseur gegangen? Seid ihr nicht zum Friseur gegangen?

2. Haben sie den Hustensaft getrunken? Haben sie den Hustensaft nicht getrunken?

3. Hast du an die Einkaufstasche gedacht? Hast du nicht an die Einkaufstasche gedacht?

4. Hat Almut geraucht? Hat Almut nicht geraucht?

Chapter 23

Phoning Home

1. Ich <u>habe</u> den Hörer <u>abgenommen</u>.

2. Ich <u>habe</u> die Telefonkarte <u>eingeführt</u>.

3. Dann <u>habe</u> ich die Telefonnummer <u>gewählt</u>.

4. Ich <u>habe</u> eine Nachricht <u>hintergelassen</u>.

5. Danach <u>habe</u> ich den Hörer <u>aufgelegt</u>.

An Actual Phone Conversation

Frau Gehring: Gehring, Hello.

Johannes: Hi, this is Johannes. May I please speak with Tanja?

Frau Gehring: One moment, please. I'm sorry. She's not home.

Johannes: When can I reach her?

Frau Gehring: I don't know when she'll be back. Would you like to leave a message?

Johannes: No, thanks. I'll call back again later. Good-bye.

Gehring: Good-bye.

They're Busy

1. Sie hat sich angezogen.
2. Er hat sich rasiert.
3. Wir haben uns gewaschen.
4. Sie haben sich die Zähne geputzt.
5. Er hat sich umgezogen.
6. Er hat sich gekämmt.
7. Sie hat sich geschminkt.
8. Er hat sich fertig gemacht.

Getting It Right

1. Ich schreibe meinem Freund einen Brief.
2. Wir lesen ein Buch.
3. Sie schreibt ihren Eltern eine Postkarte.
4. Du liest die Wohnungsanzeigen.
5. Ich lese eine Illustrierte.
6. Wolfram liest gern Kinderbücher.
7. Ihr schreibt uns jede Woche.

Chapter 24

Would You Please ...

1. Würdest du bitte oft schreiben?
2. Würdest du bitte gute Zeitungen lesen?
3. Würdest du bitte dein Medikament nehmen?

1. Ich würde gern nach Spanien fahren.
2. Ich würde gern lang schlafen.
3. Ich würde gern nur tanzen.

1. Ich würde in die Oper gehen.
2. Ich würde mehr Milch trinken.
3. Ich würde nicht alles kaufen.

You Have Three Wishes

1. Ich hätte am liebsten ein Schloss.
2. Ich hätte am liebsten ein Stück Schwarzwälder Kirschtorte.
3. Ich hätte am liebsten viel Geld.
4. Ich hätte am liebsten ein Haus in den Alpen.
5. Ich hätte am liebsten ein großes Bier.
6. Ich hätte am liebsten viele schöne Blumen.

Chapter 25

Auf Möbelsuche (on the Search for Furniture)

1. Ich brauche ein bequemes Sofa.
2. Ich brauche einen kleinen Stuhl.
3. Ich brauche eine modische Uhr.
4. Ich brauche eine helle Lampe.
5. Ich brauche einen billigen Tisch.

Auf Möbelsuche (on the Search for Furniture)

Müller's Furniture Store

Absolute guaranty of quality

We'll guarantee free furniture repair within the first two years.

We'll deliver your furniture for free.

We'll buy your old furniture back.

We ensure this absolute price and quality guaranty.

Tomorrow's Plans

1. Sie werden ins Kino gehen.
2. Er wird Brot backen.
3. Wir werden Tennis spielen.
4. Sie wird zum Zahnarzt gehen.
5. Ich werde Norbert anrufen.
6. Wir werden ein Buch lesen.
7. Ihr werdet Rad fahren.
8. Sie werden viel Deutsch sprechen.

Glossary: Linguistic Terms and Definitions

adverb　Word used to modify verbs or adjectives.

affix　A meaningful form that is attached to another form to make a more complex word, such as the –er in "small**er**" or the re- in "**re**do".

auxiliary　A verb that serves as the modifier of the main verb—it *helps* the main verb.

cardinal number　The basic form of a number; numbers used in counting.

case　The form that nouns, pronouns, adjectives, and prepositions take in a sentence, depending on their function.

cognate　Word that is historically derived from the same source. Cognates may be similar to (near-cognates) or exactly like (perfect cognates) their counterparts in another language.

colloquial　A linguistic repertoire that is characteristic of ordinary or familiar conversation; informal.

comparative form　The "more" form that adjectives or adverbs take to describe things that are dissimilar in quality or quantity, expressed in German with the suffix -*er*.

compound verb　Verb that is formed by adding a prefix to the stem verb. German has two principal types of compound verbs: those with separable prefixes and those with inseparable prefixes.

conjugation　The changes of the verb that occur to indicate who or what is performing the action (or undergoing the state of being) of the verb and when the action (or state of being) of the verb is occurring: in the present, the past, or the future.

consonants　All the letters in the alphabet other than *a*, *e*, *i*, *o*, and *u*.

contraction　A single word made out of two words. German contractions do not use apostrophes.

declension   The pattern of changes occurring in nouns, pronouns, articles, adjectives, and prepositions in each of the four cases.

definite article   The masculine (*der*), feminine (*die*), or neuter (*das*) article that precedes German nouns and corresponds to *the* in English. Unlike the English *the*, German articles show the gender and number of a noun.

demonstrative pronoun (adjective)   Pronoun (adjective) such as *dieser* (this) that allows you to point out a specific someone or something.

diphthong   Combination of vowels that begin with one vowel sound and end with a different vowel sound in the same syllable, such as the "ow" sound in "house."

direct object   At whom or what the action of the verb is being directed, marked by the accusative case.

future tense   To form the future tense, use the present tense of the auxiliary verb *werden* with the infinitive of the verb as in *Wir **werden** Suppe essen.*

genitive -s   The case that indicates possession used with case endings *–(e)s* or, with proper names, such as the *–s* in *Stephanies Vater.*

idiomatic expression   Speech form or expression that cannot be understood by literal translation, such as "hit the ceiling."

imperative form   The form a verb takes to indicate a command. In the imperative form, the understood subject is always *you.*

indefinite article   Article used when you are speaking about a noun in general, not about a specific noun.

indirect object   The object for whose benefit or in whose interest the action of the verb is being performed, marked by the dative case.

infinitive form   The unconjugated form of a verb. In German, the infinitive form of verbs ends in *-en* or, in some cases, simply *-n*. Verbs are listed in the dictionary in the infinitive form.

inflection   A linguistic addition (an affix) to a word that signals a grammatical relationship including tense, number, and degree, as in "blink**ed**," "play**s**," and "sweet**est**."

intransitive verb   Verb that does not take an object and uses the auxiliary *sein* in the perfect tense.

inversion   Reversing the word order of the subject noun or pronoun and the conjugated form of the verb, to make a statement a question, such as "**Are we** going to eat soon?"

linguistics   The scientific study of human language.

modal verb   A verb used with another verb to alter or modify its meaning. The six principal modal verbs in German are *sollen, müssen, dürfen, können, wollen,* and *mögen.*

modified or mutated verb   A verb that takes an umlaut, incurring a mutation of sound. The tongue moves forward in the oral cavity, resulting in a sound made closer to the front of the mouth.

noun marker   Any of a variety of articles, such as *der, die, das,* or *die* (the equivalent of *the* for plural nouns); *ein,* the equivalent of *a* for masculine or neuter nouns; or *eine,* the equivalent of *a* for feminine nouns.

ordinal number   Number that refers to a specific number in a series and answers the question "Which one?"

paradigm   A grammatical chart showing various forms of a word, such as a verb conjugation chart.

positive form   The form in which adverbs and adjectives normally appear, to which a comparative or superlative ending is added.

possessive adjectives   The adjectives *mein, dein, sein, ihr, unser, euer,* and *Ihr* show that something belongs to someone.

prefix   An affix form that modifies the meaning of the basic word.

preposition Word that shows the relation of a noun to another word in a sentence, such as "**with** a mouse" or "**between** us."

present tense The form a verb takes to indicate that the action is occurring in the present.

reflexive pronoun The pronoun that forms a part of a reflexive verb, in which the action refers back to the subject, such as *Chris kauft **sich** eine neue Kamera* (Chris buys **himself** a new camera).

reflexive verb A verb that always takes a reflexive pronoun because the action of the verb reflects back on the subject of the sentence, as in *Ich **kleide** mich **an*** (I get **myself** dressed).

separable prefix Verbal complements that are placed at the end of the sentence when the verb is conjugated, such as *Wir **stehen** spät **auf*** (We **get up** late).

stem The part of a verb you are left with after removing the ending *-en* from the infinitive. The stem of the verb *tanzen* (*tAn-tsuhn*) for example, is *tanz-*.

stem vowel The vowel in the stem (diphthongs are considered single vowels).

stress The emphasis placed on one or more syllables of a word when you pronounce it.

strong verb Verb whose stem vowel undergoes a change or a modification when conjugated in the past tense. Only some strong verbs undergo a vowel modification in the present tense.

subject The noun or pronoun performing the action of the verb.

superlative form The *most* form that adjectives or adverbs take to indicate the highest degree of quality or quantity, expressed in German with the suffix *–(e)sten*.

transitive verb Verb that takes an object and uses the auxiliary *haben* in the perfect.

umlaut The term for the two dots that can be placed over the vowels *a*, *o*, and *u*, indicating a sound mutation.

vowel *A*, *e*, *i*, *o*, and *u* are vowels.

weak verb Verb whose stem vowel never changes. These verbs follow a set, predictable pattern of rules in their conjugation, such as *glauben, glaubt, hat geglaubt* (to believe, believes, believed.)

word order The position of words in a sentence.

Lexicon: English to German, German to English

How to Use This Lexicon

As you learn in *The Complete Idiot's Guide to Learning German, Third Edition,* some German nouns have articles in front of them. These articles label the words as feminine (*f*), masculine (*m*), or neutral (*n*). If a word occurs primarily in its plural form and you find it listed as such in this appendix, it will bear the plural marker, *die.* Also, you know that some German words are capitalized and others are not, whereas in English all words except places and names are lowercase. Strong verb conjugations are given in parentheses. A period separates the infinitive form of separable prefix verbs.

English to German

A

a lot of   viel (*feel*)

about   circa (*tseeR-kuh*)

actor   Schauspieler (*shou-shpee-luhR*) m.

address   Adresse (*A-dre-suh*) f.

advice   Rat (*Raht*) m.

advise (to)   raten (rät, hat geraten) (*Rah-tuhn*)

after   nach (*nACH*)

afternoon   Nachmittag (*nACH-mi-tahk*) m.

ago   vor (*foR*)

air   Luft (*looft*) f.

air-conditioning   Klimaanlage (*klee-mah-An-lah-guh*) f.

airline   Fluglinie (*flewk-lee-nyah*) f.

airplane   Flugzeug (*flewk-tsoyk*) n.

airport   Flughafen (*flewk-hah-fuhn*) m.

airport gate   Flugsteig (*flewk-shtayk*) m.

alarm clock   Wecker (*ve-kuhR*) m.

all   alle (*ah-luh*)

allergic allergisch
(*A-leR-gish*)

almond Mandel (*mAn-duhl*) f.

along entlang (*ent-lAng*)

almost fast (*fAst*)

always immer (*i-muhR*)

angry ärgerlich (*äR-guhR-liH*)

ankle Fußknöchel
(*fews-knö-CHuhl*) m.

answer (to) antworten
(*Ant-voR-tuhn*)

answering machine
Anrufbeantworter (*An-Rewf-huh-Ant-vohR-tuhR*) m.

apartment Wohnung
(*voh-noong*) f.

appetizer Vorspeise (*foR-shpay-zuh*) f.

apple Apfel (*Ap-fuhl*) m.

approximately ungefähr
(*oon-guh-fähR*)

April April (*Ah-pril*) m.

apricot Aprikose
(*Ap-Ree-koh-zuh*) f.

armchair Sessel (*ze-suhl*) m.

around rund (*Roont*)

arrive (to) an.kommen
(ist angekommen)
(*An-ko-muhn*)

art Kunst (*koonst*) f.

ashtray Aschenbecher
(*ah-shun-be-HuhR*) m.

ask (to) fragen (*fRah-guhn*)

asparagus Spargel
(*shpAR-guhl*) m.

at bei (*bay*)

at home zu Hause (*tsew hou-zuh*)

at last endlich (*ent-liH*)

at the side seitlich (*zayt-liH*)

ATM Bankautomat
(*bAnk-ou-toh-mAt*) m.

aunt Tante (*tAn-tuh*) f.

August August (*ou-goost*) m.

autumn Herbst (*heRpst*) m.

awake munter (*moon-tuhR*)

awful furchtbar (*fooRCHt-bahR*)

B

back Rücken (*Rü-kuhn*) m.

backyard Hinterhof (*hin-tuhR-hohf*) m.

bacon Speck (*shpek*) m.

bad schlecht (*shleHt*)

bag Tüte (*tüh-tuh*) f.

bake (to) backen (backt, hat
gebacken) (*bA-kuhn*)

baker Bäcker (*bä-kuhR*) m.

bakery Bäkerei (*bä-kuh-Ray*) f.

balcony Balkon (*bAl-kon*) m.

bar (pub) Kneipe (*knay-puh*) f.

basement Keller (*ke-luhR*) m.

basil Basilikum (*bah-zee-lee-koom*) n.

bathe (to) baden (*bah-duhn*)

bathing suit Badeanzug (*bah-duh-An-tsewk*) m.

bathroom Badezimmer (*bah-duh-tsi-muhR*) n., Toilette (*toy-le-tuh*) f.

be allowed (to) dürfen (darf)
(*dür-fuhn*)

bean soup Bohnensuppe
(*boh-nuhn-zoo-puh*) f.

beans Bohnen (*boh-nuhn*) pl.

beautiful schön (*shöhn*)

become (to) werden (wird,
ist geworden) (*veR-duhn*)

bed Bett (*bet*) n.

bedroom Schlafzimmer
(*shlahf-tsi-muhr*) n.

beef Rindfleisch (*Rint-flaysh*) n.

beef broth Kraftbrühe
(*krAft-bRüh-uh*) f.

beer Bier (*beeR*) n.

begin (to) beginnen (hat
begonnen) (*buh-gi-nuhn*)

behind hinter (*hin-tuhR*)

beige beige (*beyj*)

believe (to) glauben
(*glou-buhn*)

belt Gürtel (*güR-tuhl*) m.

beneath unter (*oon-tuhR*)

beside neben (*ney-buhn*)

best (the) am besten
(*Am bes-tuhn*)

better besser (*be-suhR*)

between zwischen (*tsvi-shuhn*)

bicycle Fahrrad (*fah-Rat*) n.

big groß (*gRohs*)

bind (to) binden (hat gebun-
den) (*bin-duhn*)

birthday Geburtstag (*guh-booRts-tahk*) m.

black schwarz (*shvARts*)

blanket Bettdecke (*bet-de-kuh*) f.

blouse Bluse (*blew-zuh*) f.

blow (to) blasen (bläst, hat
geblasen) (*blah-zuhn*)

blue blau (*blou*)

blueberries Blaubeeren
(*blou-bey-Ruhn*) pl.

blunt stumpf (*shtoompf*)

boat Boot (*boht*) n.

body Körper (*köR-puhR*) m.

book Buch (*bu-CH*) n.

bookshelf Bücherregal
(*büh-HuhR-Rey-gal*) n.

bookstore Buchhandlung
(*bewCH-hAnt-loong*) f.

boots Stiefel (*shtee-fuhl*) pl.

boring langweilig (*lAng-vay-liH*)

borrow (to) aus.leihen (hat
ausgeliehen) (*ous-lay-uhn*)

bottle Flasche (*flah-shuh*) f.

bowl Schüssel (*shü-suhl*) f.

box Schachtel (*shACH-tuhl*) f.

boy Junge (*yoon-guh*) m.

bra Büstenhalter, BH (*bü-stuhn-hAl-tuhR*), (*bey-hah*) m.

brain Gehirn (*guh-hiRn*) n.

brave mutig (*mew-tiH*)

bread Brot (*bRoht*) n.

break (to) brechen (bricht, hat gebrochen) (*bRe-Huhn*)

bright bunt (*boont*)

bring (to) bringen (hat gebracht) (*bRin-guhn*)

broccoli Brokkoli (*bRo-koh-lee*) m.

brother Bruder (*bRew-duhR*) m.

brown braun (*bRoun*)

burn (to) brennen (hat gebrannt) (*bRe-nuhn*)

bus Bus (*boos*) m.

busy beschäftig (*buh-shäf-tiH*)

butcher Metzger (*mets-guhR*) m.

butcher shop Metzgerei (*mets-guh-Ray*) f.

butter Butter (*boo-tuhR*) f.

button Knopf (*knopf*) m.

buy (to) kaufen (*kou-fuhn*)

C

cabbage Kohl (*kohl*) m.

cake Kuchen (*kew-CHuhn*) m.

call (to) rufen (hat gerufen) (*Ruh-fuhn*)

calm ruhig (*Rew-iH*)

camera Kamera (*kah-me-Rah*) f., Fotoapparat (*foh-toh-ah-pah-Rat*) m.

can Dose (*doh-zuh*) f.

can (to be able to) können (kann) (*kö-nuhn*)

candies Süßigkeiten (*süh-siH-kay-tuhn*) pl.

cap Mütze (*mü-tsuh*) f.

car Auto (*ou-toh*) n.

carpet Teppich (*te-piH*) m.

carrot Karotte (*kah-Ro-tuh*) f.

carry (to) tragen (trägt, hat getragen) (*trah-guhn*)

carry-on luggage Handgepäck (*hAnt-guh-päk*) n.

cash Bargeld (*bahR-gelt*) n.

cat Katze (*kA-tsuh*) f.

catch a cold (to) sich erkälten (*ziH eR-käl-tuhn*)

catch (to) fangen (fängt, hat gefangen) (*fAn-guhn*)

cathedral Kathedrale (*kah-tey-drah-luh*) f.

cauliflower Blumenkohl (*blew-muhn-kohl*) m.

celery Sellerie (*ze-luh-Ree*) m.

cell phone Handy, Funktelefon, Mobiltelefon (*hahn-dee, foonk-tey-ley-fohn, moh-beel-tey-ley-fohn*) n.

change (coins) Wechselgeld, Kleingeld (*vek-suhl-gelt, klayn-gelt*) n.

change one's clothes (to) sich um.ziehen (hat sich umgezogen) (*ziH ewm-tsee-uhn*)

changeable wechselhaft (*vek-suhl-hAft*)

cheap billig (*bi-liH*)

cheese Käse (*käh-zuh*) m.

cherries Kirschen (*keeR-shuhn*) pl.

chest Brust (*bRoost*) f.

chicken Huhn (*hewn*) n.

chicken breast Hühnerbrust (*hüh-nuhR-broost*) f.

chicken salad Geflügelsalat (*guh-flüh-guhl-zah-lAt*) m.

child Kind (*kint*) n.

chocolate Schokolade (*shoh-koh-lah-duh*) f.

church Kirche (*keeR-Huh*) f.

cinema Kino (*kee-noh*) n.

city Stadt (*shtAt*) f.

city map Stadtplan (*shtAt-plAn*) m.

clean sauber (*zou-buhR*)

clean (to) reinigen (*ray-ni-guhn*), putzen (*poo-tsuhn*)

climb (to) steigen (ist gestiegen) (*shtay-guhn*)

clock Uhr (*ewR*) f.

close (to) schließen (hat geschlossen) (*shlee-suhn*)

closet Schrank (*shrAnk*) m.

clothes Bekleidung (*buh-klay-doong*) f.

clothing store Bekleidungsgeschäft (*buh-klay-doongz-guh-shäft*) n.

cloudy bewölkt (*buh-völkt*)

coat Mantel (*mAn-tuhl*) m.

cod Kabeljau (*kah-buhl-you*) m.

coffee Kaffee (*kA-fey*) m.

coffee table Couchtisch (*kouch-tish*) m.

coins Münzen (*mün-tsuhn*) pl.

coke Cola (*ko-lA*) f.

cold kalt (*kalt*)

cold (illness) Erkältung (*eR-käl-toong*) f.

comb Kamm (*kAm*) m.

comb one's hair (to) sich kämmen (*ziH kä-muhn*)

computer Computer (*kom-pyew-tuhR*) m.

come (to) kommen (ist gekommen) (*ko-muhn*)

come back (to) zurück.kommen (ist zurückgekommen) (*tsuh-Rük-ko-muhn*)

comfortable bequem (*buh-kveym*)

command (to) befehlen (befiehlt, hat befohlen) (*buh-fey-luhn*)

commuter train S-Bahn (*es-bahn*) f.

concierge Pförtner (*pföRt-nuhR*) m.

conditioner (hair) Pflegespülung (*pfley-guh-shpüh-loong*) f.

cook (to) kochen (*kO-CHuhn*)

cookie Plätzchen (*pläts-Huhn*), Keks (*keks*) n.

corduroy Kord (*koRt*) m.

corn Mais (*mays*) m.

cost (to) kosten (*kos-tuhn*)

cotton (Baumwolle) (*boum-vo-luh*) f.

cough Husten (*hew-stuhn*) m.

country Land (*lAnt*) n.

courtyard Innenhof (*i-nuhn-hohf*) m.

cousin Kousin (*koo-zin*) m.

crab Krebs (*kreyps*) m.

cream Sahne (*zah-nuh*) f.

cry (to) weinen (*vay-nuhn*)

cucumber Gurke (*gooR-kuh*) f.

cup Tasse (*tA-suh*) f.

curly lockig (*lo-kiH*)

currants Johannisbeeren (*yoh-hA-nis-bey-Ruhn*) pl.

cutlery Besteck (*buh-shtek*) n.

cutlet Schnitzel (*shni-tsuhl*) n.

D

daily täglich (*tähk-liH*)

dance (to) tanzen (*tAn-tsuhn*)

dark dunkel (*doon-kuhl*)

daughter Tochter (*toCH-tuhR*) f.

day Tag (*tahk*) m.

day after tomorrow übermorgen (*üh-buhR-moR-guhn*)

day before yesterday vorgestern (*foR-ges-tuhRn*)

debt Schulden (*shool-duhn*) pl.

December Dezember (*dey-tsem-buhR*) m.

delicious lecker (*le-kuhR*)

dentist Zahnarzt (*tsahn-ARtst*) m.

depart (to) ab.fahren (fährt ab, ist abgefahren) (*ap-fah-Ruhn*)

dessert Nachtisch (*nahCH-tish*) m., Nachspeise (*nahCH-shpay-zuh*) f.

develop (to) entwickeln (*ent-vi-kuhln*)

dial a phone (to) wählen (*väh-luhn*)

diarrhea Durchfall (*dooRCH-fAl*) m.

die (to) sterben (stirbt, ist gestorben) (*shteR-buhn*)

dining room Esszimmer (*es-tsi-muhR*) n.

dinner plate Teller (*te-luhR*) m.

dirty dreckig (*dRe-kiH*), schmutzig (*shmoo-tsiH*)

discover (to) entdecken (*ent-de-kuhn*)

dish (of food) Gericht (*guh-RiHt*) n.

dishes Geschirr (*guh-sheeR*) n.

dishwasher Spülmaschine (*shpül-mA-shee-nuh*) f.

do (to) tun (hat getan) (*tuhn*)

doctor Arzt (*aRtst*) m.

door Tür (*tühR*) f.

double room Doppelzimmer (*do-puhl-tsi-muhR*) n.

draw (to) zeichnen (*tsayH-nuhn*)

dream trämen (*tRoy-muhn*)

dress Kleid (*klayt*) n.

dress oneself (to) sich anziehen (hat sich angezogen) (*ziH An-zee-uhn*)

dresser Kommode (*ko-moh-duh*) f.

drink (to) trinken (hat getrunken) (*tRin-kuhn*)

drinks Getränke (*guh-tRän-kuh*) pl.

drive (to) fahren (färt, ist gefahren) (*fah-Ruhn*)

drizzle Sprühregen (*shpRüh-Rey-guhn*) m.

drug store Drogerie (*dRoh-guh-Ree*) f.

dry trocken (*tRo-kuhn*)

dryer Trockner (*tRok-nuhR*) m.

E

ear Ohr (*ohR*) n.

early früh (*fRüh*)

eat (to) essen (isst, hat gegessen) (*es-uhn*)

easy leicht (*layHt*)

egg Ei (*ay*) n.

eggplant Aubergine (*oh-beR-jee-nuh*) f.

elevator Aufzug (*ouf-tsewk*) m.

employee Angestellte (*An-guh-shtel-tuh*) m.

empty leer (*leyR*)

enjoy (to) genießen (hat genossen) (*guh-nee-suhn*)

enough genug (*guh-newk*)

envelope Briefumschlag (*bReef-oom-shlahk*) m.

evening Abend (*ah-buhnd*) m.

event Ereignis (*eR-ayk-nis*) n.

every day jeden Tag (*yey-duhn tahk*) m.

examine (to) untersuchen (*oon-tuhR-zew-Huhn*)

excellent ausgezeichnet (*ous-guh-tsayH-net*)

exchange rate Wechselkurs (*vek-suhl-kooRs*) m.

exit Ausgang (*ous-gAng*) m.

expensive teuer (*toy-uhR*)

eye Auge (*ou-guh*) n.

F

face Gesicht (*guh-ziHt*) n.

fall (to) fallen (fällt, ist gefallen) (*fA-luhn*)

false falsch (*fAlsh*)

false alarm blinder Alarm (*blin-duhR A-lARm*) m.

farmer Bauer (*bou-uhR*) m.

fashion Mode (*moh-duh*) f.

fashionable modisch (*moh-dish*)

fast schnell (*shnel*)

fat dick (*dik*)

father Vater (*fah-tuhR*) m.

father-in-law Schwiegervater (*shvee-guhR-fah-tuhR*) m.

fear Angst (*Angst*) f.

February Februar (*feb-Rew-ahR*) m.

feel (to) sich fühlen (*ziH füh-luhn*)

fever Fieber (*fee-buhR*) n.

fill out (to) aus.füllen (*ous-fü-luhn*)

find (to) finden (hat gefunden) (*fin-duhn*)

fingernail Fingernagel (*fin-guR-nah-guhl*) m.

finished fertig (*feR-tiH*)

fireplace Kamin (*kah-meen*) m.

fish Fisch (*fish*) m.

fish (to) angeln (*An-geln*)

fitness center Fitnesscenter (*fit-nes-sen-tuhR*) n.

flight Flug (*flewk*) m.

flight number Flugnummer (*flewk-noo-muhR*) f.

floor Fußboden (*fews-boh-duhn*) m.

floor (story) Stock (*shtok*) m.

florist Blumengeschäft (*blew-muhn-guh-schäft*) n.

flounder Flunder/Rochen (*floon-duhR/Ro-CHuhn*) f./m.

flower Blume (*blew-muh*) f.

flu Grippe (*gRi-puh*) f.

fly (to) fliegen (ist geflogen) (*flee-guhn*)

fog Nebel (*ney-buhl*) m.

foggy nebelig (*ney-buh-liH*)

follow (to) folgen (*fol-guhn*)

food Essen (*e-suhn*) n.

foot Fuß (*fews*) m.

for für (*führ*)

foreign country Ausland (*ous-lAnt*) n.

forget (to) vergessen (vergisst, hat vergessen) (*feR-ge-suhn*)

fork Gabel (*gah-buhl*) f.

French fries Pommes frites (*po-muhs*) pl.

Friday Freitag (*fRay-tahk*) m.

fried eggs Spiegelei (*shpee-guh-lay*) n.

friend Freund (*fRoynt*) m.

from von (*fon*)

from where woher (*voh-heR*)

fruit Obst (*opst*) n.

full voll (*fol*)

funny lustig (*loos-tiH*)

furnished möbliert (*möh-bleeRt*)

furniture Möbel (*möh-buhl*) pl.

G

garden Garten (*gAR-tuhn*) m.

garlic Knoblauch (*knohp-louCH*) m.

gas tank Benzintank (*ben-tseen-tAnk*) m.

Germany Deutschland (*doytch-lAnt*) n.

get oneself ready (to) sich fertig machen (*ziH feR-tiH mA-CHuhn*)

ghost Geist (*gayst*) m.

gift Geschenk (*guh-shenk*) n.

gift shop Geschenkarti-kelladen (*guh-shenk-AR-tee-kuhl-lah-duhn*) m.

girlfriend Freundin (*froyn-din*) f.

give (to) geben (gibt, hat gegeben) (*gey-buhn*)

glass Glas (*glAs*) n.

glasses Brille (*bri-luh*) f.

gloves Handschuhe (*hAnt-shew-uh*) pl.

go (to) gehen (ist gegangen) (*gey-uhn*)

go on (to) weiter.gehen (ist weitergegangen) (*vay-tuhR-gey-uhn*)

good gut (*gewt*)

good day Guten Tag (*gew-tuhn tahk*) m.

good evening   Guten Abend (*gew-tuhn ah-bent*) m.

good morning   Guten Morgen (*gew-tuhn moR-guhn*) m.

good-bye   auf Wiedersehen (*ouf vee-duhR zey-uhn*)

grandfather   Opa (*oh-pah*) m.

grandmother   Oma (*oh-mah*) f.

gray   grau (*gRou*)

green   grün (*gRün*)

grocery store   Lebensmittelgeschäft (*ley-buhnz-mi-tuhl-guh-shäft*) n.

group   Gruppe (*gRoo-puh*) f.

grow (to)   wachsen (wächst, ist gewachsen) (*vak-suhn*)

H

hail   Hagel (*hah-guhl*) m.

hair   Haar (*hahR*) n.

hair dryer   Fön (*föhn*) m.

hairbrush   Haarbürste (*hahR-büR-stuh*) f.

haircut   Haarschnitt (*hahR-shnit*) m.

happy   fröhlich, glücklich (*fRöh-liH*), (*glük-liH*)

ham   Schinken (*shin-kuhn*) m.

hand   Hand (*hAnT*) f.

hang (to)   hängen (hängt, hat gehangen) (*hän-guhn*)

hanger   Kleiderbügel (*klay-duhR-büh-guhl*) m.

happen (to)   geschehen (geschieht, ist geschehen) *guh-shey-uhn*)

hard   schwer (*shveR*), hart (*hARt*)

hat   Hut (*hewt*) m.

have (to)   haben (hat, hat gehabt) (*hah-buhn*)

hazelnuts   Haselnüsse (*hah-zuhl-nü-suh*) pl.

head   Kopf (*kopf*) m.

headache   Kopfschmerzen (*kopf-shmeR-tsuhn*) pl.

healthy   gesund (*guh-zoont*)

hear   hören (*höh-Ruhn*)

heart   Herz (*heRts*) n.

hello   hallo (*hA-loh*)

help (to)   helfen (hilft, hat geholfen) (*hel-fuhn*)

herbs   Kräuter (*kroy-tuhR*) pl.

here   hier (*heeR*)

hers   ihr (*eeR*)

high   hoch (*hoCH*)

hike (to)   wandern (*vAn-duhRn*)

his   sein (*zayn*)

history   Geschichte (*guh-shiH-tuh*) f.

hit (to)   schlagen (schlägt, hat geschlagen) (*shlah-guhn*)

hold (to)   halten (hält, hat gehalten) (*hAl-tuhn*)

horrible   schrecklich (*shRek-liH*)

horse   Pferd (*pfeRt*) n.

horseradisch   Meerrettich (*mey-Re-tiH*) m.

hot   heiß (*hays*)

hotel   Hotel (*hoh-tel*) n.

hour   Stunde (*shtoon-duh*) f.

hourly   stündlich (*shtünt-liH*)

house   Haus (*hous*) n.

how   wie (*vee*)

human being   Mensch (*mensh*) m.

humid   feucht (*foyHt*)

hunger   Hunger (*hoon-guhR*) m.

hungry   hungrig (*hoon-gRiH*)

I

ice cream   Eis (*ays*) n.

immediately   sofort (*zoh-foRt*)

important   wichtig (*viH-tiH*)

in front of   vor (*fohR*)

industrious   fleißig (*flay-siH*)

injure oneself (to)   sich verletzen (*ziH feR-le-tsuhn*)

in-laws   Schwiegereltern (*shvee-guhR-el-tuhRn*) pl.

inspect (to)   kontrollieren (*kon-tRo-lee-Ruhn*)

interesting   interessant (*in-te-Re-sAnt*)

internet access   Internetzugang (*in-tuhR-net-tsew-grif*) m.

iron   Bügeleisen (*büh-guhl-ay-zuhn*) n.

iron (to)   bügeln (*büh-guhln*)

J

jacket   Jacke (*yA-kuh*) f.

jam   Marmelade (*mAR-muh-lah-duh*) f.

January   Januar (*yah-new-ahR*) m.

jewelry   Schmuck (*shmook*) m.

juice   Saft (*zAft*) m.

K

key   Schlüssel (*shlü-suhl*) m.

kiss (to)   küssen (*kü-suhn*)

kitchen   Küche (*kü-Huh*) f.

knee   Knie (*knee*) n.

knife   Messer (*me-suhR*) n.

know a fact (to)   wissen (weiß, hat gewusst) (*vi-suhn*)

know, be familiar with (to)   kennen (hat gekannt) (*ke-nuhn*)

L

lady Dame (*dah-muh*) f.

lake See (*zey*) m.

lamb Lamm (*lAm*) n.

late spät (*shpäht*) late

later später (*shpäh-tuhR*)

lay (to) legen (*ley-guhn*)

lazy faul (*foul*)

learn (to) lernen (*leR-nuhn*)

leather Leder (*ley-duhR*) n.

leave (to) lassen (lässt, hat gelassen) (*lA-suhn*)

left links (*links*)

leg Bein (*bayn*) n.

lemon Zitrone (*tsi-troh-nuh*) f.

lend (to) leihen (hat geliehen) (*lay-uhn*)

less weniger (*ve-nee-guhR*)

letter Brief (*bReef*) m.

lettuce Kopfsalat (*kopf-zA-laht*) m.

library Bibliothek (*bib-lee-oh-tek*) f.

lie (to), be situated liegen (hat gelegen) (*lee-guhn*)

lift (to) heben (hat gehoben) (*hey-buhn*)

light Licht (*liHt*) n.

light hell (*hel*)

lightning Blitz (*blits*) m.

like (to) mögen (mag) (*möh-guhn*)

linen Leinen (*lay-nuhn*) n.

lip Lippe (*li-puh*) f.

little/not much wenig (*vey-niH*)

living room Wohnzimmer (*vohn-tsi-muhr*) n.

load (to) laden (lädt, hat geladen) (*lah-duhn*)

long lang (*lang*)

look (to) blicken (*bli-kuhn*)

look (to look for) suchen (*zew-Huhn*)

lose (to) verlieren (hat verloren) (*feR-lee-Ruhn*)

love Liebe (*lee-buh*) f.

love (to) lieben (*lee-buhn*)

low tief (*teef*)

M

magazine Zeitschrift (*tsayt-shRift*) f.

main course Hauptgericht (*houpt-guh-RiHt*) n.

make (to) machen (*mA-CHuhn*)

man Mann (*mAn*) m.

March März (*märts*) m.

market Markt (*mARkt*) m.

marry (to) heiraten (*hay-rA-tuhn*)

matches Streichhölzer (*shtRayH-höl-tsuhR*) pl.

May Mai (*may*) m.

maybe vielleicht (*fee-layHt*)

meat Fleisch (*flaysh*) n.

meet (to) treffen (trifft, hat getroffen) (*tRe-fuhn*)

melon Melone (*me-loh-nuh*) f.

men Männer (*mä-nuhR*) pl.

menu Speisekarte (*shpay-zuh-kAR-tuh*) f.

midnight Mitternacht (*mi-tuhR-nACHt*) f.

milk Milch (*milH*) f.

minute Minute (*mi-new-tuh*) f.

mirror Spiegel (*shpee-guhl*) m.

misunderstand (to) missverstehen (hat misverstanden) (*mis-feR-shtey-uhn*)

Monday Montag (*mohn-tahk*) m.

month Monat (*moh-nAt*) m.

monthly monatlich (*moh-nAt-liH*)

more mehr (*meyR*)

morning Morgen (*moR-guhn*) m.

mornings morgens (*moR-guhnz*)

mother Mutter (*moo-tuhR*) f.

mother-in-law Schwiegermutter (*shvee-guhR-moo-tuhR*) f.

motorcycle Motorrad (*moh-toh-Rat*) n.

mouth Mund (*moont*) m.

movie Film (*film*) m.

much viel (*feel*)

mushrooms Pilze (*pil-tsuh*) pl.

music store Musikgeschäft (*mew-zeek-guh-shäft*) n.

must müssen (muss) (*mü-suhn*)

mustard Senf (*zenf*) m.

my (*mayn*)

N

name Name (*nah-muh*) m.

napkin Serviette (*zeR-vee-e-tuh*) f.

narrow eng (*eng*)

neck Hals (*halz*) m.

necktie Schlips (*shlips*) m., Krawatte (*kRah-VA-tuh*) f.

need (to) brauchen (*bRou-CHuhn*)

nervous nervös (*neR-vöhs*)

never nie (*nee*)

new neu (*noy*)

news Nachrichten (*nACH-RiH-tuhn*) pl.

newspaper Zeitung (*tsay-toong*) f.

newsstand Kiosk (*kee-osk*) n./m.

night Nacht (*nACHt*) f.

night club Nachtclub (*nACHt-kloob*) m.

nose Nase (*nah-zuh*) f.

novel Roman (*roh-mahn*) m.

now jetzt (*yetst*)

nurse Krankenpfleger (*kRan-kuhn-pfley-guhR*) m.

nuts Nüsse (*nü-suh*) pl.

O

occasionally gelegentlich (*guh-ley-gunt-liH*)

October Oktober (*ok-toh-buhR*) m.

of course selbstverständlich (*zelpst-feR-shtänt-liH*)

offer (to) bieten (hat geboten) (*bee-tuhn*)

often oft (*oft*)

oil Öl (*öhl*) n.

old alt (*Alt*)

older älter (*äl-tuhR*)

onion Zwiebel (*tsvee-buhl*) f.

only nur (*nooR*)

open (to) öffnen (*öf-nuhn*)

operator Vermittlung (*feR-mit-loong*) f.

opposite gegenüber (*gey-guhn-üh-buhR*)

order (to) bestellen (*buh-shte-luhn*)

our unser (*oon-zuhR*)

outdoors draußen (*dRou-suhn*)

over über (*üh-buhR*)

P

pack (to) packen (*pA-kuhn*)

package Paket (*pah-ket*) n.

painting Bild (*bilt*) n.

pair of pants Hose (*hoh-zuh*) f.

pajamas Schlafanzug (*shlahf-An-tsook*) m.

parents Eltern (*el-tuhRn*) pl.

park (to) parken (*pAR-kuhn*)

parking lot Parkplatz (*pARk-plAts*) m.

passport Pass (*pAs*) m.

pastry shop Konditorei (*kon-dee-toR-ay*) f.

patterned gemustert (*guh-moos-tuRt*)

peaches Pfirsiche (*pfeeR-ziH-uh*) pl.

pears Birnen (*beeR-nuhn*) pl.

peas Erbsen (*eRp-suhn*) pl.

pepper mill Pfeffermühle (*pfe-fuhR-müh-luh*) f.

perfume Parfüm (*paR-füm*) n.

pharmacy Apotheke (*ah-poh-tey-kuh*) f.

pickles eingelegte Gurken (*ayn-guh-leyg-tuh gooR-kuhn*) pl.

piece Stück (*shtük*) n.

pillow Kopfkissen (*kopf-ki-suhn*) n.

pineapple Ananas (*ah-nah-nAs*) f.

pink rosa (*Roh-zah*)

pizza Pizza (*pi-tsuh*) f.

plaid kariert (*kah-ReeRt*)

plan (to) planen (*plah-nuhn*)

play (to) spielen (*shpee-luhn*)

please bitte (*bi-tuh*)

poison Gift (*gift*) m.

police officer Polizist (*poh-lee-tsist*) m.

police station Polizeiamt (*poh-lee-tsay-Amt*) n.

polka-dotted gepunktet (*guh-poonk-tuht*)

poor arm (*Arm*) m.

pork Schweinfleisch (*shvayn-flaysh*) n.

possess (to) besitzen (hat besessen) (*buh-zi-tsuhn*)

postcard Ansichtskarte (*An-ziHts-kAR-tuh*) f.

post office Post (*post*) f.

potato Kartoffel (*kAR-to-fuhl*) f.

praise (to) loben (*loh-buhn*)

produce shop Obst- und Gemüsehandlung (*opst-oot-guh-müh-zuh-hAnt-loong*) f.

promise (to) versprechen (verspricht, hat versprochen) (*feR-shpRe-Huhn*)

proud stolz (*shtolts*)

prove (to) beweisen (*buh-vay-zuhn*)

pull (to) ziehen (hat gezogen) (*tsee-uhn*)

punctually pünktlich (*pünkt-liH*)

purple lila (*lee-lah*)

purse Handtasche (*hAnt-tA-shuh*) f.

Q

quite ziemlich (*tseem-lih*)

R

rain Regen (*Rey-guhn*) m.

raincoat Regenmantel (*Rey-guhn-mAn-tuhl*) m.

rainy regnerisch (*Reyg-nuh-Rish*)

read (to) lesen (liest, hat gelesen) (*ley-zuhn*)

receipt Quittung (*kvi-toong*) f.

receive (to) bekommen (hat bekommen) (*buh-ko-muhn*)

recommend (to) empfehlen (empfiehlt, hat empfohlen) (*em-pfey-luhn*)

recuperate (to) sich erholen (*ziH eR-hoh-luhn*)

red rot (*Rot*)

regularly regelmäßig (*rey-guhl-mäh-siH*)

relax (to) sich entspannen (*ziH ent-shpA-nuhn*)

remain (to) bleiben (ist geblieben) (*blay-buhn*)

rent (to) mieten (*mee-tuhn*)

reserve (to) reservieren (*Re-zeR-vee-Ruhn*)

reside wohnen (*voh-nuhn*)

ride (to) reiten (ist geritten) (*Ray-tuhn*)

right rechts (*ReHts*)

river Fluss (*floos*) m.

roll Brötchen (*bRöt-chuhn*) n.

roll (to) rollen (*Ro-luhn*)

room Zimmer (*tsi-muhR*) n.

roughly etwa (*et-vah*)

run (to) laufen (läuft, ist gelaufen) (*lou-fuhn*)

rye bread Roggenbrot (*Ro-guhn-bRoht*) n.

S

sad traurig (*tRou-RiH*)

sail (to) segeln (*zey-guhln*)

sailboat Segelboot (*zey-guhl-boht*)

salmon Lachs (*lAks*) m.

salt shaker Salzstreuer (*zAlts-shtRoy-uhR*) m.

Saturday Samstag (*zAms-tahk*) m.

saucer Untertasse (*oon-teR-tA-suh*) f.

sausage Wurst (*vooRst*) f.

save money (to) Geld sparen (*gelt shpah-Ruhn*)

say (to) sagen (*zah-guhn*)

scarf Schal (*shahl*) m.

scratch (to) kratzen (*krA-tsuhn*)

seafood Meeresfrüchte (*mey-Ruhs-fRüH-tuh*) pl.

season Jahreszeit (*yah-Ruhs-tsayt*) f.

second Sekunde (*ze-koon-duh*) f.

see (to) sehen (sieht, hat gesehen) (*zey-uhn*)

sell (to) verkaufen (*feR-kou-fuhn*)

send (to) schicken (*shi-kuhn*)

send (to) senden (*zen-duhn*)

serious ernst (*eRnst*)

set (to) setzen (*ze-tsuhn*)

shampoo Haarshampoo (*hahR-shAm-pew*) n.

shave oneself (to) sich rasieren (*ziH rah-zee-Ruhn*)

shine (to) scheinen (ist geschienen) (*shee-nuhn*)

ship Schiff (*shif*) n.

shirt Hemd (*hemt*) n.

shoes Schuhe (*shew-uh*) pl.

shopping center Einkaufszentrum (*ayn-koufs-tsen-tRoom*) n.

short kurz (*kooRts*)

shoulder Schulter (*shool-tuhR*) f.

show (to) zeigen (*tsay-guhn*)

shower Dusche (*dew-shuh*) f.

shrimp Garnele (*gahR-ney-luh*) f.

sick krank (*kRAnk*)

side dish Beilage (*bay-lah-guh*) f.

sign Schild (*shilt*) n.

signature die Unterschrift (*oon-tuhR-shRift*) f.

silk Seide (*zay-duh*) f.

since seit (*zayt*)

sing (to) singen (hat gesungen) (*zin-guhn*)

single room Einzelzimmer (*ayn-tsel-tsi-muhR*) n.

sink (to) sinken (hat gesunken) (*zin-kuhn*)

sister Schwester (*shves-tuhR*) f.

sit (to) sitzen (hat gesessen) (*zi-tsuhn*)

skin Haut (*hout*) f.

skirt Rock (*Rok*) m.

sky Himmel (*hi-muhl*) m.

sleep (to) schlafen (schläft, hat geschlafen) (*shlah-fuhn*)

slice Scheibe (*shay-buh*) f.

slow langsam (*lAng-zAm*)

small klein (*klayn*)

smart klug (*klewk*)

smoke (to) rauchen (*rou-CHuhn*)

snow Schnee (*shney*) m.

socks Socken (*zo-kuhn*) pl.

soap Seife (*zay-fuh*) f.

sometimes manchmal (*mAnH-mahl*)

son Sohn (*zohn*) m.

song Lied (*leed*) n.

soon bald (*bAlt*)

soup dish Suppenteller (*zoo-puhn-te-luhR*) m.

sour sauer (*zou-uhR*)

speak (to) sprechen (spricht, hat gesprochen) (*shpRe-Huhn*)

spin (to) spinnen (hat gesponnen) (*shpi-nuhn*)

spinach Spinat (*shpi-naht*) m.

spine Wirbelsäule (*viR-buhl-zoy-luh*) f.

spoon Löffel (*lö-fuhl*) m.

sport shop Sportgeschäft (*shpoRt-guh-shäft*) n.

spring Frühling (*fRüh-ling*) m.

stand (to) stehen (hat gestanden) (*shtey-uhn*)

stationery Schreibwaren (*shRayp-vah-Ruhn*) pl.

still noch (*noCH*)

stink (to) stinken (hat gestunken) (*shtin-kuhn*)

stomach Magen (*mah-guhn*) m., Bauch (*bouCH*) m.

store Geschäft (*guh-shäft*) n., Laden (*lah-duhn*) m.

storm Sturm (*shtooRm*) m.

straight ahead geradeaus (*guh-Rah-duh-ous*)

strawberries Erdbeeren (*eRt-bey-Ruhn*) pl.

street Straße (*shtRah-suh*) f.

streetcar Straßenbahn, S-bahn (*shtRah-suhn-bahn, es-bahn*) f.

strength Stärke (*shtäR-kuh*) f.

striped gestreift (*guh-shtRayft*)

strong stark (*shtARk*)

study (to) studieren (*shtew-dee-Ruhn*)

stupid blöd (*blöd*)

suddenly plötzlich (*plöts-liH*)

suede Wildleder (*vilt-ley-duhR*) n.

suffer (to) leiden (hat gelitten) (*lay-duhn*)

sugar Zucker (*tsoo-kuhR*) m.

suit Anzug (*An-tsewk*) m.

suitcase Koffer (*ko-fuhR*) m.

summer Sommer (*zo-muhR*) m.

sun Sonne (*zo-nuh*) f.

Sunday Sonntag (*zon-tahk*) m.

sunny sonnig (*zo-niH*)

supermarket Supermarkt (*zew-puhR-mARkt*) m.

suspenseful spannend (*shpA-nuhnt*)

sweet süß (*zühs*)

swim (to) schwimmen (ist geschwommen) (*shvi-muhn*)

swimming pool Schwimmbad (*shvim-baht*) n.

T

table Tisch (*tish*) m.

tablecloth Tischdecke (*tish-de-kuh*) f.

take (to) nehmen (nimmt, hat genommen) (*ney-muhn*)

tea Tee (*tey*) m.

teach lehren (*ley-Ruhn*)

teacher Lehrer (*ley-RuhR*) m., die Lehrerin (*ley-Ruh-Rin*) f.

teaspoon Teelöffel (*tey-lö-fuhl*) m.

telephone Telefon (*te-le-fon*) n.

telephone number Telefonnummer (*tey-ley-foh-noo-muhR*) f.

telephone (to) telefonieren (*te-le-foh-nee-Ruhn*)

tennis shoes Tennisschuhe (*te-nis-shew-uh*) pl.

thank (to) danken (*dAn-kuhn*)

thanks danke (*dAn-kuh*)

their ihr (*eeR*)

then danach (*dA-nahCH*)

there da, dort (*dA*), (*doRt*)

therefore also (*Al-zoh*)

thin dünn (*dün*)

think (to) denken (hat gedacht) (*den-kuhn*)

thirst Durst (*dooRst*) m.

thirsty durstig (*dooRs-tiH*)

throat Kehle (*key-luh*) f.

thunder Donner (*do-nuhR*) m.

Thursday Donnerstag (*do-nuhRz-tahk*) m.

time Zeit (*tsayt*) f.

tired müde (*müh-duh*)

to zu, (*tsew*) nach (*nahCH*)

today heute (*hoy-tuh*)

toe Zehe (*tsey-uh*) f.

together zusammen (*tsew-zA-muhn*)

tomato Tomate (*toh-mah-tuh*) f.

tomorrow morgen (*moR-guhn*)

tongue Zunge (*tsoon-guh*) f.

too little zu wenig (*tsew vey-niH*)

too much zu viel (*tsew feel*)

tooth Zahn (*tsahn*) m.

toothbrush Zahnbürste (*tsahn-büR-stuh*) f.

towel Handtuch (*hAn-tewCH*) n.

train Zug (*tsewk*) m.

train station Bahnhof (*bahn-hof*) m.

transfer in travel (to) um.steigen (ist umgestiegen) (*oom-shtay-guhn*)

transfer money (to) Geld überweisen (*gelt üh-buhR-vay-zuhn*)

travel (to) reisen (*Ray-suhn*); fahren (fährt, ist gefahren) (*fah-Ruhn*)

tree Baum (*boum*) m.

trout Forelle (*foh-Re-luh*) f.

true wahr (*vahR*)

try (to) versuchen (*feR-zew-Huhn*), probieren (*pRo-bee-Ruhn*)

Tuesday Dienstag (*deenz-tahk*) m.

tuna Thunfisch (*tewn-fish*) m.

turkey Truthahn (*tRewt-hahn*) m.

turn (to) ab.biegen (ist abge-bogen) (*ap-bee-guhn*)

U

ugly häßlich (*hähs-liH*)

umbrella Regenshirm (*rey-guhn-shiRm*) m.

unbelievable unglaublich (*oon-gloup-liH*)

uncle Onkel (*on-kuhl*) m.

under unter (*oon-tuhR*)

underpants Unterhose (*oon-tuhR-hoh-zuh*) f.

understand (to) verstehen (hat verstanden) (*feR-shtey-uhn*)

underwear Unterwäsche (*oon-tuhR-väh-shuh*) f.

unfortunately leider (*lay-duhR*)

until bis (*bis*)

use (to) benutzen (*buh-noot-suhn*)

V

veal Kalbfleisch (*kAlp-flaysh*) n.

vegetables Gemüse (*guh-müh-zuh*) n.

vegetarian vegetarisch (*vey-gey-tah-Rish*)

very sehr (*zeyR*)

vinegar Essig (*e-siH*) m.

W

wait (to) warten (*vAR-tuhn*)

waiter Kellner (*kel-nuhR*) m.

waitress Kellnerin (*kel-nuh-Rin*) f.

wall Wand (*vAnt*) f.

wallet Portemonnaie (*poRt-moh-ney*) n.

want (to) wollen (will) (*vo-luhn*)

warm warm (*vahRm*)

warning Warnung (*vAR-noong*) f.

wash (to) waschen (wäscht, hat gewaschen) (*vah-shuhn*)

watch TV (to) fern.sehen (sieht fern, hat ferngesehen) (*feRn-zey-uhn*)

water Wasser (*va-suhR*) n.

weak schwach (*shvACH*)

wear (to) tragen (trägt, hat getragen) (*trah-guhn*)

weather Wetter (*ve-tuhR*) n.

Wednesday Mittwoch (*mit-voCH*) m.

week Woche (*vo-CHuh*) f.

weekly wöchentlich (*vö-Hent-liH*)

well done gut durchgebraten (*gewt dooRch-guh-bRa-tuhn*)

wet naß (*nahs*)

what was (*vAs*)

when wann (*vAn*)

where wo (*voh*)

where (to) wohin (*voh-hin*)

which welch (*velCH*)

whipped cream Schlagsahne (*shlAk-zah-nuh*) f.

white weiß (*vays*)

white bread Weißbrot (*vays-bRoht*) n.

who wer (*veyR*)

whole-grain bread Vollkornbrot (*fol-koRn-bRoht*) n.

why warum (*va-Room*)

wide breit (*brayt*)

wife Frau (*fRou*) f.

win (to) gewinnen (hat gewonnen) (*guh-vi-nuhn*)

wind Wind (*vint*) m.

window Fenster (*fen-stuhR*) n.

wine Wein (*vayn*) m.

winter Winter (*vin-tuhR*) m.

wish (to) wünschen (*vün-shuhn*)

without ohne (*oh-nuh*)

woman Frau (*fRou*) f.

wonderful herrlich/wunderbar (*heR-liH/voon-duhR-bAR*)

wool Wolle (*vo-luh*) f.

work (to) arbeiten (*AR-bay-tuhn*)

wrist Handgelenk (*hAnt-guh-lenk*) n.

write (to) schreiben (hat geschrieben) (*shray-buhn*)

wrong falsch (*fAlsh*)

X–Y

year Jahr (*yahR*) n.

yearly jährlich (*yähR-liH*)

yellow gelb (*gelp*)

yesterday gestern (*ges-tuhRn*)

yogurt Jog(h)urt (*yoh-gooRt*) m.

young jung (*yoong*)

younger jünger (*yoön-guhR*)

your dein (informal), Ihr (formal) (*dayn, eeR*)

Z

ZIP code Postleitzahl (*post-layt-tsahl*) f.

German to English

A

ab.biegen (*ap-bee-guhn*) to turn

Abend (*ah-buhnd*) m. evening

ab.fahren (*ap-fah-Ruhn*) to depart

Adresse (*A-dre-suh*) f. address

alle (*A-luh*) all

allergisch (*A-leR-gish*) allergic

also (*Al-zoh*) therefore

alt (*Alt*) old, aged

Ananas (*A-nah-nAs*) f. pine-apple

angeln (*An-guhln*) to fish

Angestellte (*An-guh-shtel-tuh*) m./f. employee

Angst (*Angst*) f. fear

an.kommen (*An-ko-muhn*) to arrive

Anruf (*An-Rewf*) m. call

Anrufbeantworter (*An-Rewf-buh-Ant-voR-tuhR*) m. answering machine

an.rufen (*An-Rew-fuhn*) to call

anschließend (*An-shlee-suhnt*) then, afterward

Ansichtskarte (*An-ziHts-kAr-tuh*) f. postcard

antworten (*Ant-voR-tuhn*) to answer

an.ziehen (sich) (*ziH An-tsee-uhn*) to dress oneself

Anzug (*An-tsewk*) m. suit

Apfel (*Ap-fuhl*) m. apple

Apfelsine (*Ap-fuhl-zee-nuh*) f. orange

Apotheke (*A-po-tey-kuh*) f. pharmacy

Aprikose (*ah-pRee-koh-zuh*) f. apricot

April (*ah-pReel*) m. April

arbeiten (*AR-bay-tuhn*) to work

ärgerlich (*äR-guhR-liH*) angry

arm (*Arm*) poor

Arzt (*aRtst*) m. doctor

Aschenbecher (*A-shun-be-HuhR*) m. ashtray

Aubergine (*oh-beR-jee-nuh*) f. eggplant

auf Wiedersehen (*ouf vee-duhR-zey-uhn*) goodbye

Aufzug (*ouf-tsook*) m. elevator

Auge (*ou-guh*) n. eye

August (*ou-goost*) m. August

aus.füllen (*ous-fü-luhn*) to fill out

Ausgang (*ous-gAng*) m. exit

ausgezeichnet (*ous-guh-tsayH-net*) excellent

Ausland (*ous-lAnt*) n. foreign country

außer Betrieb (*ou-suhR buh-treep*) out of order

aus.steigen (*ous-shtay-guhn*) to climb off

aus.ziehen (sich) (*ziH ous-tsee-uhn*) to take off one's clothes

Auto (*ou-to*) n. car

B

backen (*bA-kuhn*) *to bake*

Bäcker (*bä-kuhR*) m. baker

Badeanzug (*bah-duh-An-tsewk*) m. bathing suit

baden (*bah-duhn*) to bathe

Badezimmer (*bah-duh-tsi-muhR*) n. bathroom

Bahnhof (*bahn-hof*) m. train station

Bäkerei (*bä-kuh-Ray*) f. bakery

bald (*bAlt*) soon

Balkon (*bAl-kon*) m. balcony

Bankautomat (*bank-ou-toh-mAt*) m. ATM

Bargeld (*bahR-gelt*) n. cash

Basilikum (*bah-zee-lee-koom*) n. basil

Bauch (*bouCH*) m. stomach

Bauer (*bou-uhR*) m. farmer

Baum (*boum*) m. tree

Baumwolle (*boum-vo-luh*) f. cotton

befehlen (*buh-fey-luhn*) to command

beginnen (*buh-gi-nuhn*) to begin

Bekleidung (*buh-klay-doong*) f. clothes

Bekleidungsgeschäft (*buh-klay-doongz-guh-schäft*) n. clothing store

bekommen (*buh-ko-muhn*) to receive

bei (*bay*) at, near

beige (*beyj*) beige

Beilage (*bay-lah-guh*) f. side dish

Bein (*bayn*) n. leg

benutzen (*buh-noot-suhn*) to use

Benzintank (*ben-tseen-tAnk*) m. gas tank

bequem (*buh-kveym*) comfortable

beschäftig (*buh-shäf-tiH*) busy

besitzen (*buh-zi-tsuhn*) to possess

besser (*be-suhR*) better

Besteck (*buh-shtek*) n. cutlery

bestellen (*buh-shte-luhn*) to order

Bett (*bet*) n. bed

Bettdecke (*bet-de-kuh*) f. blanket

beweisen (*buh-vay-zuhn*) prove

bewölkt (*buh-völkt*) cloudy

Bibliothek (*bib-lee-oh-tek*) f. library

Bier (*beeR*) n. beer

bieten (*bee-tuhn*) to offer

Bild (*bilt*) n. painting

billig (*bi-liH*) cheap

binden (*bin-duhn*) to bind

Birnen (*beeR-nuhn*) pl. pears

bitte (*bi-tuh*) please

bis (*bis*) until

blasen (*blah-zuhn*) to blow

blau (*blou*) blue

Blaubeeren (*blou-bey-Ruhn*) pl. blueberries

bleiben (*blay-bun*) to remain

blicken (*bli-kuhn*) to look, glance

Blitz (*blits*) m. lightning

blöd (*blöd*) stupid

Blume (*blew-muh*) f. flower

Blumengeschäft (*blew-muhn-guh-schäft*) n. florist

Blumenkohl (*blew-muhn-kohl*) m. cauliflower

Bluse (*blew-zuh*) f. blous

Bohnen (*boh-nuhn*) pl. beans

Bohnensuppe (*boh-nuhn-zoo-puh*) f. bean soup

Boot (*boht*) n. boat

brauchen (*bRou-CHuhn*) to need

braun (*bRoun*) brown

brechen (*bRe-Huhn*) to break

breit (*brayt*) wide

brennen (*bRe-nuhn*) to burn

Brief (*bReef*) m. letter

Briefumschlag (*bReef-oom-shlahk*) m. envelope

Brille (*bri-luh*) f. glasses

bringen (*bRin-guhn*) to bring

Brokkoli (*bRoh-koh-lee*) m. broccoli

Brot (*bRoht*) n. bread

Brötchen (*bRöt-chuhn*) n. roll

Bruder (*bRew-duhR*) m. brother

Brust (*bRoost*) f. chest

Bücher (*bü-HuhR*) f. books

Bücherregal (*büh-HuhR-Rey-gal*) n. bookshelf

Buchhandlung (*bewCH-hAnt-loong*) f. bookstore

Bügeleisen (*büh-guhl-ay-zuhn*) n. iron

bügeln (*büh-guhln*) to iron

bunt (*boont*) bright

Bus (*boos*) m. bus

Bustenhalter (*boo-stuhn-hAl-tuhR*) m. bra

Butter (*boo-tuhR*) f. butter

C

circa (*tseeR-kuh*) about

Couchtisch (*kouch-tish*) m. coffee table

D

da (*dAh*) there

Dame (*dah-muh*) f. lady

danach (*dA-nACH*) then

danke (*dAn-kuh*) thanks

danken (*dAn-kuhn*) to thank

denken (*den-kuhn*) to think

Deutschland (*doytch-lAnt*) m. Germany

Dezember (*dey-tsem-buhR*) m. December

dick (*dik*) fat

Dienstag (*deenz-tahk*) m. Tuesday

Donner (*do-nuhR*) m. thunder

Donnerstag (*do-nuhRz-tahk*) m. Thursday

Doppelzimmer (*do-puhl-tsi-muhR*) n. double room

dort (*doRt*) there

Dose (*doh-zuh*) f. can

draußen (*dRou-suhn*) outdoors

dreckig (*dRe-kiH*) dirty

Drogerie (*dRoh-guh-Ree*) f. drug store

dunkel (*doon-kuhl*) dark

dünn (*dün*) thin

durch (*dooRCH*) through

dürfen (*dür-fuhn*) to be allowed to

Durst (*dooRst*) m. thirst

durstig (*dooRs-tiH*) thirsty

Dusche (*dew-shuh*) f. shower

E

Ei (*ay*) n. egg

Einkaufszentrum (*ayn-koufs-tsen-tRoom*) n. shopping center

ein.steigen (*ayn-shtay-guhn*) to climb on

Einzelzimmer (*ayn-tsel-tsi-muhR*) n. single room

Eis (*ays*) n. ice cream

Eltern (*el-tuhRn*) pl. parents

empfangen (*em-pfAn-guhn*) to receive

empfehlen (*em-pfey-luhn*) to recommend

endlich (*ent-liH*) at last

eng (*eng*) narrow

entdecken (*ent-de-kuhn*) to discover

entlang (*ent-lAng*) along

entspannen (sich) (*ziH ent-shpA-nuhn*) to relax

entwickeln (*ent-vi-kuhln*) to develop

Erdbeeren (*eRt-bey-Ruhn*) pl. strawberries

Ereignmis (*eR-ayk-nis*) n. event

Erbsen (*eRp-suhn*) pl. peas

erholen (sich) (*ziH eR-hoh-luhn*) to recuperate

erkälten (sich) (*ziH eR-käl-tuhn*) to catch a cold

Erkältung (*eR-käl-toong*) f. cold

ernst (*eRnst*) serious

etwa (*et-vah*) roughly

etwas (*et-vAs*) some

essen (*es-uhn*) to eat

Essen (*es-uhn*) n. meal

Essig (*e-siH*) m. vinegar

Esszimmer (*es-tsi-muhR*) n. dining room

F

fahren (*fah-Ruhn*) to drive

Fahrrad (*fah-Rat*) n. bicycle

fallen (*fA-luhn*) to fall

falsch (*fAlsh*) wrong

fangen (*fAn-guhn*) to catch

fast (*fAst*) almost

faul (*foul*) lazy

Februar (*fey-bRew-ahR*) m. February

Fenster (*fen-stuhR*) n. window

fern.sehen (*feRn-zey-uhn*) to watch TV

Fernseher (*feRn-zey-uhR*) m. television

fertig (*feR-tiH*) finished

fertig machen (sich) (*ziH feR-tiH mA-CHuhn*) get oneself ready

feucht (*foyHt*) humid

Fieber (*fee-buhR*) n. fever

Film (*film*) m. movie

finden (*fin-duhn*) to find

Fingernagel (*fin-guR-nah-guhl*) m. fingernail

Fisch (*fish*) m. fish

Fitnesscenter (*fit-nes-sen-tuhR*) n. fitness center

Flasche (*flah-shuh*) f. bottle

Fleisch (*flaysh*) n. meat

fleißig (*flay-siH*) industrious

fliegen (*flee-guhn*) to fly

Flug (*flewk*) m. flight

Fluggesellschaft (*flewk-guh-zel-shAft*) f. airline

Flughafen (*flewk-hah-fuhn*) m. airport

Flugnummer (*flewk-noo-muhR*) f. flight number

Flugsteig (*flewk-shtayk*) m. gate

Flugzeug (*flewk-tsoyk*) n. airplane

Flunder (*floon-duhR*) f. flounder

Fluss (*floos*) m. river

folgen (*fol-guhn*) to follow

Fön (*föhn*) m. hair dryer

Forelle (*foh-Re-luh*) f. trout

fragen (*fRah-guhn*) to ask

Frau (*fRou*) f. woman, wife

Freitag (*fRay-tahk*) m. Friday

Freund (*fRoynt*) m. friend

Freundin (*fRoyn-din*) f. girlfriend

fröhlich (*fRöh-liH*) happy

früh (*fRüh*) early

Frühling (*fRüh-ling*) m. spring

Funktelefon (*foonk-tey-ley-fohn*) n. cell phone

furchtbar (*fooRHt-bahR*) awful

Fuß (*fews*) m. foot

Fußboden (*fews-boh-duhn*) m. floor

Fußknöchel (*fews-knö-Huhl*) m. ankle

fühlen (sich) (*ziH füh-luhn*) to feel

für (*fühR*) for

G

Gabel (*gah-buhl*) f. fork

ganz (*gAnts*) quite, entirely

Garnele (*gahR-ney-luh*) f. shrimp

Garten (*gAR-tuhn*) m. garden

geben (*gey-buhn*) to give

Geburtstag (*guh-booRts-tahk*) m. birthday

Geflügelsalat (*guh-flüh-guhl-zA-laht*) m. chicken salad

gegenüber (*ge-guhn-ü-buhR*) opposite, facing

gehen (*gey-uhn*) to go

Gehirn (*guh-hiRn*) n. brain

Geist (*gayst*) m. ghost

gelb (*gelp*) yellow

gelegentlich (*guh-ley-gent-liH*) occasionally

gemustert (*guh-moos-tuhRt*) patterned

Gemüse (*guh-müh-zuh*) n. vegetables

Gemüsehandlung (*guh-müh-zuh-hAnt-loong*) f. vegetable stand

genießen (*guh-nee-suhn*) to enjoy

genug (*guh-newk*) enough

gepunktet (*guh-poonk-tuht*) polka-dotted

geradeaus (*guh-Rah-duh-ous*) straight ahead

Gericht (*guh-RiHt*) n. dish (of food)

Geschäft (*guh-shäft*) n. store

geschehen (*guh-shey-uhn*) to happen

Geschenk (*guh-shenk*) n. gift

Geschenkartikelladen (*guh-shenk-AR-tee-kuh-lah-duhn*) m. gift shop

Geschichte (*guh-shiH-tuh*) f. history

Geschirr (*guh-sheeR*) n. dishes

Gesicht (*guh-ziHt*) n. face

gestern (*ges-tuhRn*) yesterday

gestreift (*guh-shtRayft*) striped

gesund (*guh-zoont*) healthy

Getränke (*guh-tRän-kuh*) pl. drinks

gewinnen (*guh-vi-nuhn*) to win

Gift (*gift*) n. poison

Glas (*glAs*) n. glass

glauben (*glou-buhn*) to believe

glücklich (*glük-liH*) happy

grau (*gRou*) gray

Grippe (*gRi-puh*) f. flu

groß (*gRohs*) big

grün (*gRün*) green

Gruppe (*gRoo-puh*) f. group

Gurke (*gooR-kuh*) f. cucumber

Gürtel (*güR-tuhl*) m. belt

gut (*gewt*) good, well

Guten Abend (*gew-tuhn ah-bent*) m. good evening

Guten Morgen (*gew-tuhn moR-guhn*) m. good morning

Guten Tag (*gew-tuhn tahk*) m. good day

H

Haar (*hahR*) n. hair

Haarbürste (*hahR-büR-stuh*) f. hairbrush

Haarschnitt (*hahR-shnit*) m. haircut

Haarshampoo (*hahR-shAm-pew*) n. shampoo

haben (*hah-buhn*) to have

Hagel (*hah-guhl*) m. hail

hallo (*hA-loh*) hello

Hals (*halz*) m. neck

halten (*hAhl-tuhn*) to hold

Hand (*hAnT*) f. hand

Handgelenk (*hAnt-guh-lenk*) n. wrist

Handgepäck (*hAnt-guh-päk*) n. carry-on luggage

Handschuhe (*hAnt-schew-uh*) pl. gloves

Handtasche (*hAnt-tA-shuh*) f. purse

Handtuch (*hAn-tewCH*) n. towel

Handy (*hahn-dee*) n. cell phone

Handynummer (*hahn-dee-noo-muhR*) f. cell phone number

hängen (*hän-guhn*) to hang

hart (*hArt*) hard

Haselnüsse (*hah-zuhl-nü-suh*) pl. hazelnuts

häßlich (*hähs-liH*) ugly

Hauptgericht (*houpt-guh-RiHt*) n. main course

Haus (*hous*) n. house

Haut (*hout*) f. skin

heben (*hey-buhn*) to lift

heiraten (*hay-RA-tuhn*) to marry

heiß (*hays*) hot

helfen (*hel-fuhn*) to help

hell (*hel*) light

Hemd (*hemt*) n. shirt

Herbst (*heRpst*) m. autumn, fall

herrlich (*heR-liH*) wonderful

Herz (*heRts*) n. heart

heute (*hoy-tuh*) today

hier (*heeR*) here

Himmel (*hi-muhl*) m. sky

hinter (*hin-tuhR*) behind

Hinterhof (*hin-tuhR-hohf*) m. backyard

hoch (*hohCH*) high

hören (*höh-Ruhn*) to hear

Hose (*hoh-zuh*) f. pair of pants

Hotel (*hoh-tel*) n. hotel

Huhn (*hewn*) n. chicken

Hühnerbrust (*hüh-nuhR-broost*) f. chicken breast

Hunger (*hoon-guhR*) m. hunger

hungrig (*hoon-gRiH*) hungry

Husten (*hew-stuhn*) m. cough

Hut (*hewt*) m. hat

I

immer (*i-muhR*) always

Innenhof (*i-nuhn-hohf*) m. courtyard

interessant (*in-tey-Re-sAnt*) interesting

Internetzugang (*in-tuhR-net-tsew-grif*) m. Internet access

J

Jacke (*yA-kuh*) f. jacket

Jahr (*yahR*) n. year

Jahreszeit (*yah-Ruhs-tsayt*) f. season

jährlich (*yähR-liH*) yearly

Januar (*yah-new-ahR*) m. January

jeden Tag (*yey-duhn tahk*) every day

jetzt (*yetst*) now

Jog(h)urt (*yoh-gooRt*) m. yogurt

Johannisbeeren (*yoh-hA-nis-bey-Ruhn*) pl. currants

jung (*yoong*) young

Junge (*yoon-guh*) m. boy

K

Kabeljau (*kah-buhl-you*) m. cod

Kaffee (*kA-fey*) m. coffee

Kalbfleisch (*kAlp-flaysh*) n. veal

kalt (*kalt*) cold

Kamin (*kah-meen*) m. fireplace

Kamm (*kAm*) m. comb

kämmen (sich) (*ziH kä-muhn*) to comb one's hair

kariert (*kah-ReeRt*) plaid

Karotte (*kah-Ro-tuh*) f. carrot

Kartoffel (*kAR-to-fuhl*) f. potato

Käse (*käh-zuh*) m. cheese

Kathedrale (*kah-tey-drah-luh*) f. cathedral

Katze (*kA-tsuh*) f. cat

kaufen (*kou-fuhn*) to buy

Kehle (*key-luh*) f. throat

Kellner (*kel-nuhR*) m. waiter

Kellnerin (*kel-nuh-Rin*) f. waitress

kennen (*ke-nuhn*) to know, be familiar with

Kind (*kint*) n. child

Kino (*kee-noh*) n. cinema

Kiosk (*kee-osk*) m. newsstand

Kirche (*KeeR-Huh*) f. church

Kirschen (*keeR-shuhn*) pl. cherries

Kleid (*klayt*) n. dress

Kleider (*klay-duhR*) pl. clothes

Kleiderbügel (*klay-duhR-büh-guhl*) m. hanger

klein (*klayn*) small

Kleingeld (*klayn-gelt*) n. change (coins)

Klimaanlage (*klee-mah-An-lah-guh*) f. air-conditioning

klug (*klewk*) smart

Kneipe (*knay-puh*) f. bar (pub)

Knie (*knee*) n. knee

Knoblauch (*knohb-louCH*) m. garlic

Knopf (*knopf*) m. button

kochen (*ko-CHuhn*) to cook

Koffer (*ko-fuhR*) m. suitcase

Kohl (*kohl*) m. cabbage

kommen (*ko-muhn*) to come

Kommode (*ko-moh-duh*) f. dresser

Konditorei (*kon-dee-toR-ay*) f. pastry shop

können (*kö-nuhn*) can, to be able to

kontrollieren (*kon-tRo-lee-Ruhn*) to inspect

Kopf (*kopf*) m. head

Kopfkissen (*kopf-ki-suhn*) n. pillow

Kopfsalat (*kopf-zA-laht*) m. lettuce

Kopfschmerzen (*kopf-shmeR-tsuhn*) pl. headache

Kord (*koRt*) m. corduroy

Körper (*köR-puhR*) m. body

kosten (*kos-tuhn*) to cost

kostenlos (*kos-tuhn-los*) free of charge

Kraftbrühe (*krAft-bRüh-uh*) f. beef broth

krank (*kRAnk*) sick

Krankenpfleger (*kRan-kuhn-pfley-guhR*) m. nurse

kratzen (*krA-tsuhn*) scratch

Kräuter (*kroy-tuhR*) pl. herbs

Krawatte (*kRah-vA-tuh*) f. necktie

Krebs (*kreyps*) m. crab

Küche (*kü-Huh*) f. kitchen

Kuchen (*kew-CHuhn*) m. cake

Kunst (*koonst*) f. art

kurz (*kooRts*) short

küssen (*kü-suhn*) to kiss

L

Lachs (*lAks*) m. salmon

laden (*lah-duhn*) to load

Laden (*lah-duhn*) m. store

Lamm (*lAm*) n. lamb

Land (*lAnt*) n. country

lang (*lAng*) long

langsam (*lAng-zAm*) slow

langweilig (*lAng-vay-liH*) boring

lassen (*lA-suhn*) to leave, to let

laufen (*lou-fuhn*) to run

Lebensmittelgeschäft (*ley-buhnz-mi-tuhl-guh-shäft*) n. grocery store

lecker (*le-kuhR*) delicious

Leder (*ley-duhR*) n. leather

leer (*leyR*) empty

legen (*ley-guhn*) to lay

lehren (*ley-Ruhn*) teach

Lehrer (*ley-Ruhr*) m. teacher

Lehrerin (*ley-Ruhr-in*) f. female teacher

leicht (*layHt*) light

leiden (*lay-duhn*) to suffer

leider (*lay-duhR*) unfortunately

leihen (*lay-uhn*) to lend

Leinen (*lay-nuhn*) n. linen

lernen (*leR-nuhn*) to learn, to study

lesen (*ley-zuhn*) to read

Licht (*liHt*) n. light

lieben (*lee-buhn*) to love

Lied (*leed*) n. song

liegen (*lee-guhn*) to lie, be situated

lila (*lee-lah*) n. purple

links (*links*) left

Lippe (*li-puh*) f. lip

loben (*loh-buhn*) to praise

lockig (*lo-kiH*) curly

Löffel (*lö-fuhl*) m. spoon

Luft (*looft*) f. air

lustig (*loos-tiH*) funny

M

machen (*mA-CHuhn*) to make

Magen (*mah-guhn*) m. stomach

Mai (*may*) m. May

Mais (*mays*) m. corn

manchmal (*mAnH-mahl*) sometimes

Mandel (*mAn-duhl*) f. almond

Mann (*mAn*) m. man

Männer (*mä-nuhR*) pl. men

Mantel (*mAn-tuhl*) m. coat

Markt (*mARkt*) m. market

Marmelade (*mAR-muh-lah-duh*) f. jam

März (*mäRts*) m. March

Meeresfrüchte (*mee-Ruhs-fRüH-tuh*) pl. seafood

Meerrettich (*meyR-Re-tiH*) m. horseradish

mehr (*meyR*) more

Melone (*me-loh-nuh*) f. melon

Mensch (*mensh*) m. human being

Messer (*me-suhR*) n. knife

Metzger (*mets-guhR*) m. butcher

Metzgerei (*mets-guh-ray*) f. butcher shop

mieten (*mee-tuhn*) to rent

Milch (*milH*) f. milk

Minute (*mi-new-tuh*) f. minute

missverstehen (*mis-feR-shtey-uhn*) to misunderstand

Mitternacht (*mi-tuhR-nACHt*) f. midnight

Mittwoch (*mit-voCH*) m. Wednesday

Möbel (*möh-buhl*) pl. furniture

Mobiltelefon (*moh-beel-tey-ley-fohn*) n. cell phone

möbliert (*möh-bleeRt*) furnished

Mode (*moh-duh*) f. fashion

modisch (*moh-dish*) fashionable

mögen (*möh-guhn*) to like

Monat (*moh-nAt*) m. month

monatlich (*moh-nAt-liH*) monthly

Montag (*mohn-tahk*) m. Monday

morgen (*moR-guhn*) tomorrow

Morgen (*moR-guhn*) m. morning

morgens (*moR-guhnz*) mornings

Motorrad (*moh-toh-Rat*) n. motorcycle

müde (*müh-duh*) tired

Mund (*moont*) m. mouth

munter (*moon-tuhR*) awake

Münzen (*mün-tsuhn*) pl. coins

Musikgeschäft (*mew-zeek-guh-shäft*) n. music store

müssen (*mü-suhn*) must

mutig (*mew-tiH*) brave

Mutter (*moo-tuhR*) f. mother

Mütze (*mü-tsuh*) f. cap

N

nach (*nahCH*) after

Nachmittag (*nahCH-mi-tahk*) m. afternoon

Nachrichten (*nahCH-RiH-tuhn*) pl. news

Nachspeise (*nahCH-shpay-zuh*) f. dessert

Nacht (*nACHt*) f. night

Nachtclub (*nACHt-kloob*) m. night club

Nachtisch (*nahCH-tish*) m. dessert

Name (*nah-muh*) m. name

Nase (*nah-zuh*) f. nose

naß (*nahs*) wet

Nebel (*ney-buhl*) m. fog

nebelig (*ney-buh-liH*) foggy

neben (*ney-buhn*) beside

nehmen (*ney-muhn*) to take

nervös (*neR-vöhs*) nervous

neu (*noy*) new

nie (*nee*) never

noch (*noCH*) still

Null (*nool*) f. zero

nur (*nooR*) only

Nüsse (*nü-suh*) pl. nuts

O

Obst (*opst*) n. fruit

öffnen (*öf-nuhn*) to open

oft (*oft*) often

ohne (*oh-nuh*) without

Ohr (*ohR*) n. ear

Oktober (*ok-toh-buhR*) m. October

Öl (*öhl*) n. oil

Oma (*oh-mah*) f. grandmother

Onkel (*on-kuhl*) m. uncle

Opa (*oh-pah*) m. grandfather

P

packen (*pA-kuhn*) to pack

Paket (*pah-ket*) n. package

Parfüm (*pAR-füm*) n. perfume

parken (*pAR-kuhn*) to park

Parkplatz (*pARk-plAts*) m. parking lot

Pass (*pAs*) m. passport

Pfeffermühle (*pfe-fuhR-müh-luh*) f. pepper mill

Pferd (*pfeRt*) n. horse

Pfirsiche (*pfeeR-ziH-uh*) pl. peaches

Pflegespülung (*pfley-guh-shpüh-loong*) f. conditioner

Pförtner (*pföRt-nuhR*) m. concierge

Pilze (*pil-tsuh*) pl. mushrooms

planen (*plah-nuhn*) to plan

Plätzchen (*pläts-Huhn*) n. cookie

plötzlich (*plöts-liH*) suddenly

Polizeiamt (*poh-li-tsay-Amt*) n. police station

Polizist (*poh-lee-tsist*) m. police officer

Pommes frites (*po-muhs*) pl. French fries

Portemonnaie (*poRt-moh-ney*) n. wallet

Post (*post*) f. post office

Postkarte (*post-kAR-tuh*) f. postcard

Postleitzahl (*post-layt-tsahl*) f. ZIP code

probieren (*pRo-bee-Ruhn*) to try

pünktlich (*pünkt-liH*) punctually

putzen (*poo-tsuhn*) to clean

Q

Quittung (*kvi-toong*) f. receipt

R

rasieren (sich) (*ziH Rah-zee-Ruhn*) to shave oneself

raten (*Rah-tuhn*) to advise

rauchen (*Rou-CHuhn*) to smoke

rechts (*ReHts*) right

regelmäßig (*Rey-guhl-mäh-siH*) regularly

Regen (*Rey-guhn*) m. rain

Regenmantel (*Rey-guhn-mAn-tuhl*) m. raincoat

Regenshirm (*Rey-guhn-sheeRm*) m. umbrella

regnerisch (*Reyg-nuh-Rish*) rainy

reinigen (*Ray-ni-guhn*) to clean

reisen (*Ray-zuhn*) to travel

reiten (*Ray-tuhn*) to ride

reservieren (*Re-zeR-vee-Ruhn*) to reserve

Rindfleisch (*Rint-flaysh*) n. beef

Rochen (*Ro-CHuhn*) m. flounder

Rock (*Rok*) m. skirt

Roggenbrot (*Ro-guhn-bRoht*) n. rye bread

rollen (*Ro-luhn*) to roll

Roman (*Roh-mahn*) m. novel

rosa (*Roh-zah*) pink

rot (*Rot*) red

Rücken (*Rü-kuhn*) m. back

rufen (*Rew-fuhn*) to call

ruhig (*Rew-iH*) calm

rund (*Roont*) around

S

S-Bahn (*es-bahn*) f. commuter train

Saft (*zAft*) m. juice

sagen (*zah-guhn*) to say, to tell

Sahne (*zah-nuh*) f. cream

Salzstreuer (*zAlts-shtRoy-uhR*) m. salt shaker

Samstag (*zAmz-tahk*) m. Saturday

sauber (*zou-buhR*) clean

sauer (*zou-uhR*) sour

Schachtel (*shACH-tuhl*) f. box

Schal (shahl) m. scarf

Schauspieler (*shou-shpee-luhR*) m. actor

Schauspielerin (*shou-shpee-luh-Rin*) f. actress

Scheibe (*shay-buh*) f. slice

scheinen (*shay-nuhn*) to shine

schicken (*shi-kuhn*) to send

Schiff (*shif*) n. ship

Schild (*shilt*) n. sign

Schinken (*shin-kuhn*) m. ham

Schlafanzug (*shlahf-An-tsook*) m. pajamas

schlafen (*shlah-fuhn*) to sleep

Schlafzimmer (*shlahf-tsi-muhr*) n. bedroom

schlagen (*shlah-guhn*) to hit

Schlagsahne (*shlahk-zah-nuh*) f. whipped cream

schlecht (*shleCHt*) bad

schließen (*shlee-suhn*) to close

Schlips (*schlips*) m. necktie

Schlüssel (*shlü-suhl*) m. key

Schmuck (*shmook*) m. jewelry

Schnee (*shney*) m. snow

schnell (*shnel*) fast, quick

Schnitzel (*shni-tsuhl*) n. cutlet

Schokolade (*shoh-koh-lah-duh*) f. chocolate

schön (*shöhn*) beautiful

Schrank (*shRAnk*) m. closet

schrecklich (*shRek-liH*) horrible

schreiben (*shray-buhn*) to write

Schreibwaren (*shRayp-vah-Ruhn*) pl. pens, stationery

Schuhe (*shew-uh*) pl. shoes

Schulden (*shool-duhn*) pl. debt

Schulter (*shool-tuhR*) f. shoulder

Schüssel (*shü-suhl*) f. bowl

schwach (*shvACH*) weak

schwarz (*shvARts*) black

Schweinfleisch (*shvayn-flaysh*) n. pork

schwer (*shveR*) hard

Schwester (*shves-tuhR*) f. sister

Schwiegereltern (*shvee-guhR-el-tuhRn*) pl. in-laws

Schwiegermutter (*shvee-guhR-moo-tuhR*) f. mother-in-law

Schwiegervater (*shvee-guhR-fah-tuhR*) m. father-in-law

Schwimmbad (*shvim-baht*) n. swimming pool

schwimmen (*shvi-muhn*) to swim

See (*zey*) m. lake

Segelboot (*zey-guhl-boht*) n. sailboat

segeln (*zey-guhln*) to sail

sehen (*zey-uhn*) to see

sehr (*zeyR*) very

Seide (*zay-duh*) f. silk

Seife (*zay-fuh*) f. soap

seit (*zayt*) since

seitlich (*zayt-liH*) at the side

Sekunde (*ze-koon-duh*) f. second

selbstverständlich (*zelpst-feR-shtänt-liH*) of course

Sellerie (*ze-luh-Ree*) m. celery

senden (*zen-duhn*) to send

Senf (*zenf*) m. mustard

Serviette (*zeR-vee-e-tuh*) f. napkin

Sessel (*ze-suhl*) m. armchair

setzen (*ze-tsuhn*) to sit

singen (*zin-guhn*) to sing

sinken (*zin-kuhn*) to sink

sitzen (*zi-tsuhn*) to sit

Socken (*zo-kuhn*) pl. socks

sofort (*zoh-foRt*) immediately

Sohn (*zohn*) m. son

Sommer (*zo-muhR*) m. summer

Sonne (*zo-nuh*) f. sun

Sonntag (*zon-tahk*) m. Sunday

spannend (*shpA-nuhnt*) suspenseful

sparen (*shpah-Ruhn*) save

Spargel (*shpahR-guhl*) m. asparagus

spät (*shpäht*) late

Speck (*shpek*) m. bacon

Speisekarte (*shpay-zuh-kAR-tuh*) f. menu

Spiegel (*shpee-guhl*) m. mirror

Spiegelei (*shpee-guh-lay*) n. fried eggs

spielen (*shpee-luhn*) to play

Spinat (*shpi-naht*) m. spinach

spinnen (*shpi-nuhn*) to spin

Sportgeschäft (*shpoRt-guh-shäft*) n. sport shop

sprechen (*shpRe-Huhn*) to speak

Sprühregen (*shpRüh-Rey-guhn*) m. drizzle

Spülmaschine (*shpül-mA-shee-nuh*) f. dishwasher

Stadt (*shtAt*) f. city

Stadtplan (*shtAt-plAn*) m. city map

stark (*shtARk*) strong

Stärke (*shtäR-kuh*) f. strength

stehen (*shtey-uhn*) to stand

steigen (*shtay-guhn*) to climb

sterben (*shteR-buhn*) to die

Stiefel (*shtee-fuhl*) pl. boots

stinken (*shtin-kuhn*) to stink

Stock (*shtok*) m. floor

stolz (*shtolts*) proud

Straße (*shtRah-suh*) f. street

Straßenbahn (*shtRah-suhn-bahn*) f. streetcar

Streichhölzer (*shtRayH-höl-tsuhR*) pl. matches

Stück (*shtük*) n. piece

studieren (*shtew-dee-Ruhn*) to study, to look over

stumpf (*shtoompf*) blunt

Stunde (*shtoon-duh*) f. hour

stündlich (*shtünt-liH*) hourly

Sturm (*shtooRm*) m. storm

suchen (*zew-Huhn*) to look for

Supermarkt (*zew-puhR-mARkt*) m. supermarket

Suppenteller (*zoo-puhn-te-luhR*) m. soup dish

süß (*zühs*) sweet

Süßigkeiten (*züh-siH-kay-tuhn*) pl. sweets, candies

T

Tag (*tahk*) m. day

täglich (*tähk-liH*) daily

Tante (*tAn-tuh*) f. aunt

tanzen (*tAn-tsuhn*) to dance

Tasse (*tA-suh*) f. cup

Tee (*tey*) m. tea

Teelöffel (*tey-lö-fuhl*) m. teaspoon

Telefon (*te-le-fon*) n. telephone

telefonieren (*te-le-foh-nee-Ruhn*) to telephone

Telefonnummer (*te-le-foh-noo-muhR*) f. telephone number

Teller (*te-luhR*) m. dinner plate

Tennisschuhe (*te-nis-shew-uh*) pl. tennis shoes

Teppich (*te-pish*) m. carpet

teuer (*toy-uhR*) expensive

Thunfisch (*tewn-fish*) m. tuna

tief (*teef*) low

Tiergarten (*teeR-gAR-tuhn*) m. zoo

Tierpark (*teeR-pARk*) m. zoo

Tisch (*tish*) m. table

Tischdecke (*tish-de-kuh*) f. tablecloth

Tochter (*toCH-tuhR*) f. daughter

Toilette (*toy-le-tuh*) f. bathroom

Tomate (*toh-mah-tuh*) f. tomato

tragen (*trah-guhn*) to wear, to carry

träumen (*tRoy-muhn*) to dream

traurig (*tRou-RiH*) sad

treffen (*tRe-fuhn*) to meet

trinken (*tRin-kuhn*) to drink

trocken (*tRo-kuhn*) dry

Trockner (*tRok-nuhR*) m. dryer

Truthahn (*tRewt-hahn*) m. turkey

tun (*tuhn*) to do

Tür (*tühR*) f. door

Tüte (*tüh-tuh*) f. bag

U

über (*üh-buhR*) over, across

übermorgen (*üh-buhR-moR-guhn*) day after tomorrow

überweisen (*üh-buhR-vay-zuhn*) to transfer money

Uhr (*ewR*) f. clock

um.steigen (*oom-shtay-guhn*) to transfer (in route)

um.ziehen (sich) (*ziH oom-tsee-uhn*) to change one's clothes

ungefähr (*oon-guh-fähR*) approximately

unglaublich (*oon-gloup-liH*) unbelievable

unter (*oon-tuhR*) beneath, below, under

Unterhose (*oon-tuhR-hoh-zuh*) f. underpants

unterschreiben (*oon-tuhR-shRay-buhn*) to sign

Unterschrift (*oon-tuhR-shRift*) f. signature

untersuchen (*oon-tuhR-zew-Huhn*) to examine

Untertasse (*oon-tuhR-tA-suh*) f. saucer

Unterwäsche (*oon-tuhR-väh-shuh*) f. underwear

V

Vater (*fah-tuhR*) m. father

vergessen (*feR-ge-suhn*) to forget

verkaufen (*feR-kou-fuhn*) to sell

verletzen (sich) (*ziH feyR-le-tsuhn*) to injure oneself

verlieren (*feR-lee-Ruhn*) to lose

Vermittlung *(feR-mit-loong)* f. operator

versprechen *(feR-shpRe-Huhn)* to promise

verstehen *(feR-shtey-uhn)* to understand

versuchen *(feR-zew-Huhn)* to try

viel *(feel)* a lot of

vielleicht *(fee-layHt)* maybe

voll *(fol)* full

Vollkornbrot *(fol-koRn-bRoht)* n. whole-grain bread

von *(fon)* from

vor *(fohR)* in front of

vorgestern *(foR-ges-tuhRn)* day before yesterday

Vorspeise *(foR-shpay-zuh)* f. appetizer

W

wachsen *(vak-suhn)* to grow

wählen *(väh-luhn)* to dial a phone, to choose

wahr *(vahR)* true

wann *(vAn)* when

Wand *(vAnt)* f. wall

wandern *(vAn-duhRn)* to hike

warm *(vahRm)* warm

Warnung *(vAR-noong)* f. warning

warten *(vAR-tuhn)* to wait

warum *(vah-Rum)* why

was *(vAs)* what

waschen *(vah-shuhn)* to wash

Wasser *(va-suhR)* n. water

Wechselgeld *(vek-suhl-gelt)* n. change (coins)

wechselhaft *(vek-sel-hAft)* changeable

Wechselkurs *(vek-suhl-kooRs)* m. exchange rate

Wecker *(ve-kuhR)* m. alarm clock

Wein *(vayn)* m. wine

weinen *(vay-nuhn)* to cry

weiß *(vays)* white

Weißbrot *(vays-bRoht)* n. white bread

weiter.gehen *(vay-tuhR-gey-uhn)* to go on

welcher *(vel-HuhR)* which

wenig *(vey-niH)* little/not much

weniger *(vey-nee-guhR)* less/fewer

wer *(veyR)* who

werden *(veR-duhn)* to become

Wetter *(ve-tuhR)* n. weather

wichtig *(viH-tiH)* important

wie *(vee)* how

wie lange *(vee lAn-guh)* how long

wie viel *(vee feel)* how much

Wildleder *(vilt-ley-duhR)* n. suede

Wind *(vint)* m. wind

Winter *(vin-tuhR)* m. winter

Wirbelsäule *(viR-buhl-zoy-luh)* f. spine

wissen *(vi-suhn)* to know a fact

wo *(voh)* where

Woche *(vo-CHuh)* f. week

wöchentlich *(vö-Hent-liH)* weekly

woher *(voh-heR)* from where

wohin *(voh-hin)* where (to)

wohnen *(voh-nuhn)* to reside

Wohnung *(voh-noong)* f. apartment

Wohnzimmer *(vohn-tsi-muhr)* n. living room

Wolle *(vo-luh)* f. wool

wollen *(vo-luhn)* to want, desire

Wurst *(vooRst)* f. sausage

wüschen *(vün-shuhn)* to wish

X–Z

Zahn *(tsahn)* m. tooth

Zahnarzt *(tsahn-ARtst)* m. dentist

Zahnbürste *(tsahn-büR-stuh)* f. toothbrush

Zehe *(tsey-uh)* f. toe

zeichnen *(tsayH-nuhn)* to draw

zeigen *(tsay-guhn)* to show, to indicate

Zeit *(tsayt)* f. time

Zeitschrift *(tsayt-shRift)* f. magazine

Zeitung *(tsay-toong)* f. newspaper

ziehen *(tsee-uhn)* to pull

ziemlich *(tseem-liH)* quite

Zimmer *(tsi-muhR)* n. room

Zitrone *(tsi-troh-nuh)* f. lemon

zu *(tsew)* to

zu viel *(tsew feel)* too much

zu wenig *(tsew vey-niH)* too little

Zucker *(tsoo-kuhR)* m. sugar

Zug *(tsewk)* m. train

Zunge *(tsoon-guh)* f. tongue

zusammen *(tsew-zA-muhn)* together

Zwiebel *(tsvee-buhl)* f. onion

zwischen *(tsvi-shuhn)* between

Index